Fred
MacMurray
A BIOGRAPHY

Charles Tranberg

Fred MacMurray: A Biography
© 2007 Charles Tranberg. All Rights Reserved.

No part of this book may be reproduced in any form or by any means, electronic, mechanical, digital, photocopying or recording, except for the inclusion in a review, without permission in writing from the publisher.

Published in the USA by:
BearManor Media
P O Box 71426
Albany, Georgia 31708
WWW.BEARMANORMEDIA.COM

ISBN 1-59393-099-2

Printed in the United States of America.
Book design by Brian Pearce.

Table Of Contents

Acknowledgements

Fred MacMurray was one of the most durable stars in motion picture history. Fred arrived in Hollywood in 1934 and within a year he was one of the top leading men in the movie industry. He was the leading actor or one of the leads in films through 1973, when Walt Disney Studios released his final starring role in a motion picture, *Charley and the Angel*. Thirty-nine years — five separate decades. Few stars have equaled that distinction.

Of course every star career has its peaks and valleys. The initial peak of Fred's stardom was his days as a Paramount leading man, beginning in 1935 and running roughly until the end of the Second World War. Like many aging stars, the post-war years were a mixed bag for Fred. Public tastes were changing and the kinds of frothy, romantic comedies which had been his forte were going out of style. But he persevered and continued to do leading roles in a variety of pictures and from time to time found a film which registered strongly with film audiences and critics alike, such as *The Egg and I* (1947), and especially *The Caine Mutiny* (1954).

By the mid-'50s, Fred was appearing, increasingly, in that favorite genre of the aging leading man — the Western film. Eight of ten films he made between 1955 and 1960 were Westerns, not Fred's favorite genre. But they did keep his name before the public.

Then in 1959, Fred began the second peak of his career thanks to Walt Disney, who cast Fred in his studio's first live-action comedy film, *The Shaggy Dog*. Incredibly, this film, which was made for under $1 million, became the third biggest box office hit of that year, and Fred found a new audience. Over the next several years, Fred starred in a series of hugely popular family films for the Walt Disney Studios.

Then in 1960, Fred did something that solidified his new family-friendly image. He accepted the lead in a new television series called *My Three Sons*. For the next twelve years he played Steve Douglas, a widower with three rambunctious sons. Fred became *the* quintessential father figure for a new generation of kids.

4

In accepting *My Three Sons,* Fred succeeded at something that few film actors had achieved up to that time. He became a star in both television and motion pictures. Look at it this way. In 1951 when Lucille Ball began *I Love Lucy* she had already spent nearly two decades as a motion picture actress, but she never had the kind of movie fame that Fred MacMurray had achieved when he became a television star. Loretta Young began a long-running anthology series in 1953, and had been a popular and Academy Award-winning movie actress prior to that, but when she began on television her days as a film actress was over. When Fred began doing *My Three Sons* in 1960, he was enjoying a rejuvenated film career thanks to the Disney films and his superb performance in Billy Wilder's hugely popular and Academy Award-winning *The Apartment.* Fred was simultaneously enjoying popularity on both the big *and* small screens. Many film actors attempted this after Fred, including his contemporaries Jimmy Stewart and Henry Fonda, but both proved failures in their own series.

Fred MacMurray arrived in Hollywood in 1934, at roughly the same time as his contemporaries (and good friends) Jimmy Stewart and Henry Fonda. Interestingly, Fred caught on quicker with film audiences than either of those two film titans. They all came from small towns. Fred from Beaver Dam, Wisconsin. Fonda from Grand Island, Nebraska. Stewart from Indiana, Pennsylvania. They were each roughly the same age. Fred was 26 when he arrived in Hollywood, Stewart, 27, and Fonda, 29. They were each tall and dark and spoke with an accent which was distinctly American. They had each gotten their big breaks in the New York Theater, though in Stewart's and Fonda's case it was as actors and in Fred's case it was as a musician. By the late '30s, all three were established Hollywood stars.

While Fred may have initially caught on quicker than either Fonda or Stewart, and certainly became a huge star in his own right, he never acquired the legendary status of his two friends. One of the reasons for this, I think, is clear. Fred didn't appear in nearly as many classic films of the American cinema as his two friends. For instance, Stewart had *Mr. Smith Goes to Washington, Destry Rides Again, The Philadelphia Story, It's a Wonderful Life, Harvey, Rear Window, Vertigo* and *Anatomy of a Murder* to his resume, along with long-term star/director relationships with both Frank Capra and Alfred Hitchcock. Fonda appeared in *Young Mr. Lincoln, The Grapes of Wrath, The Lady Eve, The Ox-Bow Incident, My Darling Clementine, Mister Roberts* and *12 Angry Men,* and had a long-term screen relationship with director John Ford. The only films that Fred made during his lengthy career which could be classified among the true classics of the American cinema are the two he made for his best director, Billy Wilder, *Double Indemnity* and *The Apartment,* and maybe Edward Dymtryk's *The Caine Mutiny.* Of *Double Indemnity,* Woody Allen considers it perhaps the greatest American film ever made and the American Film Institute selected it number 38 in its poll of the 100 Greatest American films. (*The Apartment* also made the list, ranked #93.)

Fred worked with many outstanding directors such as King Vidor, Henry King, Michael Curtiz, George Stevens and William Wellman, but rarely more than once, and not in their best pictures. He made eight films for an excellent director, and considered one of the finest in his day, Mitchell Leisen, whose films still hold up, but is overshadowed by the writers of his best pictures: Billy Wilder and Preston Sturges. It's not fair to say that Fred ended up working most often with directors like Wesley Ruggles, Edward H. Griffith and George Marshall, because while these were journeymen directors, they also were effective craftsmen, who maybe didn't make many classic films, but did help create some very fine and enjoyable entertainments. And isn't that enough?

Like all the great screen actors of the classical era, and certainly true of Stewart and Fonda, Fred was very versatile in his choice of roles. He effortlessly went from romantic comedy (*The Gilded Lily, Remember the Night*), to wacky/screwball comedy (*Hands Across the Table, Murder, He Says*) to action films (*Dive Bomber, Men With Wings*), to *film noir* (*Double Indemnity, Pushover*), to romantic dramas (*Alice Adams*), to Westerns (*The Texas Rangers, At Gunpoint*), to historical dramas (*Maid of Salem*), and even an occasional musical (*Coconut Grove, And the Angels Sing*). Within the framework of his guy-next-door persona, Fred was remarkably versatile, and often excelled in roles which cast him as a heel (*The Apartment, The Caine Mutiny*), or murderers (*Double Indemnity* and *Pushover*). The French filmmaker Jean Pierre Melville called Fred "the inventor of underplaying, you can't help being astonished by the economy of means with which he achieves his effects."

Three men were largely responsible for Fred's comeback to the front ranks of Hollywood stardom in 1959-1960. They are Walt Disney, who thought that Fred performed comedy, particularly slapstick comedy, "like nobody else in the business" and cast him in several top box office hits from 1959-1967. Billy Wilder, who once again cast Fred against type, as a philandering heel in *The Apartment*. When Billy sent Fred the script, Fred was horrified to see he would be playing such an immoral character and one at odds with his new Disneyfied image. And a television producer named Don Fedderson, who wouldn't give up when Fred initially said "No" to playing Steve Douglas on *My Three Sons*. His perseverance became legendary and allowed Fred to enjoy one of the most unique deals ever agreed upon for an actor's service in a television series.

In his private life, Fred was considered by most in Hollywood as a stable family man who was devoted to both women he married. His first wife, Lily, was by all accounts the first woman he truly loved, and he was married to her for 17 years, until her untimely death in 1953. It is said that the first months after Lily's death were the saddest of Fred's life. He delved into work, initially *The Caine Mutiny,* a film script that Lily had read before her death and urged Fred to do. When he wasn't working, he spent his time with his two children, Susan and Robert. He finally came out of his shell when he met the vivacious singer-actress June Haver at a Christmas party in late 1953. June, too, was going through a rough patch following the death of her fiancé, and as a result she spent a period of months in a convent contemplating becoming a nun. Both of these lost souls found somebody they needed and needed them and to the surprise of many in Hollywood, Fred remarried a year after Lily's death. Still, because he was Fred MacMurray, and his character was so well known, marrying so soon after his first wife's death didn't raise any scandal clouds.

He and June, 17 years younger, were, if anything, even happier than Fred had been with Lily. Together they adopted two little red-headed girls and led a very happy second family life. If you are reading this book looking for dirt on Fred MacMurray, I'm sorry to disappoint you, but this is the story of a stable, happy man who was one of the most durable film stars in Hollywood history, and one who has, if anything, been underestimated as an actor. If he had any faults, it was his reputation for being in real-life what Jack Benny was on stage, a tight-wad, but even the stories told about his parsimoniousness are done with a smile because here was this extremely wealthy man who would ask his business manager permission to buy a fly-fishing rod! In "real-life" Fred and June MacMurray supported many charitable causes.

It has been a true pleasure telling Fred's story.

As always when writing a book there are many people to thank for the time they spent with me sharing their memories about Fred MacMurray, the actor and the man. They include: Ray Bayley, Sid Bloomberg, Martha Crawford-Cantarini, Arlene Dahl, Lyda Fischer, Anne Francis, Beverly Garland, Don Grady, Darryl Hickman, Claude Jarman, Jr., Sybil Jason, Hank Jones, Tom Kirk, George Lindsay, Joan Leslie, Dawn Lyn, Leonard Maltin, Rose Marie, Randall McKinstry, Lester Martin, Cynthia Pepper, Elliott Reid, Gene Reynolds, Mel Shavelson, Dave Smith, and Jane Wyman.

Derek Tague, as he did on my previous books, *I Love the Illusion: The Life and Career of Agnes Moorehead* and *Not So Dumb: The Life and Career of Marie Wilson,* helped my research immeasurably thanks to his work at the Billy Rose Library in New York City, where he assembled dozens of newspaper articles on Fred MacMurray from their vast archives.

I also would like to thank and commend the staff of the Margaret Herrick Library in Beverly Hills, California, who provided me with pertinent information from the papers of legendary Hollywood columnist Hedda Hopper, including unedited interviews with Fred and June MacMurray from the late '50s that Hopper used as the basis for newspaper articles on the couple. The staff of Arizona State University Archives in Tempe, who sent me information regarding Fred from the papers of Hollywood columnist Jimmy Starr. Starr was a Hollywood columnist going back to the '30s, who after the passing of the classical era of Hollywood and the passing of the fan magazines ended up working for *The National Enquirer*, and Fred, ever loyal to his friends, continued to give him interviews well into the 1970s. The staff of the Wisconsin State Historical Society, here in my hometown of Madison, Wisconsin, which as always, does yeoman service. They house the papers of Claude Binyon, a close friend of Fred's who wrote several of his best films. We owe a great debt of gratitude to these libraries and archives for the work they do.

Fellow authors are equally indispensable and always willing to help. I especially want to say a big thank you to Robert Nott, who provided me with a detailed transcript of an interview he conducted with *My Three Sons* producer Ed Hartmann, as well as other useful information. My biggest thank you to Mr. Nott is for helping me locate Tom Kirk, who worked with Fred in four Disney films, and gave some great insight into that studio and working with Fred. Sandra Grabman, a wonderful author, was incredibly helpful to me with suggestions and improvements. Laura Wagner kindly made copies of some articles from her files regarding Fred, which I was able to use in the text. My publisher, Ben Ohmart, also a prolific author himself, I thank for his encouragement of this book.

I would also like to give thanks to these authors for some incredible source material: James Robert Parish, who, along with Don Stanke, wrote a highly informative chapter on Fred in his essential book *The All-Americans;* David Chierichetti, the author of *Hollywood Director,* a splendid biography of Mitchell Leisen; and Dan Falatico, who wrote a comprehensive study of *My Three Sons* for *Television Chronicles.* These publications and others were of immense help to me. Finally, my thanks to a wonderful and legendary writer named Charles Stumpf for his encouragement, as well as my friends and family.

Charles Tranberg
Madison, WI.
December 7, 2006

Introduction

BY DON GRADY

Every once in a great while something happens in life that is miraculous.

It was early 1960. I was 15 years old, building a cedar bench in the garage of our Burbank, California home when my father appeared, suitcase in hand, and announced that he was leaving us. I was so confused and angry I pounded nails into a two-by-four for hours.

At the same time, over the hill in Brentwood, legendary film star, Fred MacMurray, was losing contact with his teenage son Rob who, according to Fred, had rejected their lifestyle for an alternate experience in a commune in northern California.

My Three Sons was in early rehearsals when I got the call. The producers had cast another actor to play "Robbie" but, for reasons I never found out, they needed to replace him. I was summoned to a hastily held audition at noon, and by 3pm I was cast as the new Robbie. My acting abilities probably helped, but I still believe the reason I got the part was because the cleft in my chin looked like Fred's!

So there we were a few weeks later, Fred and I, one who had lost touch with his son Rob, and the other who had lost touch with his father, playing Rob…standing face to face. Well, we hardly stood face to face…he was 6'2" and I was 5'7"! Still, there we were, about to bond in a way that neither of us expected.

Fred was always nice and very polite, but not an easy man to get to know. He towered over me like one of those monuments to big business on Wilshire Blvd. I felt inconsequential standing in his shadow. All I was looking for was a nod of acceptance, and I finally got it the day Fred took out his sax and I accompanied him on piano. I remember the twinkle in his eye and the connection I felt. Music bridged the unspoken gap between us, and a deep friendship began.

Fred often spoke to me about Rob. It bothered him deeply that he couldn't connect with his only son. Gradually I came to see Fred as a man who was longing to have the same relationship with Rob, as Steve Douglas had with his sons…a relationship that he created on screen and would continue to re-create for twelve years. I've always felt that one of the reasons the show was so successful was because there was really very little acting going on!

In becoming a Douglas, I was able to live out a family life that probably most of us never had. True, the Douglases didn't have a mother…but I didn't care. I had a great one at home. On Stage 11 at Desilu Studios, Fred would take me under his wing five days a week, and advise me about all sorts of things…how to deliver certain lines, what foods were healthy to eat, what I should and shouldn't do with the girls I was dating (oh, those were some fun talks!), and what was proper to wear. Every time I put on a suit and tie, Fred would come over and tie it for me…explaining how this side goes over that side, then this part goes through there, etc. I literally didn't tie my own tie for years! It was Fred's way of fathering me, of showing me he cared. And I soaked it up. He loved me like a father, I loved him like a son…and I'll never forget him.

Through his TV sons, Fred found the chance to express his love for his son. Through Fred, I found the chance to experience a father-son relationship, which I eventually had with my real dad. And through the Douglas family, a lot of people found that many of life's difficulties could be conquered with a lot of warmth and a little humor.

How much of that is miraculous? I suppose it depends on where you are in life, and how much of a miracle you need. For me, Fred MacMurray was the miracle I needed.

Hollywood, 1938

By 1938 Fred MacMurray was one of the top leading men in the motion picture industry. He had teamed with the likes of Claudette Colbert, Carole Lombard, Sylvia Sidney, Katharine Hepburn and Joan Bennett in such glittering films as *The Gilded Lily, Hands Across the Table, Alice Adams, The Trail of the Lonesome Pine* and *Thirteen Hours by Air.* At 30 years of age he had fame and fortune, as well as a happy marriage. Despite making his home in Hollywood, he was essentially the same small-town boy who grew up in Beaver Dam, Wisconsin enjoying such pastimes as hunting, fishing and athletics. Throughout his life, he never forgot where he came from or the people he knew growing up as "Bud" MacMurray.

As it so happened, in the summer of 1938 members of the Beaver Dam (WI) American Legion band traveled out to Los Angeles to attend the national American Legion Convention. Many members of the Beaver Dam American Legion band were young kids just out of high school. It turned out that the Legion ranks had thinned and, as long as they had a minimal number of actual Legionnaires in the band, they could recruit other members such as those recent high school graduates. One of the boys who excitedly arrived at Union Station in Los Angeles with his fellow band mates was Ray Bayley. Ray was excited for a couple of reasons—one, to march in the parade at the convention and two the possible opportunity to meet one of Beaver Dam's own favorite sons — Fred MacMurray.

"When we disembarked in the Union Depot," Bayley recalled years later, "I called a friend of my mother's, Fred MacMurray's mother. Although I dutifully relayed news bits from back home, my real mission was obvious. She graciously arranged for me to visit Fred at his home." On the day of his visit Bayley was up early and, skipping breakfast, he caught a bus which took him out to Fred's house. He arrived at the appointed hour, knocked on the door and was greeted by Fred's wife, Lillian. "Lillian struck me as an extremely gracious lady," recalled Bayley. "There was no real reason to be kind to this celebrity-hanger-on from his hometown who never knew him! She showed me around the house and yard ..." She also explained with an apology that Fred was still in bed, "[He] had been up until midnight and, not accustomed to that, he was still in bed."

Mr. Bayley recalls that Fred's home was "not showy, though it was very nice; a sign of opulence was the swimming pool, unusual in those years. As I recall, there were flowers galore." Within a few minutes, Fred was up and joined them. He invited the young man to have breakfast with him. "The breakfast nook where we ate consisted of a long table against a wall, with chairs at the ends and available for the long side," Bayley remembered. Bayley, having skipped breakfast, was hungry, so Fred asked his maid to bring him some. As they ate and talked, Fred suddenly noticed that the young man didn't have a napkin. "He moved as if to call the maid, but instead said, 'Here, take mine; I'm through with it.' And tossed it to me." From that moment forward, Bayley says his appreciation for Fred really began, "he was folksy and unassuming."

Fred had invited the other Beaver Dam legionnaires to have lunch with him that afternoon at Paramount Studios. Bayley felt that, since he was meeting with Fred at his home, he should skip the lunch at the studio. When Fred heard this, he prevailed upon Bayley to come along and invited him to ride with him to the studio. It was an opportunity the young man wasn't about to pass up. Fred drove himself and Bayley — he didn't use a chauffeur. When he arrived at the studio and parked his car, Bayley would recall that "Fred became the movie star when we alighted from the car into public view, and put on sunglasses which fooled nobody."

Of Paramount Studios itself Bayley recalls it as "unpretentious and practical. Its parking lot, even then, was spacious; we walked a distance from his car to the building where we had lunch, coming upon the bus which had brought the rest of our band group to arrive at the same time as we did." Bayley felt he had dominated enough of Fred's time and wanted to let the others have an opportunity to talk to the hometown boy made good. But Fred had other ideas and invited Bayley to sit next to him at the U-shaped table at which they all enjoyed luncheon.

At the lunch Bayley says he "witnessed what I have often referred to as Fred MacMurray's best job of acting." Many of the people at the table knew Fred from Beaver Dam, but others didn't. It was a thrill to all of them to meet with him at the studio for lunch because they were in the presence of a bona-fide star. "Fred would interact cordially," Bayley recalled. "Then, leaning toward me with his napkin over his mouth, he would ask, 'Who am I talking to?'"

Bayley would later write, "I was deeply impressed by his plainness, his modesty and his humility. Fred MacMurray, the Beaver Dam boy who had gotten a job in Los Angeles, made a major difference in my life — a difference, that, in my mid-80s, I still recognize and appreciate."

Fred in Hollywood, around 1938.

CHAPTER ONE

Small-Town Boy Makes Good
1908-1934

When Fred MacMurray was born on August 30, 1908, in Kankakee, Illinois, his parents knew only two things for certain. If it was a girl, her name would be Rose and if it was a boy he would be named after his father, concert violinist Frederick MacMurray. A baby boy was born and he was named after his father, but to the family he was known as "Bud," as in Rosebud — this pleased Fred in later years because, "Man, how I hated that 'Frederick' when I was a kid."

Both of Fred's parents had ties to the small Middle Western town of Beaver Dam, Wisconsin. As a matter of fact, Beaver Dam would pride itself on two things for many years: being the hometown of Fred MacMurray and its selection as the typical American small town. Frederick MacMurray was the son of the Rev. T.J. MacMurray, former pastor of the First Presbyterian Church of Beaver Dam. Fred's mother, Maleta Martin, was the eldest daughter of a prominent Beaver Dam family, whose father was the president of the Beaver Dam Telephone Company. Frederick MacMurray, who traveled the country performing concerts, had not lived in Beaver Dam for many years when he returned in 1903 for a concert. It was here that he met the fetching, dark-haired Maleta and they fell in love.

Maleta's family disapproved of the romance. Maleta had long been considered "the most popular girl" in Beaver Dam. Her parents believed that she should not be involved with somebody who was in show business. It was a typical reaction of the times against an industry considered loose morally. Frederick, being a traveling musician, did not lead the kind of conservative and stable life that Jacob and Lena Martin envisioned for the suitor of their vivacious daughter.

Jacob Martin was a self-made man. His obituary makes this clear: "Mr. Martin received his education in the public schools and in the hard school of practical experience." His first job was as a cabinet maker's apprentice at age thirteen. He went on to manufacture cigars and then launched a popular Beaver Dam restaurant, Bon Ton Buffet, and later the Bon Ton Bottling Works. Besides owning his own successful businesses, Jacob became the manager of the local telephone company. When he took on this job in 1889 the exchange consisted of only a single subscriber, but through his energetic efforts, within a few years it had over 1500 members.

Maleta was a headstrong girl who knew her own mind, and despite the opposition of her parents, she and Frederick eloped to Chicago and were married on June 20, 1904. She would travel off and on with her husband over the next several years. When she wasn't with Frederick on one of his tours, she would return to the family home in Beaver Dam. However, because she had disobeyed her father and eloped, Maleta wasn't allowed to stay in the main living quarters of the family home. When she did come home, she stayed in the room occupied by her youngest sister Hazel with whom she was very close to.

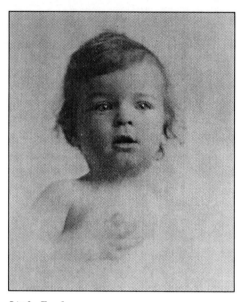

Little Fred.

Maleta was with her husband when he was performing at a concert in Kankakee, Illinois in August 1908 when she delivered their son Fred. There is some evidence that while staying in Kankakee Maleta and the baby were taken in by Dr. Charles Geiger and his wife, Katharine. He was an eye, ear, nose and throat specialist and wasn't the doctor who delivered Fred. Years later when Fred was an established Hollywood star, Kankakee resident Ida Bird Holmes sent Hollywood columnist Hedda Hopper copies of Dr. Geiger's obituary and asked Hedda to pass them on to Fred writing, "Will you kindly give the two enclosed clippings to Fred MacMurray for I know how good Dr. and Mrs. Geiger were to Fred and his mother when he was born in Kankakee. It seems they took them into their home and kept them until the father was able to see for them. Dr. Geiger always referred to Fred as 'my boy.' He was a grand man and Kankakee will mourn him always ..."

The pressures of the road finally got to be too much for Maleta. She eventually left her husband and returned full time to Beaver Dam with little Fred. When Fred was a toddler, his mother took him to the circus. "I wept because a clown knocked another clown's head off — although the head was papier-mâché," Fred recalled years later. "For some time I refused to go into the theater because of that." He had recovered from this shock sufficiently to appear on stage with his father in a theater when he was five years old, accompanying his father on the violin, an instrument that the son didn't particularly care for as his father did. Little Fred played the violin while standing on a chair. "I played a duet with my father," Fred later recalled. "I trembled. I shook. I had trouble fingering the strings. I loathed every second of it, but I did it. I still sweat profusely when I'm forced to face a live audience. I duck that whenever I can."

It was shortly after this that Frederick MacMurray and Maleta Martin MacMurray separated for good. Apparently Fred never knew for sure what became of Frederick. Fred's cousin, Lester Martin, would later state that Fred often wondered why, when he became famous, his father never tried to contact him, but assumed he probably had died.

Fred as a baby, probably in Beaver Dam.

Years later Fred and his second wife, June Haver, would be sitting in their living room listening to a concert on television. At one point in the concert there is a violin solo and June looked over to Fred and noticed tears in his eyes. She realized he was thinking of the father that he barely remembered. It is perhaps ironic that Fred MacMurray, the ultimate TV dad, grew up basically with no father and in a household dominated by females. Maleta's father, Jacob Martin, died in December 1911 at only 58 years of age when Fred was just three. His major influences growing up would be his mother, his grandmother Lena and his aunt Hazel. Perhaps it was due to his understanding and respect for the feminine influences of his early life that when Fred did become a Hollywood star he worked with nearly all the great actresses of his day without being overshadowed by them or losing his masculinity. He was in constant demand by the female stars to be their leading man.

Despite growing up with an abundance of female influences, Fred was, by all accounts, a typical American boy. He was creative — he liked to draw and paint. He was musically inclined and would eventually play a variety of instruments. He also enjoyed outdoor recreations such as hunting, camping and fishing and eventually developed into an all-star athlete. He and Maleta did occasionally move around. Maleta sought work as a secretary in Madison, and for a short time they lived there. Fred also was enrolled in military school for a while, but, by and large, his boyhood was spent in Beaver Dam.

"He was always himself; he never was a big shot or even tried to be — he was a quiet fellow," his boyhood friend Randall McKinstry said of Fred. As boys, McKinstry recalled that he and Fred loved to "wake up early and go fishing" at a time before the sun came up and when the fish would hungrily go for a squirming worm on a fishing hook. But Fred was notorious for being a heavy sleeper and according to McKinstry, Fred would tie a string to his big toe and sleep with the

A boy and his dog, Fred at around eight.

string hanging outside the window, so that when it was time for them to go fishing, McKinstry would pull on the string hanging outside of Fred's window as a means of waking him up. The two boys became close friends (a friendship which lasted Fred's entire life) in part because they lived in close proximity to one another. "We lived on Washington Street here in Beaver Dam," McKinstry later explained, "and he lived on Park Avenue with his grandmother and mother. The two properties connected at the back, and that's how we became so well-acquainted." Randall McKinstry's nephew, Robert, would later say that Fred was "just a very friendly man. Very down to earth — he didn't put on airs and he was not Hollywoodish — just very congenial and we in Beaver Dam were very proud of him." He added that his uncle Randall "was not in awe of Fred even after he became a huge star because he was just 'Bud' to him and they had been friends since they were children." Fred enjoyed his youth in Beaver Dam, saying, "Life was fun. No problems. Two blocks and you were in the country. I used to fish a lot."

Besides Randall McKinstry, Fred formed close friendships with two other local boys, Howie Louden and Myron Bartell. Louden recalled Fred as "a nice guy, and he always treated everybody the same. He never said much, but he was very artistic and one very nice person." With Louden and Bartell Fred played basketball and football — and excelled in both. His height, he was over six feet tall by the time he entered high school, made him a natural for basketball. But one of his most remembered feats of athleticism happened on the football field in a game which pitted Beaver Dam against rival Portage on November 22, 1924, when Fred was sixteen and already a senior in high school. On that night, according to both men, Fred helped Beaver Dam achieve a 13-6 victory over Portage with a 45-yard dropkick which sent the ball sailing in the wind. "They argued and argued that it was really a punt," Bartell later recalled. "Heck, nobody kicked 45-yard dropkicks, now called field goals, in those days." In his high school career Fred ended up winning ten letters in athletics as well as an American Legion medal which awarded him fifty dollars.

The kids could be mischievous as all kids are, but it was an innocent type of mischievousness. Fred later recalled, "All the kids in the big classroom on the second floor of the old high school, the old Wilson school, would move their feet in unison while studying (and apparently while there was no teacher present in the room) and it would shake the ceiling below." The boys might take a bottle of wine out into the country and split it — "that was the worst we did," Fred remembered during the far more turbulent '60s, when he was confused and perplexed by the youth of that day.

As a teenager, Fred held a variety of odd jobs. In the summers he worked in the local pea canning factory where, "the wages were twenty-five cents an hour and when the rush was on you canned peas twenty hours a day or took a chance of drowning in them." He also worked for a time in another local business, the Malleable Iron Range Company, which each year gave a yearly diploma and prize of fifty dollars as a scholarship. In 1924, Fred won this prize.

Fred inherited a love of music from his father and while he didn't take to the violin, he did learn to play a variety of musical instruments, including the piano, banjo and the instrument in which he would become most famous for playing and for a time earn his living with — the saxophone. In the mid-'40s he told a reporter, "No, I have no complaints against the saxophone. I went through school and quite a way into college on it. In youth it sheltered me, and I'll protect it now." Fred was rarely as passionate about anything in an interview as he was about the saxophone.

Fred also tried out for the school play, but was rejected because he couldn't sing. (Fred later sang in several of his films and sounded fine.) "Isn't that funny?" asked Randall McKinstry's wife many years later. "He never made it. He wasn't good enough. [But] it didn't bother him at all." He may have been rejected as well due to stage fright. Fred would recall that when he graduated from the eighth grade, he had to give a speech. "My first two lines were, 'In a dingy garret in the lonely city of London lay a dying man. His legs were clothed in long, military boots,'" Fred recalled. "That's as far as I got. That's as far as I can get now. I sat down and shut my mouth."

His height, wavy dark hair and amiability made him attractive to the girls at school. "He was considered very handsome by us girls and I recall he had dark curly hair and was quite a dream boat," recalled Lyda Fischer, one of Fred's classmates. (Miss Fischer was actually a grade behind Fred.) "He was involved in athletics, I believe he was on the football team, plus he was interested in music — I think he played in a local boys band — and played the sax and of course he came from a musical family — his father being a violinist, so apparently he inherited a love of music." Miss Fischer went on to say, "When he lived in Beaver Dam he was considered just a nice — regular fella. He got along with everybody and was very popular. Later on when he became famous he came back several times — sometimes we in town knew about it and other times we didn't. He would just come and visit his friend Randall McKinstry."

When Fred wasn't working at the Iron Range Company or canning peas, he earned money, with Bartell, playing in a two-man band during the summers of 1923 and 1924. Bartell recalled that they played in a "gin joint" on the shores of Beaver Dam Lake — and this was during Prohibition! Bartell said that the owner would have the two of them — Bartell on piano and Fred on sax — play to attract people inside and then again when they started to leave. In an early profile of Fred, shortly after he became a leading Hollywood star, the experience at the Road House on Beaver Dam Lake was remembered this way, "... he became tangled up with one Mynie Bartell, who was a piano playing kid at school who had formed an orchestra which got a job at a barroom on the lake. Either the beer was bad or the orchestra was short of excellence because nobody ever came out to the place and the management never paid the band. They put the thing down to experience and tried to work it out, without success with pretzels."

Fred graduated from high school on June 4, 1925. He was only sixteen at the time. The class of '25 consisted of 62 members, "the largest of Beaver Dam High School" up to that time. In the newspaper announcing the names of the students graduating and on his diploma itself his name is the dreaded "Frederick" MacMurray. Due to his excellence in athletics Fred was given a scholarship to Carroll College in Waukesha, Wisconsin — which badly wanted him on their football team.

II

Carroll College boasted one famous alumnus when Fred began his college career in the fall of 1925. Stage actor Alfred Lunt had attended the school, but while Lunt was making a name for himself in the New York Theatre he had not yet attained the greatness of his later teaming with wife Lynn Fontanne. Fred's scholarship paid his tuition and books but no other expenses. To survive Fred needed to get a job, and his most likely avenue would be through music. He joined up with a six-piece orchestra called

Tom Joy's Gloom Chasers, which played five nights per week at the Blue Mounds Inn, paying Fred $25 per week. "It was a swell place," Fred recalled a decade later when he was already established in Hollywood. "I'd be working my head off around there but all the time thinking about the good free meal I'd get after the rush was over — and then I'd be so tired I couldn't eat." In addition to his work with the band, Fred helped wash dishes at the Inn to earn a few extra bucks. Fred wrote his buddy Randall McKinstry back in Beaver Dam that he was having fun where he was living, but had done precious little studying. In fact, working in a band all week, and not getting home until three or even four in the morning, and then having to get up and go to classes and then football practice in the afternoons, took its toll on Fred's energy and grades. "I didn't have to tell them I couldn't do jazz bands and football and classes — they told me."

After Fred left Carroll College (by mutual consent) he went off to Chicago where he planned to try his luck at the Chicago Art Institute. He stayed with an aunt, sleeping on her davenport while he sought out jobs by day and took classes by night. One of the temporary jobs was selling sporting goods at Marshall Fields Department Store. Music was more of a passion for Fred than art (or sales for that matter), so after only a few classes he left the Art Institute when he got an interview with a bandleader named Morrie Sherman. Sherman had his own band, but also booked bands all over the Middle West. At his audition, Sherman had him play a piece on his sax, and Fred selected a swing version of the Sam Lewis and Joe Young hit "Dinah." Fred performed it all the while shaking in his boots and perspiring from his brow. Sherman didn't think that Fred was right for his band, but felt he did show potential, so he connected him with a bandleader named Jack Higgins, who had a band called The Royal Purples which played out of Loyola University. With Higgins and the Royal Purples Fred played several months worth of dates around the Chicago area and at a summer resort in Twin Lakes, Wisconsin. In addition to playing sax, Fred also began doing some singing and, to his shock, did surprisingly well, reminding his audiences of the then popular Rudy Vallee.

In 1928 Fred's mother and Aunt Hazel decided to go to California to visit their mother who had moved to Los Angeles a few years earlier. Fred wasn't getting anywhere with the Royal Purples, so he decided to go along and offered his services as chauffeur, and off they all went to the west coast. Fred was also thinking ahead in other ways too. "I was looking ahead to the time when I'd have to support my mother and grandma and I wasn't missing any tricks. My father played the violin, but I thought the sax would be more commercial — jazz and stuff coming up like mad, you know. I had an eye out for a loose buck." Fred believed, like many people, that California was a land of opportunity.

In fact, they all did. Maleta and Aunt Hazel decided to stay on in

California as well. For a time they all lived in the grandmother's house. One of the reasons why Fred's grandmother had moved to California was because a favorite brother, Charley, had moved there when doctors had advised him that he should live in a warmer climate due to his health. According to Fred's cousin, Lester Martin, Charley bought an orange grove near Whittier, which had proved to be profitable.

It was shortly after arriving in California that Fred had a terrible experience which caused him to have a lifelong aversion of the sea. Like many people who come to California, one of the first places they like to stop is at the beach. Fred was no exception. He went swimming alone in the Pacific Ocean and after a few minutes he was caught in a riptide which threatened to take him under. He battled it fiercely and finally was able to reach shore. "I just crawled in," he recalled forty-five years later. "I was scared. I really didn't think I was going to make it." Fred loved to fish, but he never became a fan of deep-sea fishing due to this experience and he was often to say in interviews that he didn't care to even go boating in the ocean.

Fred began looking for band work and ended up playing for a bandleader named Lou Woods. Woods found Fred to be amiable and a fine musician, but not a particularly memorable personality. Years later, after Fred had attained great stardom, Woods was asked what he recalled about Fred MacMurray. "Well, there was one thing," Woods said. "Peanut butter. The guy was a fool for it and his mother was always sending it to him."

It was while in Los Angeles in 1928-1929 that Fred decided to try his luck in the movies. He had been doing some laboring work around the studios, and with his tall good looks several people suggested that he try to make a go in motion pictures. So he registered with the central casting office for work as an extra in films. He got a few jobs in that time. Fred always downplayed these early jobs and told the same story over and over again about the time he was cast as an extra in a crowd scene, and because he towered over many of the other extras (due to his height) he was noticed by the director who called out to him, "You! Do you think you can come up here and say, 'We won't stand for it!'?" It was a moment that most of the other extras would have given up their right arm for, but Fred always claimed that he immediately and defiantly shouted "No!" Fred did recall one of his extra jobs in a film called *Girls Gone Wild.* "That was a film everybody's forgotten but for me," Fred later claimed. "Sue Carol and Dixie Lee were the stars. Later one married Alan Ladd and the other Bing Crosby. I earned $10 wearing a dress suit which cost me $5 to hire. Naturally I went back to shoving timber and scenery on the lot. But every now and then a director would get me a small part." In actuality Fred does have two lines in *Girls Gone Wild.* He is first seen with a group of fellow schoolboys who rush in yelling, "Hooray! The Girls are here!" and then later has a solo line where he says, "Is that Sally?" before disappearing to the back of the crowd.

But it wasn't to be films which would ultimately lead to his big break — it was music. By 1930 he was playing sax with a pit band at a Los Angeles theater. In addition to playing with this band he also did a few songs with a trio. Fred's baritone voice caught the ear of another act on the bill, a group of young men who wore blazers, straw hats and gloves which made their fingers look like black and white piano keys. They called themselves The California Collegians. Fred thought they were being kind when they complimented him on his act and was making casual conversation when they asked him if he knew how to read music — he did — so, he was flabbergasted when the band asked him to join them — they had an opening, one of their players had quit and they needed somebody in a hurry. While they certainly did like Fred's sax work and his easy-going style with a song, it was the fact that he could read music which sealed the deal. It turned out that none of the Collegians (Fred is the only member who actually spent any time at all in college) knew how to read music, and because of this they were playing the same tired tunes over and over again and desperately needed to update their material. Fred eagerly accepted their invitation. Fred would later recall that the Collegians were "one of the first performing bands to go on the vaudeville circuit." In addition to their musical abilities the boys liked to clown around on stage. "The vaudeville part of the Collegians' act was real wild," Fred later recalled. "At one point they pretended to be seals and went flippering across the stage. I flippered across the boards too. At another point we wore bald-headed wigs, and we did an organ number."

The boys made their way to New York, where they found work in a revue opening on Broadway called *Three's a Crowd*. The show starred Libby Holman, Clifton Webb and Fred Allen. The Collegians played in the orchestra, but Fred's good looks got him noticed, and he was brought up on stage to be sung to by Libby Holman. The song was "Something to Remember You By," and originally it was going to be sung in an up-tempo, comedic fashion, but it was later decided that it would be more effective being sung as a ballad. Fred was dressed as a sailor on leave and while Holman is singing this love song to him his back is to the audience much of the time. She sings the song and then at the conclusion the whistle of his ship sounds and he begins to make his exit and utters, "See you around, baby." Fred's cousin Lester Martin contends that Fred being chosen to appear on stage with Holman was a lucky circumstance. "There was an actor who was to stand on stage with Libby Holman as she sung to him and he didn't show up so they had Fred go on stage and do it. That was his first real introduction to acting."

Fred recalled Holman as, "the hottest torch singer of the day," and the experience itself as terrifying. "I wasn't just a kid. I was born in 1908. Three's a Crowd opened in 1930 so that made me twenty-two, but being sung a hot song by Libby Holman and trying to react in an undopey way was murder.

At the conclusion of Libby's song I was so self-conscious that I wanted to break away and stumble off the stage. But I had to pull an anchor from my uniform give it to her and say, 'see you later, babe.' The first three nights my hands shook. I had trouble getting that anchor off. I fixed that by attaching it to a hairpin. After that I plucked it off easier."

Following the New York run of *Three's a Crowd* the show began its national tour. Even though it did well in New York the farther it got from the Big Apple the fewer ticket buyers there were. The show was supposed to go as far as the west coast, but closed in Des Moines. The California Collegians then experienced a dry spell which was interrupted by a gig at a resort hotel in Marblehead, Massachusetts. After that they did find some work in nightclubs and vaudeville, and then they got another big break with a job in yet another Broadway show.

III

Roberta, based on the novel *Gowns by Roberta*, by Alice Duer Miller, was about a football player who inherits a Paris dress shop after his aunt dies. Producer Max Gordon, who had an illustrious record of hits on Broadway including *The Jazz Singer*, *Three's a Crowd*, *The Band Wagon* and *Cat and the Fiddle*, bought the novel and arranged for Otto Harbach to write the book for the play. Harbach was best known for his book and music of the phenomenally successful 1920s Broadway musicals *No, No Nanette* and *Sunny*. For Roberta, Gordon hired Jerome Kern to do the music with Harbach writing the lyrics. Luckily, Max Gordon had employed the Collegians in *Three's a Crowd* and had enjoyed their work and signed them on for his new show.

Ray Middleton was cast as John Kent, the football player who inherits the dress shop. Bob Hope, an up-and-coming comedian who had appeared in a few Broadway shows, got his big break playing Middleton's best friend, a bandleader named Huckleberry Haines. George Murphy played Billy Boyden, Huckleberry's manager and best friend. Tamara Drasin, or simply Tamara, was cast as the manager of "Roberta's," the dress shop in the story, and the love interest to Middleton. Since Hope's character Huckleberry Haines was a bandleader he had to have a band, and that's where the California Collegians came in. They were the on-stage band and participated in several sketches and numbers. In one sketch Fred does what was described as a ten-second impression of Rudy Vallee. George Murphy recalled that Fred's bit went over well with the audiences and, on a personal level, he "was such a nice guy we all loved him." In addition to being part of the California Collegians, Fred was asked to be Ray Middleton's understudy — a task he accepted somewhat apprehensively. Even though he was much more comfortable on stage, Middleton was one of the leads in the play and if he ever missed a performance, Fred wasn't sure he would be able to carry it off.

Despite the talent involved in the show the tryouts were not going well, particularly an early one in Philadelphia. "I knew we were in real trouble when at the end of the first act, I saw the stage carpenter go to the telephone and place a call to New York," recalled George Murphy. "He was already looking for another job." But Gordon had faith in the show, particularly the show-stopping song "Smoke Gets in Your Eyes." To keep the show afloat he asked all the players to take a ten-percent pay cut, which they all grudgingly did. He also solicited advice from the other players. Bob Hope later recalled, "Because it's such a stand out in the memory of all theatergoers old enough to remember it, it's hard to realize now that *Roberta* had rough going when it opened in Philadelphia; that it was decided that it needed extra staging ... I myself suggested a few jokes and an idea or two." One of the ideas Hope says that he suggested was to have the California Collegians do the "organ bit" that they had perfected on the vaudeville stage. "The Collegians wore gloves which looked like organ keys. I played those keys. Each time I touched a glove it brought a different note." By creating some new comedy material and staging a reprise of "Smoke Gets in Your Eyes" in the second act — the show showed steady improvement and shortly after it premiered at the New Amsterdam Theater in New York on November 18, 1933 it became a solid hit.

Despite George Murphy's assertion that everybody loved Fred, there is some evidence that Bob Hope felt some jealousy toward the younger (Fred was Bob's junior by four years) and better-looking man. According to film historian and author Lawrence J. Quirk in his biography of Bob Hope *The Road Well-Traveled*, "Hope began stepping on toes right from the first. Jealous of Fred MacMurray's good looks (and Fred was a looker, as all the showgirls noted, as would millions of filmgoers two years hence), Hope patronized him as a green kid and former saxophone tootler who couldn't put over comedy." According to Quirk, Fred wasn't the only one that Hope gave trouble to. Also in the cast was the rotund character actor Sydney Greenstreet, eight years before his tour de force role as Gutman in the Humphrey Bogart version of *The Maltese Falcon*. Greenstreet was getting irritated by the continual fat jokes that Hope was making at his expense and decided to turn the tables on him and started giving Hope acting tips, "much to Hope's annoyance."

Quirk maintains that years later when he asked about Bob Hope, Fred kind of hesitated and then said, "He was tough — very tough. He thought he was right on everything and everyone else was wrong. No middle ground for him. He was a pain in the ass." Despite this, legend has it that Fred and Bob Hope were old friends and there is some evidence to support this as well. But it may be that they were more like professional friends. They had experiences working together in later years on television shows, but that outside of the studio they rarely saw each other. While both were avid golf-ers, Bob Hope didn't really participate in other MacMurray passions such as fishing and hunting. They did occasionally golf together, but usually as a foursome rather than being alone one on one.

The showgirls did find Fred attractive but only one caught his eye, a tall, statuesque brunette in the show named Lillian Lamonte. Lillian would make her nightly appearance in the show during the "Smoke Gets in Your Eyes" number as one of the models in the background. "I saw a girl named Lillian Lamonte," Fred later recalled, "and smoke got in my eyes." For the rest of their lives together the song "Smoke Gets in Your Eyes" would be considered "their" song. They met when the show was in rehearsals in New York in August 1933. Fred found the courage to ask her out and she accepted. Because both were limited of funds, they had a romantic but inex-pensive courtship. One early article describes it as a "courtship of quiet din-ners in cheap tearooms, long walks, occasional movie shows, and many rides on the tops of Fifth Avenue buses." It was love at first sight and very soon afterwards Fred was telling Lillian (whom he called Lily) that he loved her and wanted to marry her. They got into the habit of taking Sunday after-noon walks during which they would window shop and plan the kind of apartment they ultimately would share. "There must be at least four rooms," Lillian would tell him. "You can't put a six foot, three'er into one of those stingy kitchenette affairs." But Fred made it clear he didn't want to marry her until he was a success and had some money behind him. "You'll get money, Frederick," Fred recalled Lily telling him. "Plenty of it. I know! Sure we'll get married." Fred would always recall Lily as someone who gave him confidence and believed in him and sometimes provided the extra push he occasionally needed when it came to his professional career.

Nobody can say for sure if Fred remained a virgin during those years on the road with the band, but he certainly did have a reputation for it. Fan magazine writer Jerry Asher later told Lawrence Quirk, "If Fred had ever gotten drunk by his band mates and ensconced in a whorehouse when he was 21 or so, or if he ever had blundered into something promiscuously casual on tour, I think he would have been as guilt-ridden as any Catholic choirboy. The quick romance was not for this boy. He was a romantic and idealistic when it came to women, under all that rakishly casual exterior of his. Of course he was so sexy that women conceived elaborate strategies to get him in bed." Fred's chaste reputation even became the butt of a private joke attributed to Jack Benny (but author Laurence Quirk in his book *Bob Hope: The Road Well-Traveled* thinks it is more likely to have been originated by Hope) which doesn't bear repeating but suggests that Fred had a lot of time on his hands for masturbation.

It was almost as if Lily was clairvoyant about an upturn in Fred's for-tunes. A short time into the run of *Roberta* Fred went to the pick up his mail, which had been sent in care of the booking office. (Since the group was accustomed to traveling, members' mail was sent care of the booking office instead of the theater.) It so happened that the booking office was in the New York Paramount building. Fred would later remember it this way: "… a young fellow, Dave Jonas, who worked in that office, asked me, 'Why don't you go into the movies?' We were in the Paramount Building, and Oscar Serlin, who was head of Paramount's talent department, had his office upstairs. "Come on upstairs,' Jonas said. Serlin looked me over and asked, 'What are you doing?' I said, 'I'm in *Roberta.*' He asked, 'What do you do in the show?' I said, 'I'm with the stage band on stage, I have a few lines, and I understudy the lead.'"

Serlin arranged for Fred to read the part he was understudying for in *Roberta* and was sufficiently impressed with this reading and with Fred's romantic good looks that he arranged for Fred to make a screen test. It turned out that in the screen test Fred was to appear as something of a dandy. He was asked to wear a tuxedo, top hat and carry a cane. He had the tuxedo he wore in the show, but didn't have a top hat or cane to go with the ensemble. He thought of Bob Hope, who was considered a young man about town. "So, I went into Bob's dressing room," Fred later recalled. "And I said, 'Bob … I've got the chance to do a movie test.' And he said, 'No kidding!' He was surprised. I said, 'Well … I've got to have a top hat — can I try yours?' He said, 'Sure … try it on.' Luckily we both had big heads, so he lent it to me.'" Hope had had a Hollywood screen test himself a few years earlier which hadn't been successful and, "when MacMurray told Hope about the offer, all Hope could think of was what happened to him … He figured they'd kick MacMurray's brains out on the coast …"

Fred made the screen test and was sure it was a disaster. "Of course, it will be terrible," Fred told Lily. "Imagine what my acting must look like. Why, they wouldn't let me blow on a sax and that's the only way I'm natural." Then the day of reckoning came. "Word came back," Fred recalled. "'Send him out.' I drew the standard seven-year contract with options at the end of each six months.'" Fred gave his notice to the producers of *Roberta* and by February 1934 he was in Hollywood. During this time Lily stayed in New York with *Roberta.* Fred wanted to see if his first six-month option would be picked up before he would allow Lily to give up her job in the show.

While in California, Fred stayed with his mother and grandmother. He was also finding out that being signed by a major Hollywood studio doesn't automatically mean that he would be working — Fred later recalled that he wasn't assigned any parts for the first five months he was at Paramount. That isn't all together true because he was loaned out to Warner Brothers shortly after he arrived in Hollywood to do a bit in the Charlie Ruggles comedy *Friends of Mr. Sweeney,* but his part was so quick that he wasn't much noticed by filmgoers or critics. When he returned to Paramount he appeared in screen tests with other actors, and was apparently considered for a film to star Sylvia Sidney, but this didn't pan out. He also took acting lessons at the studio's drama school under the guidance of Phyllis Loughton, later Phyllis Seaton, the wife of director George Seaton and considered one of the top acting teachers in Hollywood. Loughton was described in a Screen and Radio Weekly article from 1935 as being "inordinately proud"

Fred with Charlie Ruggles in Friends of Mr. Sweeney.

of Fred and the progress he made within a year of his coming to Paramount. She also described what a young contract actor would go through as part of her acting school, "... we usually have at least 20 who give great promise of screen talent. At present we conduct our plays and coaching periods on one the sound stages, which is always especially arranged to suit the settings of our plays, whatever they are. We present one play a month and the audience consists of the studio personnel. We do not attempt anything too heavy or dramatic, but on the other hand we do not confine ourselves to the very lightest comedies. We try modern up-to-date things."

Fred was sure he was going to be dropped when the studio decided to loan him out again rather than cast him in a Paramount production. But this time the loan out was for a featured role rather than a walk-on, in an RKO film called *Grand Old Girl,* which starred May Robson and Mary Carlisle. Of his role in this film, Fred said, "I ... played a truck driver who delivered ice cream to Mary Carlisle. We had a little romance going, but the important thing was that I ate popcorn at a football game." The film wrapped in early October 1934 and Fred returned to Paramount with his first real role in a major film under his belt. Little would he know that within a few weeks one of the biggest stars at Paramount would ask for his services in her next film — a film which would propel Fred from juvenile to major star — thanks to his ability to eat popcorn in a natural way.

Fred with Mary Carlisle in his first big role, Grand Old Girl.

CHAPTER TWO

Paramount Leading Man

1935-1940

In 1934 Claudette Colbert was the biggest name actress under contract to Paramount Pictures. That year she and Clark Gable were generating heat, and big box office receipts, in the nation's movie theaters in the brilliant Frank Capra-directed comedy *It Happened One Night.* Their on-screen chemistry was potent in a story about a runaway heiress and a reporter on a cross-country bus trip. The film was not produced by either Paramount or MGM (where Gable was under contract), but by Columbia Pictures, long considered a border-line "poverty row" studio. Columbia was still a minor studio when compared to Paramount and MGM but, thanks to Frank Capra, who was Columbia's biggest name director, the studio had produced some solid hits, including *The Miracle Woman* and especially *Lady for a Day.* Still, both Colbert and Gable were somewhat insulted that they had been loaned out to a studio which they felt lacked a certain amount of stature. But once they began working on the film they knew they had something special. The film became a huge box office success and swept the Academy Awards for the year 1934 (earning, among other awards, Best Picture, Best Director, Best Actress and Best Actor), and Colbert and Gable returned to their respective studios more powerful, demanding and popular than ever.

Paramount decided to capitalize on Colbert's newfound popularity as a film comedienne. Up to this point she had been best known for such dramatic spectacles as *The Sign of the Cross* and *Cleopatra* (famously taking a pre-Code milk bath) and popular soap operas like *Imitation of Life. It Happened One Night* dramatically altered her career and from this point forward she was increasingly cast in romantic comedies. Paramount had a script titled *One Night Like This* ready and waiting for Colbert.

Paramount had established a formula of presenting three stars in comedy love triangles. It worked box office magic for Miriam Hopkins, Herbert Marshall and Kay Francis in *Trouble in Paradise,* and Hopkins, Fredric March and Gary Cooper in *Design for Living.* Both of these films had been released prior to the establishment of the Production Code, which was Hollywood's voluntary system of censoring its own pictures, so that the government wouldn't take over the task for them. Both *Trouble in Paradise* and *Design for Living* were full of sexual innuendo and imagery. It seems clear that in *Design for Living* both March and Cooper enjoyed a sexual relationship with Hopkins. Now with censorship in place Hollywood writers had to be more imaginative in establishing sexual innuendo in their films — a hidden meaning here, and a wink and nod there. Paramount was the most European of studios with cultured and sophisticated directors like Josef von Sternberg (Marlene Dietrich's Svengali), Rouben Mamoulian, and especially Ernst Lubitsch (the director of both *Trouble in Paradise* and *Design for Living*). MGM, which had "more stars than in the heavens," under the guidance of the paternal L.B. Mayer, believed in stories which epitomized mother, apple pie and all that is good about the USA. Warner Brothers had a reputation for undertaking gritty social commentaries. Fox had Shirley Temple, the biggest box office star in the world. Universal was making a mint churning out successful horror films like *Dracula* and *Frankenstein*. Paramount films involved worldly sophistication and elegance with a dash of sex and they had the stars (bar Greta Garbo) who most appealed to European audiences: Chevalier, Colbert and Dietrich (even if her films were fading in the United States).

One Night Like This told the story of a New York stenographer (Colbert) who meets an Englishman (the rising Ray Milland) and falls in love with him. She finds out that the Englishman is a nobleman and then is heartbroken to find out that he is also engaged. There is a third character — the more pivotal male role, actually — a platonic friend, a reporter, who writes a series of articles about the girl who refuses nobility. When the stories reach the masses she (Colbert) becomes a member of café society. Ultimately, the Colbert character must choose between the nobleman and the reporter. Which man will she select? The nobleman is not written as an out-and-out scoundrel, and, as played by Ray Milland, is quite attractive. But the pivotal role of the reporter hadn't yet been cast, but he had to be attractive enough to compete with the darkly handsome Milland. Paramount attempted to borrow Franchot Tone from MGM, but since they had just loaned him to Paramount for *The Lives of a Bengal Lancer* they were not about to allow Paramount to borrow him for a second picture in a row.

There was some thought of 30-year-old Cary Grant for the reporter, but with his slight cockney accent he was not considered American enough. It was at this point that Charlie Ruggles spoke to his brother Wesley, the director of the film, now retitled *The Gilded Lily*, about a tall handsome young man who he thought had "something." The young man that Ruggles spoke to his brother about was, of course, Fred, who Ruggles had recently worked with on the film *Friends of Mr. Sweeney.* (Charlie Ruggles, who would work with Fred again in the 1937 film *Exclusive* and then later in the 1966 Disney film *Follow Me, Boys!*, once called Fred "the most comfortable actor in Hollywood"— alluding to Fred's easygoing nature rather than the great wealth he later acquired.) Accepting his brother's suggestion, Ruggles screened *Friends* and agreed that the young man had an imposing screen

Fred and Claudette Colbert on a New York City park bench debating the virtues of popcorn vs. peanuts in **The Gilded Lily.**

presence despite his rawness. He also screened the film that Fred had just made on loan-out to RKO, *Grand Old Girl*, and took interest in one scene which particularly impressed the director. It's a scene where Fred eats popcorn while attending a football game. He was able to chew and deliver his lines without difficulty, not as easy as it seems. This was important because in *The Gilded Lily* there is a plot point where the platonic friends, the stenographer and reporter, habitually meet on a bench outside of the New York City Public Library to debate such vital issues as peanuts vs. popcorn. Ruggles wanted to give him a chance, but this was to be a high-profile film, and the studio expected that a bigger star name would appear opposite Colbert. Ruggles decided to try and enlist the support of Colbert (who had casting approval) behind Fred.

In his autobiography, George Murphy recalls that he is the one instrumental in getting Wesley Ruggles to select Fred for *The Gilded Lily*. "Later in Hollywood, I helped Fred get started in pictures. I had run into the director Wesley Ruggles at a party one Sunday. He said, 'I've got a great part for a young man in a picture starring Claudette Colbert. Everyone in town is working. Do you know anyone who needs a job?'" (I'm wondering if Murphy himself wasn't just a bit resentful that he himself wasn't asked!) Murphy relates that he told Ruggles about a "hell of a nice guy" he worked with in *Roberta*. Ruggles told Murphy to have Fred come and see him.

Colbert later recalled Ruggles telling her, "We've got a new fellow here and all the girls on the lot are just crazy about him!" He asked her to watch a screening of *Grand Old Girl*, and this convinced Colbert of Fred's suitability for the role. She appealed on Fred's behalf with the Paramount front office, which was still uncertain about casting Fred, in only his third picture, in a big part in such an important film. Colbert, however, had the clout to impose her will on the front office and it was primarily due to her insistence that Fred was cast in *The Gilded Lily*. When Fred received word that he'd been assigned to *The Gilded Lily*, and that Colbert had requested him as her leading man, he felt like "all the air had been let out of me." He told the casting director, "Me? You're kidding." He was absolutely awestruck that this huge star had requested a "nobody" to be her leading man. The night before he was to report to the set for the first day of shooting he was hardly able to sleep at all, and "the next morning I practically had to drag myself onto the set." When he saw Colbert walking toward him he said he was "a basket case" and "felt all empty and hollow inside and weak in the knees. I felt drained. My mouth was dry and I was hyperventilating. I practically collapsed." But Colbert understood and immediately attempted to put her co-star at ease. "When Claudette saw me standing there petrified, she put her hand on my arm and with a grin on her face quietly said, 'Now what are you so frightened about?'" Colbert found her new co-star "adorable and quiet" and attempted to put him at ease. "Fred and I had our first scene, a long shot, where we were coming out of a subway station. He was holding my arm and shaking like a leaf. I said, 'Relax, the camera is a mile away'"

But the worst was yet to come, the love scene. It is ironic that throughout Fred's career he was destined to work with virtually every great leading lady in Hollywood and would enact dozens of love scenes, but always claimed that they were his least favorite part of doing any film. It made him nervous to enact love scenes with the crew standing just inches away while he was trying to be romantic with his leading ladies. It was particularly trying in this first film with Colbert. "We had a big emotional scene," Fred later recalled. "Kissing Claudette before the crew, the props and the electricians had me so embarrassed I didn't know what I was doing ... Claudette rumpled my hair and kidded me, and finally I made it." Fred later maintained that he wasn't a great lover on the screen. "Sometimes a writer writes in scenes for people who just say 'Hi' to indicate they're in love. I play those scenes very well." Fred would always credit Colbert with giving him the push and the confidence to do a credible job despite his rawness and nerves. *The Gilded Lily* was the first of seven films which teamed Fred with Claudette Colbert, establishing them as one of the great romantic comedy teams in motion pictures (only one of their films was not a comedy). Making the film was not easy and there was even some talk midway through of replacing Fred, but Colbert was insistent on keeping him, and director

A typical scene in one of Paramount's romantic love triangles, Fred, Claudette Colbert and Ray Milland in The Gilded Lily.

Ruggles (a "morose man," according to Ray Milland), a keen observer of talent, was also supportive of the young and relatively untried actor.

Depression-era audiences wanted to laugh and were eager to see Colbert in a new screwball comedy as a follow up to *It Happened One Night* and in doing so they discovered a new leading actor, Fred MacMurray. Bob Hope would recall his surprise when walking in Time Square and coming across a movie theater with a marquee which read "CLAUDETTE COLBERT IN THE GILDED LILY with Fred MacMurray," the musician he had leant his top hat to for a Hollywood screen test a year or so before. "There was Mac just floating through his part like an old master," Hope later wrote. "He'd skipped the usual drudgery of playing bits and was a star from the start." Fred himself was apprehensive about being compared to Clark Gable. "I hate to follow Clark Gable in a part like the one I'm playing now," he told a reporter. "You know, this is a reporter role, and Gable in *It Happened One Night* was a newspaperman too. Both lean to comedy. Coming so close together, I'm afraid there's bound to be some comparison between the two — and woe to me!" After seeing the film the reporter assured Fred there was nothing to worry about, he more than held his own with a breezy style that was all his own. Fred's tall, dark wavy good looks not only appealed to younger women but also to mothers and grandmothers. His non-threatening masculinity made him appealing and non-threatening to men. Within a short period of time he was getting 3,000 fan letters per month.

The critics also found much to like about *The Gilded Lily* when it was released in January 1935. *Variety* in the first paragraph of its review stated, "Audiences will sit back in their seats with the feeling that five people got together for the avowed purpose of making entertainment for them." (The five people being director Ruggles, writer Claude Binyon, Claudette Colbert, Fred MacMurray and Ray Milland.) Hollywood's top entertainment reporter Louella Parsons applauded the film and Fred: "I like Mr. MacMurray — he has a certain appealing wholesomeness." The response to the film when it hit local neighborhood theaters was also heartening. The *Bridgeport (CT) Herald* said the picture "succeeds by the deftness of its direction, story treatment and tongue in cheek performances, *The Gilded Lily* will be compared with last year's most delicious cream puff, *It Happened One Night.* The comparison is scarcely necessary, *The Gilded Lily* can and will stand on its feet as an expertly mixed cinematic cocktail." The review called Fred a "newcomer who becomes box office in his first major film vehicle." While the film didn't score any Academy Award nominations it did make a hefty profit at the box office and was placed on the National Board of Review's list of 1935's ten best films. Fred later commented, "*The Gilded Lily* turned out to be a big hit and I was lucky. According to the critics, I had a fresh bread and butter quality." He would always credit Colbert for her work with him in this, the first important picture of his career. "I'll never forget how kind Claudette was," he recalled years later. "I didn't have the slightest idea what I was doing, but she was so patient with me. She worked and worked with me and got me through it. She was so positive, so kind-hearted, and so unselfish with other players … Her work with me in *The Gilded Lily* set the pace for my future work, and the style, for that matter. Thanks to playing off her, I discovered I had a talent for light comedy I didn't think was in me."

According to Colbert's biographer Lawrence Quirk, "the secret of the successful MacMurray-Colbert chemistry was the constant contrast between his gentle, low-brow bullying and her sophisticated and urbane femininity." Movie historian James Robert Parish called Fred's style "lumbering casualness." Paramount, of course, wanted to cash in on the successful teaming with more, but they also wanted to exploit the chemistry between Fred and Colbert in the fan magazines by fostering the idea that they were a romantic item off screen as well as on. Colbert had recently been divorced from her first husband and Fred was engaged to Lillian, and living in a small house with his mother, but that didn't sound too exciting to the studio publicity hounds. Fred was totally devoted to Lillian, but according to Quirk, Colbert may have felt a "little disappointed that she and Fred didn't catch fire off-screen as well as on." According to director Mitchell Leisen, who would later direct Colbert and MacMurray several times, "Claudette got around between her first and second marriages, but was damned quiet about it." Fred was later quoted as saying that Colbert was "a little rich for my blood romantically, though as a friend and a co-worker, she was A-number one."

The success of *The Gilded Lily* enhanced Fred's career and Paramount wanted to cash in by casting him in a series of films which both showcased his versatility as well as his romantic quality. RKO requested him to play Arthur Russell in an adaptation of Booth Tarkington's famous novel *Alice Adams* opposite Katharine Hepburn and directed by George Stevens. Such was Hepburn's reputation that she was able to dictate not only the director, choosing Stevens over her usual favorite George Cukor, but also her leading man. Based on Fred's performance in *The Gilded Lily* she chose him over Randolph Scott. The film is one of Hepburn's very best, about a socially awkward young woman who tries, too hard, to fit in with the socially powerful town clique. Rarely in the early stages of Hepburn's career did she allow herself to play a character so vulnerable, sweet and insecure. It is a credit to Stevens' direction that he was able to so successfully bring these qualities out in Hepburn. But it wasn't always easy as both Hepburn and Stevens had very definite ideas about the character of Alice and her motivations. Many times Hepburn saw things one way and Stevens the other. "I knew the Alice Adams people intimately," Stevens later said. "Better than she did, intuitive and brilliant though she was." Fred saw their war of wills first hand on the set. "I remember a scene on a porch; Kate was in a porch swing and I was sitting in a chair. Her concept of the scene was entirely different from George's. He was quietly definite, and she was less quietly definite. Finally, he said, 'Let's shoot it.' We did it over and over, most of the morning, and we broke for lunch. We did it over. He said, 'It's not the way I want it.' After eighty takes, all day, at last she did it the way he wanted it." Hepburn liked strong men and eventually, according to various biographies of the star, she and Stevens ended up having a love affair off camera. Hepburn, like Colbert and Carole Lombard, proved helpful to Fred as well. "You'd think they might resent a punk without experience getting breaks other people have to work years for — but they don't," Fred said at the time. "Miss Hepburn helped me all through *Alice Adams,* and the others have been very nice to me."

Alice lies about her own family's social prominence and wealth and is invited to a party held at the house of the socially prominent Russell family where she meets Arthur, the handsome son, and falls in love with him. One of the highlights of the film has Arthur invited to dinner at the Adams' faded home (where the family attempts to put on airs), and is played humorously and poignantly at the same time. Hepburn's Alice is not secure enough to understand that Arthur would love her for herself not because of any supposed social standing she might have. Hollywood writer Ruth Waterbury later wrote that Fred "was perfect in *Alice Adams* as the aristocratic suitor of shy Katharine Hepburn's underprivileged nice girl. In fact he was very sensitive and aware in that picture. You felt his honest sympathy and concern for the girl. I always saw Fred as a nice boy, nicely brought up, and he saved any itches he had in his pants for marriage. That kind of decent level headedness in a handsome film actor is something anybody can respect. Many people in Hollywood admired and looked up to him for that." The film was well received by critics and audiences alike and Fred and Hepburn work very well together, so well that when Stevens and Hepburn worked together again, on the film *Quality Street*, they again considered Fred for the leading male role, but ultimately choose Franchot Tone instead. It's a pity that she and Fred never worked together again, because Fred is one of the few leading men that Hepburn worked with, in the period prior to her on-screen teaming with Spencer Tracy, where she was allowed to be so vulnerable and feminine on screen. Film historian Foster Hirsch put it this way: "In *Alice Adams* (1935) and *Woman of the Year* (1942) Stevens uncovered a lovely naturalness beneath Katharine Hepburn's usual hauteur; pairing her with straightforward, homespun actors like Fred MacMurray and Spencer Tracy, Stevens released her from her mannerist excesses." The film went a long way toward furthering Fred's career as a romantic leading man.

With Fred's future seeming bright thanks to *The Gilded Lily* and his work in *Alice Adams*, his real life Lily took the plunge and left New York to join Fred in California. She found herself a flat which she made sure had a decent kitchen so that she could make home cooked meals for Fred. To support herself she found a job modeling gowns in a Hollywood department store. While Fred had filmed *The Gilded Lily*, it had yet to be released and he was still a relative unknown. When Fred would come and pick Lily up at the department store the other shop girls would gawk at the handsome young man and tell one another how lucky Lily was to have such a good-looking and considerate boyfriend.

II

In August 1935 Fred began production on another romantic comedy, *Hands Across the Table*, which brought yet another enduring team partnership, with the delectable Carole Lombard. *Hands Across the Table* tells the story of a manicurist, Regi Allen, who has struggled financially all of her life, and her determination to marry a rich man. She meets her match in Theodore (Ted) Drew III, whose supposedly wealthy family had actually lost its wealth in the 1929 stock market crash. Most people still believe that the Drew family is rich, but Ted has the same goal as Regi, to marry into a rich family. In fact, when he meets Regi he is engaged to the daughter of "the Pineapple King," Vivian Snowden. There is another complication (in keeping with Paramount's tradition of love triangles) thrown in — a former aviator named Allen Macklyn, who is now confined to a wheelchair after a plane crash. Macklyn also falls in love with Regi. Who will the gold-digging Regi choose? The fortune hunter or the crippled aviator? With whom will the audience's sympathies lie? There is also a role reversal in this picture; it is the woman, rather than the man, who is the pursuer while the man (seemingly) is more passive — not the first time this would be the case in a MacMurray film.

Fred was assigned to play Ted after Gary Cooper proved unavailable. Lombard, who had director and star approval for the first time on a film, had approved him after viewing *The Gilded Lily*. Ralph Bellamy was chosen for the role of the aviator. Bellamy was Hollywood's most successful also-ran, an actor who played the "other man" in romantic triangles with flair and good humor, though his role in *Hands Across the Table* contains a good measure of pathos as well. Mitchell Leisen was selected to direct.

This film was the first to be tailored for the considerable charm and talent of Carole Lombard. She was one of the great stars of the 1930s, and while she played in a variety of pictures, she had proved in Howard Hawks' *Twentieth Century* that she was an expert screen comedienne. Nearly everybody who came to know Lombard was captivated by her beauty, humor, vitality and bawdiness. Lombard was known in the industry as the "profane angel" because she looked like an angel, and as Mitchell Leisen would later state, "swore like a sailor." Fred was amused by this contradiction later recalling, "You never knew what she was going to do or say." He also admitted, years later, to his second wife, June Haver, but never publicly, that of all of his leading ladies Lombard was "the most fun to work with." Film biographer Foster Hirsch pointed out that many of Lombard's leading men caught her "light, swinging style and her daffy energy" when working with her, among them, William Powell and Fred MacMurray have never been livelier, and in *Nothing Sacred* she even manages to loosen up Fredric March."

For Fred the other fortuitous opportunity offered by *Hands Across the Table* was working for Mitchell Leisen for the first of eight times. Leisen was by this time, with the exception of Cecil B. DeMille and Ernst Lubitsch (who was now acting as Paramount's production head), Paramount's most profitable director. Leisen began his career as a set and costume designer for DeMille before becoming a director of his own films in the early 1930s. His first two films were in collaboration with another director (though those later interviewed for David Chierichetti's splendid study of Leisen's career state that Leisen, in fact, directed most, if not all, of those first two films). His first solo credit as a director was *Cradle Song*. (UCLA owns the only print, a Nitrate copy of the film.) He went on to direct such diverse films as *Bolero* (with George Raft and Lombard), *Murder at the Vanities* (with Kitty Carlisle and Victor McLaglen), *Behold My Wife!* (with Sylvia Sidney and Gene Raymond), *Four Hours to Kill!* (with Richard Barthelmess), but his most famous film from that period, and still one of his best known today, is *Death Takes a Holiday* with Fredric March. Leisen didn't specialize in any one genre but directed all types of pictures: comedies, romances, musicals, dramas, mysteries and adventures.

The biggest gripe that some critics, including screenwriters Billy Wilder and Preston Sturges, had is that Leisen put more effort in how a film looked rather than how it played. Film historian Steven Bach later wrote, "Leisen was competent and stylish at his best. He could always make a picture look better than it was, but never play better, for he had no sense of material." Wilder later stated that he believed Leisen "hated writers" and would refer to him not as a director but as a set designer. Yet two of Leisen's greatest films come from Wilder screenplays (in collaboration with Charles Brackett), *Midnight* (1939) and *Hold Back the Dawn* (1941). These two films are not only gorgeously filmed, but also directed with flair and sophistication, and the performances in each are uniformly superb. Film historian Leonard Maltin would later state that he believes that Leisen gets a "bad rap," but concedes that it was also true that Leisen was "often more interested and involved with the look of his films than the performances of his cast." (In later years, Leisen employed an assistant whose job was to help guide the actors while he worked on sets, costumes, and camera angles.) Yet, Maltin also says that when Leisen had good material, "I think he delivered first rate films."

Personally, Leisen was a cultured man who enjoyed beautiful objects and beautiful women. He formed long-lasting friendships with many of the actresses he worked with including Lombard, Paulette Goddard, Dorothy Lamour and Claudette Colbert. They adored him because he did care about how they looked on screen and took the time to make sure that they appeared as attractive as possible, especially years later when they were aging actresses. But he was not simply a "woman's director," the same rap which was given to George Cukor. Leisen was instrumental in forming the early cinema careers of such leading men as Fredric March, Ray Milland and Fred MacMurray. Leisen was married but lived apart from his wife for most of their marriage. He was bisexual and later had a long-lasting relationship with a prominent set designer named Billy Daniels. Was Fred the recipient of unwelcome sexual advances by Leisen? Leisen's biographer, David Chierichetti, thinks so. "I know Leisen's passes troubled Fred

MacMurray a great deal." Chierichetti further states that during the 1940s Leisen "got so audacious ... that he really seemed not to care. He'd do very outrageous things, like making passes at his leading men." Writer Gavin Lambert believed that Leisen was able to bring out sexiness in Fred on-screen that other directors weren't able to tap into. "You look at Leisen's movies," Lambert later stated, "and Fred MacMurray is very sexy. He's not sexy in anybody else's movies. Obviously Leisen was attracted to him and brought that out." Certainly, Leisen contributed a great deal in making Fred a viable romantic leading man, but the truth is that Fred's diamond-in-the-rough romantic quality was exploited by several directors early in his career including Wesley Ruggles, who directed Fred more often during his early romantic leading man period (roughly 1935-1942) than Leisen, including the first film that Fred made a serious splash in, *The Gilded Lily*. If Leisen did "come on" to Fred it certainly didn't scare him off from working with the director. Years later, even after he left Paramount and was a freelance actor, Fred returned to work with Leisen in the film *Suddenly It's Spring*, and called on him in the 1950s to direct him in a live television program. But there is evidence, as we shall see later, that when Fred felt that others might be affected by Leisen's attentions he turned his back on the director.

After Cooper had proved unavailable for *Hands Across the Table* the studio had thought of Ray Milland for the part of Ted. Leisen had just worked on a picture with Milland and felt that the actor could handle the job, but Milland backed off because at this point in his career, despite *The Gilded Lily*, he felt uncomfortable performing comedy. Again, the studio thought of Franchot Tone, but when Lombard saw *The Gilded Lily* all bets were off. Lombard's biographer would later write, "Carole certainly knew who Fred MacMurray was. She had danced to music generated by local bands that employed him as a saxophonist, before she had made her first real dent in pictures." Leisen would later state, "I took a flying leap and put Fred MacMurray in, and I was terribly worried since it was only his third picture."

Leisen discovered, to his relief, that Fred, "had a natural flair for comedy," but he would have to work hard to draw it out of him because of his natural shyness and relative inexperience. He approached Lombard, whom he admired greatly ("She could do anything") and asked her to work with Fred ("She worked as hard as I did to get that performance out of him"). Lombard's prescription for helping Fred relax in front of the camera appears to have involved a huge dose of physical discomfort. One day, to his amusement, Leisen arrived on the set to discover Lombard sitting on top of Fred and pounding his chest with her fists and saying, "Now, Uncle Fred, you be funny now or I'll pluck your eyebrows out." In the scene where Lombard and Fred are sitting together at Regi's manicure table (and practically torturing the character Fred is playing as she gives him a manicure),

Lombard kicked Fred in the shin just before the cameras would roll and smiled sweetly at him and purred, "Loosen up, you big ape! It isn't going to hurt." Fred later said that Lombard "did all she could to make me feel at ease." He recalled that the first scene they shot together was of Fred playing hopscotch on the linoleum of the hotel where Regi works ("Something I wouldn't do in a million years"), but Lombard worked with Fred and made

Is Carole Lombard kicking Fred in the shin? Hands Across the Table.

sure this nonsensical scene depicting a 6'3" man playing hopscotch in a hotel lobby was played as naturally as possible, and served as an excellent introduction to his somewhat zany and certainly unorthodox character. "I owe so much of that performance and my subsequent career to her," Fred would later say of Lombard.

Lombard did make Fred relax as their scenes together testify. There is one scene in *Hands Across the Table* where Lombard pretends to be a long distance telephone operator ("Bermuda Calling, Bermuda Calling") so that Fred can convince his wealthy fiancée that he is actually in Bermuda rather than spending time with Lombard in New York City. Leisen later told David Chierichetti, "When they finished that take, Carole and Fred collapsed on the floor in laughter; they laughed until they couldn't laugh anymore. It wasn't in the script, but I made sure the cameras kept turning and I used it in the picture. It is so hard to make actors laugh naturally - I wasn't about to throw it out." There is another scene in the picture which demonstrated Fred's growing confidence as an actor, not to mention his sense of ease working with Lombard. According to Fred, it involved an "obstreperous cat." "We tried to keep it on cue," Fred recalled, "even going so far as to stuff my ears with herring, but this ball of fluff was a born scene stealer and show stopper." There is a scene where Fred is to answer a ringing phone; the cat lunged at the phone, Fred brushed the cat aside, and ad-libbed, "Never mind, Whitey, I'll get it."

At the time they were filming *Hands Across the Table* Fred was engaged but not yet married to Lillian Lamont. He would later recall Lillian asking him, "Well, how did it go with Carole Lombard?" Fred told her, "I never heard such profanity from anybody, man or woman — she's wonderful!" Fred greatly enjoyed working with Lombard. "If Fred could get a laugh out of the beloved Lombard — herself known for her practical jokes — it set him up for the day," a friend recalled. Fred and Lillian and Carole and her future husband Clark Gable became good friends and often socialized together, sometimes they would go to nightclubs together on a Saturday night, or they would get together for a California-style barbecue on a Sunday afternoon, the only day of the week when Fred, Carole and Gable didn't have to go to the studio in those days of six-day work weeks. So close did Lillian and Lombard become that Carole would later refer to Lillian as "really the most decent person I've met in Hollywood."

Hands Across the Table opened in November 1935 (in time for Thanksgiving) to solid box office revenues and excellent reviews. *Variety* called the film "first rate entertainment" and "Miss Lombard and MacMurray both are blessed with highly amusing material." The review in *The New Republic* was even more positive: "In this picture Carole Lombard and Fred MacMurray make an all-time copybook example of how to play a movie for what it is worth - with subtlety, much resource in the matter of visual expression, and the open, sustained kind of charm that can be projected through the shadows of a mile of celluloid ..." Years later in her book *5001 Nights at the Movies,* Pauline Kael found the film predictable but of its two leads she wrote, "... MacMurray knows how to read a good line when he gets one, and though he isn't the subtlest of farceurs, that works just fine with Lombard because of her gift for uninhibited comedy." The studio was as delighted with the Lombard-MacMurray teaming as they had been with the Colbert-MacMurray teaming earlier in the year, and 1935 turned out to be a banner year for Fred who successfully played opposite three reining screen goddesses, Colbert, Hepburn and Lombard, without being bowed over by their very distinct personalities. Not only that, but all three pictures had been critical and box office hits.

Fred went almost immediately from *Hands Across the Table* into the Walter Wanger production of *The Trail of the Lonesome Pine*. The film received a great deal of publicity because it was the first outdoor picture to be filmed totally in Technicolor. The story, however, was as old as the hills. The story tells of two Kentucky hill families, the Falins and the Tollivers, who have been feuding for generations over reasons nobody now recalls. Fred is cast as the educated Jack Hale, a city engineer who brings the railroad to Lonesome Pine. He also is related to the Tolliver family. His nephew Dave Tolliver (Henry Fonda) is engaged to marry his cousin June (top-billed Sylvia Sidney). A love triangle is formed when June falls for the more educated and worldly Jack. The chief asset of the film (as the reviews would testify) is the magnificent scenery filmed in glorious Technicolor. The film was shot partly on location in Big Bear, located in the San Bernardino Mountains. The film's shooting schedule also included four nights of outdoor photography in the Santa Susana Pass. Outdoors man Fred would later recall, happily, that between scenes he and Fonda would go fishing at Big Bear Lake, where they would sit quietly for long periods of time without saying a word; not that they didn't get along, but because both Fred and Fonda were essentially shy men who didn't say much but enjoyed each others company just for the pleasure of having somebody to fish with. It was the first of three films that Fred and Fonda would appear in, but the only one in which they really shared any scenes. (The two others were the episodic *On Our Merry Way* (1948) and the all-star disaster *The Swarm* (1978), made in the twilight of both men's careers.)

Sylvia Sidney was by far the biggest name at the time and her salary proved it. Walter Wanger, the producer, paid her a flat fee of $50,000 for roughly two months' worth of work. By contrast, Fred, loaned to Wanger by Paramount, which would distribute the picture, was paid his usual $1,250 per week for roughly eight weeks of shooting. Coming in the rear is Fonda, a Wanger contract player, who was an up and comer, billed third in the picture and paid $937.50 per week. He ended up earning slightly more money than Fred did, but only because he worked a few weeks longer on the picture. The director was Henry Hathaway, who had just come off of the very successful *The Lives of a Bengal Lancer* with Gary Cooper (and was paid $19,305.16 for his directing of this film). Sidney would remember *The Trail of the Lonesome Pine* as, "a difficult film to make. It was the only on-location picture I had done, and I had no idea of the discomfort involved. It was so cold. When I showered my legs would turn blue!"

As stated, the reviews focused on the color photography, but many critics also liked the story itself. Frank Nugent of the *New York Times* wrote, "When to the story is added a cast of unusual merit and a richly beautiful color production, then it becomes a distinguished and worthwhile picture, commanding attention no less for its intrinsic entertainment value than as another milestone in the development of the cinema." According to *Film Daily*, "With or without color, this production has been so effectively done from screenplay and casting to direction and editing that it can't miss." The film had its world premier in Miami on 2/18/36 and Edgar Hay, the movie critic of the *Miami Herald*, went so far as to proclaim *The Trail of the Lonesome Pine*, "The most important picture in nearly a decade - since *The Jazz Singer* made the screen articulate." Today, the film doesn't seem nearly as impressive, but the color photography is still quite stunning.

Fred and his leading lady Sylvia Sidney in The Trail of the Lonesome Pine.

Two weeks following the completion of *The Trail of the Lonesome Pine*, Fred was back on a Paramount soundstage working for Mitchell Leisen in the adventure-comedy *Thirteen Hours by Air*. This time his leading lady is Joan Bennett, playing an heiress who boards a transcontinental flight from New York to San Francisco piloted by Jack Gordon (Fred). The heiress is on her way to San Francisco to stop her younger sister from marrying somebody she feels is unsuitable for her. Midway through, the flight is hijacked by an escaped convict. The film includes a solid supporting cast, including ZaSu Pitts, John Howard, Alan Baxter and Brian Donlevy, and predates the *Airport* pictures by 35 years. The film wasn't without incident. A second unit crew obtaining aerial footage crashed, but fortunately nobody was seriously injured. United Airlines cooperated with the making of the film and were allowed to see a preview of the picture where they expressed disappointment with how the film ended; they found the original depiction of an emergency landing to be unrealistic and so it was reshot. Leisen would later explain the title of the film this way to his biographer, "Actually it took at least fif-

Joan Bennett and Fred in the Mitchell Leisen adventure-comedy **Thirteen Hours by Air.**

teen hours to fly across the continent in those days, but I knew that sooner or later they would get the time down, so I decided to call it *Thirteen Hours by Air* and get a jump on them." Leisen got another excellent performance out of Fred, this time extenuating his masculinity, and he enjoyed working with Bennett, too, who Leisen called a "doll." But he was amused by the fact that Bennett was near-sighted and yet so vain as to not wear glasses even off camera when she was doing needle-point, saying she would "stick the thing about an inch from her eye to see what she was doing." Joan Bennett enjoyed working with Fred so much that she requested him as leading man for her next film, a comedy-mystery titled *Big Brown Eyes*. But her director, Raoul Walsh, insisted on giving the part to another Paramount leading man who was still struggling in the second ranks, Cary Grant. *Thirteen Hours by Air* would be the first of three films shot over the next five years that would depict Fred as a pilot, the others being *Men with Wings* (1938) and *Dive Bomber* (1941).

During the filming, the company did location work at the Alhambra Airport, shooting scenes aboard a snowbound plane. To make the scenes as realistic as possible Leisen made sure the set inside a hangar was as cold as possible. "The corn flakes were flying (representing snow flakes, corn flakes were used painted white), the wind machines were howling and it looked like Christmas in Eveleth, Minnesota." But outside the temperature was in the 80s and between scenes Fred, Alan Baxter, John Howard and some stagehands occupied time between scenes played baseball with the sun beating down on them. Then it was back inside the ice cold hangar. The result from the contrast in temperature was Fred coming down with a case of pleurisy. "How do I feel?" Fred said. "I feel like a damned fool ... Pleurisy in the hottest January in California history."

Fred was moving from one picture to another with hardly any time off between assignments. But he enjoyed the steady work and unlike many leading men did not spend his money frivolously. He helped support his mother and grandmother but spent as little as possible on himself. He was developing a reputation for being tight with a buck. As the years went by many stories of alleged or real MacMurray stinginess would surface. One of the first to notice was Mitchell Leisen. Leisen would later say that he was sure "Fred had the first buck he ever made." He also noticed that Fred's personal wardrobe, while practical and comfortable, was hardly stylish and befitting of that of a top leading man, which Fred was. When Fred was cast in one of his films and because they were roughly the same build, Leisen began loaning Fred suits and other clothing from Leisen's own personal wardrobe because his clothes looked more stylish and fit the characters Fred was playing than Fred's own clothing (this was at a time when actors wore clothes from their own wardrobes when making a "modern day" picture). Later, Leisen states, he found out that Fred didn't even cash some of his payroll checks because he was "certain he wouldn't last as a movie actor."

Fred was next reunited with Claudette Colbert and director Wesley Ruggles in another screwball farce, *The Bride Comes Home*. It's another love triangle. Colbert plays Jeanette, a society girl, who is bored with her nothing life and wants to get a real, meaningful job. Her view is reinforced when she finds out from her father that they are broke, casualties of the Depression. When her friend Jack (Robert Young) inherits three million dollars he decides to buy a magazine and hires Jeanette to be assistant editor to Cyrus (Fred), a can-do self-made man who is contemptuous of people of great wealth. Jeanette and Cyrus constantly quarrel and yet are attracted to one another and slowly fall in love, but, of course, Jack is also in love with her and wants to marry her as well.

The film was scripted by Ruggles' frequent collaborator, writer Claude Binyon, who was fast becoming one of Fred's best Hollywood friends too. Binyon was a big man, and, like Fred, basically shy, but they shared a love of the outdoors and activities such as camping, fishing and skeet shooting. It wasn't unusual for Fred and Binyon to take a couple of weeks off and go hunting when their schedules allowed. In Fred, Binyon found what he later called the "perfect personification of the American male," stating, "I think he always gives a good performance. It's a habit ... There is a kind of character I always like to write and Fred plays him perfectly." He would script

Another Paramount love triangle comedy: Robert Young, Claudette Colbert and Fred in The Bride Comes Home.

many MacMurray films all the way up to 1964's *Kisses for My President.*

The Hollywood Reporter called *The Bride Came Home* a "swell comedy ... suburb playing, smart direction, with writing that sparkles." The review went so far as to call Colbert's performance ("without discounting roles in *It Happened One Night* and *The Gilded Lily"*) her "best." As for Fred, "MacMurray ... does his talents full justice" and Robert Young "holds up his end splendidly." In its Monday, January 13, 1936, review, *The Chicago Tribune* commented on the Saturday box office attendance at the Chicago Theater where 24,600 moviegoers turned out. Theater manager Roy Bruder used the adjective "phenomenal!" to describe the scene. The reviewer himself called the film a "delightfully modern, gay and carefree romantic comedy that glitters with enough comedy situations to keep the audience continuously mirthful." Fred was described as "one of Hollywood's fastest climbing screen stars" and he "enhances his position considerably" due to his presence in *The Bride Comes Home.*

Fred, being a fast rising star, was often invited to glittering Hollywood parties, and no invitation was more sought after or potentially valuable, than being invited to spend a weekend at the fabulous home of the powerful publisher William Randolph Hearst. With his vast publishing empire Hearst could, and did, help many studios build up stars with the help of columnist Louella Parsons, the most powerful columnist in Hollywood, whose flagship newspaper was the Hearst-owned *Los Angeles Examiner*. An invitation to Hearst's home, called San Simeon, was tantamount to a command. The invitation from Hearst to Fred came via a phone call by Louella Parsons. Fred politely told Parsons that he was sorry but he couldn't make it because he had a date for Saturday night. Then an idea popped into his head, "could I bring my date, my fiancée, along?" Parsons, perhaps somewhat embarrassed, explained to Fred that it would be impossible for him to bring Lily because "Mr. Hearst already has another guest chosen to be your partner." Fred, probably stunning Louella, told her, "Then, I guess I won't be able to make it." Despite this brush-off of Hearst's invitation it didn't seem to hurt Fred as Louella Parson continued to be a booster of his in her syndicated columns. If anything she may have thought more of him for his fidelity to Lily.

III

Carole Lombard had signed a big new contract with Paramount which, among other things, gave her script, director and co-star approval. The script she approved was a shipboard romance, *The Princess Comes Across*. The co-star she approved was George Raft, also a former lover. It's the story of a woman who impersonates a Swedish princess on an ocean liner making its way to New York. Along the way she falls in love with the ship bandleader. The comedy-mystery also involves blackmail, and an escaped killer, who has stowed away under an assumed identity.

In the rushes Raft was proving to be dead weight as a light comedian, but Lombard had worked with him before and liked him, so she went to bat for him. But after a few days of shooting even Raft was looking for excuses to get out of the picture and finally found one, he didn't approve of the cameraman, Ted Telzlaff, and wanted him removed from the picture. However, Lombard did approve of Telzlaff and ultimately it was Raft who left, probably as he intended. Lombard's biographer also points out that Raft's ego may also have been at stake, because in their previous two films together it had been Raft who had been the undisputed star, and now here he was playing second fiddle to Lombard. With Carole's approval, Paramount cast Fred in the role of the bandleader who falls for the princess, in the end much better casting than George Raft. It would not be the last time Fred would benefit from being offered a role Raft was initially considered for.

Carole insisted that Fred be given billing above the title with her and at this point she also advised Fred to begin demanding a raise since he was still being paid a relatively paltry $1,250 per week despite having appeared as the lead actor in several top box office and critical hits over the past year and a half. When Fred had his agent approach Paramount about renegotiating his contract he was given the brush off. When this happened Lombard suggested that Fred go on strike. Despite some apprehension, Fred did as Lombard instructed. "I was living with my mother in a little apartment on Franklin Avenue," Fred would recall years later. "And every day I went out to spend the day with Lily. Every evening I came back to find notes from the studio saying I would be fired if I didn't come back the next day." Fred was distressed by the studio intimidation and not being familiar with the ways of Hollywood contract negotiations he would call up Lombard for advice, who would attempt to reassure her nervous friend. "Don't go back until they offer you a lot more money. You're worth it, they know it and sooner or later they'll have to give it to you. Besides I'll tell them I won't make *The Princess Comes Across* with anybody else." She suggested that he go down to Palm Springs to show Paramount that he means business. Again, Fred took her sage advice. After a few days in Palm Springs the studio sent word that they were now willing to renegotiate his contract and Fred went back to Hollywood. The new deal called for four pictures per year but as Fred would recall, "The money was a lot better [about $3,500 per week with yearly hikes], and I think they respected me a little more. I owe all of that to Carole."

Within two weeks of shooting Paramount considered shelving the picture because it didn't seem to be jelling as a comedy. The director, William K. Howard (a contract director not well remembered today despite some interesting films), offered to resign, but the ever-loyal Lombard stood up for him too, and, according to her biographer, told Howard to just take care of the camera angles and that she and Fred would "establish the pace and style of the comedy." Lombard also rewrote sections of the script, to make the picture less talky. The dailies improved and Paramount continued on with the picture. Despite lukewarm reviews, the film nevertheless did well at the box office and today it is one of the best of the Lombard-MacMurray comedies.

Gary Cooper was Paramount's top leading man and many of the studio's best scripts were first submitted to him, and if he turned them down, then other contract players were considered, especially Cary Grant, Ray Milland and Fred. The studio had a Western they were preparing, *The Texas Rangers*, directed by King Vidor, that they wanted Coop to do. Cooper was to play Jim Hawkins, one of three outlaws who split up to evade the law. Two of the outlaws reform and join the Texas Rangers and the third one continues on his life of crime. However, Cooper was already filming an "outdoor" picture and one of his rules was that he didn't want to do two in a row, so he backed out of *The Texas Rangers*. (Another story has it that Cooper's agent didn't want Coop to work with the scene-stealing Jack Oakie, who was cast in a prominent role. According to director King Vidor, "He thought Oakie had too many stunts, too many tricks of acting, and would dominate Cooper's slow easy manner.") This opened up the part for another actor and once again Fred was tapped to replace Cooper. But there was one problem with Fred doing a Western: he didn't know how to ride a horse. But, according

Fred's first Western, and one of the best of the '30s, The Texas Rangers.

to Vidor, Fred got "busy and practiced riding for a month or so before we started … He worked at the stables every day with the wrangler attached to the film, and came through as a darn good rider."

It wasn't an easy shoot. Much of the film was shot on location near Gallup and Santa Fe, New Mexico and included the reenactment of an 1876 battle between Texas Rangers and Apaches. Over 500 extras, including members of three Indian tribes, were used in reenacting the battle. (Vidor recalls that "We had to set up three separate camps for them. They demanded different corrals and separate food. They had brought their own horses, and wanted to remain apart from each other.") Production was delayed for several days due to a severe dust storm. For interior shots showing the inside of the Texas

Rangers office, a 125-year-old building in Gallup was utilized. According to the studio publicity bulletins, Paramount shipped 50,000 rounds of blank cartridges, 500 bows and 5,000 arrows to Gallup for the reenactment of the climactic battle between the Rangers and Apaches.

Jack Oakie was cast, along with Fred, as the other Texas Ranger who reforms (Lloyd Nolan was the one who kept on his outlaw ways) and there

Fred, with his leading lady Jean Parker, in **The Texas Rangers.**

may have been something to the apprehension of Cooper's agent that Oakie would try and upstage him. There is a scene where Fred has to say good-bye to the leading lady, Jean Parker. "I stood there and waited for Oakie to say goodbye and leave," Fred recalled years later. "I waited and waited and waited, and finally Oakie said, 'Goodbye, honey!' and backed out into me —

maneuvering me right thru the door ahead of him [Fred was supposed to be the last to leave]. Well, darn it, as soon as Oakie came through that door I ran right back into the scene before the camera stopped rolling, and said goodbye again. When I went through the door the second time, I was sure I had at last gone through the door after Oakie, but King Vidor yelled, 'Cut!, say Fred, let's take it again and this time let's just cut out that last goodbye.' See what I mean? Nobody gets out the door after Oakie!" (Incidentally, Hollywood legend has it that in 1940 when Paramount was casting a buddy comedy, *Road to Singapore*, both Fred and Oakie were approached to star in it. Fred would be a smooth-talking bandleader/con-man and Oakie his stooge best friend. They reportedly turned it down and Paramount cast Bing Crosby in the role intended for Fred and Bob Hope as the best friend. Dorothy Lamour, who was inevitably the sarong-clad girl the boys fight over in all but the last *Road* film, writes in her autobiography that "neither Oakie nor MacMurray recalls that story.")

Fred and Lillian shortly after their 1936 wedding.

When the film was completed on June 19, 1936, Fred was supposed to rush into production on his next film, *Champagne Waltz*. But then he was told that the picture was being delayed for three weeks. With this unexpected hole in his schedule Fred and Lily decided to get married. They eloped to Las Vegas. According to one later account of the elopement (written in 1945), "When he makes up his mind, it's apt to be sudden and solid. Back in 1936, deep in 1936, deep in the month of June he decided that June had some significance, so he and fashion model, Lillian Lamont, and his mother jumped into an airplane along toward morning and flew up to Las

Vegas ... They got a judge up a little early and had a sort of sunrise ceremony in the county clerk's office with Mrs. MacMurray and a newspaper-
ing friend as a witness." With equal precision, Fred also made reservations
to leave the day after the wedding on a ship bound for Hawaii and was able
to book a last-minute cabin. Fred was never one to gush about his feelings
in public but there is little doubt that he was deeply in love with Lillian and
she with him. When he did speak of her publicly, he would call her "the
finest woman I've ever known" and credit her for giving him the "push" to
achieve the career he had. He would also demonstrate his love and devotion to Lillian in the years of their marriage due to her fragile health. While
on a ship heading to Hawaii for their honeymoon Lillian caught influenza
and while in Hawaii she regained some strength, but had not recovered sufficiently and suffered a relapse when they returned home. For the entire first
year of their marriage she was so ill at times that it seemed that she was not
going to pull through. Sheilah Graham wrote that Fred acted as a "nurse
for the sick Lillian Lamont during one year of marriage." She was to be in
fragile health for the remainder of her life. There may have been another
reason for Lillian's poor health throughout her marriage to Fred. According
to Lester Martin, Fred's cousin, Lillian suffered from what is known today
as Bulimia, an eating disorder where a person eats a great deal in a short
period of time, binging and "purging" as a way to keep from gaining weight.
As a former model, Lillian had been very weight-conscious and unlike today
there wasn't a lot of focus on the disease and its effects during her lifetime.

Gary Cooper had been the first choice of several films which Fred had
appeared in, including *The Gilded Lily* and *Hands Across the Table*, but Fred
also had been the first choice of some features which Cooper later did,
including the 1936 film *The General Died at Dawn*. The Hollywood press
noticed and began writing stories about the "competition" between Cooper
and Fred. But, really, there was no serious competition. Cooper was and
always would be the bigger film star who got the first shot at the best roles.
But the publicity value of linking Fred's name with Cooper's was priceless. Fred and Cooper also got along fine and occasionally were hunting
companions. Fred also recalled that early in his career "Coop" offered the
younger actor some sage advice which he took to heart. "Do as little talking
as possible," Fred recalled Cooper telling him. "And leave the speechmak-
ing to the women and the little guys ... I decided then and there that since I
wasn't naturally talkative maybe I'd better let things go as they were."

The last two years had been particularly awarding for Fred. He had
appeared in eight films, working with some of the most successful actresses
of the day: Claudette Colbert, Katharine Hepburn, Carole Lombard, Joan
Bennett and Sylvia Sidney. He had gained a reputation as a reliable leading
man who could work smoothly in many different genres, including comedy,
drama, adventures and Westerns. The studio had acknowledged his grow-

ing popularity with moviegoers by giving him a big pay raise. By August 1936 *The Los Angeles Times* was writing that Fred was emerging as Robert Taylor's chief rival among new film stars and was becoming a "rapidly growing favorite." But the crowning event was in his personal life when he and Lillian finally became man and wife.

IV

In 1937 Fred would have five films released, with mixed results. One was a so-so musical, two were fair to good comedies, one was a disastrous historical drama and one was a superb comedy-drama, one of the best films of his career and certainly one of the best of the twenty-odd films he made during the 1930s.

The musical is *Champagne Waltz*, which Paramount was giving a big publicity campaign, calling it their "silver anniversary film of the year." The studio was also trying to make a star out of its leading lady, Gladys Swarthout, a famous diva of the Metropolitan Opera. Swarthout was to be Paramount's answer to Jeanette MacDonald. This was problematic because Paramount was not known for its musicals. Yes, they had Bing Crosby, who was very popular at the box office, but whose Paramount musicals certainly, with a few exceptions, did not equal those of MGM or even the Warner Brothers' efforts of the 1930s. They were essentially star vehicles tailored to Bing's easygoing charm and way with a song. Swarthout's first film for Paramount, *Rose of the Ranchos* (1936), died an agonizing death at the box office despite a huge publicity campaign on behalf of Swarthout and the film. Her second film was *Give Us This Night* (1936), which was better and had a book by Oscar Hammerstein, but the film still didn't bring in ticket buyers. So, after two straight operatic misfires they attempted to bring her down a peg or two and put her in a lighter musical with a well-known leading man, Fred MacMurray, in a story which Billy Wilder is one of the four co-authors, and set in a location which Wilder knew well, Vienna. Fred plays a bandleader who brings his swing band to Vienna where they play at a club located next to a classical music hall where Swarthout performs, naturally opposites attract. *Time* magazine in its review called the film a "heavy-footed musical" and dismissed it as yet another "perennial and expensive attempt to make a Grace Moore out of Gladys Swarthout." You would think that three strikes and you're out, but Paramount gave her two more chances, including a role in a non-musical, all to no avail. Still, while *Champagne Waltz* is one of Fred's more disappointing films from the 1930s, it is probably Swarthout's best.

The following month Paramount released *Maid of Salem*, which reunited Fred and Claudette Colbert for the third time, and the first in a dramatic story. They should have stuck to romantic comedy since this film, a historical drama set during the Salem witch hunts, is a bore. Fred seems out of place in this film; you expect him to wake up in 1937 America wondering if it was all a dream. Colbert, who did this type of material in the past for DeMille, seems more at ease, but isn't helped by the script. The film did at least try to correct the historical record that people accused of being witches were burned at the stake; in fact, in the United States, they were hung. Joseph Breen of the Production Code wanted to make sure, too, that members of the clergy were not represented unjustly. "While there is of course ample historical grounds to prove that many of the clergy were caught up in the hysteria of the time, it might be well to counter-balance this in your picture by introducing briefly another minister ... who will typ-ify the more rational element among the clergy." In another letter to the filmmakers, Breen wrote, "... in their characterizations of ministers should not be used in comedy, villains, or as unpleasant persons," and demanded specific changes with regards to the characterization of Rev. Parris. The film at least had the attraction, for the cast and crew, of being shot on a farm near Santa Cruz, California (where the village of Salem was reproduced on forty acres) and the Pacific Ocean overlooking Carmel. A sneak preview of the film in December 1936 was found to be unsatisfactory and the actors were recalled for several days of retakes. The climax, in particular, received unin-tentional laughter, with Fred vigorously riding a horse to save Colbert from the gallows and arriving just in a nick of time saving Colbert's character just as she is about to be hung, with Claudette dramatically collapsing into Fred's arms. At that point the people figure out that they had been duped into believing that Colbert was a witch by a vengeful little girl (who else but Bonita Granville) and they call for the burning of the tree at Gallows Hill and the film then ends. In the revised version, the information absolving Colbert is received prior to Colbert going to Gallows Hill and the governor signs a decree abolishing the trial for witchcraft and orders the tree to be burned, and then Colbert emerges from her cell where she embraces Fred. The changes didn't help and the film was a box office and critical disappoint-ment. Fred felt that he was miscast in this film and years later would recall with a laugh, "I was the Irish cavalier. I can remember one review after the picture came out that said, 'At any minute we expected Fred MacMurray to take a saxophone out from under his cape.'"

Fred next appeared in back to back films with Carole Lombard. Many critics believe that Fred didn't really have a substantial dramatic role until he appeared in Billy Wilder's *Double Indemnity*, but Fred's performance as Skid Johnson in Mitchell Leisen's dramatic-musical *Swing High, Swing Low* fore-shadows Walter Neff by seven years. Like Neff, Skid is full of bravado with women he has just laid eyes on. In the film Skid meets Lombard's Maggie King as her ship is going thru the Panama Canal, which he is guarding on his last day as a sentry along the Canal Zone. He engages her in some smart-alecky, come-on pick-up lines which reminded one of Neff's initial meetings with Barbara Stanwyck in the later film. Maggie seems repulsed *and* intrigued by Skid at the same time. Later, Maggie runs into Skid again when she goes ashore and they end up visiting a cabaret where Skid proves that there is talent behind the bravado when he plays the trumpet, mesmerizingly causing Maggie to fall in love with him. He is her diamond in the rough and things get rough soon when a Spaniard (Anthony Quinn) tries to pick Maggie up — she barely notices him, but Skid does and a fight breaks out which ends up with Skid and Maggie being arrested. Maggie is so taken with Skid that she stays on in Panama — moving in with Skid and his best friend. But Skid, like Neff, is also reckless and lives for the moment. He pawns his trumpet so he would have the money to bet on a cockfight. But Maggie — who believes in him — arranges to get him a job in a nightclub and in doing so confesses to the club's owner that she and Skid were secretly married. But loyalty is a word which cannot be applied to Skid and when he meets a voluptuous vixen (played by Dorothy Lamour). Skid eventually gets a chance at stardom and leaves Maggie behind in Panama, instead taking with him the vixen, who played Skid for the sap he is. Eventually, Maggie follows him to New York and attempts to get him back, but, finally realizing it's a lost cause, she divorces him — all the while Skid acts as if it doesn't faze him at all, but in reality he is devastated and begins drinking heavily which causes much havoc to his career as well as his health. But Maggie still believes in him and in the film's climax he is given one last chance at redemption by appearing on a radio broadcast, though he barely has the strength to stand. Maggie appears at the studio to try and give him the spark to get through the performance and he literally leans on her as she stands in front of him — one of his arms feebly around her shoulder as she clutches the arm with both hands and together — him on trumpet and she singing the song that had mesmerized her so when he first played it, "I Feel a Call to Arms":

> *When you blow that horn you thrill me,*
> *To the marrow of my bones you chill me,*
> *There it goes,*
> *I feel a call to arms.*

While his playing of this song in his weakened state doesn't have the intensity or spark of his initial rendition, for instance he isn't able to sustain the final note of "I Feel a Call to Arms" for over thirty-seconds as he was able to do when he was stronger, his rendition has a sad poignancy of its own. Skid is "just a shadow of ... his former glory," according to Leisen's biographer David Chierichetti, "and yet, somehow, there is a vague hope. Leisen, ever optimistic, ends the film on that note."

Interestingly, Fred was touted as early as August 1935 as the male lead in this film opposite Sylvia Sidney, in the role which Lombard eventually played. But so potent was the Lombard-MacMurray teamings that when Carole expressed interest in the film, Sidney (who was slipping at the box office) was reassigned to another picture. Lombard later placed her performance as Maggie King as one of her personal favorites.

In preparing for the role of Skid Johnson, Fred "walked up and down the set practicing on that trumpet until you thought you would go out

Fred, Carole Lombard, director Mitchell Leisen and Paramount founder Adolph Zukor on the set of Swing High, Swing Low.

of your mind," recalled Leisen. "But he got the lip movements just right." Fred's trumpet playing was dubbed by two trumpet players who, Leisen would recall, "could hold their notes longer than anybody else." The scenes where Fred holds Lombard in his arms and plays as she sings was devised by Leisen, and it's one of the most memorable images in the film. While it was necessary to dub Fred's trumpet playing, Lombard was insistent to Leisen that her singing similarly be dubbed, "but I said that nobody could have the same quality of voice and it would be unbelievable. So she did it and it came out beautifully."

As usual Fred had a hard time with love scenes. Leisen later recalled a line in the script which read, "I love you, and will you marry me?" And Fred, petrified that he would have to deliver this line, objected to its use, insisting that, "Skid Johnson would never say that." Leisen asked Fred what he thought Skid would say, but Fred wasn't sure. So before the next take he approached Lombard and cautioned her to be ready for whatever Fred says. Fred thought that they were only going to rehearse the scene but Leisen waved his hand to the camera operator who photographed the scene and the line Fred came up with turned out to be brilliant: "Gee, I'm kinda sick to my stomach, but will you marry me?" It was the kind of flip line that Skid would throw out without any hesitancy. According to Leisen, after the take, Lombard threw her arms around Fred and said, "Bless you, that was wonderful."

There is another scene, near the end, where Skid, very ill and hardly able to stand on his free will, but unwilling to admit it to Maggie, holds on to her when his legs give out and he slides down her body collapsing to the floor. Leisen would recall that Fred had rehearsed that fall and did it in one take and was "fantastic." But Lombard had not expected Fred to fall the way he did and had waved her hand when he fell and felt that she had ruined the scene. Leisen, knowing that he probably couldn't equal the initial take Fred had just performed, asked Lombard to withhold judgment until she watched it in the dailies the next morning. "We went to the projection booth the next morning," Leisen recalled to Chierichetti, "and ran it. It was one of the greatest things I'd ever seen and Carole came out sobbing. She said, 'I was watching as closely as I could, but when Fred collapsed, I couldn't see myself anymore. Nobody will ever notice what I did."

Swing High, Swing Low was only Dorothy Lamour's second film in a featured role and she was delighted to be working with a woman she had always idolized, Carole Lombard. In her autobiography, Lamour pays tribute to her: "Not only a great star, Carole was a beautiful woman inside and out and a great humanitarian. She did more for people in need than anyone I ever met in Hollywood — and she did it quietly. From the lowest to the highest paid, everybody at Paramount loved her and I was absolutely thrilled to be in the same picture." During its shooting Lombard took Lamour under her wing in much the same way she had Fred in *Hands Across the Table.* Lamour and Fred also got along well, remaining friends for the remainder of his life and making one more film together several years later.

Despite the excellent performances, strong script, direction, camera work and general atmosphere, *Swing High, Swing Low* received mixed reviews when it was first released. Some reviewers felt it was just another reworking of an old chestnut (the film was based on a popular Broadway play of the '20s *Burlesque,* which had been filmed before). *The New York Times'* Frank Nugent would write, "Carole Lombard and Fred MacMurray skip through the formula devices of *Swing High, Swing Low* with their usual ease at the Paramount, raising a routine story to a routine-plus picture. The plus is extremely small, sometimes being almost invisible." But others thought differently. *Variety* opined, "With Carole Lombard and Fred MacMurray topping a strong cast, plus the basic entertainment ingredients, no reason to believe that 'Swing High' will not jam 'em at the gate." Fred's performance was called "expert." Film historian David Thomson would write of *Swing High, Swing Low*, "When it is funny and happy it is as light as play; in love it nearly swoons; but when it turns somber it is a love story *noir* in 1937." The film went on to be one of Paramount's biggest grosser of the year.

Fred and Lombard next went on to make what would be Lombard's last film for Paramount, *True Confession*, and the last film they would appear together in. The film reunited them with one of Lombard's favorite directors Wesley Ruggles, and Fred with his favorite writer, Claude Binyon, in a story about a woman (Lombard) who is a pathological liar and causes no end of trouble for her attorney husband (Fred). In the story she goes so far as to admit to a murder she didn't commit! Naturally, with a storyline like this, the Production Code would be expected to be vigilant — and they were. They couldn't condone a story where the, for lack of a better word, heroine is a pathological liar. In a letter to Paramount producer John Hummel, Production Code Agency (PCA) Director Joseph Breen wrote, "There [was] no attempt to indicate that the 'processes of law' are to prevail ... there should be some indication at the end of this story that Helen's technical perjury is to be confessed to the proper legal authorities ... we think you might easily meet with this technical objection under the code by the insertion of a line, spoken, possibly by MacMurray, suggesting that he feels bound to make known to the judge, or the district attorney, or whoever is the proper person, that his wife has been guilty of perjury and that she will have to take the consequences — that he is helpless to save her — or some such line ..." A Paramount inter-office communication, dated September 3, 1937, and found in the papers of Claude Binyon, and directed to Hummel (probably written by the film's producer in consultation with Ruggles and Binyon), makes for fascinating reading of how the filmmakers responded to the PCA either by giving in to the Code, tweaking a scene or piece of dialog to make it less objectionable or by standing up to the Code and insisting that it will be done the way they want to do it:

1) We shall try to add a sentence indicating that something will be done about Helen's technical perjury.
2) We do not like the spanking ending but will try to devise an alternative protective ending which we will submit to you.
3) I am at a loss to understand the objections to the words, "kidney trouble" and we are not changing this.
4) The scenes of Helen and Ken on the divan will be handled with good taste.
5) There are no offensive decorations in Krayler's study.
6) The word, "quuims" will be dropped.

7) The line, "I am knitting little things," will be dropped or a protective take made.

8) We will take a chance on the word, "fry."

9) The judge will be handled with dignity. Our intention being, as Mr. Breen advised, to get our comedy as much as possible with other characters in the courtroom.

10) The line, "Because Mr. Krayler gave me a fifty dollar raise," is a sure-fire laugh and does not seem to me to be offensively suggestive. It certainly could not possibly mean anything to a child and wouldn't corrupt an adult. If possible, we would like to take a chance on this line and if censorship boards object, it can be removed from the picture very easily.

11) I have advised Mr. Ruggles of the possible objection to the judge's action of grimacing and clapping his hand to his forehead.

12) The phrase, "…gold would buy womankind's most priceless possession — her honor," will be read without undue stress.

13) We are not changing the line "…defending that which is womankind's prime heritage."

14) Since this is not a public beach we feel that Ken need not wear a swimming shirt in addition to his trunks.

15) It is already clearly indicated in the script that Daisy will be fully clothed.

16) Care will be taken in the handling of the dialogue between Helen and Ken.

17) As explained above, we shall try to find another alternative ending in place of the spanking.

Some mild changes were made, and on September 27, 1937, Breen once again wrote to Hummel decreeing the film unacceptable. "We refer to the play upon Helen's suggestion that she is pregnant and the further action and dialogue which suggest that Ken carries her into the bedroom for the purposes of making her lie come true. We earnestly recommend that you delete from your picture all suggestions having to do with the sexual relationship between Ken and Helen … the business of showing Helen taking Ken's trousers from him should be dropped. The dialogue about the baby and the doctor should also be dropped. Particularly important is the necessity for deleting the line, 'Well, it could be true,' which plants and points up the suggestiveness of Ken carrying her into the bedroom."

Apparently, the latest denial from the Code angered director Ruggles enough that when he went into a meeting with the Production Code on September 30 he told them that he wanted to know what the "score" was, and that the Code "read dirty things into scripts." A few more concessions were made, but the Code still wasn't satisfied. Paramount then appealed to the head of the PCA, President Will Hays, who, finally, on November 19, 1937, gave a stamp of approval to the film, but with qualifications. "I have directed Mr. Breen to issue the formal certificate of approval for this production. In doing this, I wish to make it clear, for the record, that it is my judgment that the scenes under discussion are of questionable acceptability and are saved from positive offense by the general farcical nature of the entire production and the grotesqueness of the scenes in the court …"

When the film premiered just before Christmas it received excellent reviews. Frank Nugent of the *New York Times,* who was so lukewarm regarding *Swing High, Swing Low,* positively raved about this film. "Although *True Confession* had a pulpwood sound, it proved yesterday to be a highly polished, smoothly grained Yule log which deserves to crackle right merrily at the Paramount from now until well after Christmas." Still, its reputation, perhaps because of the faded reputation of its director Wesley Ruggles, a virtual non-entity today, has declined over the years while *Swing High, Swing Low* has risen. Leonard Maltin in his capsule review gives *True Confession* only one-and-a-half stars out of four and calls the film "alarmingly unfunny."

Next, Fred went into production with a newspaper comedy-drama called *Exclusive.* Originally, the squeaky-voiced Jean Arthur (just off the triumph that was *Mr. Deeds Goes to Town)* was announced as Fred's co-star, but she was under contract to Harry Cohn at Columbia and in the end he decided against a loan-out of one of his few star contract players. (Though he did consent to loan her out to appear with Cooper in *The Plainsman.)* Instead, Paramount assigned an actress they considered to be up and coming to the leading female role, Frances Farmer, who had just scored a hit in Howard Hawks' *Come and Get It.* The film was made without incident and was received by audiences and critics alike unenthusiastically. Fred ended 1937 as popular as ever with those who worked at Paramount by being selected by the extras as their favorite actor due to his politeness and consideration for them and others.

V

In 1938-1939 Fred would appear in six more films, but compared to the films he made between 1935-1937 they did seem to be a tad of a let down. Fred was now considered enough of a star that he didn't always need to be teamed with a high-powered leading lady. An example of that was his first release of 1938 in a nice little musical called *Cocoanut Grove.* Fred was again cast as a bandleader and his leading lady was a band singer who was making the transition to movie actress and had just scored well in the Astaire-Rogers film *Follow the Fleet,* Harriet Hilliard, who was the girl singer for her husband Ozzie Nelson's band. Of course, Ozzie and Harriet would later go on to television immortality with their long-running family comedy *The Adventures of Ozzie and Harriet.* Harriet and Fred were also old friends because she had once sung with the California Collegians. Eve Arden had a supporting role in this film and was excited to be in the picture because Fred was a "big favorite" of hers, and recalled in her autobiography a "funny moment" during the making of the film. There was a scene where Fred was continually blowing his lines and he appeared (to Arden) to be "terribly nervous." Arden recalls Fred "kept blowing his lines ... I cringed each time the sound man would identify the beginning of the scene with 'Take 64'; then 'Take 65'; as poor Fred muffed it again. Finally some perceptive soul got to the sound man and warned him that he was making Fred more nervous with his bellow. So, on the next take, the contrite sound man hissed softly, 'Take 66,' and the tense set erupted in laughter, in which Fred joined heartily — and the next take was perfect."

In 1938 for the first time in his career Fred was cast opposite not a strong leading lady, but a strong leading man, playing Bing Crosby's dependable brother in *Sing, You Sinners*. The film was considered to be a departure for Crosby in that he was playing the less than reliable brother who even tried to steal Fred's girl away from him. Initially, Fred's role was to be played by Don Ameche, who was under contract to Fox, and a third brother was to be played by Mickey Rooney, an up-and-comer at MGM, and soon to be the number one star in the movies. But eventually it was decided to cast Fred and young Donald O'Connor in those parts. The film was a reunion between director Wesley Ruggles and screenwriter Claude Binyon, two of Fred's perennial favorites. According to Bing Crosby's biographer, "*Sing, You Sinners* was Claude Binyon's baby ... he and director Wesley Ruggles had developed an enviable track record with a series of edgy screwball comedies that advanced the careers of Paramount players Claudette Colbert, Fred MacMurray and Carole Lombard," and now Ruggles and Binyon were collaborating on a story to give Bing a new depth. After reading the script, and understanding that he was to play the no-account brother, Bing reportedly said, "I guess I can play myself." He also expressed his glee that he wasn't the guy who gets the girl in this picture. "The only break I get in the picture is that I don't get the girl — Fred gets her. And believe me that's a relief. I've made enough love scenes in the past five or six years. And I haven't got a one in *Sing, You Sinners*. Whoopee! What a break."

Fred and Bing enjoyed making the film together. They were both golf enthusiasts and outdoorsmen. A visiting reporter recorded the following exchange between the two leading men between filming:

Fred: Say Bing a friend of mine just got back from Bishop with a whole limit of trout and there wasn't a one under ten inches.

Bing: Izzat so?

(They looked at each other speculatively for a moment. Stanley Goldsmith, the assistant director, was standing nearby casting dirty looks in the general direction of MacMurray.)

Fred: You know I just checked up and I can get away Friday night. It's only 300 miles. We could fish Saturday and Sunday and drive back Sunday night. Can you get off Saturday?

Bing: Oh Stanley, do I work Saturday?

Stanley: Well, there's that tea cart routine.

Bing: Aw, Stanley, have a heart.

Stanley: — but I know we're not going to get to it. Yes you can get away but remember now —

Bing: I'll be fresh as a daisy Monday, Stanley.

(The two stars almost danced a jig with glee and started excitedly discussing tackle, flies, etc. until Goldsmith broke it up by calling Crosby to work.)

The Crosbys and MacMurrays also socialized as couples. Fred had appeared as an extra in a film which starred Dixie Lee in 1929, before she retired to her new full-time job as Mrs. Bing Crosby, and Lillian and Dixie were good friends as well. As mentioned, Fred and Bing had a shared passion for golf. Fred told a reporter that "if it were up to Bing and me we would spend all our waking hours on the golf course." At around this time Bing and Dixie had formed a club called the Westwood Marching and Chowder Club and would occasionally put on shows for benefits or for just fun. One such show was titled *The Breakaway Minstrel Show*, which performed under a huge tent which was erected on the Crosbys' tennis court. Bing rounded up friends like Fred, Wesley Ruggles, Bill Frawley, Andy Devine and Edward Sutherland to perform. Fred chose to perform a song which young Donald O'Connor sang in *Sing, You Sinners* called "Small Fry," but there was a major difference in Fred's rendition as part of the Minstrel show, he would sing the song in drag.

Fred's big 1938 release was William Wellman's production of *Men with Wings*, an aviation film he starred in with Ray Milland. (*The Hollywood Reporter* had at one time reported that Cary Grant and Randolph Scott were locked into making this film, but as would happen with great frequency in Hollywood the studios announced an actor for a film and later changed their mind or something would happen which would prevent the actor from appearing.) Wellman was one of Hollywood's supreme action directors and had a particular feeling and love for aviation films. His greatest film up to this time was the 1927 silent screen classic *Wings*, which included some of the most amazing aerial shots ever made for a motion picture — then and now. Wellman would go to great lengths on this film to get the kinds of aerial shots necessary as well. Interestingly, Fred had thought of being a pilot when he was growing up and as things would turn out he would appear in several films as a pilot — such as the earlier *Thirteen Hours by Air* and later *Dive Bomber*. But Fred later said that when he first got in a plane he got motion sickness and with that went his ambitions of being a pilot, yet thanks to the wonders of acting he was now able to act out his boyhood dreams. "In this business," Fred would later state, "one gets to be and do everything one wishes to be or do, everything life previously had prevented." To top that off doing these aviation films seemed to ultimately cure Fred of the motion sickness he used to get.

Wellman would later state that "we wanted to get that feeling that every

Fred playing the hero in William Wellman's aviation drama **Men with Wings.**

man has who flew in the war. That restlessness, it's hard to describe." He tried to instill in Fred this spirit of adventure and awe that he believed that pilots, especially those in dangerous situations, experience. "I think he caught the idea." *Men with Wings* had an unusually long production schedule — for those days — from pre-production to its final editing took nine months with principal photography beginning in early May 1938 and continuing into September. When the film premiered in New York a huge premier was held in Times Square before large crowds and several pilots were awarded with "Men with Wings" citations. The film went on to be a big success and there was even talk of Fred being cast in Wellman's next film, *Beau Geste,* but that fell through when Gary Cooper expressed interest.

Fred ended the decade by appearing in three comedies opposite two leading ladies — Madeleine Carroll and Irene Dunne. Carroll was a cool English beauty who excelled at playing one of Hitchcock's blonde heroines — icy on the outside and full of passion on the inside. She made a fine counter balance to Fred's all-American diamond-in-the-rough masculinity and they would go on to do several films together over the next decade. Their first film was *Café Society* with Carroll as the daughter of a wealthy and prominent member of New York society. She uses reporter Chick O'Bannon (Fred) to get her name printed in the society pages of the paper he works for and goes so far as to lure him into marriage. Chick later overhears how she lured him into marriage and decides to get even by writing an expose about his wife. In classic screwball fashion they decide to get a divorce, but discover that they really do love each other. Also in classic screwball comedy fashion the film is full of violence — usually at Carroll's expense. Sure, she slaps MacMurray, but he gets in his licks too. There is a sequence toward the end where Carroll's character is forced to hold on for dear life to water skis while Chick drives the speed boat and yet they are able to spar back and forth — he comes out fine, but she ends up cutting up her hands. But the sequence actually brings them back together as he apologetically asks, "Those ropes certainly cut them up, didn't they?" to which the Carroll character, now smitten and humbled (as always, the rich dame in screwball comedy is humbled by the ordinary man), gushes, "Yes, I never met a man before who'd do a thing like that to me!" In the end, Carroll vows to reform and be the kind of wife an average Joe like Chick would want.

Of his leading ladies, Fred was often asked by reporters if he had a favorite — he gallantly never complied with this request, but he did once add that, "There have been a few who were my non-favorites," but, again, never naming names. But there appears to be some evidence that one of his non-favorites may have been the coolly regal Madeleine Carroll. Former movie publicist Sidney Bloomberg would recall that Fred "didn't particularly care" for Carroll and says that Fred told Allan Jones, who played the third lead opposite Fred and Carroll in the 1938 film *Honeymoon in Bali,* that he didn't want to do another picture with Carroll but that "Zukor [Adolph Zukor, head of Paramount] was adamant about teaming them" due to their box office popularity. Movie still photographer John Engstead once told the following story, which may give one example of why Fred was less than enamored by Carroll: "We had to do a session once with Fred MacMurray, and he had finished the picture, *Virginia* or whatever, and he had it in his contract that he had to have two weeks off between pictures. Well, he was on his two-week layoff and the assistant director called me up and said I could do these stills for the film this afternoon. He said, 'But you've got to get Fred, and you can have Madeleine at 3:30 or 4:00.' And so I called Fred's house, and Lilly said he's out at Lake Sherwood and he's fishing with Zeppo Marx, who was his agent. So I called Lake Sherwood and told him, 'Fred, I got to have these stills of you and Madeleine,' and he said, 'Oh, well, I guess I can do that.' But I said, 'Fred, you can't add it to your layoff, because you can't break your layoff with these pictures,' so, because he was really a friend and helping me out, he said, 'Well, okay, but call Lilly and tell her to bring a dark suit to the studio, because we're going to go right to dinner from the studio.' So he came in, and I went to the set about 3:30 to get Madeleine, and Madeleine said, 'Nobody told me about this. I'm not going to do this today, I couldn't possibly.' I said, 'Madeleine, Fred's coming in especially,' and she said, 'That doesn't matter. I'm not going to do it.' And this poor guy had come in especially on his off time to do this, while she was working anyway

Fred and Madeleine Carroll in 1939's **Honeymoon in Bali.**

and her filming had finished early. And, you know, this is just being a bitch. I was just disgusted with her."

Fred slapped around a good share of his leading ladies and still came out of it, usually, as a decent guy — and, frankly, Fred was getting sick and tired of it. "I had to slap Carole Lombard," Fred told a reporter with tongue firmly in cheek. "I had to slap Claudette Colbert. I had to slap Madeleine Carroll. Every time a writer heard he was working on a picture I was to be in, he dashed off a little scene in which I took a punch at the star. I used to have nightmares, terrible dreams of enraged and aroused womanhood descending upon me in a body and slapping me silly. Dreams where I was tied to a stake and a parade of women a million miles long walked by, each one taking a poke at me!"

So when he heard that he was to play opposite one of the esteemed ladies of the screen, Irene Dunne, he wanted to make sure that she gets her revenge on him for all the women he took a poke at in his earlier films. "When Wesley Ruggles told me he wanted me for *Invitation to Happiness* ... the first thing I did was to get Claude Binyon, the writer fellow who thinks it's funny for me to slap some girl, to go on a hunting trip with me." As one of Fred's best friends it didn't take much to get Binyon to go off with him. "Suffice to say that the only punching I do in this picture is to Eddie Hogan. Hogan's a heavyweight fighter, and he socks me plenty, right back." And Binyon wrote in the scene where Dunne gets even with Fred for all the slaps he gave to his past leading ladies. "It happens on a park bench," Fred recalled. "She chases me out there. So I start telling her about a swell blonde I know in a night club. 'I ought to slap your face,' says Irene. So I go right on telling her more about my swell blonde. And then I say, 'With all your class and fine clothes you're a woman. Just the same as that blonde. There's something about me that's got to you.' Right there is where Irene bangs one on me. And boy! she delivers. We made six takes ... afterwards she told me she was avenging Carole and Claudette and Madeleine and Marion [Martin] ... and all the rest of them. It's all okay with me. The gals are even — and my friends are calling me by name again."

Fred had appeared in twenty-two films in just over five years. He was one of Paramount's top stars. He was their all-purpose leading man adept at light comedy, adventures, Westerns and dramas. Warner Brothers had such a leading man in George Brent, but Brent never attained the popularity or stardom that Fred did, and while Brent appeared opposite some of the biggest female stars, he, unlike Fred, was often overshadowed by them. While Hepburn, Lombard, Colbert and Dunne were considered bigger names than he was, Fred was no pushover. Fred more than held up his end of the pictures he appeared in. But, with the possible exception of *Swing High, Swing Low,* Fred had not been given a truly meaty role, one he could sink his teeth into and prove he was an actor — and to Fred this was just fine. He was popular, he was highly paid, he was happily married and he had scores of friends and enough time to enjoy his outdoor pursuits. He was quite content with being one end of a seesaw.

CHAPTER THREE

Highest Paid Actor in Hollywood
1940-1944

In early 1940 Fred was asked to critique the kissing style of some of the leading ladies he had worked with since arriving in Hollywood. Apparently he was asked to do this because of his reputation for working with the most delectable women in the business. Fred, or a Paramount publicity man, came up with a pretty good list and the results are worth including. He prefaced it by stating, "They're all wonderful — and they're all different too":

Katharine Hepburn: "Unpredictable in auscultation as in temperament. The esthetic kiss was preferred, but it had to be a thing of beauty — and camera angles."

Sylvia Sidney: "A kiss is just a kiss ... just a smack and let's get done with it." (Also Fred's preference.)

Claudette Colbert: "A happy medium between realism and make-believe."

Ann Sheridan: "In the objective class — while kissing for the customers, she doesn't forget for an instant that she's acting." (What makes me think that Fred had at least a say on this list and it wasn't totally the job of a Paramount publicity writer is the line "kissing for the customers." Fred often referred to movie audiences as his "customers.")

Jean Arthur: "Extremely shy off screen she parks her inhibitions when the camera begins to roll and kisses must mean something."

Frances Farmer: "Her's had to be casual — sort of off the elbow in spirit."

Gladys Swarthout: "She prefers a good health-salad to a kiss in front of the camera." (Of which Fred could identify — though he preferred peanut butter sandwiches.)

Louise Campbell: "The proper sort of gal who likes her kisses to be formal."

Barbara Stanwyck: "Like [Campbell] she is equally deliberate though more thorough."

Madeleine Carroll: "The soulful smackeroo — ethereal, moonlight and roses stuff." (I can just hear Fred going "Yuck" after this.)

Carole Lombard: "Likes 'em rapturous and enthusiastic."

In July of 1939 Fred began production on one of the best films of his career and perhaps the best of his long collaboration with director Mitchell Leisen. The film was *Remember the Night* and it was the last film Preston Sturges would write without directing. Sturges, like fellow Paramount contract writer Billy Wilder, longed to direct his own screenplays and would soon get his chance in the 1940 film *Christmas in July*. Sturges was present on the set during much of the making of this film, unusual for a writer once a screenplay is completed, and certainly unusual for Sturges. According to Sturges' personal assistant of the time, Edwin Gillette, Paramount had to "squeeze the work out of him ... What he wanted really was to play around, to entertain freeloaders at the Players [a club which Sturges owned], to go out on his boat. He loved to hang around and be the great raconteur, but he had to work to get the money to enjoy himself, but he stretched things out until the studio screamed." But not this time because he wanted to keep his eyes on Leisen, who he didn't trust, but also because he wanted to be on his best behavior so Paramount would allow him to direct his own films.

Remember the Night casts Fred as a Manhattan Assistant District Attorney prosecuting a shoplifter (Barbara Stanwyck) just before Christmas. When Stanwyck's public defender, a windbag from the old school, orates before the judge so long that MacMurray is able to arrange a continuance of the case until after the holidays, it means that Stanwyck has to spend the holidays in jail. Fred feels guilty about this so he arranges for her bail until after the holidays. When he finds out that they both are from Indiana he offers to drive her home so she can spend Christmas with her mother, who

Stanwyck hasn't seen in years. Meanwhile, he will drive on to his mother's farm. When they arrive at her mother's house, Stanwyck is devastated when her mother viciously turns her away, not wanting anything to do with her. MacMurray invites her to spend an old-fashioned Christmas with him, his mother (the ever-wonderful Beulah Bondi), his aunt (Elizabeth Patterson) and a slightly dotty farm hand (Sterling Holloway). And an old-fashioned

Barbara Stanwyck was one of Fred's favorite leading ladies and this is from their first of four films together, Remember the Night.

Christmas is what is had, complete with chestnuts, apple bobbing, and popcorn popped over an open fire. Stanwyck finally gets to know what a loving family is really like while falling in love with Fred — and he with her. Will the DA compromise his principles and allow her to escape or will she pay her debt to society with Fred waiting for her when she gets out of jail? That the film doesn't have the same holiday following of *It's a Wonderful Life* is a shame because both films share a hardened sentimentality about them. George Bailey discovers that no man is a failure as long as he has friends after he contemplates suicide, while Stanwyck's Lee Leander discovers what a loving family unit is all about after being disowned by her own mother. But *Remember the Night* has not had the exposure that *It's a Wonderful Life* and many other Christmas classics have enjoyed. One problem with the film that dates it and may cause contemporary audiences to cringe at is the inclusion of MacMurray's slow-talking, slow-witted Negro valet (played by Snowflake) in a couple of short scenes and played as the kind of "comedy relief" that stereotyped many African-American actors of that period.

While this is a Sturges screenplay, Leisen made it his film. According to David Chierichetti, "... it might be assumed that Sturges and not Leisen was the main creative force behind _Remember the Night_. Such an assumption is unwarranted. Certainly Sturges' screenplay is excellent, one of the best Leisen ever directed. The screenplay, however, was very different from the final film, and in modifying it to suit his own tastes, Leisen markedly changed the concepts of the characters and the whole emotional tone of the piece." Sturges' 130-page screenplay was overly sentimental and included such scenes as Stanwyck being profoundly moved by a Christmas Day sermon; it was such scenes and sentimentality which Leisen decided to tone down without unduly hardening the film or the characters, but keeping them and the situations more real. The film was shot in 34 days and came in eight days ahead of schedule with a savings of $50,000. For this, Leisen would always credit Stanwyck, one of his favorite actresses, stating to Chierichetti that she "set the pace and everybody worked harder, trying to outdo her." Fred was equally a pro, both he and Stanwyck had a clause in their contracts which allowed them to finish up work by six every evening, but both, when called upon to stay later, did so without hesitation.

As usual, the only real problem Leisen had with Fred was the filming of the love scene with Stanwyck. As was the case with Colbert and Lombard and most of his other leading ladies, Fred was shy when it came to shooting love scenes and especially since this was his first picture with Stanwyck, somebody he didn't know very well at the time. According to Eleanor Broder, Leisen's dialogue director, Stanwyck was prepared. "We all dreaded having to shoot the love scene at the end of the picture, because Fred was terribly shy and love scenes were the hardest thing for him to do. But Barbara knew how to handle that. For days before we did it, she kept saying, 'This is going to be something, doing a love scene with Fred' to everybody on the crew and even to Fred. All this ribbing really got his dander up and he decided he'd get it right in spite of himself. The day came, Fred gritted his teeth, and he did it perfectly."

Leisen wasn't the only one who came away from the experience of filming _Remember the Night_ admiring Barbara Stanwyck. Preston Sturges took Stanwyck aside on the set and told her that one day he would write "a great comic role" for her — a promise he kept within two years with his classic comedy _The Lady Eve_. But Sturges wasn't nearly as enthusiastic about Fred, who he felt "showed neither the nimble wit nor commanding presence" that Sturges felt his DA should encompass. Apparently Sturges' criticism of Fred's performance didn't escape Fred's ears and there was no love lost between the two. When filming was completed Sturges told Fred, "It's been a pleasure working with you." Fred apparently thought that Sturges was being two-faced complimenting him to his face while criticizing him behind his back and told Sturges, "I wish I could say the same about you." Years later Fred recalled the encounter and said, "I don't like to be that way, but he was terrible, really cruel."

Ironically, Fred did work again briefly with Sturges. In 1941 Fred made a mediocre film called *New York Town*. When newly placed Paramount production head Buddy DeSylva previewed the film in his private screening room he came away considering the Charles Vidor-directed comedy "lousy" and didn't want such a poor picture to be the first product released under his reign. He called in Sturges and asked him to write and direct a new ending which he hoped would help the film. Sturges, who wanted to gain some credit with the new head of production, agreed to do this as a personal favor, but provided that DeSylva didn't publicize his efforts — which DeSylva readily agreed to. According to Sturges biographer James Curtis, "There was obviously little Sturges could do, other than to rethink a limp and inconclusive ending and add a little noise and slapstick. He turned the last five minutes of the picture into a boisterous scrap between Robert Preston and Fred MacMurray over the hand of wide-eyed Mary Martin. Sturges kept the noise high and the expressions broad and brought the film briefly to life."

When released in January 1940, *Remember the Night* became a box office and critical success. In its first week at the New York Paramount Theater the film grossed $45,000, setting a new record. *Variety* complimented the leads. "Stanwyck turns in a fine performance. MacMurray is impressive as the serious minded prosecutor, but loosens up for the comedy stretches." The Sturges-composed script was called "deft" while Leisen was complimented for his "fine piloting."

Remember the Night would be the first of four films which united Fred with that most prolific of actresses, Barbara Stanwyck, continuing his streak of working more than once with the great leading ladies of the screen. There was one leading lady who was an exception. She worked with Fred only once and apparently she didn't quite take to his humor. The lady was the talented comedienne Jean Arthur and the film was *Too Many Husbands*. The film is the old chestnut about a woman (Arthur) who remarries thinking that her first husband is dead. He then returns and complications arise. Fred played the missing and thought deceased first husband with Melvyn Douglas as Arthur's new spouse. Arthur was Columbia's biggest leading lady as well as one of Frank Capra's favorite — he had cast her in both *Mr. Deeds Goes to Town* and *Mr. Smith Goes to Washington*. On screen she was incomparable with her distinctive voice and split-second comedic timing, but off-screen she was so insecure of her talent and camera shy that she would occasionally vomit before and after a take. According to Arthur's biographer, John Oller: "Her insecurities continued to spill over onto the shooting set. In *Too Many Husbands* ... her character was subjected to a tug-of-war between new husband Melvyn Douglas and first husband Fred MacMurray, who has returned after supposedly drowning years before. Off screen, she fretted constantly that she was not attractive enough to make a convincing object of the rivalry. MacMurray joked at one point that she needn't worry since they could shoot the next scene with an Indian blanket over her head. Furious, Arthur asked whether she really looked that bad, and burst into tears."

Around 1940 Fawcett Publishing wanted to come up with a superhero that could compete against Superman. Writer Bill Parker and artist C.C. Beck created the character of Captain Marvel. According to many sources Fred MacMurray served as the inspiration for how Marvel looked. "Captain Marvel himself was based on the actor Fred MacMurray, who was known as a pretty down-to-earth guy," Beck later said. Beck later went on to say, "At the time, Fred MacMurray was a very popular actor and I used him as the basis for Captain Marvel. He had kind of a slanted forehead, wavy hair, and a big chin." According to other sources, other leading movie stars were inspiration for Captain Marvel characters:

Fred supplemented his income by appearing in print ads such as this, which also touted his upcoming films.

Judy Garland was the model for Mary Marvel, Betty Grable was the source for Beautia Sivana, Danny Kaye inspired Sivana Junior, Tyrone Power inspired Ibis the Invincible and W.C. Fields is considered the model for Uncle Marvel. Interestingly, Fred would don a superhero outfit complete with cape in a fantasy sequence of the 1943 film *No Time for Love.*

II

Fred and Lily were living in a modest, by Hollywood standards, home in Brentwood, twelve miles west of Hollywood. The house was described as "a small, early-American affair whose sole Hollywood feature is a swimming pool." The house was at one time the home of Margaret Sullavan and her then-husband, agent extraordinaire, Leland Hayward. On the property was a red barn which the Haywards had built as a place to house their children, which Fred converted back to a barn and also used as a workshop. Fred would later say that the swimming pool had "never been worth what we put into it, but apparently you can't sell a house around here without it, so there it is." That statement said a great deal about Fred's business sense. The pool was more or less not for show but to make the house more of an investment should he ever sell it. In fact, Fred was gaining a strong reputation in the film colony not only for his amiability but for his business sense and in the meanwhile fast becoming one of the richest men in town. Much of his financial gain came courtesy of the man who was his financial advisor and the advisor to many of the stars of the day, Bo Christian Roos.

Roos would one day become a controversial figure when some of his clients found that the investments that he had made on their behalf were bad and they lost their fortunes and had to start over again. (John Wayne is the primary example of this. At one time he was one of Roos' most famous clients but when Wayne was financing his dream project, the film *The Alamo*, in the late '50s, he asked Roos to give him a report of how much money he had from his investments that he could sell and then use to finance the film. Roos tried to put him off but eventually had to admit the awful truth that Wayne had lost virtually everything. Wayne immediately fired him and even had him investigated for fraud, which couldn't be proved.) But in the early 1940s Roos and his seventeen-employee company, Beverly Management Corporation, was at its peak and had a client list which was the envy on Hollywood: Wayne, Merle Oberon, Bing Crosby, Ray Milland, Red Skelton, Johnny Weissmuller, Lupe Velez, Joan Crawford and Marlene Dietrich. Roos soon found that Fred was the ideal client because of his incredible fidelity to the extraordinary budget that he often placed his famous clients on.

John Wayne told of Roos telling "doleful tales of once-famous, and formerly wealthy, movie stars now living from hand to mouth." Roos would take over total management of his client's finances and put them and their spouses on an expense account. He invested their money in real estate, including apartments, hotels, parking lots, oil wells, cattle, and common stocks. So while supposedly his clients would get very rich by these investments (and many did, including Fred), they would have to live well within their means and this meant being put on a stringent (for Hollywood standards) budget. By this time Fred was getting $5,000 per week as a contract player at Paramount, excellent money. In his first interview with Fred Roos asked him point blank "how much money do you want for pocket money," Fred said $35 per week! (When Roos asked John Wayne if he could live on $50 per week, the Duke virtually laughed in his face!) "MacMurray never had any idea of going Hollywood," Roos later said.

Roos' Beverly Management paid the MacMurray's mortgage and utility bills and allowed Fred his $35 per week walking around money and set Lily up with a household allowance for food and other necessities as well as a modest budget for clothing. Meanwhile, the bulk of the money that Fred earned was invested. By 1945 Fred was the part-owner of a golf-and-tennis club, the outright owner of a Los Angeles apartment house (nine stories high on Wilshire Blvd.) and the co-owner of three other apartment houses. He also was the owner of a knitting mill and invested in an oil company. He also bought a working cattle ranch of over 900 acres near Santa Rosa in northern California along the Russian River. Fred got great enjoyment out of this investment and often when he was between pictures he, Lily and their young daughter Susan (adopted in 1941) would spend a great deal of time at the ranch which was described as having one of the "finest herds of milking shorthorns on the Pacific coast." Fred would always insist that the ranch was not only for pleasure but was a money-making operation. "It's stocked with a breed of Hereford cows rather new to the Pacific Coast," Fred explained. "They're dual-purpose cattle — good milkers and good meat animals too. When one of those cows goes dry, you've still got something."

Unlike some of Roos' other clients Fred took an active interest in how his investments were faring which may be one of the reasons why Fred didn't suffer the same fate as John Wayne. According to one account, Fred "never has to sign a check or look at a bank statement, if he doesn't want to. He regularly attends, however, what Roos calls 'Board of Director' meetings, which consist of just Roos and MacMurray. In the middle of these, the star will occasionally interrupt the discussion of six-figure finance to ask, naively enough, if it's O.K. with Roos if he orders a new fishing rod."

In August 1941 Roos, who enjoyed a bit of luxury himself, took Fred, John Wayne, Ray Milland and Ward Bond in his forty-foot cabin cruiser on what had been called a "pleasure cruise" to Mexico. While they were in Acapulco Roos convinced the foursome (plus Johnny Weissmuller who wasn't along on this trip) to invest in a resort hotel which stood high above a cliff along the Acapulco beach. The 28-room hotel was a wise investment and many of the investors would often come and stay or allow their friends to stay for free. All but Fred, who believed in people paying their own way and, besides, if enough people stayed for free in the hotel it would eventually lose money. The MacMurrays weren't much for going out on the town either. They enjoyed a quiet domestic life. When Fred was working, he liked to come home and enjoy a quiet dinner with Lily and then take some time to play

Fred and Lily in their greenhouse.

with Susan. For recreation he enjoyed listening to music, read magazines (like *Field and Stream* and *Outdoor Life*) or a few favored radio programs in the evening. Then he would often study lines for the next day's shoot and then try to get to bed by ten P.M. When he wasn't shooting a picture he would often go hunting and fishing with his sportsman buddies and spends periods of time at his ranch with his family. Even though Lily was often in frail health she did a lot of the cooking herself, though the MacMurrays did employ a part-time cook and maid. Fred's mother was also a frequent visitor, especially when Lily had periods when she was not at all well and had to take to her bed. She would take over the running of the household as well as cooking chores. At most, Fred and Lily would go out on the town no

Fred and Lily taking a stroll around their pool.

more than 2-3 times per year. Lily would recall that on these occasions they would arrive at a nightclub and Fred would immediately ask her, "Do you want your dance right away or would you rather wait and have it just before we go home?" Lily would tell interviewers (on the few occasions when she was interviewed) that she liked being a housewife and mother and enjoyed such activities as making her own hats, "just for the fun of it." She later told

The Saturday Evening Post that it "amused" her when she was named one of the "Ten Best-Dressed Women" in Hollywood. Likewise, one account of the MacMurray home life indicated that "Fred and Lillian swim, play tennis, fish, play Monopoly, go to the races, go to the fights, go to the homes of friends, just fritter away their time."

Occasionally, Fred and Lily did enjoy entertaining in their own home and one of their parties has long been considered part of Hollywood legend because of the delightful antics of Carole Lombard. Joan Crawford would recall that Fred and Lily "had one of the few happy and well-adjusted marriages in Hollywood." She also recalled that Lily "didn't approve of swearing," which so frustrated the foul-mouthed Lombard that one night she jumped into the MacMurray swimming pool wearing an expensive white gown. "For the rest of the evening she wore Fred's pajamas, but she didn't utter a blue word." Another account of this party indicates that when Lombard did this her husband, Clark Gable, "laughed and laughed, saying, 'Isn't she wonderful? Isn't she darling? Isn't she marvelous?'" Crawford would recall the MacMurray parties as "divine." On another occasion Fred and Lily were among those invited to the Gables' for a dinner party. Clark Gable's biographer would later write that "The Gables threw parties only for close friends." This particular party was held in July under a big tent on the Gables' tennis court with the Brown Derby catering. There was even a bandstand but as always with the unpredictable Carole Lombard there was no band. The idea was to have the guests be the band. So Fred brought along his saxophone while Gable played the drums and a flute and another man played bass fiddle "and everybody else hummed." Fred was the only one who was actually proficient with his instrument!

For some years the MacMurrays had wanted children, but couldn't conceive, possibly because of the fragile nature of Lily's health. In 1940 Fred and Lily took in a newborn blonde and blue-eyed baby girl. They named the little girl Susan, or Susie for short. The adoption was effective in April 1942 when Fred and Lily went to court to officially legalize the adoption. They tried to shield little Susie from the newspaper cameras that were at the courthouse where Juvenile Judge Robert H. Scott officiated. "It's just that we want her to grow up like any other normal child and not be constantly recognized," Lily explained. Judge Scott approved the formal adoption based on the glowing reports submitted by child welfare officials who observed the relationship between child and prospective parents for the 21 months that Susie lived with them. Though there was little doubt this would happen, the MacMurrays were overjoyed.

III

In the late spring of 1941 Fred was invited to take part in his hometown of Beaver Dam's Centennial celebration. Fred wasn't certain he could attend because he was busy shooting *Dive Bomber.* As it turned out Fred got away just in time to fly home. At almost the last minute he notified the event organizers that he would attend and arrive on July 3. The headline of the hometown paper blared out on its front page:

FRED MACMURRAY TO ATTEND CENTENNIAL EVENT

Fred traveled overnight with his mother from Los Angeles to Chicago, where he was met by Beaver Dam dignitaries, including his uncle, Lester Martin. Together they then drove to Beaver Dam, where Fred arrived in time to crown the "Queen of the Centennial" that night. After spending the night with his childhood friend Randall McKinstry and his family, Fred participated in the big parade held on July 4 riding in an open car down Main Street to the fairgrounds. Once at the fairgrounds and on the platform, "MacMurray gave his classic exhibit of forgetfulness. After watching him fidget around for several minutes ... someone suggested that, maybe he could sing something. He chose 'On Wisconsin' but halfway through the third line, he stopped - the words had escaped him." The appearance of Fred was the highlight of the centennial event and would long be remembered by old-timers. "He showed his support and loyalty for Beaver Dam when he came in 1941 for the Centennial and many remember that," recalled McKintry's nephew years later.

Shortly after the Centennial, Fred, Randall McKinstry and another Beaver Dam friend, Dr. R.B. Schoenwetter, went off on a fishing trip to Canada where, like in his hometown, Fred's presence caused excitement. When word got out that Fred and his friends were coming to little Kenora in Ontario, the town turned out. Main Street was shut down for about an hour-and-a-half as more than 1,000 people "many of them feminine waited to catch a glimpse of Fred MacMurray, Hollywood screen star." When he got to town, Fred ended up needing the assistance of two policemen to get through the crowd of well-wishers, occasionally stopping to sign autographs. Fred's cousin Lester Martin, Jr. recalled that Fred was "always nice to the public. He never turned down anybody who asked for his autograph." And despite Fred's "cheap" reputation he never pulled anything like Cary Grant later did— charging twenty-five cents for autographs! Fred and his friends stopped into a nearby hotel restaurant and ordered steaks with McKinstry telling a reporter, "This is the most excitement we've run into on our trip." The waitress who served Fred seemed impressed. "He was very nice and gave me 65 cents for a tip." The females in the crowd seemed to approve of his week-long growth of whiskers, "After all, I'm on a holiday," Fred said.

The film Fred was working on prior to going to Beaver Dam, *Dive Bomber,* was shot by Warner Brothers beginning in the spring of 1941. Fred, a Paramount contract actor, was borrowed by Warner Brothers in exchange for the services of Olivia de Havilland, a Warner Brothers contract actress, for the Mitchell Leisen film *Hold Back the Dawn* at Paramount. *Dive Bomber* was to be one of Warner Brothers' prestige pictures of the year. They cast their top contract actor of the time, Errol Flynn, as a doctor researching how to avoid Altitude sickness which caused pilots to blackout and crash. Because the film was budgeted at more than $1.5 million (a high amount for the time), Warner Brothers wanted to insure top box office receipts by putting another popular actor along side Flynn, especially since there is little in the way of a love interest in the story. Enter Fred as a squadron leader who is suspicious of Flynn, but ultimately realizes the benefits of his work and becomes Flynn's human guinea pig. Also cast was Ralph Bellamy. Michael Curtiz, one of Warner's top contract directors (he was a year away from directing *Casablanca)*, was selected to helm this production.

Much of the film was made on location at the San Diego Naval Station with the stars and crew quartered at the legendary Hotel de Coranado. The Navy kept a tight rein on the movements of the stars and according to one account the stars "were at all times transported by naval cars and drivers and under surveillance continually." Fred, Flynn and Bellamy spent a week on the aircraft carrier *Enterprise*, which was conducting military maneuvers at sea. "We didn't need all that time," recalled Bellamy. "But it was the only way we could get the shots we needed." Bellamy would recall that the brass on the carrier was not thrilled with having a Hollywood film company on board especially when they were doing maneuvers. But because Hollywood was actively working with Washington to prepare the country for the possibility of war, Navy Secretary Frank Knox had personally sanctioned Navy cooperation with the production, there was little that the brass could do except get their little digs in by making the cast as uncomfortable as possible. "We were in the way and they really let us know it," Bellamy would recall. "The first night out, they kept up battle practices and most of us didn't get any sleep."

Curtiz could be a tyrannical director, almost a dictator on his sets, but Bellamy recalls that on this picture he had never seen Curtiz so "humbled." "Curtiz had to be on his best behavior on that picture," said Bellamy. "He was used to calling the shots, but this time the Navy was doing the ordering. Many of the aviation sequences had to be done in one take because they [the Navy] were not about to do another." Not only that but when filming on the airbase in San Diego, the sounds of hundreds of engines from departing and returning planes, often drowned the company out. The noise level got so bad that Flynn and Fred would rehearse some scenes in pantomime.

The company returned to the Warners' Burbank lot and Fred and a fellow pilot, played by Regis Toomey, were filming a scene showing the kind of physical and mental fatigue that pilots go through at high altitudes against a process screen in the background. Apparently neither Fred nor Toomey was registering ample amounts of physical torture that Curtiz was looking for.

Neither actor seemed to be suffering enough for his taste. Curtiz was looking for the right words to inspire his actors and he finally threw his hands in
the air and bellowed, "Please — Everybody sweat now!"

Despite all of this the picture, shot in Technicolor, came out well and
generally won praise for its moral building story. It also became a big hit at
the box office, grossing more than $3 million and becoming the second most
successful film of the year.

Following *Dive Bomber*, Fred had a two-month layoff until September
when he was loaned out to work with Marlene Dietrich at Columbia in
the Mitchell Leisen-directed comedy *The Lady is Willing*. According to the
book *Hollywood Director* Leisen and Fred were loaned to Columbia "apparently for a simple payment of money instead of the usual exchange of talent." Another reason was that Columbia didn't have as many name stars,
especially male stars, under contract and they often had to borrow actors
from the other studios. Fred's value as an actor with box office viability was
especially evident in the early 1940s since several studios were requesting his
services. Fred appeared in 18 films between 1940 and 1944 and six, or one-
third of his output, was on loan out from Paramount. (*Little Old New York* at
Fox, *Dive Bomber* at Warner Brothers, *Too Many Husbands* at Columbia, *The
Lady is Willing* at Columbia, *Flight for Freedom* at RKO and *Above Suspicion*
at MGM.).

Dietrich apparently made the film so she could help finance an upcoming USO tour, and was also, according to her daughter Maria Riva, flat-
tered by the film's producer Charles Feldman. "She accepted without knowing the director, full script, or leading man," according to Riva. "Charlie
Feldman was pleased ... she trusted him ... Once installed in her dressing room at Columbia, reality hit a little, but unfortunately, not strongly
enough." Dietrich's daughter maintains that Leisen "worshiped" Marlene.
It is clear that she did become one of his favorite actresses and Leisen later
said that he considered Marlene's performance in *The Lady is Willing* to be
one of her best performances, which is a bit of a stretch. The film tells the
story of a stage star (Marlene) who tries to convince a physician (Fred) to
marry her so she can adopt a baby.

In her biography of her mother, Riva is condescending of Fred. "Poor Fred
MacMurray," she wrote. "Ever the dependable workhorse of Hollywood's
leading men, found himself in the midst of this gay extravaganza, and in his
unflappable way, never said a word, did his job, took his paycheck, and like
any normal breadwinner, went home to his little woman. No love was lost
between the stars. Actually, the way everyone behaved, there was only one
star in the film — Dietrich."

Perhaps one of the reasons why there was no "love lost between the stars"
is because Marlene was perplexed that for once one of her leading men
wasn't trying to take her to bed. She allegedly had had flings with sev-

eral of her previous leading men, including Gary Cooper on *Morocco*, James Stewart on *Destry Rides Again* and John Wayne on *Seven Sinners*. She was used to her leading men falling in love with her, so she was apparently displeased when Fred, who she did find attractive, didn't respond properly to her allure. "One thing she couldn't understand," recalled Leisen, "was why Fred MacMurray didn't fall madly in love with her? I said, 'Listen, Marlene, Fred's so much in love with his wife Lily, he couldn't care less about any other woman, so you lay off. Just make the picture." Film publicist Sid Bloomberg, who knew Dietrich well later, said, "Marlene hit on everybody. She believed it helped a film's chemistry if she slept with her leading men. Fred was an exception and she never forgave him for it. He was too devoted to Lillian — it truly annoyed Marlene." Leisen would later say that Fred was "embarrassed" by Marlene and her transparent attempts to get him in the sack.

Marlene Dietrich teamed only once with Fred in 1942's The Lady is Willing. *The lady was indeed willing, but Fred was not.*

Despite all of this, the filming went smoothly except for an accident involving Dietrich. According to Riva, "A baby figured prominently in the story. One day, carrying it in her arms, she tripped, stumbled and fell. As she couldn't very well toss the child like a forward pass, she twisted her body to avoid squashing it and broke her ankle." Apparently Dietrich, who was an avid follower of astrology, had been advised that she might have an accident that day and had tried to be especially careful, but couldn't avoid this on-set accident. But Dietrich was a professional and, according to Leisen, she didn't allow the injury to slow down production and "went right on." Fred would recall another on-set incident which occurred after the mishap with the baby which compounded the original injury and was a testament to her professionalism: "Marlene was amazing. She never showed her pain, and wouldn't go home. She had to be mounted on a small 'dolly' to give the impression we were walking together

Fred with Marlene Dietrich.

against a back projection of a street. She managed to move her shoulders to suggest she was in motion normally. Then something crazy happened. To show we were going down a slope, the set had to be cantilevered. Without warning, Marlene and the little 'dolly' took off! They vanished in the wings! She picked herself up off the floor, put on some orthopedic shoes, and came back and did the scene without the 'dolly.' Is there anyone like that?"

Just weeks after completing this film both Fred and Leisen were back at the Paramount lot where they were to begin shooting *Take a Letter, Darling* with Rosalind Russell, in one of her patented lady executive roles, with Fred (in the usual role reversal) cast as her secretary, and naturally they fall in love. Leisen wasn't the original choice to direct this piece of froth, nor for that matter had Russell been the original choice for Fred's leading lady. Originally, Preston Sturges had been assigned to the picture as director, but due to his clout with the studio, he insisted that he would only direct screenplays he wrote. (The writer of this film was Fred's good friend Claude Binyon.) Claudette Colbert was originally announced for the leading role,

Rosalind Russell and Fred in the first of their two on-screen teamings in Mitchell Leisen's **Take a Letter, Darling.**

but decided to opt out of it and do *The Palm Beach Story* for Preston Sturges instead. No matter, Russell was an excellent comedienne and this type of material was right up her alley.

The secondary male lead was assigned to a new Paramount contract player, Macdonald Carey, in his first film. Carey and Fred hit it off right away and became lifelong friends. Because he was so new to filmmaking Fred became a mentor to Carey, just as Colbert and Lombard had been mentors to him when he was just starting in pictures. "Fred became a good friend, a sort of mentor who showed me the ropes," Carey later recalled. "He was never a great actor but a very rudimentary guy who had done a remarkable job of surviving. Actors then not only had to please an audi-

Take a Letter, Darling *proved to be a box office and critical success.*

ence but had to have the political sense to please people around them as well. Fred learned all of this." Carey recalled that Fred made him feel more at ease in front of the camera and that even though he believed that Fred "never fell in love with acting as acting himself, just working with him, you felt comfortable. He's reassuring to be with."

Carey would later write that Fred was a man who is "worth adoration." In his autobiography, he even included a poem he wrote about Fred and how he "hero worshiped" him. He considered Fred to be "one of the pools of 'the best people' in the movie business, what passed for movie society." Carey wasn't the only person who felt so, even his then wife, Betty, enjoyed Fred's company. "She likes him in person as much as she thought she would when she had a crush on him on the screen."

Carey found that Leisen was another booster of his; indeed Leisen would use Carey in several of his films. "He really took a shine to me and was grooming me," Carey would later recall. "I was one of the few actors who could do comedy as well as serious roles. If I hadn't gone off to war, which left a gap of several years in my career, I probably would have been brought along at Paramount like Fred MacMurray."

Indeed, war did interrupt several Hollywood careers when it came crashing down on December 7, 1941. The film had been in production for about three weeks and would have several more weeks of shooting. It was a Sunday and the actors were on their one day off when word came in the early afternoon that Pearl Harbor had been attacked by the Japanese, and everybody knew this meant war. When the cast and crew of *Take a Letter, Darling* gathered again the next day, a "somber feeling permeated all around the set," Carey later recalled.

The final day of shooting on *Take a Letter, Darling* was January 16, 1942 and in the early evening hours of that day, after completing a war bond drive the night before in her home state of Indiana, Carole Lombard was in a rush to return home and willing to risk flying in less than ideal weather. Along with her mother and twenty others (mostly servicemen) on board, the plane she was flying in went down on a mountainside outside of Las Vegas. All perished. Her death shook the Hollywood community which so loved her. Leisen was devastated by the loss. He would recall being at Paramount when he ran into Claudette Colbert, who understood what he was feeling because, she felt the same thing herself. She took him behind the corner of a soundstage and told him, "Nobody's looking. You can let go." And he did. Fred later paid tribute to Lombard, "A wonderful girl. Swore like a man. Other women try, but she really did. She was like one of the fellas, yet there she was, this beautiful girl." Fred and Lily were among the handful of Hollywood stars invited by the devastated Clark Gable to attend Lombard's funeral.

Apparently after Pearl Harbor Lombard had begun prodding Gable to enlist, and this is what he did shortly after Lombard's death. Several

Hollywood celebrities enlisted, including James Stewart, Henry Fonda, Robert Montgomery, Tyrone Power, Robert Taylor and Macdonald Carey. According to Fred's daughter, Kate, Fred wanted to enlist but a punctured ear drum kept him from serving. Not to mention that he had a wife who was, at best, a semi-invalid, and a new young daughter. But as late as September of 1942 there was still speculation about whether Fred would enlist, such as in

this blurb from *The Hollywood Reporter*, dated 9/3/42: "If Robert Taylor, Mickey Rooney, Cary Grant, Fred MacMurray and others go in [the service] as reported, the financial loss [to agents] would mount tremendously." As it turned out Taylor and Rooney did eventually go in, but Grant and Fred did not. Still, Fred, like many of the others who stayed on the home front during the war, did his best to support the war effort through raising money for war bonds and generally making films which would raise morale and entertain on the home front. He also served as the air raid warden in his Brentwood neighborhood and made the rounds at night to make sure his famous neighbors had their blinds drawn. Fred also joined

Russell played an Amelia Earhart-based pilot, with Fred as her love interest in 1943's **Flight for Freedom.**

the Hollywood Anti-Nazi League (HANL), which, according to the book *Radical Hollywood*, "almost overnight, HANL fund-raising played a key role in the Hollywood whirl" in raising money to support the war effort. The HANL members put on shows to raise money which included "standard HANL performers" such as Judy Garland, Sophie Tucker, Dorothy Lamour, Ray Bolger, Benny Goodman, Fred (who played saxophone or sang), Ben Blue, The Ritz Brothers, Bert Wheeler and Martha Raye.

With so many leading men heading off to war, Fred's services were even more valuable to the studios. Unlike John Wayne, who almost single-handedly won World War II on the screen in such wartime films as *Flying Tigers, The Fighting Seabees, Back to Bataan* and *They Were Expendable*, Fred didn't appear in any films which could be referred to as "war pictures," but he did make a couple of films which raised the patriotic colors. Among these was on loan-out to RKO for *Flight to Freedom,* which was a barely disguised fictional biography of Amelia Earhart with Rosalind Russell as a female aviator who gets competition and romance from a sexist pilot, played by Fred.

Fred also appeared opposite Joan Crawford in MGM's *Above Suspicion,* which is set in 1939 and cast Fred as an American-born Oxford professor

Fred on loan out to MGM appearing opposite Joan Crawford in Above Suspicion.

who marries an American girl in England. While on their honeymoon, they plan to travel to southern Germany. Into the picture comes an old associate of the professor's who's now a spy for the foreign office. He asks the honeymooners to help track down a scientist, who has information regarding a magnetic mine the Germans are developing. He felt that as American tourists on their honeymoon they would be considered "above suspicion."

The script for the film had been sitting on an MGM shelf for a couple of years when it was finally dusted off for Fred and Joan Crawford. Apparently, it had originally been intended for William Powell and Myrna Loy, but after the war broke out Loy took a leave of absence from Hollywood to concen-

Fred and Claudette Colbert in the Mitchell Leisen comedy, **No Time for Love** *(1943).*

trate on her work for the Red Cross. At that point Powell also backed out, clearing the way for Crawford and Fred (on loan-out from Paramount). This was also to be Crawford's last film for MGM after an association of eighteen years. She decided to leave the studio because she felt that they were not giving her the kinds of projects necessary to advance her career. Certainly, while *Above Suspicion* had the usual top-notch MGM production values, the script was lackluster and some of the dialogue ridiculous. Crawford herself would later state that both she and Fred realized that the script was "bad" and that they worked hard "to put some life into the film." Like Dietrich, Crawford had enjoyed occasional sexual relationships with her leading men, but she respected the MacMurray marriage, and, besides, according to her biographer, "Joan enjoyed working with Fred MacMurray, whom she found likeable and charming, if not necessarily her cup of tea sexually."

But mostly what Fred appeared in during the war years were morale-boosting comedies (designed to relieve the tensions of a world at war for an hour-and-a-half or so) opposite such leading ladies as Claudette Colbert (in two comedies for Mitchell Leisen, *No Time for Love* and *Practically Yours*), Paulette Goddard (*Standing Room Only*, which had essentially the same plot as the more superior *The More the Merrier*, which starred Jean Arthur and Joel McCrea and had been released a year earlier by Columbia Pictures and dealt in a humorous way with the housing shortage in Washington, D.C.

Betty Hutton and Fred in the 1944 musical, And the Angels Sing.

during World War II), and Betty Hutton in *And the Angels Sing* (which was a remake of *Sing You Sinners*, which Fred had appeared in with Bing Crosby six years before).

Practically Yours cast Fred as a navy pilot who, when preparing to sink a Japanese carrier by crashing his fighter plane into it, radios his buddies on another bomber. Believing that he is on a suicide mission begins talking about how much he will miss walking in Central Park with "Piggy" and "kissing her on the nose." He does crash his plane into the carrier and he becomes a national hero back home. His "final" words to his buddies were recorded and everybody thinks that "Piggy" was "Peggy" (Claudette Colbert), a woman he worked with at a typewriter company, when in fact "Piggy" was his dog! Even Peggy thinks he is talking about her — and is stunned to find out that he was in love with her. The truth comes out because the pilot actually survived the crash.

This was to be the final film under Claudette Colbert's contract for Paramount and her final with Mitchell Leisen. None of the principles were

overly enthused with the film. Leisen, who viewed the film in the early
'70s with his biographer David Chierichetti, said "it was a pretty dreary job"
watching the film. He went on to say that the film is supposed to be a comedy, but it was "about as funny as a crutch to me." Neither Fred nor Colbert
thought that they were right for their parts. Both were in their late 30s
playing characters that were at least a decade younger. During the making
of this film Fred took Colbert aside and said, "Claudette, the trouble with
this picture is that we're both too goddamn old for it!" Colbert was ready
to make the transition to more mature roles, which she did later that year
in David O Selznick's *Since You Went Away* playing the mother of two teenage girls.

The war years were Fred's most financially satisfying as a motion picture
actor. Since his services were in such demand, he worked almost continually. The pay-off came in 1944 when he was named the highest paid actor
in motion pictures, earning $438,000. Fred, typically, downplayed this. He
attributed it to the fact that so many of his fellow leading men were away
fighting in the war, and he was just filling in the void until they returned.
He also downplayed the report which named him the highest paid actor in
Hollywood as misleading. "Quite a few Hollywood folk made more than
I do, but their incomes come from several sources, such as radio fees and
record royalties. All that extra money doesn't show in the report featuring
straight salaries." To Fred it had nothing at all to do with any kind of box
office appeal he might have. (Indeed, during the war with so many leading men gone, new leading men were created; among the most popular to
appear were Van Johnson and Gregory Peck.)

In between filming *Standing Room Only* and *Practically Yours* Fred did
make one film which was neither war related nor morale building, but dealt
with the darker impulses of the American psyche in a surprisingly (for its
day) daring way. The film would contain his finest screen performance and
become one of the American screens all-time classic motion pictures. And
to think Fred didn't even want to do it.

CHAPTER FOUR

"A Pair of Cobras in Action": Double Indemnity

Billy Wilder and Charles Brackett were two of the most prolific and successful film writers in Hollywood. Like Fred, they were under contract to Paramount Pictures where they wrote such intelligent and diverse films as *Bluebeard's Eighth Wife, Midnight, Ninotchka, Arise My Love, Hold Back the Dawn* and *Ball of Fire*. (Actually, *Ninotchka* and *Ball of Fire* were written on loan out to other studios.) They were opposites who attracted. Wilder was an Austrian-Hungarian who immigrated to the United States from Berlin shortly after Hitler came to power. He was an outrageous liberal who was well known around the studio for telling racy stories and sleeping with young starlets. Brackett was a dour conservative from New York who was considered long suffering because of his devotion to his alcoholic wife. Brackett was also a member of the Hollywood establishment in a way that Wilder never could be. Together they were magic.

The Wilder-Brackett formula was heavily influenced by Ernst Lubitsch and his famous "touch." They wrote in a witty scintillating style, which included more than a touch of risqué dialog which somehow got past the censors due to the ingenious way they were able to camouflage the true essence of a scene or a line. They wrote films for the biggest stars in Hollywood, Gary Cooper, Claudette Colbert, John Barrymore, Greta Garbo, Charles Boyer, Bing Crosby and Barbara Stanwyck, and had a seamless way of adapting the scenarios around the stars' established personas.

In 1940 Paramount gave Preston Sturges the chance to write and direct his own films and Wilder also desired to do so. Like Sturges, Wilder complained bitterly about how some of his screenplays were diluted by directors who, he believed, had no understanding of the written word. He was particularly irked by Mitchell Leisen, who had directed two of Wilder and Brackett's best screenplays, *Midnight* and *Hold Back The Dawn* (for this film Wilder was especially displeased by Leisen refusing to film a scene where Charles Boyer has a conversation with a roach). He viewed Leisen more as an interior decorator concerned with how the sets looked and what the leading lady wore than the integrity of the characters and script. (In Leisen's defense, it is hard to see how either Billy Wilder or Preston Sturges could have improved on the films which Leisen directed of their screenplays. Those four films: *Easy Living, Midnight, Remember the Night* and *Arise, My Love* are among Leisen's best and are well regarded to this day.)

Paramount finally gave in and allowed Wilder the opportunity to direct his next film for them. To bone up for this he was a constant presence on the set of *Ball of Fire*, a comedy he and Brackett had written for Samuel Goldwyn and which starred Gary Cooper and Barbara Stanwyck. He was forever observing director Howard Hawks, who he greatly admired, and Stanwyck, who he knew he wanted to direct in one of his own films.

The first film that Wilder directed was a trifle of a comedy called *The Major and the Minor*, which starred Ginger Rogers as a woman impersonating a child so she could get half fare on a train. Ray Milland plays the major who takes the Rogers character into his stateroom for her own protection since he believes her to be a child alone on the trip. True to typical Wilder form the major eventually finds himself, to his consternation, attracted to this "child." Wilder brought the film in ahead of schedule and below budget and the film went on to perform well at the box office. That was enough for the studio to entrust another film to Wilder, an espionage thriller, *Five Graves to Cairo*, which also performed well.

For his third picture as writer-director Wilder wanted to adapt a James M. Cain story, "Double Indemnity," which had been serialized in *Liberty Magazine* in 1936. The story was based on a real-life 1927 murder where a wife killed her husband with the help of her boyfriend, a corset salesman. Hollywood had long been interested in filming the story but felt its subject matter wouldn't get past the censors, who were operating under strict rules at the time. As early as 1936 Joe Breen, the head of the Censorship office in Hollywood, told MGM head L. B. Mayer that if they attempted to film this story that it would almost certainly result "in a picture which we would be compelled to reject." That was enough for Mayer, who was more into producing wholesome family entertainment like the *Andy Hardy* series than a story about an adulterous wife and her murderous boyfriend. Subsequently, both Columbia and Warner Brothers, which may have been more at home with this type of material, also passed because of the problems presented by the Production Code.

When Wilder expressed interest in making this film, Paramount warned him that it would be difficult to get it past the Production Code and had a copy of the original letter sent to Mayer to back them up. Part of the reason the Code had rejected *Double Indemnity* was because in the novel the murderous pair cheat the authorities and jointly commit suicide rather than pay for their crimes in a court of law. Wilder believed that he could film the basic story but allow the characters to pay for their crimes in a way which would satisfy the Production Code. Paramount decided to green light the project.

Wilder's next problem was his collaborator, Charles Brackett. They had always had a stormy relationship, but in the case of *Double Indemnity* Brackett flat out refused to cooperate on the adaptation of the novel because he considered it "immoral." Cain himself was tied up writing another film, so Wilder approached a couple of other writers before detective novelist Raymond Chandler was hired to collaborate with him on the script. Chandler was selected because his writing style was considered similar to Cain's. It was not a collaboration made in heaven. According to Jay Rozgonyi in *Films in Review,* "Chandler liked to smoke his pipe constantly, but he hated to open the windows (he thought the daytime air in Los Angeles was unhealthy). Wilder was an excitable and volatile man, continually pacing and shouting, and often brandishing a riding crop. When Chandler became too much for him to handle, Wilder would retreat to the bathroom, sit on the toilet seat, and light up a cigarette. While Wilder was gone, Chandler would make detailed notes of the various ways in which the director was abusing him." Chandler also didn't like Wilder's womanizing ways and odd hours, while Wilder objected to Chandler's drinking. Chandler would later write that working with Wilder "was an agonizing experience and has probably shortened my life." For Wilder's part, Chandler gave him "more aggravation than any writer I ever worked with." But they got through it and produced a masterpiece.

While the novel provided the framework Wilder and Chandler had to change important elements, including the ending. But they also created some scenes to add dramatic suspense and dramatic punch on a cinematic level. Wilder was content to use much of Cain's dialogue from the novel, but one of Chandler's enduring contributions to the screenplay was convincing Wilder that much of what the characters say in the novel is fine in that form but sounds wooden or even laughable when spoken. Chandler's contribution to the dialogue of the film is evident throughout, especially in the way Walter Neff narrates the story and the witticisms he uses throughout the film. It certainly has the same flavor as such Chandler novels as *Farewell, My Lovely* and *The Big Sleep.*

Double Indemnity is the story of a cocksure insurance salesman, Walter Neff, who is introduced in the first scene arriving in the middle of the night (injured in some way, though the audience isn't sure at this point how) at his insurance company where he goes to the office of Insurance Claims investigator Barton Keyes and begins narrating his story into Keyes' Dictaphone. Neff is the star salesman at his insurance company, and believes he is smarter and savvier than it turns out he actually is. He more than meets his match with Phyllis Dietrichson, an icy blonde whose anklet cuts into the long legs

Neff can't take his eyes off of when she appears at the top of the stairs after Neff forces his way past the maid and into her home for the purpose of selling her husband some insurance. It is lust at first sight and Phyllis knows it and is ready to take advantage of it. The dialog which Wilder and Chandler write to introduce the characters to one another is steamily suggestive:

> *Phyllis: (indicating her husband, who is at work)* He'll be in
>   then.
> *Walter:* Who?
> *Phyllis:* My husband. You were anxious to talk to him,
>   weren't you?
> *Walter:* Yeah, but I'm sort of getting over the idea, if you
>   know what I mean.
> *Phyllis:* There's a speed limit in this state, Mr. Neff, forty-five
>   miles an hour.
> *Walter:* How fast was I going?
> *Phyllis:* I'd say around ninety.
> *Walter:* Suppose you get down off your motorcycle and give
>   me a ticket.
> *Phyllis:* Suppose I let you off with a warning this time.

Fred admiring Barbara Stanwyck's anklet in Double Indemnity.

Walter: Suppose it doesn't take.
Phyllis: Suppose I have to whack you over the knuckles.
Walter: Suppose I burst out crying and put my head on your shoulder.
Phyllis: Suppose you try putting it on my husband's shoulder.
Walter: That tears it.

To Phyllis, Walter is nothing more than a patsy who she will use to rid herself of the ineffectual husband who can't satisfy her needs, sexually or monetarily. Walter is taken in by her hook, line and sinker and truly believes that they will settle down together after a cooling off period. He has allowed his libido to dominate his brain. Together they come up with a plan to insure her husband under a "double indemnity" clause in his insurance policy, and wait for the perfect opportunity to strike. When Neff finds out that her husband is taking a train to attend a football game at his alma mater he realizes this is the break they need because the statistics involving accidental death from a fall from a train are astronomical. He hides in the backseat of the Dietrichson car and as Phyllis drives her husband to the train station she unexpectedly drives down a dark alley and then Walter comes up from behind him and strangles him to death. But the camera is not focused on this gruesome act of violence; it is focused on Phyllis as she looks straight ahead with a satisfied smirk on her face.

When they get to the train station, Walter impersonates Dietrichson, who had broken or sprained his ankle, and using/ Dietrichson's crutches and wearing his hat low, he boards the train. He makes his way to the observation deck, where he finds another man having a smoke. This is a distraction because Walter must jump off the train before it gets moving too fast or too far, Phyllis is waiting for him by a preordained location. Walter convinces the man to go back for a package of cigarettes just in the nick of time. Walter then jumps off the train and together with Phyllis they take the dead body of the real Dietrichson and lay it on the tracks, to make it seem as if he slipped off the observation car.

They realize they need to lay low until this blows over and Phyllis collects her money. Walter also believes that he can handle the claims investigator for the insurance company, Barton Keyes, who always trusts his "little man," more specifically his intuition. Walter and Keyes have a complicated relationship. Film historian Foster Hirsch thought that Billy made Keyes a "submerged homosexual," explaining, "His character is a tireless investigator married to his job who acts as a father/surrogate for a young co-worker who is destroyed by just the kind of heterosexual desire from which [Keyes] is isolated." One of the plot devices is to continually have Keyes searching his pockets for a match to light up his cigar but never finding one and then Walter always offering him one of his matches. They have a father/

son type of relationship and Keyes is impressed enough to offer Walter a $50 per month *reduction* in pay to come and work with him in the claims department, which Walter turns down. "I always thought you were smarter than the others," Keyes tells Walter, "but you're only taller." The character of Keyes was greatly enhanced from the original novel, with his relationship to Walter much closer than depicted in the book. In an interview published more than thirty years after the film was released, Billy Wilder said that the "idea was to write a love story between the two men and a sexual involvement with the woman."

Walter is convinced that Keyes is "playing on our team," but, after some further thought, Keyes comes to the conclusion that Dietrichson's death couldn't have been an accident. When Keyes gets one of his feelings, there is no stopping him from pursuing every nick and cranny. This puts Walter and Phyllis on the defensive and begins to eat away at their relationship. As time goes by Walter finally comes to the conclusion that Phyllis was using him as a sap, especially after he finds out that Phyllis, prior to marrying Dietrichson, was the nurse to Dietrichson's wife when she was recovering from pneumonia and that *somehow* during a cold night the windows of the first Mrs. Dietrichson's room were left open causing her death. Shortly afterwards, she married Dietrichson.

The climax has Walter coming to Phyllis' house. He knows he has been played for a sap and believes that Phyllis has also been involved with another man, her stepdaughter's boyfriend. He plans to kill her. Phyllis anticipates that this is Walter's plan (remember she is smarter than he is and is always one step ahead) and hides a gun for her own protection. Phyllis admits that she was using the stepdaughter's boyfriend. "I was working on him ... I kept hammering into him that she was with another man so he'd go into one of his jealous rages and then I'd tell him where she was. And you know what he would have done to her, don't you, Walter?" To which, Walter replies, "Yeah. And for once I believe you, because it's just rotten enough."

> *Phyllis:* We're both rotten.
> *Walter:* Only you're a little more rotten. You got me to take care of your husband for ya. And then you get Zachretti [the jealous boyfriend of the stepdaughter] to take care of Lola, maybe take care of me too Then somebody else would have come along to take care of Zachretti for ya. That's the way you operate, isn't it, baby?
> *Phyllis:* Suppose it is. Is what you've got cooked up for tonight any better?

At that point Walter walks over to the window in the living room; she pulls the gun and shoots him, wounding him. For a moment she hesitates and is unable to shoot him again, which gives Walter his opening. He walks over to her and she clings to him and admits, "I never loved you, Walter, not you or anybody else. I'm rotten to the heart. I used you just as you said. That's all you ever meant to me. Until a minute ago, when I couldn't fire that second shot. I never thought that could happen to me." Walter isn't buying it, and, as he coldly says, "Goodbye, baby," he plugs two bullets into her as she is still embracing him.

Just as Walter is about to leave the scene the jealous boyfriend of the stepdaughter, Zachretti, arrives. It would be easy to pin this on him and make it seem as if Phyllis and he were conspiring from the beginning, but Walter finally has a change of heart and talks the hot-headed Zachretti into calling Lola from the corner drugstore and reconcile with her. Walter plans to escape to Mexico, but first goes back to the insurance company to dictate the true story into Keyes' Dictaphone. As he is coming to the end of the story, he notices Keyes in the doorway entrance, listening in on his narration. "I wanted to straighten you out on that Dietrichson case," Walter tells him. "Kind of a crazy story with a crazy twist to it, one you didn't figure out."

Walter asks Keyes to give him a couple of hours to get to the border, but Keyes tells him that he would never make it in his condition. (It was the night janitor who called Keyes in after finding a trail of blood left by Walter leading to Keyes' office.) Just as Walter has reached the office door, he collapses, his strength sapped. Keyes calls for an ambulance and then comes over to Walter:

> *Walter:* You know why you couldn't figure this one, Keyes? I'll tell ya. 'Cause the guy you were looking for was too close, right across the desk from you.
> *Keyes:* Closer than that, Walter.
> *Walter:* I love you, too.

Walter then struggles to light a cigarette and is unable to. Keyes then assists Walter, lighting the cigarette for him in the fade out.

II

Wilder knew at once that he wanted Barbara Stanwyck to play Phyllis. He saw her as the kind of blood-and-guts actress who didn't mind getting her hands dirty by playing such an amoral bitch. Stanwyck wasn't so certain at first if she wanted to play an "out and out bitch." She deferred her decision for the time being.

Wilder understood that it would be tougher to find a leading man to play Neff. Not only was Neff a murderer but he was also a sap. For some inex-

plicable reason, Wilder pursued George Raft, who would have been obvious casting. When Billy approached Raft, he told Wilder he didn't read
scripts and to just tell him the story. Billy began reciting and about halfway
through Raft stopped him and said, "Ok, when do I pull out the badge?"
Billy incomprehensibly asked, "What badge?" Raft explained that there had
to be a moment in the film when the audience is made aware that Neff is
really a cop. "Sorry, Mr. Raft," Billy explained, "but that's not the case in
this story." Raft took a pass. (Raft had a reputation for turning down good
roles such as *High Sierra* and *The Maltese Falcon,* two roles which eventually went, thank goodness, to Humphrey Bogart.) Alan Ladd and Brian
Donlevy, both Paramount contract players, also took a pass when they heard
the details. One actor who practically begged Billy for the part was singer
Dick Powell, who later established himself as an excellent anti-hero in such
films as *Murder My Sweet* and *Cornered,* who might have made a good Neff,
but couldn't get out of another film obligation.

One day while looking over a list of Paramount contract players one
name immediately hit Billy's eye: Fred MacMurray. According to Wilder's
biographer, Ed Sikov, "What Wilder saw was MacMurray's grinning, guy-
next-door affability. He wasn't glamorous and aristocratic. Or rugged.
Or callow. What he was — purely, indistinguishably — was American.
Fred MacMurray could play a glad-handing everyday salesman. In Billy's
mind at least, he would be perfect as a scheming killer on the make." It
would also be the kind of against-type casting that would shock the audience. When Fred MacMurray is introduced as Walter Neff, the audience
wouldn't at first expect that the "guy next door" would wind up killing
Barbara Stanwyck's husband. So it comes as a shock, especially to 1944
audiences.

While Neff was a murderer and sap, Wilder also wanted to have the audiences sympathies with him. "I just wanted the audience to go with Walter,"
Wilder explained, "to make him a murderer all right, but with redeeming
features. The Keyes relationship, and ultimately the gesture of letting the
innocent man off the hook. If he confesses, then it has to be motivated by
him, by his sense of justice. Perhaps he'd done it, but within that murderous
act there is still an element of compassion and decency." With this in mind
the ultimate casting of Fred MacMurray as Walter Neff makes a great deal
of sense. In effect, what Wilder wanted to do by casting Neff was to show
the dark side of his "regular guy" persona.

Billy wasn't shocked, however, with MacMurray's reaction to the offer
to play Walter Neff, given how Raft, Ladd and the others had reacted.
"MacMurray greeted Billy's offer with open disbelief," according to Sikov.
"He thought the idea of playing a murderer was suicidal in terms of his
career, and besides he simply could not imagine that Paramount, with which
he was under contract, would ever permit him to stray so far from the happy

Fred and Edward G. Robinson in Double Indemnity.

niche they had carefully tailored for him." According to Wilder the dialog went like this:

Fred: You're making a mistake — that part requires acting.

Billy: Yes, it does — but you've got to make the big step. You've got to get over being a saxophone player ... You don't want to just do comedies with Claudette Colbert and Ginger Rogers.

Fred: But I do!

Fred later said, "I held off saying I would do it, because in the first place, I wasn't sure that I was able to, never having done anything like that type before. And then, also, I thought, people aren't going to like me if I kill somebody's husband." But Fred also understood what Billy was out for. "Wilder wanted me to do it because he thought it would add a lot to the character. Say he got Bogart to do it, or somebody, why the audience would say, 'They're going to knock off the husband any minute now.'"

Billy pestered Fred every day until he wore him down. Finally, he said yes, but he was sure that even with his agreeing to do the picture that the head honchos at Paramount wouldn't allow it. Little did he know. Fred was playing hard ball at the time with the studio. His contract was soon going to be up and he wanted a big increase in money and more control over what films he did. Paramount decided to let Wilder have Fred, as if to teach him a lesson. The studio thought that the public would never accept Fred in this type of role, the very apprehensions that Fred had about accepting it.

Meanwhile, Billy was also courting Stanwyck, who continued to be apprehensive. "I was used to being the bad girl," Stanwyck would later recall. "But with redeeming qualities, so the audience could be with me. I was afraid my fans would confuse me with the character of Phyllis and not like me anymore." When Billy told her that he thought he would be able to get Fred to play the Neff role Stanwyck's interest perked up. "In that case, I'll think about it," she told Billy. Wilder used the same ploy on Fred telling him, "If you agree, Barbara will do it." This, more than anything, including the powers that be at Paramount, seemed to convince Fred, who later said, "There being nobody, then or now whom I respect more, not only as an actress but as a person, I said ok." Billy finally had his two leads.

The third lead role of Barton Keyes, the moral conscience of the film, went to Edward G. Robinson, but even he was apprehensive about taking this role, not because of the film or its subject matter, but because this would mark the first time on screen since he became a star that Robinson wouldn't have the leading male role, "It was designed to be MacMurray's film," but he finally agreed.

Filming began on September 27, 1943 and continued for almost two straight months, wrapping on November 24. The filming went smoothly and included many location shots in and around the Los Angeles area. For some reason, perhaps because he felt that she would look sluttier, Wilder put Stanwyck in a gaudy blonde wig. When one Paramount executive saw rushes of Stanwyck he remarked to Billy, "We hire Barbara Stanwyck and here we get George Washington!"

Fred continued to be nervous during the making of the picture. Stanwyck would recall, "Fred was very very unsure about whether he should be doing *Double Indemnity.* I tried to reassure him, but I didn't have anybody to reassure me. So I reassured myself." Wilder would recall that Fred was a "notorious line-muffler" and, in fact, according to Sikov, during the filming of Fred's Dictaphone monologue ("You were pretty good in there for a while, Keyes. You said it wasn't an accident. Check. You said it wasn't suicide. Check. You said it was murder. Check …"), he kept going up on his lines and they had to do one take after another. After another take in where he went up on his lines Fred, "without missing a beat … continued, in character, speaking directly into the microphone, 'Memo to Wilder — MacMurray blew his topper again.'" As time went on Fred did become more confident and, according to Stanwyck, he did something which he rarely did before, or after — he went to the daily rushes — and when Stanwyck asked him how they *really* were, Fred, "very candidly … looked at me and said, 'I don't know about you, but I was wonderful!'" A remark which Miss Stanwyck thought was entirely proper because "actors only look at themselves."

One day during the shooting of the picture, Billy left the set to meet a

starlet for a noontime rendezvous. He got into his car and found the ignition wouldn't turn over. He missed his rendezvous, but he got to thinking
that this would be a wonderful piece of suspense to add to the picture. In
the novel after Walter and Phyllis leave Dietrichson's body on the tracks
they drive off. Billy got to think that they and the audience should have a
moment of suspense by not having the car's engine turn over. Fred would
recall this as "the most successful scene in the picture." He later recalled
how he and Stanwyck performed this scene. "I remember we did it on a
process stage with rear projection for the trees, y'know, the scenery behind
us. Barbara and I sat in this dummy car. Just a car seat. No dashboard. No
ignition key to turn. We faked it, pantomimed it. When I changed places
with her and turned the key I remember I was doing it fast and Billy kept
saying, 'Make it longer, make it longer,' and finally I yelled, 'For chrissake,
Billy, it's not going to hold that long,' and he said, 'Make it longer,' and he
was right. It held. It held — that was how much the audience was involved
in the story."

About a week before the picture wrapped production Wilder shot a
scene which was initially going to be the films ending, Walter Neff's execution in a gas chamber. It was a vivid scene with Keyes attending watching Neff being put to death. Wilder spoke of this scene, which was ultimately deleted from the film, at a seminar at the American Film Institute.
"I shot an ending which I chopped off, where Fred MacMurray was exe-
cuted in the gas chamber, and there was a kind of thing between him and
Eddie Robinson, who was watching it. It was all done with minute precision. I had the priest from San Quentin and I had the warden and the doctor. Everything was just absolutely perfect, but as I was proceeding with the
picture I wrote a scene where he tries to go to the elevator and get into his
car and go to Mexico, and he collapses and can't even light the match anymore the way he always did. And in the distance you hear the police car
or the ambulance, so you knew what the outcome was going to be. And I
ended it there, because the rest would have been anti-climatic. We knew he
was guilty." According to James Naremore, in his excellent essay on *Double
Indemnity* for *Film Comment*, "Wilder photographed the step by step procedure of execution, emphasizing its coldly mechanical efficiency. There was
no blood, no agonized screaming, and, for once in the movie, almost no dialogue. Much of the sequence was shot from Walter's point of view, looking
through glass windows at the spectators outside the chamber - an angle creating a subtle parallel between the chamber and the 'dark room' of a movie
theater. When the fatal pellets dropped, clouds of gas obscured the windows, and we could barely make out Keyes standing amid the witnesses,
turning his head away..." It was a powerful scene, but in December of 1943
Wilder got a memo from the Production Code indicating that this scene
would be "too gruesome" for the audience, and this may have been the real

The deleted execution scene from **Double Indemnity.**

reason why it was not used. But I tend to agree with Wilder that the film ends just right with Walter badly injured in the doorway of the insurance office and Keyes looking over him with the sound of an ambulance in the background ... after that scene everything else would seem anti-climactic.

When the film was previewed at the Fox Theater in Westwood, Stanwyck's entrance elicited wolf whistles from the audience. This, Wilder felt, meant the film was probably going to be a failure. He then quickly realized that her first appearance on screen was incredibly sexy — she had been draped in nothing but a towel and anklet. The preview was a smashing success and Paramount was sure they had a hit on their hands. But the best compliment of the night came from James M. Cain, who attended the preview. "I got a very high compliment," Wilder recalled, "... and there standing in the lobby was Cain, and he put his arms around me and he said that this is the first time that somebody did a decent job with any of my... and he was very, very, happy with it." One 13-year-old fan who attended another preview of the film would fondly recall the occasion many years later. "When I was 13 and in love with movies, movie stars and collecting every autograph I could, one star stood far and above the others — Fred MacMurray. After the preview of *Double Indemnity* in Glendale, California, the lights went on, and MacMurray was spotted in the loge. I ran to where he was sitting and signing autograph books. I was leaning over the seat in front of him and realized I did not have mine. No problem. 'What's your name?' he asked. He took a book from another girl and wrote 'Margaret, best wishes always.' Then he tore the page out and handed it to me. That was 47 years ago, and I have never forgotten his kindness."

When the film was released in September 1944, the reviews were, on the whole, very good. *Variety* called it "rapidly moving and consistently well developed." Fred "has seldom given a better performance. It is somewhat different from his usually light roles, but is always plausible and played with considerable restraint." *PM* said the film is "certainly the most fascinating little case history of red-hot passion, conscienceless killing and needle nosed detection that has come along … It is something like watching a pair of cobras in action." The star trio "plays it for every ounce of drama." Alton Cook in *The New York World Telegram* called it "the perfect movie" and complimented Fred on "shedding his musical comedy bluster." "MacMurray … shows up as a top flight dramatic actor in a role that is a new type for him," gushed the *Brooklyn Eagle*. James Agee in *The Nation* was a little more guarded. "Casting of Fred MacMurray, Barbara Stanwyck and Edward G. Robinson is perceptive," but "in many ways *Double Indemnity* is really quite a gratifying and even a good movie, essentially cheap I will grant, but smart and crisp and cruel … but if at the same time you are watching for all that could have been gotten out of it, you cannot help being disappointed as well as pleased." The bottom line, which the studio cared the most about, was also good; the film was one of the top performers at the box office in 1944.

When the Academy Award nominations were announced for the year 1944, *Double Indemnity* was nominated for four key awards, Best Actress, Best Picture, Best Director and Best Screenplay. Inexplicably, Fred was not among the five

Newspaper ad for **Double Indemnity.**

names nominated for Best Actor, nor was Robinson nominated for the Supporting Actor award, though both clearly deserved to be. (During their long careers neither Fred nor Robinson would ever be nominated for an Academy Award, a huge oversight, though Robinson did receive an Honorary Oscar posthumously.) It's not as if there was no room on that list of nominees for Fred. The five actors nominated for 1944 were Bing Crosby for *Going My Way*, Charles Boyer for *Gaslight*, Barry Fitzgerald for *Going My Way*, Cary Grant for *None But the Lonely Heart* and Alexander Knox for *Wilson*. Crosby won for his relaxed and easygoing Father O'Malley in the warmly sentimental *Going My Way*, but was Crosby really any different in that film than he had been in most of the other 30-odd pictures he had made up to that time, except for wearing a priest's collar? Grant was nominated twice during his career for performances which really cannot be considered his best. Knox was good, but didn't really add anything spectacular to his portrayal of Woodrow Wilson and *Wilson* was probably nominated because it was *the* prestige picture of 1944. Fitzgerald was very good as the elderly priest in *Going My Way*, but why was he nominated for Best Actor and Best Supporting Actor for the same performance? (He won the supporting award.) Of the five nominations Boyer's is probably the one which deserved to win. Why wasn't Fred nominated for a performance which absolutely dominated one of the most successful films of 1944? Because Paramount didn't go to bat for him. By the time the nominations were announced Fred had made the final film under his Paramount contract and had signed with Fox. So Paramount had no reason to put its forces behind securing a nomination for him. Instead, they pushed Bing Crosby, the biggest star at Paramount in the biggest box office hit of the year.

Double Indemnity has stood the test of time. James Naremore called it "a definitive *film noir*, and one of the most influential movies in Hollywood history." Its influence is clearly seen in many of the *noir* films which followed, especially in an adaptation by MGM in 1946 of another great Cain story, *The Postman Always Rings Twice*. In fact, it could be argued that any film which followed about an adulteress wife or husband who plans to kill their spouse owes a debt to *Double Indemnity*. Billy Wilder, one of the most successful and revered Hollywood directors, made many classic motion pictures but even among his pantheon of films *Double Indemnity* ranks high. It could be argued that among Wilder films only *Sunset Blvd.* (made very much in the *film noir* fashion and also with the lead actor narrating the story) is a better film. When the American Film Institute selected the one-hundred greatest films ever made (a Herculean task, which can be debated endlessly), *Double Indemnity* ranked #38 overall. In 1945 Wilder and Charles Bracket made *The Lost Weekend* and swept the Oscars for that year. "I think we did so well," Wilder later explained, "partly because they didn't give me any Oscars for *Double Indemnity* in 1944, so, in '45, they made up for it."

While Fred wasn't nominated for an Academy Award for *Double Indemnity* he got a reward of another sort, the recognition by the writer of the material, James M. Cain, who was overcome by Fred's performance. Cain sent autographed copies of *Three of a Kind* to each of the principal actors in the film, and, according to Cain's biographer, Cain thought that Fred, "particularly, had done a superb job." In a note to Fred accompanying the book Cain wrote, "The way you found tragedy in his shallow, common-place, smart-cracking skull will remain with me for a long time and, indeed, reinforce an aesthetic viewpoint that many quarrel with; for if I have any gift, it is to take such people and show that they can suffer as profoundly as anybody else. If, harkening to clamor, I ever weaken and begin to pretty my characters up; I shall remember your Walter and be fortified."

Double Indemnity allowed Fred MacMurray to be more than a depend-able light leading man who had a way with a witty or flip line and made it possible for other dramatic roles which challenged him more as an actor, *Pushover, The Caine Mutiny, There's Always Tomorrow* and *The Apartment*. The film also made Fred a devotee of Billy Wilder, who was, bar none, the greatest director he ever worked with. Fred would later state, "I'd make any picture Billy wanted me to [this turned out not to be the case, as we shall see]. I respect his talent and judgment. Also I enjoy working with him." He also, like most others who study these things, considered *Double Indemnity* his best film. "I enjoy comedy more than anything, I guess, but I honestly have to come back to *Double Indemnity* and say, that's my best role."

CHAPTER FIVE

Leaving Paramount, Fox Trilogy and Career Doldrums

1945-1949

Logically, given the accolades that Fred's performance received from *Double Indemnity*, he should have been a perfect candidate for more substantial roles than he had been playing up to that time. For instance, Dick Powell, who practically begged Wilder to allow him to play Neff, got the chance to show off his stuff in another 1944 *film noir*, *Murder, My Sweet*, playing hardboiled private-eye Philip Marlowe. Up to that point Powell had been best known for his singing, especially in a string of successful Warner Brothers' musicals during the 1930s. The film was successful and Powell had a new career as a tough guy. Over the next decade he would appear in fifteen more films and in only one of them did he sing. Such was not the case for Fred. *Double Indemnity* certainly proved Fred could handle meaty dramatic roles but of the forty-three films he would make over the next thirty years only a handful would stretch his abilities in the way *Double Indemnity* did. He also miscalculated. In 1945 he was invited to play the role of the older married veteran who returns home in Samuel Goldwyn's prestigious *The Best Years of Our Lives* but turned it down reportedly because he considered the part "third banana." (Fred wasn't alone: Olivia de Havilland turned down the part of the wife for the same reason.) Instead, the part went to Fredric March, who ended up winning the Academy Award for it.

Following the filming of Leisen's *Practically Yours*, Fred made what was to be the final film of his Paramount contract and one of the best comedies he ever made. The title of this film was based on a popular song sung by Betty Hutton in the film *Happy Go Lucky*. This is a hilarious black comedy in the tradition of *Arsenic and Old Lace*. Shot between April and late June of 1944 *Murder, He Says* gives Fred an opportunity to use many of the tricks he would delight audiences with in his later Disney comedies. There is plenty of slapstick to spare and the unmistakable MacMurray double-or-triple takes

Marjorie Main, Fred and Peter Whitney in, arguably, Fred's best comedy, 1945's Murder, He Says. *Photo courtesy Robert Nott.*

and arched left eyebrow, which became his trademark in those later films. He also isn't the glib and self-assured character of many of his earlier films, especially since much of the humor comes from him trying to escape from a family of lunatics who are out to kill him. The timing by director George Marshall is frenetic and the acting is outstanding, producing a film that Charles Higham and Joel Greenberg in their book, *Hollywood in the Forties,* called "a neglected masterpiece and perhaps the forties' funniest farce."

Fred plays Pete Marshall, a pollster who is trying to locate a missing colleague. Way out in the country he comes upon the town of Plainville. His search for his colleague brings him together with a mountain family, the Fleagles, at their old rickety farmhouse. The family matriarch is played by Marjorie Main with Porter Hall as her hen-pecked husband. There are also two dim-witted gun-toting lookalike sons, Mert and Bert Fleagle (played by Peter Whitney), who Ma uses a bullwhip on to keep in line. There is a daughter (Jean Heather), who takes a liking to Pete, and a dying grandmother (Mabel Paige), who glows in the dark. The Fleagle family has a habit of doing away with intruders, which is exactly what happened to Pete's unlucky colleague and what they intend to do to Pete as well. They don't want any intruders to know that they are searching for $70,000, which their cousin Bonnie (Barbara Pepper) stole in a robbery and has hid somewhere on their property. Into this wackiness comes Claire Matthews

(Helen Walker), the daughter of another man who was implicated in the robbery — her motive is to try and clear his name. The climax of the film finds Pete and Claire trapped by the Fleagles in the barn and they manage to escape by trapping each in a bale of hay using a hay compression machine into which Pete and Claire also fall into but emerge on the conveyer belt together embracing in a bale of hay.

The backstory behind this film is almost as chaotic as the film itself. First and foremost, Fred was having contract problems with Paramount. His contract was almost up and Fred believed that after a decade as one of the most successful box office stars at the studio he deserved a big raise and more say in the selection of his projects. By this time *Double Indemnity* had opened and was performing well at movie theaters around the country and most of the reviews praised Fred's against-type work. Fred thought that this would be an additional feather in his cap in contract negotiations, but it really wasn't. Paramount didn't even have a new project ready for him. Fred felt that the studio was spending more time building up newer stars like Alan Ladd and John Lund than they were in furthering his career. Paramount felt they had done quite well with Fred over the past decade and an indication of this was his continued popularity and the fact that he was one of the highest paid actors in the industry. They came to an impasse. Twentieth Century-Fox was waiting in the wings and very much wanted to bring Fred over to their studio with an offer of $125,000 per picture and the ability to do outside projects as well. They even told Fred they were holding a big-budgeted biographical film based on the life of World War I flying ace Eddie Rickenbacker for him. One of the primary reasons why Fox wanted Fred was because they had lost a huge roster of their top male stars to the war effort, including Tyrone Power, Henry Fonda and Victor Mature. They needed some major star power, which Fred would represent. Fred was ready to jump over to Fox, but he still owed Paramount one last picture and they had nothing on the plate for him.

At this point Paramount was just as unbendable and all too willing to allow Fred to leave and so they went to veteran director George Marshall to put something together as a final MacMurray film. George Marshall was one of the most prolific film directors in Hollywood history whose career began in silent pictures and continued into the 1970s. He eventually directed over 400 films and while few of them became classics, the closest he came in that category would probably be *Destry Rides Again* (1939), but several of them were well-done entertainments which made money at the box office (*You Can't Cheat an Honest Man, Tap Roots, The Ghost Breakers, Houdini, How the West Was Won* and several Martin and Lewis films). He was a journeyman director with no recognizable signature attached to his films which stamped them as a "Marshall picture" in the way one would look at a movie and immediately tag it as a "Hitchcock" or "Ford" picture. He did a competent job and delivered competent pictures and sometimes a few which were better than that.

So Paramount gave their journeyman director the job of preparing Fred MacMurray's finale film for the studio. "Fred had one picture left to go on his contract, and there was no film ready for him," Marshall later recalled. "We did have an idea which we had worked on for a Bob Hope film. It was similar to *The Ghost Breakers*, but it was merely an idea. It had not been reduced to a screenplay. I was told to prepare it at once." Fred wanted something immediately, so Marshall went to him to get him to wait until a script was ready. "He refused," according to Marshall, "he said he wanted out and would do anything they gave him. Then he asked what I was working on for him. All I could tell him was that we had two gags. A dog lights up and an old lady lights up, but nothing that tied anything together. Fred replied 'Fine! Just let me know when you are ready.'"

From here Marshall got hold of one of his old writers going back to the days when they had slapped out silent comedies, Lou Breslow, and together they managed to work out a synopsis of the idea which became the crux of *Murder, He Says.* "It was comparable to stringing up popcorn on a string in order to get all the little pieces into line," Marshall said. With this synopsis finished Marshall was ready to begin shooting even though there wasn't a completed script. "We would start in the morning at the place we had left off the night before, then the crew would have to wait until we had the scene written, before the cameras could be placed." In short, they would write the film as they went along, just as Marshall had done in his silent days.

Many stars when presented with this kind of circumstance would balk, not knowing what would come next, but not Fred, according to Marshall. "One characteristic concerning MacMurray was that he never created even the smallest problem, because of his studio arguments. In fact, it was just the reverse. He would sit down on the set with Breslow and myself, helping out with our routines. He frequently gave us some ingenious suggestions. For example, we would say 'Let's see now. Yesterday we left Ma chasing one of the twins, outside. Pa was in the basement doing one of his experiments. Grandma was in bed upstairs, so that leaves us one twin and the zany daughter to start off with.' Fred and the rest of us chimed in with suggestions to move the story forward." Because of filming without a completed script, the movie was shot in continuity. "Without my early training, I never would have been able to make such a film," Marshall later said. "Another fact that now becomes salient is that we had to stay in direct continuity, otherwise we would have been lost ... *Murder* ... is such a perfect lesson in creative filmmaking and improvisation. We made scene after scene without having the slightest idea as to the next one. So it was necessary to take the one we had just made and improvise from that."

Marshall was pretty much on his own during the making of this picture. He ignored the producer assigned to the film and the studio's production chief Buddy DeSylva was in South America during the shooting. But Marshall guessed that DeSylva had been getting frantic reports about the making of the film while he was away because when DeSylva returned from South America and Marshall passed him in the hall one morning, he was greeted by DeSylva in a less than cordial fashion and told that he would be sending for him. "Finally I was summoned to DeSylva's office," Marshall later recalled. "He was laughing when I arrived. He said 'That's the craziest picture I ever looked at, but thank God for your early comedy experience. It was the only way you could have made it.' He then apologized for his rather arch attitude on the preceding morning. He explained that all sorts of wild rumors had reached him concerning the film, even one wherein my producer was contemplating suicide."

From the most chaotic shooting circumstances came Fred's final film as a Paramount contract player. *Murder, He Says* has strong claims toward being Fred's all-time best comedy. It certainly foreshadowed the befuddled characters he would later become associated in such films as *The Absent Minded Professor* and the father figure of *My Three Sons* and given that much of the film was improvised on the set it leads one to the conclusion that Fred himself had a great deal to do with the creation of this later more farcical persona. When the film opened nearly a year after it was completed in June 1945 it won decent reviews and performed solidly at the box office. Over the years the reputation of *Murder, He Says* has grown. In discussing the movie *Arsenic and Old Lace* in her book *Kiss Kiss Bang Bang* film critic Pauline Kael wrote, "But nobody paid much attention to a funnier, less labored movie in the same genre, the 1945 *Murder, He Says.*"

Fred's contract at Paramount was up in the summer of 1944 and Fred decided not to renew. Fred decided to sign with Fox. Cleveland Amory in *The Saturday Evening Post* (incidentally one of Fred's favorite magazines to relax to and read) put it this way: "Fox hung out the STAR WANTED sign in earnest. They needed no ordinary leading man. They had all sorts of pictures lined up. They must have a man who could do almost anything, and do it fast and well. He must be a real draw and at the same time no type - a man equally at home in musical extravaganzas and boudoir comedies. He must be either 4-F or old enough to be beyond at least probable immediate drafting. Above all, he must be someone who would not be impressed with his own importance. Clearly it was no spot for a Hollywood big head."

While the Rickenbacker biography was being prepared, Fred began work on a musical-fantasy called *Where Do We Go From Here?* This was actually a very ambitious project for the studio. They didn't spare expenses and filmed it in Technicolor. In some respects it is similar to MGM's *DuBarry Was a Lady*, in which the protagonist of the picture is taken back in time, to the court of Louis XVI. Our hero, Bill Morgan, who's unable to become a marine because of his 4-F status, works as a guard at a salvage yard. While working he finds an old lamp and, intrigued, he begins to polish it — and lo-and-behold a genie appears and offers him the obligatory three wishes. Morgan, a true patriot, says he wants to be in uniform. The genie therefore sends him back to Valley Forge, puts him aboard the *Santa Maria* with Christopher Columbus and then makes him an agent on Manhattan Island who buys the Island from an Indian chief (played by Anthony Quinn).

The film is interesting for another reason because it teamed him with June Haver, a popular Twentieth Century-Fox musical-comedy star who was dubbed the "pocket Grable" due to her relative shortness (5'2") but otherwise striking resemblance to Betty Grable, the top box office actress at Fox during the war years. This was the only film that Fred and Haver, who would become his second wife in 1954, would appear together in. Haver would later recall that when shooting this film she was impressed by Fred's devotion to his wife Lillian and their two adopted children. She would remember telling her mother that she wished that someday she too would meet and marry a man like Fred MacMurray.

The film has another leading lady, Joan Leslie, who was loaned to the studio by Warner Brothers. (She was best known for her work with James Cagney in *Yankee Doodle Dandy* and danced superbly with Fred Astaire in

Fred and June Haver worked together in 1945's **Where Do We Go From Here?** *nearly a decade before their 1954 marriage.*

The Sky's the Limit.) Leslie would later say that she was delighted when she learned of the loan out because her leading man would be Fred MacMurray. "He was a big name who was really a good actor — and a very solid actor," Leslie recalls. "He always kept a part of his real-life personality in the roles he played, which is what all the great actors did." She recalls Fred as being very easy to work with and somebody who always tried to be helpful. There was a particular scene in the picture where she and Fred ride a chariot through the air thanks to the Genie's magic. "We are in the chariot and Fred tells me, 'Joan, I want to tell you something. Mr. Ratoff [director Gregory Ratoff] has a habit of shooting a scene without any rehearsing.' I said, 'You gotta be kidding!' I was very nervous about doing a scene without actually rehearsing it, especially one that was so technical in nature. So Fred suggested that we run through the scene ourselves. Well, Mr. Ratoff, who was a bit eccentric, came to us and said, 'You kids know what you're doing, let's just shoot it.' But I would not have made it without Fred and his help; he was a very generous actor." When asked why so many actresses wanted to work with Fred, Miss Leslie didn't hesitate. "He was tops! A very good actor and made a splendid appearance, was recognizable. If it was a Fred MacMurray picture, it will be fun, he could do it all. He had a very modest way about him and he never acted [off screen] the part of the star. He had a very workman-like attitude."

The film was one of the most ambitious and hyped musicals that Fox had ever made and was to be one of their big pictures of the year. Its cost was an astronomical (for that time) $2.4 million, but it ended up taking in only $1.75 million at the box office. It was not helped by mostly negative or indifferent reviews.

As it turned out Fred's pact with Fox would produce only three films before they more or less amicably parted company. It was thought that the biopic of Eddie Rickenbacker would be a sure-fire hit with World War II audiences. It is obvious that the studio was heavily influenced by the 1941 Gary Cooper film *Sergeant York* and hoped for the same box office and critical reaction. The film opens with Rickenbacker on an army plane that is shot down in the South Pacific in the early days of the Second World War. Eddie and a group of survivors are huddled on a make-shift life raft and to keep their minds off their predicament and lift their morale Eddie begins to tell them, via flashback, his life story — from the time he was twelve years old and fibbed to get a job to help support his widowed mother to his storied military and flying career.

To help prepare for his role Fred read some 765 pages of biographical notes and also received coaching from Rickenbacker himself. According to Fred, Rickenbacker offered advice on many subjects including how he should play love scenes! "He asked me to go a little easy on the love scenes," MacMurray said. "He said his love-making was persistent, but not too ardent." Of course this suited Fred just fine. Despite the extensive notes and the cooperation of Rickenbacker himself, Fred later said he felt "odd" playing a real-life living person. Typically, Fred downplayed his performance as Rickenbacker. When asked by a reporter if he hade made a "special effort to get inside the personality" of Rickenbacker, Fred answered, "Nope. I played that my regular way. I asked myself how would I behave in the situation the script called for — and then just went on and acted myself ... Rickenbacker seemed to like the picture."

Darryl Hickman acted in *Captain Eddie*, portraying Rickenbacker as a boy. While he obviously didn't share any scenes with Fred, he did get a chance to observe Fred when he visited the set or dined in the studio commissary. Hickman was excited and honored to be in a film based on the life of a national hero. "I knew who he was and I was very aware that he was an American hero ... I was very proud." There was only one thing which caused Hickman some mild anxiety. "I remember I had a conversation with my mother and asking her if she thought I looked like Fred MacMurray. Because I didn't think I did, but that didn't matter to Fox." Hickman first met Fred during filming when Fred visited the set when Hickman was filming a scene with the great character actor Charles Bickford, who plays Rickenbacker's father in the film. "I remember Fred as being one of the shyest men I've ever met. He was just very quiet and laid back," Hickman recalls. "The director, Lloyd Bacon, introduced us and I recall that we discussed playing Rickenbacker, me as a boy and him as the man, and he had no ego problems and was very, very sweet and pleasant to me." But it was Fred's shyness which really caught Hickman's attention. "The hub of the Fox studio was its commissary, it was a wonderful commissary and there was constant activity and catching up with friends," Hickman recalls. "Fred would come in with his newspaper and sit down away from anybody else and put the newspaper up to his face so no one would see him sitting there. I would walk by and suddenly hear, 'Hello, Darryl' - and it was Fred with his face hidden behind his newspaper! -and he would say hello and then just go on reading." Hickman contrasted Fred's behavior with that of Clark Gable and Spencer Tracy, who he recalled loving being the center of attention in the MGM commissary. Despite this, Hickman emphasizes that Fred was not "standoffish," a word his mother liked to use; "everyone liked him and recognized that he was just basically a shy man." Hickman believes that Fred's appeal and longevity as star was that he acted like "the average guy ... he didn't act like a movie star — he acted like an insurance salesman."

As it turned out, the film, which cost slightly more than *Where Do We Go From Here?*, was a colossal flop, grossing a little more than a million dollars. By the time the film came out the war was nearly over and Americans had had their fill of patriotism for four years and were looking for lighter diversions. Among those who did see the film the word of mouth couldn't have been helpful because in the hands of journeyman director Lloyd Bacon, Fred's performance is pretty wooden. Darryl Hickman recalls Bacon fondly. "He wore a special baseball cap all the time and was very direct. He never said after a scene 'print it,' but if he liked a scene he would jump out of his chair and yell, 'That's It!'"

Rickenbacker's biographer, W. David Lewis, called the film a "syrupy melodrama" with Fred "bringing out nothing of the intensity of Rickenbacker's life and experiences." Rickenbacker, himself, writes Lewis, was "proud of it and went on tour to promote it." Fred's first two efforts for Fox left both star and studio a bit bewildered by the lack of audience appeal given the care, budgets and talent involved.

But things couldn't be better in Fred's personal life. He and Lily added to their family. In addition to blonde-haired Susan the couple added a little brother for her, adopting a year-and-a-half-year-old blond-haired and blue-eyed little boy and naming him Robert, or Bob for short. It was a family affair, with Fred's mother living close by and often joining them for long weekends at the MacMurray ranch near Santa Rosa. Meanwhile, Fred's aunt (the sister of his mother), Hazel Martin, was put in charge of his fan mail, which averaged 5-6,000 cards and letters per week. "Miss Hazel Martin, takes care of this avalanche of words with no interest whatsoever from Fred, but with the assistance of two secretaries," reported *The Saturday Evening Post.* "A motherly type, she is addicted to the personal touch, and likes to write colorful homilies to MacMurray's youthful admirers. In answering letters from older fans, she will, when the impulse strikes her, insert a candid snapshot of Fred instead of the routine posed studio photograph. Sometimes, even to feminine fans, she does something that would give any self-respecting Hollywood press agent goose flesh - she includes a picture of Fred and his wife together. 'Don't tell Bud, she says coyly, 'but I do it quite a lot.'" But there was an occasional dust-up, such as when a group of tenants in an apartment building he owned brought suit against Fred for allegedly raising the rent from $90 to $300. But Fred's attorney was able to justify the increase because the apartments on Wilshire Boulevard had been altered from unfurnished to furnished units.

Since his contract with Fox wasn't exclusive, it gave Fred the opportunity to do outside projects and one such project turned out to be the first picture he produced, a comedy of mistaken identifies called *Pardon My Past,* which would be distributed by Columbia. Fred stars as a soldier just out of the service who is returning to his hometown (the producer made sure the hometown he is headed for is Beaver Dam, Wisconsin) to start a mink farm along with his army buddy Chuck (William Demarest). While in New York the two ex-GIs decide to stop in a tailors shop and buy new suits, and while there Fred is mistaken for a playboy who owes a gangster $12,000 in gambling debts. Fred plays a duel role as the ex-GI who only wants to settle down on a mink farm in Beaver Dam and a carefree playboy who has been hiding out in Mexico.

Marguerite Chapman was cast as Fred's leading lady in the picture. She had just come off of a film called *Counter-Attack* and found *Pardon My Past* more fun to work in. On the first day of shooting Fred came up to her and asked, "Which is your favorite side?" and she admitted, "My left." He told her, "You're going to get your right. My neck is out of joint from having to keep playing to Claudette's left side!" An allusion to Colbert famously insisting that she be photographed from the left side because she thought it was her best side. Chapman knew who was paying her check on this picture and told him, "Okay, boss." On another occasion she showed up late, oversleeping due to forgetting to set her alarm clock. She was worried what the reaction of her co-star-cum-producer would be. "I was apologizing when I noticed that Fred wasn't even there and thought, 'My God, he's walked off because of me!' They later told me he'd gone to the dentist but I never knew whether or not he went because I wasn't there. We came in way under budget though."

Fred chose his good friend

Pardon My Past, a 1946 comedy, was produced by Fred.

and golfing companion, Leslie Fenton, to direct. He came away from the experience of producing with ambivalent feelings. He was glad he did it and got it out of his system, but from now on he would be content with being a working actor, a "hired hand." "It's too much work being a producer," he later commented. "You have to deal with any and all sorts of problems on the set and it can cause some hard feelings. From now on I'm content just to say my lines, take a check and head home."

From here Fred went back to Fox for what would be his final film under the contract he signed with them. Given the box office results of the first two collaborations Fox was only too willing to part company and besides the war was fast coming to a conclusion and their contract players, including Tyrone Power, Henry Fonda and Victor Mature, would be returning, making Fred's services at $125,000 per picture less necessary. The third film of the Fox trilogy was *Smoky*, filmed over two months between July and September of 1945 and based on a popular children's novel by Will James. The studio had bought the rights to the novel in 1933 for $15,000, but it had been sitting on the story development shelf until producer Robert Bassler found the property and the studio decided it was the right project for Fred. Fred plays a cowboy who has

Studio portrait of Fred from Smoky, *the only hit of the Fox trilogy.*

been riding from one rodeo to another to make a living that finds and captures a wild stallion and tames him, not by intimidation but by kindness. He wants the horse to be treated gently and worked on a cow farm rather than at hard labor, but his brother has other ideas which leads to the horse, named Smoky, eventually being stolen by the brother, along with some cattle being rustled, and sold for a high price to a ranch which will work Smoky hard. Eventually, of course, Fred is able to free Smoky and allows him to freely roam the pastures and woods surrounding his ranch.

As it turned out, this film became a big box office success. Costing under $2 million to shoot on beautiful locations in Kanab, Utah and Northern Arizona, the film brought in over $4 million in rentals, becoming one of Fox's biggest hits of the year. At least at his third time at bat Fred came out a winner. Fox had been readying another picture for Fred at the time of the mutual decision to terminate his contract, it was an interesting *film noir* called *The Dark Corner*, which would co-star Lucille Ball and Clifton Webb (in one of his typically acerbic roles). With Fred out of the picture the role went to Mark Stevens, who the studio was grooming for stardom.

Another studio portrait of Fred from
Smoky.

II

Fred quickly followed up by signing a non-exclusive contract at Universal which, along with other studios, kept him busy over the next several years. Of the ten films he appeared in that were released between 1947 and 1951 six were comedies with familiar leading ladies like Claudette Colbert, Paulette Goddard, Madeleine Carroll, and Irene Dunne, but without the effervescing spark of their earlier teamings. One was a rather stiff adventure which gave him a new leading lady in Ava Gardner, but hardly used either star at their best. Then there were the two "Miracles": *A Miracle Can Happen* (a trilogy film, a.k.a *On Our Merry Way*) and *Miracle of the Bells*, a supposedly inspirational film which featured Frank Sinatra invading Bing Crosby's territory by playing a singing priest. Then there was a film which couldn't make up its mind whether it was a romantic comedy or a *film noir*, *Borderline*, so at times it was both. Needless to say, Fred kept busy but his box office appeal, like that of many aging stars, began to wane.

Paramount asked him to return in 1946 to team up with Paulette Goddard in the passable Mitchell Leisen comedy *Suddenly, It's Spring*. Also

Fred and Paulette Goddard in Mitchell Leisen's Suddenly, It's Spring, *the final film that Fred would make with both Leisen and Goddard.*

in the cast was Macdonald Carey, in his first picture since returning from the war. It's actually a fairly adult story with Fred and Goddard playing a married couple who have been separated by the war for a number of years and inevitably it takes a toll on their marriage. Fred's character has fallen in love with another woman and wants a divorce; Goddard wants to win him back. The film was scripted by Fred's good friend and hunting buddy Claude Binyon, who also acted as the producer of the film. "Claude Binyon was Fred MacMurray's favorite writer and Fred always tried to get him on any picture he did," recalled Leisen's assistant, Eleanor Broder. But in this case, with Fred no longer at Paramount, it was producer Binyon who wrote the screenplay with Fred in mind for the leading man.

Originally, the plan was to cast Fred with Claudette Colbert, who was considered a superior farceur as compared to Paulette Goddard, but that fell through and Goddard got the part. Although Goddard was once married to Charlie Chaplin and featured in two of his brilliant comedies, *Modern*

Times and *The Great Dictator* as well as other comedic roles, she didn't feel comfortable about her abilities as a comedic actress. She was so insecure about the screenplay that she would badger Binyon for better lines. "Binyon was very shy and every morning, when he came on the set, he looked around nervously and asked, 'Where is she?'" recalled Broder, "because as soon as Paulette laid eyes on him, she rushed over in her peppy way, saying, 'Oh, come on, Claude, give me some better lines' and that got on his nerves.'" Goddard's biographer would later write, "Fred MacMurray was expert at comedy timing, but Paulette wasn't. Those on the film remember that she would play a scene either too fast or too slow, and it would take many attempts before she got it right. In some instances, she never did get it right, and it was up to the film's editor to cut the scene so it would work."

The film did well at the box office and Hollywood writer Erskine Johnson decided to rub some salt in Paramount's wound for letting Fred get away from them. "Fred MacMurray turns in the best comedy performance of his career in *Suddenly, It's Spring*. Paramount executives who DIDN'T renew his contract are gnashing their teeth." This was Fred's last big screen teaming with director Mitchell Leisen.

Fred followed this film by reuniting with Colbert at Universal for one of the biggest box office hits of either of their careers (and really the last big hit at the box office that Colbert would enjoy) with the adaptation of Betty MacDonald's semi-autobiographical novel, *The Egg and I*. The novel was a runaway success that stood on the bestseller lists for a full eighteen months. Fred and Claudette play a couple who decide to uproot themselves from the city (really more the husband's idea than the wife's) and move to the country and buy a chicken farm. Of course, they have the inevitable problems of adjusting to country life and fitting in. The wife is also in for some competition when one of their neighbors (played by Louise Allbritton) decides to try and steal Fred away from her.

Fred and Colbert play as effortlessly together as ever and after so many years of screen partnership they seem very much like a long-married couple who could finish each other's sentences. "Claudette and I worked darn hard," Fred would later recall. "We were both at the turn of 40 then and it isn't as easy to keep the ball in the air - to keep it sparkling and spontaneous. I know Claudette was a big asset to the film. It wasn't easy for her getting all dirtied up, sliding off roofs and what not, but she was a wonderful sport, as always." But the film itself is stolen by a country couple with large brood of children, Ma and Pa Kettle, played delightfully by Marjorie Main and Percy Kilbride. Ma was boisterous and domineering while Pa was lazy and quiet, so completely and effortlessly do they steal the film that it led to a series of *Ma and Pa Kettle* sequels over the next several years which were hugely profitable for Universal. Audiences may have initially come to *The Egg and I* based on its strong popularity in bookstores and for the Colbert-MacMurray teaming, but it was the word of mouth regarding Main and Kilbride which kept audiences coming back. They also stole the reviews, Main in particular. James Agee (*The Nation*, 5/10/47) didn't care for the film itself but complimented Main on her characterization. "Marjorie Main in an occasional fit of fine, wild comedy, picks the show up and brandishes it as if she were wringing its neck." Main was nominated for an Academy Award as Best Supporting

Claudette Colbert and Fred in one of their biggest box office hits, The Egg and I.

Actress for her work in this picture and considered "Ma" her favorite character. "Ma was good for a lot of laughs and I would rather make people laugh than anything else." She publicly stated that the other reason why she enjoyed working in *The Egg and I* was due to Claudette Colbert, an experience she "thoroughly enjoyed." Yet in an interview she gave years later with author Boze Hadleigh, Main was asked how she liked working with Colbert and replied, "She was very grand" and Hadleigh, egging her on, asked, "Very grand?" to which Main responded, "She thought she was." As for Fred, Main curtly dismissed him, telling Hadleigh that he "lacked warmth."

Louise Allbritton, who plays the scheming other woman in the film, would have pleasanter memories of working with Fred. At first she found him distant and relatively uncommunicative, except for perhaps throwing an occasional "good morning" her way. One day they were shooting a scene where she had to stroke a cow, a horned Hereford, on the nose and she was a little scared about doing it. "Don't be silly," the assistant director told her, "just get on with it." Finally, Fred, who had been quietly sitting in his chair off to the side with a newspaper folded in his lap, piped up, "The lady is absolutely right. Hereford's are dangerous. The foreman at my ranch was gored by one. Cut this scene out." From that point forward Allbritton would recall a much more communicative MacMurray. She later told a

Fred and Ava in **Singapore.**

reporter that he talked constantly about his "two little ones" at home.

He was working almost as constantly in the late forties as he was at his romantic peak in the mid-'30s, but the films were at best mediocre. In the next two years he would be reunited in films with such past co-stars as Claudette Colbert, Madeleine Carroll and Irene Dunne all of whom were — like Fred — past their prime. Fred's next film for Universal is one of his weakest of the lot but at least had the novelty of teaming Fred with a new leading lady, the up-and-coming beauty Ava Gardner.

Gardner, who was 24 at this time, had just achieved a breakout role in the classic *film noir The Killers* while on loan-out from MGM to Universal. Her smoldering, uninhibited beauty filled the screen and a new sex symbol was born. Prior to this, despite appearing in fifteen films (mostly B's at MGM), she was best known as the wife of first Mickey Rooney and then bandleader Artie Shaw. She was just completing a part in *The Hucksters* with Clark Gable and Deborah Kerr when she was told that MGM was again loaning her out to Universal for ten weeks at $5,000. According to her biographer Roland Falmini, "She was rushed to Universal and onto an oriental set, introduced to the star of the picture, Fred MacMurray, and told to make passionate love to him. Only after that was she taken aside and told the plot of the film."

Fred was cast as Matt Gordon, one of the many anti-heroes who populated the screen during the late '40s. He just got out of the Navy after serving five years during World War II and has returned to Singapore to pick up on his pre-war vocation, that of pearl smuggler. When he arrives at his favorite hotel, he can't help but reminisce about his pre-war life and the woman he loved and was engaged to be married, Linda (Gardner), who disappeared without a trace during the Japanese attack. The story then goes back to the present and that night Matt goes to a nightclub where he is startled to see Linda on the dance floor dancing with another man and further surprised when he approaches her and she doesn't remember him. It turns out that Linda has a case of amnesia and is now married to another man, a rich British planter. Meanwhile, Matt sets out to find the pearls he smuggled years earlier and somehow remind Linda of her true identity and of the love they once shared.

The filming went relatively smoothly until the day that Fred and Gardner shot a fire sequence which got out of hand when part of the burning ceiling caved in just narrowly missing Gardner but setting Fred's white tropical suit on fire. But since the studios routinely had a fire squad available on the set when filming such scenes Fred was able to run over to the side and they quickly put the fire out. The two stars got along fine but didn't forge any long lasting attachments and this would be their only film together. (According to one of Gardner's biographers Ava referred to Fred as "great.") Apparently Gardner did like to gossip about other stars and she assigned coded nicknames for them so that she could gossip about them on the set with other friends without actually saying their real names. Barbara Stanwyck was called "short lips," Deborah Kerr was "Miss Continuation" ("because her voice never changed from one film to the other"), Hugh O'Brian was referred to as "tight-ass" and Fred had the rather innocuous coded name of "Mr. Gordon." As for Gardner, director John Brahm would later say, "She didn't have a brain in her head." The film didn't go anywhere at the box office despite its New York opening, where the first one hundred women at the box office were given a string of pearls.

Next, Leslie Fenton directed Fred and William Demarest in an episode of the anthology film *A Miracle Can Happen,* which included an all-star cast in three different episodes. Besides Fred and Demarest the cast included James Stewart, Henry Fonda, Paulette Goddard, Burgess Meredith (who produced the film) and Dorothy Lamour. Two directors were credited, Fenton and King Vidor, with two others non-credited (George Stevens and John Huston). The MacMurray-Demarest episode is about two con men that meet up with a runaway, and, believing the kid to be from a wealthy family, plan to return him to his guardian in hopes of getting a big reward. It turns out that the guardian doesn't want the spoiled brat back. Despite the cast and an interesting premise, the film got generally poor reviews (the Stewart-Fonda teaming turned out best) and didn't succeed at the box office. The *New York Daily News* may have summed it up best when its critic wrote, "A million dollar cast in a ten-cent film."

Between mid-July and late September of 1947 Fred filmed *The Miracle of the Bells* for producer Jesse Lasky at RKO. Fred headlined a cast including Valli (on loan-out from David O. Selznick) and Frank Sinatra (on loan out from MGM). Despite Sinatra's casting as a young priest, the film is no *Going My Way*, it's a much darker story and Sinatra sings only one song, much to the chagrin of his fans.

The Miracle of the Bells is based on a best-selling novel by Russell Janey and casts Fred as a press agent for a recently deceased actress (Valli). Much of the film is told in flashback about how the press agent found the girl, Olga, as a dancer in a chorus line and promotes her into the lead role in a film about Joan of Arc without knowing that she is dying of a lung ailment, probably Tuberculosis, caused from a childhood being brought up in an impoverished coal town and her exposure to the coal dust. Olga dies just a day after completing the Joan the Arc film and the press agent, who had fallen in love with her,

Another print ad Fred gave his name and image to from the late '40s.

arrives in her hometown to make funeral arrangements. He is determined that the town remembers her and makes an arrangement with the churches to ring their bells continually for three days straight in her honor leading up to the day of her funeral. At the funeral a "miracle" occurs which reawakens the faith of the community and while it turns out that there is a rational explanation for the "miracle" the press agent calls on a young Catholic priest (Sinatra) to back up the miracle theory or else it will tear away the newfound faith of the community and, probably more importantly to the press agent, extinguish Olga's role as the catalyst of the "miracle."

Lasky was one of the early movie pioneers and formed Famous Players-Lasky Studio which eventually evolved into Paramount Pictures. He spared no expense on this film. It was budgeted at $3 million, a very high budget for a film in those days, especially at RKO, which was experiencing a financial downsizing. But the novel had proved to be very successful; and the studio was gambling that with a best-selling book as the basis of the story and stars like Fred, Valli (a new discovery), and Sinatra that the picture would be successful. Lasky chose Irving Pichel, a sometime actor, to direct. Pichel was best known for such films as *The Most Dangerous Game, She* and *They Won't Believe Me*. Soon after making *The Miracle of the Bells*, Pichel's name had been muddied by the House Un-American Activities Committee as one of the so-called "Hollywood 19," which consisted of mostly writers (13 of the 19) who didn't cooperate with the committee. Pichel's name was later cleared when it was discovered that he had no affiliation with the Communist Party and he was able to work until practically the day he died. The film was written by Ben Hecht and Quentin Reynolds. Hecht was considered one of the best movie writers in Hollywood, often used by David O. Selznick and Alfred Hitchcock. In addition to his own projects he was often asked to "polish" somebody else's screenplay. Hecht considered himself a playwright more than a screenwriter; his most famous play was *The Front Page*, which was adapted into a film at least four times over the years. That Hecht was reportedly working on three other screenplays at the time he was writing this film may have something to do with why the script seems to be underwritten in spots. It fell to RKO writer DeWitt Bodeen (*Cat People, The Seventh Victim*) to add some spice and atmosphere to the script when Hecht and Reynolds proved unavailable. All in all, with the names associated with this film, expectations were high.

Lasky planned a huge promotional campaign, but, according to *The Films of Frank Sinatra*, one aspect of the promotional campaign probably backfired: "Aware of the sensitive feelings surrounding their production, Lasky and RKO attempted to devise a suitably tasteful promotional campaign. The result stands as one of the worst posters in movie history. Plugged as Russell Janney's *The Miracle of the Bells*, to keep that bestseller link in the public's mind, the title lettering is flanked by multiple swinging clappers. On the bottom left of the poster are dreadful renditions of MacMurray and Valli, both of whom appear to have penciled eyebrows and red-glossed lips. Slightly elevated on the bottom right, his eyes raised in the general direction of heaven, Sinatra looks for the entire world like a drag queen in search of his wig. Lipstick, eyelashes, eyeliner, eyebrow pencil, the lot. If the Mob stories about him had been true, at least one Hollywood graphic designer would have been given a new concrete wardrobe." The principle actors were all contractually obligated to appear in San Francisco for the premier of the film (Sinatra tried to get out of it, but Lasky appealed to him as a personal favor), which went well enough, but the film itself, while not exactly a box office failure, didn't recoup its investment.

For Fred this was his third straight box office disappointment, so it was back to basics with a trio of comedies. First up was *Don't Trust Your Husband* (a.k.a., *An Innocent Affair*), which reunited him with Madeleine Carroll for the first time since *One Night in Lisbon* seven years earlier. This was also Carroll's first film in six years and she demanded $100,000 for her services. She wasn't one of Fred's favorite leading ladies, but he recognized that their teamings had always been successful and since he owned a piece of the picture he urged the producers to hire her at her price. "She's worth it," he later told Hedda Hopper. Unfortunately for both leads this comedy of marital misunderstanding failed at the box office.

Next, Fred was cast opposite Claudette Colbert in *Family Honeymoon*. It was their seventh and final picture together. Where in *Practically Yours*, five years earlier, Fred had complained that they were "too old" for their roles in that film they were at least their basic ages here with Colbert playing a widow with three children (she was 43 by the time she made this film) who falls in love with a professor (the now 40-year-old Fred) and get married, but find it hard to consummate their wedding vows when her children end up accompanying them on their honeymoon. The stars' expertise with dialogue still brought about some laughs from the Claude Binyon script, but Fred and Claudette realized that their teaming was running out of gas. "We had been getting together for 14 years," Fred would later recall, "and by 1949 Claudette knew as well as I did that things run their good and proper course and then they are simply over. We had a long run, and a rewarding one, and there are no complaints to offer in retrospect." The film did better than most of his previous several films at the box office, but the reviews were lukewarm and an acknowledgement that perhaps the MacMurray-Colbert teaming, which had been contemporary and frothy in the mid-'30s, was becoming dated and static by the late '40s. "The stars bravely maintain the characteristics that have endeared them to the public," wrote the *New York Herald Tribune*, "but in this case they cannot intrigue anyone."

Fred's final feature of the '40s and the last of this comedy trio cast him with a new leading lady, the fiery, Irish, red-headed Maureen O'Hara, in yet another domestic comedy, *Father Was a Fullback*. The film, shot at Twentieth Century-Fox, was about a football coach who has to contend with problems on the field and off, especially those involving his two daughters (played by Betty Lynn and young Natalie Wood). Helping the proceedings along immeasurably are the acid comments of sharp-tongued Thelma Ritter who plays their maid. What stood out in O'Hara's mind of this film was a challenging director in John Stahl who didn't seem to know what he was looking for because he "shot sometimes as many as fifty takes. You'd say, 'Mr. Stahl, is there something we should change?' and he'd say, 'No no no, do it again.' And then you'd be shocked because he might print take three and you'd think, 'What was he looking for?' He would be the same with Natalie as he was with me and Fred MacMurray." Stahl's approach, while exasperating to the actors, was similar to that of William Wyler, one of the most acclaimed directors of the time, who would similarly make several takes and then often print one of the earlier ones he shot. This was the first of two films which Fred made with Natalie Wood, one of the most promising child actresses of her time who came to public consciousness due to her precocious performance in the classic *Miracle on 34th Street* two years earlier. Fred would later comment that he "never saw a child of such energy and delightful innocence" as Wood. But Gigi Perreau, who was an even younger up-and-coming child actress and would work with Fred and Wood in 1950's *Never a Dull Moment*, would recall Wood as overly ambitious, "to the point of sometimes being very obnoxious," but put much of the blame on Natalie's mother, nicknamed Mud, who was an exceedingly pushy and domineering stage mother. The film, which cost about $1.2 million to produce, grossed $1.8 million, producing a small profit for Fox and allowing Fred to breathe a little easier.

In the late '40s Dashiell Hammett was in discussions about bringing his best-selling novel *The Maltese Falcon* to the New York stage. In a letter to his sister, Hammett wrote that such a production would only proceed "if we can get a good script and if we can get a good cast." Fred was one of two actors on the short list to play Hammett's hard-boiled private eye Sam Spade (the other being Howard Duff, who played Spade on radio). But Fred had little or no interest in returning to the stage and ultimately nothing became of Hammett's attempts to launch a stage production of *The Maltese Falcon*.

Since *Double Indemnity*, Fred had made a string of films which hardly stretched his abilities as an actor. Of the fourteen films Fred made after *Double Indemnity* only one can be considered an honest to goodness classic today (*Murder, He Says*), while two were hugely successful commercial hits (*Smoky, The Egg and I*). Most of the films were a rehash of better material from earlier days, often teaming him with familiar faces and did so-so to disappointing at the box office. If Fred needed a career boost Billy Wilder was prepared to give it to him. When Montgomery Clift got cold feet about playing a gigolo to Gloria Swanson's faded silent screen star in Wilder's biting *Sunset Blvd.* and dropped out of the picture, Wilder approached Fred. Even though at 40 Fred was a little too old for the part (he was only a decade younger than Swanson herself, who had to be made up to look older than she actually was) he certainly could have captured the world-weariness of Joe Gillis, a man beset by creditors while undergoing a dry spell as a Hollywood screenwriter. Gillis is ready to pack it in and return to his more stable middle-western existence where he could be a big man in a small pond while in Hollywood he was a little man in a very large pond. Fred read the script and despite previously saying he would do "anything" that Wilder offered him, he turned the part down finding the Gillis character too "morally repellent" to do. It's puzzling that Fred, who would play an insurance man who gets involved with a married woman and ends up killing her husband, found Gillis - a desperate man, but not really a bad guy - repulsive. Needless to say, William Holden, who was ten years younger than Fred, gleefully accepted the role and finally cemented his stardom. He even won an Academy Award nomination for his work. Like *The Best Years of Our Lives*, it was another lost opportunity for Fred.

Fred in a studio portrait from the late '40s.

CHAPTER SIX

A New Life

1950-1954

In 1950 instead of basking in the glow of Billy Wilder's classic *Sunset Blvd.*, Fred appeared in two routine films. The first was opposite Claire Trevor in the schizophrenic *Borderline*, a film which couldn't decide whether it was a romantic comedy or *film noir*, and wasn't too successful in either way despite good chemistry between Fred and Trevor. Then, he teamed with Irene Dunne in *Never a Dull Moment*, about a city woman who marries a rodeo rider and moves to his ranch. It reminded critics and audiences alike of the similarly-themed *The Egg and I*, without the same result on screen or at the box office.

His film pickings improved in 1951, starting with a first-class comedy, *A Millionaire for Christy*, opposite a new leading lady, the beautiful and versatile Eleanor Parker. Parker was not widely known for her comedy roles. She had just come off of making the prison drama *Caged* for which she was nominated for a Best Actress Oscar. She leaped at the chance to do an old-fashioned screwball comedy and even went so far as to dye her hair blonde as a tribute to one of her favorites, Carole Lombard. The plot was good. Parker plays Christy, legal secretary who is sent to inform a down-home radio humorist (played by Fred) that he inherited

Fred teamed for the second time on screen with Irene Dunne in 1950's **Never a Dull Moment**, *which some critics considered a rip-off of* The Egg and I.

$2 million from a dead uncle. Parker's best friend advises her to romance the MacMurray character first so that he will fall in love with her and then break the news to him that he is a millionaire. At first Christy protests that she cannot lower herself to become a "gold-digger" but as she thinks more about it, it takes on a certain attraction, and, needless to say, she does fall in love with the MacMurray character. Complications arise when Fred finds out that she knew all along that he had inherited $2 million. Further complicating matters is that the MacMurray character is already engaged to be married. The film is smoothly directed by George Marshall, who demonstrates that he had not lost his zest for slapstick in the seven years since he and Fred filmed *Murder, He Says*. The picture, which was filmed in about four weeks between mid-January and mid-February of 1951, was praised as an "old fashioned romantic comedy" by several critics but it failed to catch on with audiences which led Fred to comment several years later that its failure had convinced him that his kind of comedy had gone out of fashion and he had better start concentrating on other types of roles if he was going to sustain his career.

But first he went to MGM to film another comedy, *Callaway Went Thataway*, which was actually a satire on the early television phenomenon of the "kiddie" Westerns such as Hopalong Cassidy and Red Ryder. William Boyd, who played Hopalong Cassidy for several years in "B" Westerns, and whose career had been on the wane, found that the rebroadcast of the "Hopalong Cassidy" films in the early days of television rejuvenated his career and made Boyd more famous and popular than ever, especially with kids. In *Callaway Went Thataway*, television does the same thing for another cowboy actor whose career has been on the skids, "Smoky" Callaway. The problem is that Callaway doesn't even realize it, and besides nobody even knows where he is. The television network which shows the old Callaway movies wants Smoky to do a series of promotional appearances around the country so they assign two of their top promotional people (played by Fred and Dorothy McGuire) to find Smoky and hire him for the promotional tour. When they do locate "Callaway" they find he is a useless drunk. Luckily, while visiting a dude ranch in Colorado, they find "Stretch" Barnes, who is a dead ringer for Callaway and hire him to impersonate Callaway. Meanwhile, the real Callaway comes to realize that an imposter has been hired to play him and is pocketing money that should be his and decides to come out of hiding, which complicates matters. Howard Keel gives a superb performance as both "Smoky Callaway" and his lookalike "Stretch Barnes."

According to a *Variety* article (11/15/51), William Boyd's manager demanded to see a print of the film so that he could "ascertain if it reflected unfavorably on Boyd" since the storyline of the film had many parallels with Boyd's return to the good graces of audiences. The article went on to state that after seeing the film Boyd's manager proclaimed it a "satire" and a "good, well-done picture." Still, the producers deemed it necessary to tack on a disclaimer at the end of the film, which read: "This picture was made in the spirit of fun and was meant in no way to detract from the wholesome influence, civic-mindedness and many charitable contributions of western idols of our American youth, or to be a portrayal of any of them." Thus, they

Fred in a scene from Callaway Went Thataway *with guest star* Clark Gable.

hoped they would be protected just in case some cowboy star (like Boyd, Gene Autry and Roy Rogers) suddenly took offense to the film's story.

Howard Keel always considered *Callaway Went Thataway* as one of his favorite films. For one thing, it allowed him to act rather than just sing. He would recall the reaction to the sneak preview of the film as "excellent," but that when it was released into theaters, "it laid a bomb" because "the public wouldn't accept satirizing them" [television Westerns]. According to Keel, he had lunch with John Wayne who told him, "Kid, it won't work today. You can't kid in Westerns and cowboys." As for the making of the film Keel considered it "great fun." He thought that Dorothy McGuire was an "amazing actress" but a "little strange," primarily because when she came on the set in the morning she was made up and looked beautiful, but when she got done for the day she would "come out looking like another person entirely. Apparently she didn't like all the froufrou and cosmetics. She painted a self-portrait for me, and it's very unusual."

As for Fred, the film gave Keel a chance to get even with him. It turns out that when Keel was younger he had a job parking cars in Hollywood and much of his income came from tips. "Fred MacMurray used to park there," he recalled. "I'd brush off his car and keep it in a special place, but no tips! I called him on that a couple of years later when I starred in *Callaway Goes Thataway* with him." At a get-acquainted party Keel approached Fred and said, "I already know you, Fred. I'm the skinny kid that used to park your car in front of Paramount. I used to keep it all nice and clean, and you never tipped me one dime. Maybe you can make up for it by helping me with my acting now that we're better acquainted." Keel doesn't write what Fred's reaction to all of this was.

Fred had a reputation in the industry of being parsimonious and dozens of stories have emerged through the years, real or imagined, of his frugality. But most of the stories are not told in a mean-spirited way and most of the storytellers seemed amused by Fred's parsimonious reputation. For one thing, most people in the industry realized that Fred did support many worthwhile causes, including cancer research, The City of Hope and The Special Olympics. Fred de Cordova, who directed Fred on *My Three Sons*, tells in his autobiography a famous story, certainly not true, of Cary Grant and Fred MacMurray having dinner together in a restaurant. Grant also had a "cheap" reputation, and according to de Cordova when the check came neither man made a move for it and ended up staying for breakfast because neither of them would pay the dinner bill! But in the same book de Cordova points out that "nobody in the industry was as generous to charitable causes as Fred and June MacMurray." Still, when it came to his personal life it does appear that Fred did like to save a buck or as Mitchell Leisen said, "I'm sure Fred has the first nickel he ever made." Here are some examples of alleged MacMurray frugality:

Director Burt Kennedy tells this story in his autobiography, *Hollywood Trail Boss: Behind the Scenes of the Wild, Wild West:* "Another movie star who was frugal was Fred MacMurray. I remember writer John Lee Mahin used to go duck hunting with Clark Gable and Fred MacMurray up in Bakersfield, California. There was some marshland up there, and this outfit had built some duck blinds. They would drive up there in the middle of the night so they could be in the blinds at dawn. John Lee said that they'd get into the blinds at five o'clock in the morning, when it was still dark and stay there till almost noon. Gable and John always carried a little paper bag with their lunch, fried chicken or whatever, and they had a thermos of coffee. MacMurray would never bring anything. When they'd start to eat, they'd feel a bit guilty, and they'd say, 'Fred, aren't you hungry?' And he'd say, 'Well, no, I'll just eat whatever you leave.' And that's exactly what he did."

Writer-Producer Ed Hartmann, from a 1994 interview for *FilmFax* magazine by Robert Nott: "He was one of the nicest guys I've known and the stingiest! You could write a whole book of anecdotes on what he did to save money. This first year of the show [Hartmann came on as producer of *My Three Sons* in 1963] my wife and I and Fred and his wife June went out to dinner once a week at Chasen's. I always picked up the check and never thought twice about it. The second year of the show he came up to me and said, 'Ed, you and Julia have been taking us out to dinner all the time. June and I want to take you out, but I don't know anything about restaurants so you pick the place and make the reservations.' I said, 'Fine, Fred, just let me know when you want to go and I'll take care of it!' I produced the show for ten years and we never went out to dinner again!"

Hartmann again: "He was one of the richest men in Hollywood, and he lived like a guy who had nothing. He had a big home in Brentwood, and he sealed off half of it and they lived in the other half. They prided themselves on the fact that they made everything they needed, like their own bread."

One final Hartmann story (almost certainly not true): "Bill Demarest, who was a hell of a guy, went over to Fred's trailer, where Fred would go every day at noon with his little brown bag and eat lunch by himself. Well, Bill went over to talk to him at lunch, and afterwards he came over to me and said, 'You'll never believe this. Fred was finishing his lunch, and he reached into his brown bag and brings out a purple egg.' Now this was late August. And Fred held it up and said to Bill, 'Well, that's the last of the Easter eggs!'"

Writer-Director Gene Reynolds (*My Three Sons*): "I was amused by Fred's frugality. Often in the scenes which took place in Steve's bedroom we would show Fred practicing with his putter or something and when Fred found out that we were paying somebody $20 to rent their clubs for the scenes, Fred began bringing his clubs in and we [laughs] ended up paying *him* the $20 per day when we used his golf clubs! And he was one of the wealthiest actors in Hollywood!"

Director Mel Shavelson tells a similar story: "He was supposedly very tight with the dollar. In a scene in one film, he was to come in carrying a set of golf clubs. When he asked what it cost to rent them for the film, and was told, '$65,' Fred went home, got his own clubs, and took the $65 for himself."

My Three Sons production supervisor John Stephens: "I'm going to a prizefight one time with Fred, Bill Frawley and his driver Phil Tanner, Gene Reynolds the director, Sid Sidman, and Carl Nugent. The fight is going to be shown live on a big screen at the Pantages Theater. First we go to Nickodell's, a well-known restaurant at the time, for dinner. At Nickodell's we meet Cissy Wellman, daughter of the famous Hollywood director William Wellman. She's a fun gal, an actress, who would hang around the set and had worked on a few *My Three Sons*. We finish dinner, and the waitress presents the check to Fred, who proceeds to go down each item and tell us what we owe. 'John, you owe $3.75 and thirty-five cents for the tip.' And so on. We aren't surprised and give him the money. I get a little gutsy and say, 'Fred, don't you think you could at least pay for Cissy Wellman?' 'Absolutely not, her father has plenty of money; she can pay her own way like everyone else!' We get to the Pantages Theater parking lot. The parking fee is two dollars. As we pull in, Fred looks at us -there are eight of us — and says, 'That'll be twenty-five cents apiece.' On the way to the theater, Fred gives Carl Nugent a quarter and tells him to buy a fifty-cent candy bar. 'We'll split it.'"

Stephens also tells a story of how he and his wife went to the famous Hollywood eatery Chasen's for their anniversary. They were disappointed that they were given a less than desirable table "almost out the back door" and, recalling that Fred was good personal friends with Dave and Maude Chasen, he calls up Fred to see if he could arrange for them to get a table. Fred told Stephens, "John, don't leave the table." About five minutes later Maude Chasen comes over to the table and makes apologies and takes the Stephens to a better table and also presents them with a bottle of champagne, compliments of Fred and June MacMurray. A few minutes later Maude Chasen comes back to the table and inquires, "Excuse me, but who exactly are you and what do you do?" Stephens tells her he is the production manager on *My Three Sons*. "Well, Dave and I have known Fred MacMurray for years," Maude Chasen tells them, "and he's never bought anything, let alone a bottle of champagne. We figured you had to be very important people. A production manager?"

Don Grady, who played "Robbie" on *My Three Sons:* "His frugality was certainly a part of his reputation … like Jack Benny's … I do remember one Christmas when he bought all of us, the cast and all of the crew, these very special 24-carat Gold cufflinks that were cast in the shape of the *My Three Sons* logo … the 3 pair of legs. We were all amazed at this incredible and very expensive gift of generosity. I later found out that he wanted these made for just a few of the producers and cast. The secretary got her signals crossed and had them made up for everybody. It must have been quite a shock for Fred when he got the bill, but he never showed it."

Beverly Garland, who later played opposite Fred on *My Three Sons:* "I remember once the wardrobe man coming in and saying, 'Fred, I really think that we should buy a dozen new shirts for you.' And Fred replied, 'Buy a dozen new shirts? Why don't you just turn the collars around?'"

Bob Hope once observed that people were always saying that he was the richest man in Hollywood but "I'm a pauper compared to MacMurray." Fred always downplayed his wealth, going so far as to tell Hollywood columnist Sheilah Graham in a 1959 interview, "Sheilah, you keep building this myth that I'm a multimillionaire," but reports following his death indicate that he left an estate worth some $500 million. Fred himself would occasionally kid about his parsimonious reputation. "Being Scottish, I'm probably a little tight, or, as the Scots say, 'Yer cautious with yer money.' I don't think that's the worst thing in the world to be." Lester Martin, Fred's cousin, summed it up this way, "Fred was not frugal — he just didn't throw his money around on useless things."

II

Fred was off the screen from early June of 1951, when he finished filming *Callaway Went Thataway*, until late June of 1952, when he went into *Fair Wind to Java*. This was the longest period of inactivity of Fred's career up to that point. It has been said that the primary reason for his inactivity during this period was because Lily's health again took a downward spiral. In fact, the last two years of her life she would often be bedridden as she battled various ailments, including kidney and heart problems. She had been declining for some time and then would seem to rally again. In April 1948, Louella Parsons had written in her column, "Mrs. Fred MacMurray, who has been sick since Christmas, is so much better she may be able to go to Europe with Fred in May." (Neither went). It is said that during this period of filming inactivity Fred spent much of his time with Lily because her prognosis wasn't good. When Lily was bedridden Fred would often be at her side and he would read to her or they would play cards. When she was feeling better they would take drives so she could get some fresh air. After Lily died, Fred acknowledged that "people felt sorry for me because Lily was sick for so long, but I got so used to caring for her."

Fred wasn't totally inactive during this period. In 1951 he signed a three-year contract paying $100,000 per year to star on a new radio show with Irene Dunne called *Bright Star*, which would be syndicated throughout the country. *Bright Star* was a newspaper comedy-drama with Fred as a crusading reporter and Irene as the more restrained editor of the paper. Their relationship is further complicated by their obvious attraction to one another. The show ended up running only one season, producing 31 episodes, and was easy enough to do, requiring Fred only to show up one day a week for some rehearsing and then transcribing the show for airing at a future date.

Fair Wind to Java might be the nadir of Fred's screen career, though it might be a toss-up between this film and what turned out to be Fred's last film, *The Swarm*. It was filmed at Republic, not one of the major studios in Hollywood, but it did turn out mostly efficiently-made "B" films, and over the years it had also turned out an occasional "A" product, the most recent being the John Ford classic *The Quiet Man,* which had been filmed on location in Ireland and starred John Wayne and Maureen O'Hara along with a superb supporting cast including Victor McLaglen, Ward Bond, Mildred Natwick and Barry Fitzgerald. It turned out to be an enormous hit for Republic and went on to be one of the five nominees for Best Picture of the year for 1952.

Fair Wind to Java, *made at Republic Studios, represented the nadir of Fred's early '50s film career.*

Fair Wind to Java was to be one of Republic's more important pictures for 1953. It was based on a best-selling novel by Garland Roark, who had also written the novel *Wake of the Red Witch,* which Republic had produced as a motion picture in 1948 with John Wayne, and had scored a big success with at the box office. In fact, Herbert Yates, the president of Republic, wanted Wayne for the lead in *Fair Wind to Java* Wayne had been one of Republic's biggest stars, his career blossoming during World War II. (Wayne didn't serve in the war and due to the shortage of leading men, Wayne, like Fred, was constantly busy during the war years in one picture after another.) Wayne was ready to sever his ties with Yates and Republic because Yates had reneged on a pledge to allow Wayne to make *The Alamo,* which Wayne would film, largely at his own expense, seven years later. It turned out that *The Quiet Man* would be Wayne's final film for the studio. With Wayne out of the picture, Yates needed another name actor for the lead role and ended up sending the script to Fred. After a year without working on a film while he stayed close to home and Lily, Fred decided to take the job. He also thought it might be a good change-of-pace role since his last several pictures, all comedies, had done mediocre business at the box office.

The film is set near the end of the nineteenth century in the Dutch East Indies. Fred plays a captain of an American merchant vessel that is looking for a sunken Dutch vessel containing a fortune in diamonds. He is told by a Chinese junk captain that he has "cargo" which will help lead him to the diamonds. The "cargo" turns out to be a woman named Kim-Kim, a dancer from a sultan's palace who was kidnapped and made into a slave by the Chinese. The captain buys her from the Chinese and has to secretly smuggle her aboard his ship, or else he may be charged with white slavery. His first mate discovers her and then blackmails the captain for half the fortune. She leads him to an island where the diamonds are hidden away while being pursued by others. The problem is that the island contains an active volcano which has been threatening throughout the picture to blow at any minute. Will the captain make it in time or will he and Kim-Kim be buried under the ash and lava of the volcano?

While second unit crews filmed some location shots in Hawaii, most of the picture was filmed on soundstages at the Republic backlot, where the studio also constructed a lagoon and a volcano. Some shots were also filmed at Point Dume in Malibu, California. Since it was meant to be one of Republic's prestigious pictures of 1953, a high budget was set, reportedly $2 million, which exceeded the budgets of many "A" films at the major studios in that day. Fred was reportedly paid $150,000 for his services.

And who would Yates get to play Kim-Kim? None other than Yates' wife and the studio's leading actress (if only because Yates insisted she be its leading actress), Vera Ralston. Ralston is certainly attractive enough but her acting ability had never been one of her strong points. A better choice for the Trucolor production might have been Maureen O'Hara. Yates assigned his top contract director, Joseph Kane, to direct the proceedings. Kane was a competent director who would make some minor classics for the studio, most notably *Jubilee Trail* in 1954. In the book Kim-Kim was a fourteen-year-old girl, and Kane wanted her to be cast as such in the film, but Yates wanted an adult love story between Fred and Ralston. He insisted on Ralston. "I was ready to walk out," Kane later recalled. "My agent told me things were slow and to stay put. Maybe I should have quit, but it takes a lot to dislodge a man with family responsibilities when he'd been there as long as I had. I finally agreed to do the picture with Vera and Fred MacMurray in the role of Captain Boll, master of the gerrymander." Kane had other grandiose ideas for the film as well and thought he hit the jackpot when he located a large four-masted sail-ship in Seattle. "It was ideal because, in addition to its sails, it had an auxiliary diesel power plant. My idea was to shoot aboard ship on the way to Hawaii and use one of the islands for the Java location." Yates rejected this idea, according to Kane, because he and Ralston had just gotten married and such a grandiose plan would interfere with their honeymoon plans. As it is, the film was not one of Republic's three-week quickies, but extended from late June through mid-October of 1952, so half of a sailing ship was constructed on a Republic soundstage and was mounted on rockers and surrounded by a huge painted backdrop showing the sea and clouds.

Claude Jarman, Jr., who captured the hearts of moviegoers in 1946 as Jody in *The Yearling*, was cast as Chess, one of the ship's crew members in *Fair Wind to Java*. The actor was 17 when he made the film and recalls it as, "another one of Herb Yates' attempts to make Vera Ralston, who was his lover and later his wife into a star." By this time, Jarman calculated that he had made eleven films and *Fair Wind* is the one he's "least proud of" because of its phony soundstage look and ridiculous storyline. But he still had a good time making it because he got to work with people like Fred and Victor McLaglen, "we had good camaraderie on the set. I loved working with Vic McLaglen; I had done *Rio Grande* with him a couple of years before. It's just the end result that was so disappointing." Jarman recalls Fred as "very affable, never temperamental. Very professional. I was taken by his sense of professionalism and he was a very down to earth guy. I also remember him being a big guy. I was a big kid for my age, but most people in Hollywood weren't all that tall, so I was struck by how tall he was." Jarman recalls a scene in the film where Fred was surrounded by several exotic dancers and he and Vera Ralston were supposed to enact a "passionate" love scene. When the scene was completed, Fred turned to a bunch of the guys on the set and said, "I have to be nuts to be in this film." Jarman added, "He pretty much summed up how most of us felt."

Film publicist Sid Bloomberg recalls *Fair Wind to Java* as the only time he ever saw Fred blow up at one of his leading ladies on a film set. "I saw Fred blow up only once. The leading lady was Vera Ralston, the mistress and then wife of the studio head, and she was basically an ice skater and not an actress. Vera kept blowing scene after scene and Fred wasn't used to it. He was used to working with professionals like Colbert and Goddard, and Ralston was not in their league and he almost walked. I couldn't blame him." When asked why he was doing swashbuckling types of films usually associated with the likes of Errol Flynn and Alan Ladd, Fred said, "I might as well ... No reason why those guys should keep adventure pictures to themselves. Nobody seems to be making comedies anymore. So adventure is the thing for me now." Unfortunately, the film didn't recoup the money which Republic invested in it.

Following the completion of *Fair Wind to Java* in October 1952 Fred was off a Hollywood soundstage again for several more months as Lily's health further deteriorated and again she was confined to her bed. In April 1953 he did accept a role opposite Barbara Stanwyck in a Western filmed in 3-D, *The Moonlighter.* It would be a quick shoot, with production lasting just over a month and filmed only miles from his home at the Motion Picture

Fred reunited with Barbara Stanwyck in the 1953 Western The Moonlighter.

Center Studio in Hollywood. Some outdoor scenes were shot at the Gene Autry Ranch in New Hall, California as well as the Semi Valley. A climactic waterfall scene was shot at Peppermist Falls in the High Sierras. Fred and Stanwyck are their usual competent selves, but a boring script, along with lackluster direction by Hollywood workhorse Roy Rowland, lets the two stars down. The film didn't generate much business at the box office perhaps because the movie-going public didn't understand the meaning of the title. *The Moonlighter* refers to cattle rustlers who apply their trade at night by the light of the moon. The *New York Times* was scathing in its review. "Exactly why the protagonists of *Double Indemnity* should have elected to participate in such cowtown petty larceny is a mystery." There is one good scene early in the film where Fred attends a funeral, supposedly his own, but in actuality a mob had lynched the wrong man. Fred delivers a eulogy for the dead man and warns those at the funeral that the ghost of the dead man would seek revenge on the lynchers. In some ways this scene predates such Clint Eastwood Westerns such as *Hang 'em High* and *Pale Rider*, where a ghostly "hero" returns to exact revenge. Unfortunately, what follows in *The Moonlighter* isn't up to that standard.

Due to her precarious health Lily had little she could do except lie in bed and read. She still took an active interest in Fred's career and at some point she read a script that had been sent for Fred's consideration. It was based on the best-selling Herman Wouk novel *The Caine Mutiny*. Producer Stanley Kramer wanted Fred for the part of Lt. Tom Keefer, a cynical aspiring novelist and psychologist. Keefer makes a diagnosis of the captain of the *U.S.S. Caine* as mentally unstable and fully supports the actions of fellow officer Lt. Steve Maryk to commit an act of mutiny and remove the captain from command of the ship when the captain can't function during a typhoon at sea. When called upon to testify on behalf of Maryk's defense, the cowardly Keefer shifts all blame to Maryk to save his own ass. Lily, who had read and liked the novel, thought the script was superb and it offered Fred the kind of change-of-pace role which might rejuvenate his film career. Given the popularity of the novel and a stage play based on it (*The Caine Mutiny Court-Martial*), the prospect that the film would be a huge success was very strong indeed.

Lily read the script while Fred was up north dealing with a problem at his Sonora ranch. Fred would later recollect that she telephoned him at the ranch and told him that she had read *The Caine Mutiny* script and that she wanted him to accept the role of Lt. Keefer. "I didn't even read the script," Fred said. "I came home and signed to do the picture even though Keefer, as you know, was-well, shall we say, a stinker? But he does motivate the whole story." It was on Lily's recommendation that Fred signed on to play Keefer, joining a cast which included Humphrey Bogart as Queeg, Van Johnson as Maryk, Jose Ferrer as Maryk's defense attorney Lt. Barney Greenwald and young Robert Francis as Ensign Willie Keith. Edward Dmytryk was selected by producer Stanley Kramer to direct.

Unfortunately, Lily would not live long enough to see the realization of one of Fred's finest screen performances. In early June 1953 Lily was admitted to St. John's Hospital in Santa Monica, California following a heart seizure. Her kidney problems further complicated her recovery, and according to her physician, Dr. Robert J. Kositchek, Lily was in grave condition. Fred was at her side all through the final days and was often observed holding Lily's hand. On June 20, while in the hospital, Lily and Fred celebrated their 17th wedding anniversary. She died two days later with Fred at her side. Lily was only 45. Lester Martin, Fred's cousin, maintains that it was Lillian's Bulimia which caused the serious side effects which affected her kidneys and heart and kept her in poor health for much of her marriage to Fred, and, in particular, the last two years of Lily's life. Lily died on a Monday, June 22, and on Wednesday, a private funeral service was held at the Church of the Recessional at Forest Lawn. Nearly every obituary observed that the MacMurray marriage had long been regarded as "one of the film colony's happiest." Fred later maintained that "everybody had the wrong idea about Lily's illness, she was not sick all the time, and although we could not make trips together, we had a wonderful life." He also said that his marriage was "so perfect" and that in her last months Lily had been "so brave that I can't get over my loneliness now." The next several months were difficult for Fred. "Stricken with grief, Fred occupied his mind with the thing best known to him - movie acting," writer James Robert Parish later wrote. "He kept himself busy with work, but hibernated at home, after hours, with his mother, and his two children." Lester Martin recalled of Fred during this period after Lily's passing, "I knew he was sad, but he didn't want to discuss it - he wasn't the type of person who was open with his emotions, and I didn't want to pry."

III

Independent producer Stanley Kramer had several critically acclaimed films to his credit (*Champion, Home of the Brave, The Men, High Noon*) when he purchased the film rights to Wouk's Pulitzer-prize winning novel in August 1951 for somewhere between $60-70,000. He initially engaged Wouk to write the screenplay, but his contribution was considered "a disaster" according to Edward Dmytryk. Stanley Roberts then rewrote the script, which came in longer than two hours. Columbia Pictures chief Harry Cohn insisted that the film be no more than two hours and demanded cuts, which led to Roberts quitting rather than make the cuts the front office mandated. Kramer then assigned to the project writer Michael Blankfort, who then proceeded to trim almost fifty pages from the screenplay in accord with Cohn's directive. Cohn imposed other tough terms on Kramer's production. He did so because several of the past films that Kramer had released through Columbia had not met box office expectations. Cohn insisted that Kramer maintain a $2 million budget and 54-day shooting schedule, both difficult tasks given the scope of the novel. *The Caine Mutiny* was the last film Kramer made under his existing contract with Columbia and he later wrote, "What I liked best about *The Caine Mutiny* was that was the last picture I had to make for Harry Cohn."

Another condition of Cohn's, to ensure box office success, was to employ an all-star cast. Of Bogart, Kramer later wrote, "I've never seen anybody who did his job more carefully. For example, he didn't hesitate to stop the whole process if he didn't have the motivation for a scene clearly in his mind, several times holding up shooting. In many cases his questions and doubts helped improve the script and the film in general--he was a very painstaking actor." Kramer described the other lead actors around Bogart as "a calm bunch by comparison." Kramer maintained that Van Johnson was just happy to have a part in a serious film after he had "suffered through so many flimsy roles." Jose Ferrer, "being from the theater was always serious about his work." Perhaps forgetting that he had just lost his beloved wife of 17 years, Kramer wrote, "Fred MacMurray was a spectator in the scene of life, both in his work and in personal relations. He seemed strangely to have retired within himself." He also praised Dmytryk's direction, especially in

The Caine Mutiny is one of the high points of '50s cinema and contains one of Fred's best screen performances.

the way he handled such a high-powered cast. "There were several marvelous performances in that picture, and he, as the director, deserves a lot of credit for that, even though he was working with highly skilled actors. Sometimes great actors work very badly together, either because of ego problems or poor direction. When you put Bogart, MacMurray, Ferrer, and Van Johnson in the same picture, you have an interesting mix of personalities. They might not have blended, but under Dmytryk's direction they did, and I didn't hear any of them complain about him." Still, according to authors A.M. Sperber and Eric Lax, "The cast was not a chummy one ... Fred MacMurray, whose wife had just died, also kept to himself. Kramer said he gave him the role to help him get through his mourning. [Wrong, Fred had the part before Lily died]. His part of Lt. Tom Keefer was very much against type: Keefer is the villain of the piece and MacMurray normally played all-Americans."

The cast did some location shooting in Hawaii. One of the first scenes shot was one involving Johnson, Fred and Robert Francis approaching and boarding the aircraft carrier. The actors had only one day to shoot the scene and Dmytryk was under the gun to get the scene shot in a timely manner because Kramer was being similarly pressured by Cohn. They had 2,000 real-life sailors as extras and they were shipping out the next day. All of these boisterous extras caused a problem for Fred, according to Dmytryk, "We got down to the business of shooting our dialogue scenes outside the bridge. Two thousand noisy sailors were watching, the light was getting yellow and MacMurray was getting nervous and lousing up his lines. He stopped short and turned to me with a request. Since the background of the scene was a mere few square feet of bulkhead, which could be duplicated at the studio for a few hundred dollars, wouldn't it be possible, he asked, to skip the scene and do it back on the lot? It was a reasonable request. I turned to relay it to Kramer, who was sitting some distance behind me, but he had heard Fred. He suddenly jumped up and shouted, 'No!' There could be no waiting - it was now or never! Somewhat abashed, we went on with the scene and got it in the can--not good, but serviceable--with just enough time left to get off the ship before it sailed for Japan."

Fred would later recall his most "unforgettable scene" in the film as the one at the end of the picture in which Jose Ferrer's attorney Greenwald confronts Keefer for his cowardice while testifying before the commission. The climax of the confrontation is when a drunken Greenwald violently tosses a glass of champagne into Fred's face. Initially, Fred felt that piece of business seemed "a little extreme," but then realized his apprehensions about doing the scene "were based on the fact that I wasn't used to being treated like a villain after playing so many nice guys." While this scene was at the end of the picture, it was one of the first to be filmed at the studio after returning from Hawaii. According to Sperber and Lax, "the actors rehearsed the scene several times." On the first take Ferrer decided to lighten the mood on the set. As the camera was filming the door opens and into the scene enters Ferrer "on his knees, 'Anybody want to buy a painting?'" he asked, breaking the cast and crew up.

Fred was pleased by his work in *The Caine Mutiny*, as were most critics. *The New York Times* called his performance "excellent." There was also some talk around town that Fred would be nominated for a Best Supporting Actor nomination for his work, but Fred typically downplayed such talk. "Be that as it may," Fred said, "I'm keeping my eyes open for the first good comedy role that comes around." In the end the only *Caine* actors nominated were Bogart and the veteran Tom Tully, who was the experienced captain that Queeg replaces on the *U.S.S. Caine*. Not all were impressed with Fred's work, however, according to John Huston, Bogart was "rather well satisfied with [his] performance as Queeg, but didn't think too highly of Van Johnson and MacMurray." As good as Bogart is in the film, his crack-up scene during the hearing seems a little over baked, especially when he pulls out the marbles, that scene has been parodied many times since. Fred, as always, underplays and is effective in doing so, and more than holds his own with the rest of the cast.

Fred's next picture was also for Columbia and he was brought in it to bolster the new leading lady that Harry Cohn was marketing in her starring debut. The actress was Kim Novak, a beautiful blonde just a month shy of her twenty-first birthday when production began. She was not a natural screen actress, but for this picture and several that followed, her ethereal beauty drove men to detraction or destruction whether it is James Stewart, who becomes obsessed by her in the classic Hitchcock film *Vertigo*, or Fred, a cop who she easily seduces, in *Pushover*.

Fred is back in *Double Indemnity* mode once again. A pillar of the community, a career cop who goes bad over a dame. And not just any dame. Fred's a cop in his 40s and Novak, the *femme fatale*, more than twenty years younger. She needs a sucker, a "pushover," and, as always when Fred plays a heavy, he is confident on the outside but a marshmallow on the inside, easily manipulated by a woman he thinks he is one up on, but in actuality she is always one step ahead of him. Novak plays the girlfriend of a bank robber who got away with over $200,000 in cash and in the process kills a man. The plan is for Fred, undercover, to befriend Novak and gain her confidence so that she will spill the beans on the boyfriend and help lead the cops to him as well as get the money back. Things go too far and Fred ends up having an affair with the Novak character. Then she finds out he is a cop, and correctly assumes that he was just using her, so she decides to use him. She tells him they can run away together and share the money. At first Fred is horrified and turns her down, but soon changes his mind. He makes a plan to get the money and run away with her. A fellow detective, near retirement, gets wise of Fred's plan and Fred ends up killing him, and trying to make it appear that he committed suicide. (Fred's character also kills the bank robber/killer.) Many things don't add up and that's when Fred begins sweating and trying to cover his tracks. Just like in *Double Indemnity* Fred's character in this film is wounded by a gun shot and he admits his guilt and remorse over being played a chump by a woman.

The working title of the film was *The Killer Wore a Badge*, which sounded too pulp novel-like, so it was changed to *Pushover*. The film was budgeted at $400,000 (including $75,000 for Fred's salary). The film was to be marketed as the second half of a double bill and, according to the producer, Jules Schermer, "this was all *Pushover* was ever intended to be." For the film's leading lady, according to Novak's biographer, "the producer knew he needed somebody who could hold her own against the natural chemistry of MacMurray," and auditioned ten different women, some were blondes, some were brunettes and a couple were even redheads. They thought they had found the right girl ("she read the lines with a lustiness that betrayed her prior stage experience") but when she was filmed the camera couldn't capture that charisma and so she was reluctantly discarded. Harry Cohn was incredulous that when testing ten different girls they still couldn't come up with the right one. It was then that the studio's chief of production held up a photograph of Kim Novak and suggested that she be tested. Cohn was not convinced; he knew she was a new contract player at the studio and didn't think that she would be ready for months. Head of production Jerry Wald believed otherwise. "Look, Harry, you will never make a Bette Davis or a Joan Crawford out of her ... She's going to get by on her sultry voice and her incredible face and body. Let's try her." Cohn thought about it and agreed to test her.

According to Cohn's biographer, *Pushover* "was not an Academy Award picture, but it offered Kim a showy role and a chance to play opposite a polished performer, Fred MacMurray." Columbia also wanted to make sure that Novak was handled with care because with her looks they believed that she could potentially be another Marilyn Monroe. Cohn insisted that the right director be chosen (one "sensitive to her inexperience") and had several directors direct a scene with Fred and Novak (as tests) until they found the right one to direct the picture. They finally decided on Richard Quine, a 33-year-old former actor, whose first big film this would be. He would shoot scenes over and over with Novak until he got what he wanted and she soon learned to trust him and together they went on to make three more films together, as well as develop a strong personal relationship. As for Fred, he and Novak got along fine, and, understanding all too well what it is to be wet behind your ears and to be thrown into a major motion picture, he didn't mind the attention that she got or the number of times that their scenes together had to be re-shot until she got it the way Quine wanted it.

IV

After Lily's death, Fred told a reporter he wasn't sure he would ever marry again. "I have my two children, and they require a lot of attention." By the holidays of 1953 the loneliness he felt over the loss of Lily was as acute as ever. John Wayne was having a "Gay Nineties" party a few days before Christmas and invited Fred to come. Fred was hesitant to go and was ready to decline Wayne's offer, but his friend and business manger Bo Roos and his wife urged him to come with them. Fred finally agreed to come, but since he didn't have a date he would bring along his saxophone and see if he could sit in with the band. It would be one way to get through the night.

Singer and dancer June Haver was also invited to the party and was also hesitant about attending. She had recently returned to Hollywood after nearly a year at a Catholic convent. Haver, the "pocket Grable" at Fox, was the daughter of a strong-willed stage mother whose own hopes for a show business career never panned out. Haver was "as sweet a human being as I met, a delightful woman," according to Darryl Hickman, who knew Haver better than he had Fred. Hickman believes that he first met Haver through his mother who knew Haver's mother, both being devout Catholics who became friendly doing church work together. Actress Sybil Jason recalls Haver as being "cute as a button and very warm and hospitable." On the other hand, Jason says that June's mother was a "darker version" of the daughter.

The past several years Haver's personal life had been an emotional shambles. She had a short-lived marriage with musician Jimmy Zito and when that marriage fizzled out she got back together with a former boyfriend, dentist John Duzik. Their relationship prospered so well that they eventually got engaged. Duzik was then hospitalized for what was considered a minor operation when complications set in and he died. The grieving Haver, a devout Catholic, made a pilgrimage to Rome and Jerusalem in the aftermath of Duzik's death as a way of dealing with the tragedy. She even managed an audience with Pope Pius XII. She returned to Hollywood still feeling numb and hoping for something more in her life and wondering if she was meant to be in a loving marriage. She surprised Hollywood when in 1953 she gave up a $3,500-per-week contract with Twentieth Century-Fox and became a novice nun at the Sisters of Charity Convent in Xavier, Kansas. Haver spent eight months at the convent before she realized that she was unable to adjust to life as a novitiate. "I think I made the right decision to go into the convent and try it out," she said many years later, "and I made the right decision to leave." Darryl Hickman sympathized with this. When he was twenty, he briefly entered into a male convent and, if it isn't a true calling, the life could be "very difficult." When she called up John Wayne to decline his invitation, he told her to get on with life again, but she wasn't totally convinced until her friends Betty Lynn and Dick Clayton talked her into coming with them.

At the party June would recall being asked to dance by British film actor Laurence Harvey, who "had just come over from Britain, very tall, very handsome." As she and Harvey were dancing around the bandstand, she noticed Fred was up on it playing his saxophone. "I'd known Fred a little ... and I knew this was unusual for him to perform." Even though she was dancing with the recently arrived and handsome Harvey her thoughts were on Fred. "I tried, every time we passed by the band, to make him laugh — something no one can do playing the sax." When dinner was announced a mutual friend, Harold Rose, came over and told June that "there was a nice fellow sitting without a date and since I was without a date, could he come over and join me? Pretty soon Fred came over carrying his steak and his beer."

June would later state that "I think I knew right away" that she could fall in love with Fred. After all, this was the same man she worked with a decade earlier who impressed her as the kind of man she would want to marry. "I can't put it into words," June recalled, "but when you love someone, you love him. It's not the color of his eyes or anything like that. It's just the man, Fred. He was kind of a challenge. I wanted to know what he was really like."

They spent the rest of the time at the party locked in conversation together, pretty much ignoring everybody else. He took her home that night, but always a gentleman he didn't stay for the night. But the next day, Sunday, he came by June's apartment with his tools and fixed the plumbing in her bathroom where the pipes had been leaking. June had casually mentioned the night before her plumbing problem. "The next thing you knew," June said, "there he was, lying on his back on the bathroom floor, working on those pipes."

On New Year's Eve Fred took June to a party at the home of producer Harriet Parsons, the daughter of Hollywood columnist Louella Parsons. June recalled that at Midnight, "everybody kissed, so did we, and Harriet said, 'That's the couple to watch.'"

Fred was playing it close to the vest by having some casual dates with Ann Sothern and Eleanor Parker. By late January 1954, while Fred was filming *Pushover* with Kim Novak, Sheilah Graham was asking Fred in her syndicated column about rumors linking him to Sothern, Parker and June. "Ann is an old friend of Lillian's," Fred told Graham, "and people call me and ask to call for different girls and bring them to parties. I brought Ann to the Bill Goetz party and to Jimmy Stewart's. I saw Eleanor Parker in New York before she left for Egypt and we went out a couple of times. As for June Haver, she's a wonderful girl. But I'm not getting married to anyone." Fred added that this was the first time in his life he had ever had this kind of publicity. "When I came to Hollywood in 1934, I was engaged to Lillian," Fred said. "So there were never any romantic items with anyone else. We married in 1936. But now for the first time in my life I'm an extra man." Graham ended her column by writing,"… when he does decide to marry again, you can envy the girl. He has millions, he's attractive, considerate and about the best husband this town ever had."

Despite this, Fred was now exclusively being seen on the town with June. By March 1954 the romance had become serious enough that Fred invited her to join him and some twenty-five other entertainment figures for a good-will tour to South America. According to one account of the trip, "They spent three hectic weeks in Rio de Janeiro and Buenos Aires. They got to know each other better, to see each other under a very special set of circumstances. And they liked what they saw. Despite all the South American attractions, they had eyes only for each other."

When June and Fred, along with the Errol Flynns, got off the plane in Panama rumors of an elopement became widespread. One of the stars on the good-will tour was Joan Fontaine, who was quoted as telling airline personnel that Fred and June had gotten off in Panama because they were eloping. Fontaine later denied that she had ever said such a thing stating, "We explained that June and Fred had gotten off in Panama that morning. So had Errol and Pat Flynn. The Flynns have a home in Jamaica. I think Errol keeps his yacht there. Someone said that the Flynns had taken a plane for Kingston, Jamaica. Somehow, June and Fred were mistaken for Errol and Pat. The Miami newspapers were phoned, and the story went out that they were eloping to Jamaica." June must not have heard Fontaine's story or thought that she was just covering her tracks when she later told the press, "I don't know what could have made Joan say such a thing. Fred and I have just been sort of drifting along. The subject of marriage might come up, but I don't think Fred would consider marrying so soon after his wife's death." This was March 1954, only nine months after Lily's death.

While they were in Panama and staying at the El Panama Hotel, a reporter did get a chance to ask Fred if he and June were planning to marry and Fred's response was not so coy: "It could happen." But he emphasized it wasn't going to happen then nor would it happen in Panama. When Fred and June arrived back in Los Angeles his children were waiting at the airport as was the Hollywood press and he tore into them explaining that the false rumors "embarrassed everyone concerned including my two children." Fred went on to say that he told his kids, "I wouldn't run off and get married without taking you into my confidence." When he said this, his daughter Susie turned to her younger brother, "See, I told you dad wouldn't do anything so silly." Bo Roos told the press that the erroneous story about an elopement "is likely to slow things up because Fred and June are self-conscious now ... they were just beginning to enjoy themselves again when this elopement report broke." But something very serious did happen on this trip. An employee at the El Panama Hotel told the *New York Daily News*, "When they danced, or just sat in the patio and talked, they seemed comfortable, like they belonged together." Also, tellingly, when June returned to Hollywood she began efforts to receive a Papal Dispensation annulling her marriage to Jimmy Zito.

Meanwhile, Fred began work on a new film, *Woman's World*, produced by Twentieth Century-Fox. The film, directed by the cultured Hungarian director Jean Negulesco, boasted an all-star cast, including Clifton Webb, June Allyson, Lauren Bacall, Van Heflin, Arlene Dahl and Cornel Wilde. The screenplay was written by Claude Binyon, who was originally going to direct until studio head Darryl Zanuck decided that the project needed a more polished touch and brought in Negulesco. Webb, who has most of the film's best lines, plays a corporate boss who has to choose a new successor. The candidates are played by Fred, Heflin and Wilde. Webb decides that the man he will choose will be the one with the stablest marriage because in big business the impression the wife makes is almost as important as the impression of the man himself, so he invites the candidates and their wives to his country home for a weekend in which he can evaluate the wives and the states of their marriages.

Fred plays Sid with Lauren Bacall cast as his wife Liz. According to notes in the Claude Binyon papers of a meeting between Binyon and Zanuck, Bacall was always the front runner for this part. (In contrast, the role that Webb ultimately got was a toss up between him and William Powell.)

Fred and Van Heflin in a scene from Woman's World, *one of Fred's best films of the '50s.*

Zanuck's general comments, as recorded from that meeting, indicate that he wanted a tighter script with more suspense as to which man gets the job. In the original script draft Sid seems to disqualify himself early on with the audience's sympathies because he was too much of a "yes-man" to Webb, so Zanuck suggested to Binyon that "Sid should not be a guy who agrees with the boss in every instance in an effort to cinch the job. He should be brilliant, and Gifford [the Webb character's name] should be impressed by him. There should be several times when it seems certain that Sid will get the job, and the audience should root for him not to get it, for it will mean the end of his marriage. Sid should be wildly ambitious, but he should not be petty." With the revisions making the character of Sid less unsympathetic, it was decided that Fred was capable of bringing out the unsavory aspects of Sid, while still making him attractive enough for a woman like Bacall to love as well as to retain audience sympathy. Zanuck also suggested that there should be a scene where Sid, seemingly the most ambitious of the three men contending for the job, should say, "To hell with it! I'm going to tell Gifford I don't want the job!" in an effort to save his marriage.

Of the three couples, the dynamic between Fred and Bacall is the most interesting. He has long been married to his work and she has borne the brunt of it for years, and is planning on leaving him, but understands how

Fred and Lauren Bacall play a tenuously married couple in 1954's Woman's World.

important the job is to him, so she decides to go with him for the weekend and put on a happy domestic face. She still loves him, but she can't stay married to him especially if he assumes even more responsibility at work. He knows that by actively campaigning for and getting the job it will surely mean the end of their marriage. In the end Sid rediscovers his love for Liz and determines to change his ways even if it means losing the promotion. It is a complex, interesting and three-dimensional characterization and Fred pulls it off well. *Woman's World* gives Fred a good opportunity and he takes advantage of it and it is one of his best films of the '50s.

The set of *Woman's World* was a happy one. A big part of it was because love was in the air. Fred and June were falling in love at the same time Arlene Dahl was being romanced by Fernando Lamas, who she would soon marry. Miss Dahl later recalled with a laugh that "June and I would get together and chat about our romances with Fred and Fernando." The set was also happy because of the director Jean Negulesco, who the cast and crew adored. Miss Dahl recalls Negulesco as "an authentic flirtatious Hungarian" who would "flirt with each of us [Dahl, Bacall and Allyson] and take us out to lunch, separately." Miss Dahl quickly adds that while he would flirt it never went beyond that stage because Negulesco was married to "a top model, Dusty, who he adored." Of the film itself Miss Dahl believes it "holds up well." Dahl believes that June helped bring Fred "out of his shell." She recalls the courting couple as being "very affectionate and sweet to one another, just very loving." June had a "wonderful sense of humor," according to Dahl, as did Fred, but Fred's humor was "drier, not everybody understood it." Dahl also observed that Fred, basically a shy man, would blush, especially in the presence of women. "I would see the red from his neck rise to his face!"

There was a scene in *Woman's World* where everybody sits down to a banquet dinner and the scene was an intricate one because of all the different angles and close ups which needed to be shot. The set was extremely hot and to make the point of just how hot it was Fred brought a thermometer and placed it on the table. The temperature registered 115 degrees. It was a good, if uncomfortable picture to make.

June was clearly smitten with Fred. She described him as "unassuming, has a wry sense of humor, and lives like he would if he were still back in Beaver Dam, Wisconsin. This is a man who is happy in his work and could be just as happy if he weren't an actor at all. He is absolutely egoless and charming in that he is just a man who could be living anywhere doing anything ... he's himself, Fred MacMurray, and I was in love with him."

June knew too that he was in love with her, but he wasn't the type of man to go around announcing his feelings to the press or even to her. When asked about June, Fred would say, "All I'm going to say is that June is a fine girl. I consider it a privilege to have her as a friend." When pressed for more he would just grin and add, "Okay, she's a good friend." Yet she realized how deeply his feelings were for her when he began to introduce her to his two children. Susan was fourteen by this time and Robert was ten. She began to get to know the kids and spend time with them. They would go on picnics together and she would cook dinner for all of them. June would later say, "It was not always easy with a ready made family, especially at their ages, but I was lucky. I loved Robbie and Susie and they knew it."

By May 1954 June felt it was time to ask reticent Fred the big question, "When are we going to get married?" She would later recall that Fred just grinned and said, "Oh, we are? Well, I guess I'd better get you a ring." She suggested "something simple-a little pearl would be fine, that's my birthstone."

But Fred didn't want just a simple ring for June, he wanted her to have a diamond and even had one in mind, "...Red Skelton's good luck ring, the one he wore on his pinky." It turned out that Fred's business manager also handled Red, so he approached Red about the diamond, probably just to find out where he had gotten it so he could have an exact duplicate made. When Red heard that Fred admired his diamond pinky ring so much that he wanted to have a copy made for June, he told Boo Roos that he would willingly let Fred have the diamond. Fred wouldn't hear of it and arranged to buy it and then have the diamond made into a ring.

Fred, true to form, chose a distinctly unromantic way to give the ring to June, probably as a way of throwing her off. One of his kids was sick and Fred and June went to a local drugstore to fill a prescription. When they arrived back at Fred's house and just as Fred and June were getting out of the car Fred said to June, "Say, there's something for you in the pocket of my suede coat." June found her "lovely" engagement ring. June later said, "It's a great compliment to a woman when a man who has been happily married remarries, and I had a man who knew what marriage was about and who is a strong man."

Unfortunately, the Catholic Church denied June's annulment, which led June to make what she called "a great decision — one of the greatest of my life." June decided to renounce her faith so she could marry Fred. The door wasn't totally closed on the chance that her marriage to Zito could, one day, be annulled. But she was told that "it could take years" before a final judgment was made and June and Fred were not willing to put off their marriage for that long. Fred and June decided they would marry the first week of August. Fred wanted to wait for two reasons. He wanted to finish *Women's World* and, most importantly, he wanted to wait at least a year after Lily's death before he remarried.

However, Fred and June sprang a little surprise which caught friends and the press off-guard. They held their civil ceremony in Ojai, California on June 28, a week earlier than they had announced. The ceremony took place at the Ojai Valley Inn, in the room of Dr. and Mrs. Don Burger, the owners of the hotel. According to press reports, Fred slipped a circle of diamonds on June's finger while June gave Fred a plain gold band. A small group of friends and family had been invited. Fred was 45 and June was 27. Darryl Hickman was somewhat surprised that Fred and June ever got married because on the surface they seemed mismatched. June was outgoing while Fred could be a hermit. But, as it would turn out, they had one of Hollywood's most happy and enduring marriages. Hickman said that Hollywood is a town where "bad news travels fast" and he never heard anything bad about June or Fred or their marriage.

As for the newlyweds, they took off for Jackson Hole, Wyoming, where Fred was to begin location shooting for a new movie, *The Far Horizons,* a biography of the Lewis and Clark expedition which also starred Charlton Heston. Fred gave his "cheap" image a boost when he announced that they were honeymooning on "company time." But they had a lovely time. When Fred wasn't working, they went fishing and sightseeing and spent their nights in a beautiful lodge. June was the prefect complement to Fred, where he was shy and withdrawn she was an extravert and outgoing. Their mutual friend actress Joan Leslie would say that June was a "shiny bright light, so tiny and beautiful, and so very spiritual." Fred's cousin, Lester Martin, contrasted June with Fred's first wife. "Where Lillian was reserved and straight forward, very princess like, June was just the reverse, but they were both wonderful ladies and Fred was devoted to them both — and they to him. He often commented to me on how lucky he was to be blessed with two happy marriages."

CHAPTER SEVEN

Career Resurrection

1955-1959

I

Following their wedding the newlyweds traveled to Moran, Wyoming, where Fred began location work on his new motion picture, *The Far Horizons*, a dramatization of the Lewis and Clark expedition. Fred was cast as Lewis with the fast-rising Charlton Heston cast as Clark. Fred and June were sharing their honeymoon with about 150 members of the movie company. It isn't that they were exactly roughing it in the wilds since they were spending their nights at a beautiful lodge, and on Fred's off days they took trips into nearby Yellowstone National Park where they would spend hours fishing and taking in the majestic scenery. On one such day off some members of the crew, knowing that Fred and June were spending the day fishing, followed them and while they were only a few hundred yards away they quietly and efficiently decorated Fred's rented gray Cadillac with signs written in lipstick. Among the signs: "Kiss Me, Cutey" and "OO, la, la," while on the windshield somebody wrote "June is Busting Out All Over," and on the trunk was "The End of a Perfect Day." The newlyweds had a good laugh, and then drove to a nearby service station where they promptly washed it clean.

Just before they got married Fred bought a new home for himself, June and the kids. He couldn't bear to live in the same house that he and Lily had shared. Fred needed to make a clean break with the past. He bought a ten-room colonial mansion in Brentwood from singer Nelson Eddy. Fred found that there were certain places and things he couldn't do or see because they reminded him of Lily. "The thing I like best about June," Fred said at the time, "is her understanding. I talk about Lil. After all, that's natural. When June and I go some place I mention having been there with Lil, and June understands. She's a wonderful girl." His new marriage also seemed to make Fred more open and accessible as well. One reporter wrote that Fred, "once a moody and sometimes unsociable actor, has acquired a friendlier personality" since his romance and marriage to June.

Shortly after Fred and June married, Lily's will was made public. She left an estate of over one-million dollars, with Fred as the chief beneficiary. The Department of Internal Revenue also released the customary lien on a portion of the couple's real estate property, so that Fred could sell the home that he and Lily had shared together. Fred made plans to sell the property to the Novitiate of the Daughters of Mary and Joseph for $105,000 and then borrow $25,000 on the property. The will, which Lily had signed in 1945, left Fred all her personal effects and stated that his share of community property should go directly to him. After leaving some modest legacies to her sisters and brothers, the remainder was put in trust, with the provision that the income be paid to MacMurray during his lifetime and then the principal be divided between their children upon his death.

II

The Caine Mutiny was still packing movie houses in 1955 and was one of the most popular films of 1954-1955. In March it was selected as the best picture of 1954 by *Film Daily* in its 32nd annual "ten best pictures" poll. (*The Caine Mutiny* led the list, followed by *On the Waterfront, Rear Window, The Country Girl, The High and the Mighty, Seven Brides for Seven Brothers, Sabrina, Executive Suite, The Glenn Miller Story* and *Three Coins in a Fountain.*) There had been talk by several Hollywood columnists that Fred was a "shoo-in" for a Best Supporting Actor Oscar nomination for his performance in *The Caine Mutiny*, but when the Oscar nominations were made public early in 1955 Fred was once again ignored. As with *Double Indemnity,* Fred didn't have many good opportunities to follow up his acclaimed performance in *The Caine Mutiny* and was once again finding himself in mostly mundane films.

Mundane is a good description of the picture he made following *The Far Horizons,* a remake of *The Rains Came* called *The Rains of Ranchipur.* Fred is the third lead after top-billed Lana Turner and Richard Burton. Fred is (mis)cast as an alcoholic who once loved the Turner character. Film historian James Robert Parish later wrote of this film, "The Merle Miller script is wordy and heavy, and the story, as delineated on the CinemaScope color screen, sagged and dated itself badly." The atmosphere on the set between Turner and Burton was frosty since Turner, apparently, was one of the few leading ladies that Burton had worked with who could resist his amorous charms. As for Fred, he went his own way, and the only problem he encountered was when the script required him to pick up and carry Lana Turner. "I've been carrying Lana Turner all day and it's no joke," Fred told writer Joe Hyams. "Actually the carrying isn't so bad; it's the putting down that's tough. I'm tired and my back aches ... When I bent down to get her for the first time I heard a crack and out went my back. From then I was relying upon memories of the day when I was younger and stronger."

Just before making this film, Fred had completed a quick three-week shoot on his first Western since *The Moonlighters*. The film was *At Gunpoint*, filmed for Allied Artists on a low budget. Fred was starting a new phase of his career in Western films, not his favorite genre, but six of the next eight pictures he made would be so-called "horse operas." Like Randolph Scott, Joel McCrea and other aging leading men, Fred was finding Western roles

Fred walking through The Rains of Ranchipur.

to be a new lease on his movie life. The six Westerns he made from the mid- to late fifties varied in quality, but they did have one thing in common; they were cheaply and efficiently made. Westerns were at their peak during these years not only at the movies but on the television screens as well.

By the late fifties Western series such as *Gunsmoke, Bonanza, Have Gun - Will Travel, Wagon Train* and *Bat Masterson* dominated the airwaves. The films that Fred made were not of the quality of the John Wayne-John Ford, James Stewart-Anthony Mann or Randolph Scott-Budd Boetticher collaborations and were released mostly as second features which filled a bill and which kids at a Saturday afternoon matinee might eat up. The other reason

Fred made several Westerns between 1955 and 1959, this is from one of the better ones, At Gunpoint, *with Dorothy Malone.*

for declining screen opportunities for Fred, and others of his generation, was the end of the studio system, which, by the mid-'50s, meant that most actors who were once under contract had been let go by the studios which, consequently, were producing fewer films.

At Gunpoint is one of Fred's better Westerns. Fred plays a mild-mannered storekeeper, who has never even shot a gun before, but when the bank is robbed by a notorious outlaw gang he gets off a lucky shot which kills one of the robbers. Fred is proclaimed a hero by the townspeople and made the new sheriff, but then reality sets in when the outlaw gang plans revenge on him and the town. Like Gary Cooper, in the superior *High Noon,* the

townspeople desert him when he seeks help and he must face them alone —
he even has a wife, not unlike the Grace Kelly character in *High Noon*, who
urges him to run away from the danger. The production values are sparse,
but the film's 81 minutes fly by and the role suits Fred like an old suit. He
is the everyman who gets involved in a situation which goes beyond his
control, and yet will not shirk from his responsibilities and, in true Western
fashion, will "do what a man's got to do." The director of *At Gunpoint* was a
studio workhorse named Alfred Werker. Werker had been in films dating
back to 1917 and while most of his output was of the "B" level he did direct
a few pictures which were a few notches higher, such as the Basil Rathbone-
Nigel Bruce *The Adventures of Sherlock Holmes* (1939, Twentieth Century-
Fox). *At Gunpoint* is another of his higher-grade films. In his book, *The
Western*, film historian Phil Hardy writes, "For the greater part of his career,
Werker's work was routine and nondescript, but the westerns he made in
the 50's at the end of his career are distinctive for their sober realism and
bitter edge."

Fred was asked by the studio to undertake a 14-city tour to publicize the
film. He was doing this in part because television had a glut of Westerns
and why would anybody want to go out to a movie theater when they could
watch one at home for free? In Dallas he optimistically told reporters, "In
every city where I appeared, I discussed business conditions with theater
managers. Without exception they spoke optimistically about the future.
They made it clear that their optimism stems from a good box office upsurge
during the past two months." *At Gunpoint,* while hardly a blockbuster, did
make money, and its appeal, like most of the low budget Westerns that Fred
made during these years, came not from major metropolitan areas like New
York, Chicago, and Los Angeles but from small towns and rural communities and second-run theaters. On a personal note, one of the highlights of
the tour was a side trip to Beaver Dam that Fred took when he was promoting the picture in Milwaukee. It gave him a chance to introduce his hometown to June (who accompanied him on the 14-city swing) and gave them
a chance to frolic in the winter snow.

This was followed by *Quantez,* which featured Fred as one of a gang of
outlaws trying to escape to the Mexican border, but encountering rivalry,
exhausted horses and Apaches along the way. *Gun for a Coward* is another
slightly-above-average Western which cast Fred as the mature older brother
of sensitive Jeffrey Hunter and hot-headed Dean Stockwell. The brothers take over the ranch left to them by their late father. The "coward" in the
script is not Fred, but Hunter. The story is a morality play as the middle
brother essentially believes in non-violence while the younger brother is
quick with his temper and his gun. When the younger brother is killed in
a gunfight, the brother played by Fred unjustly blames Hunter for not coming to Stockwell's assistance. Naturally, by the end, MacMurray realizes

he is wrong and defends Hunter. Western film historian Phil Hardy later wrote that one of the highlights of the film is watching the "contrasting acting styles" of the lead actors, especially between the naturalistic approach of Fred and the "James Dean inspired histrionics" of Dean Stockwell.

Stuntwoman Martha Crawford-Cantarini, who received the coveted Golden Boot Award for her work in western films in 2005 recalled her

Gun for a Coward, *released in 1956, is one of Fred's better '50s Westerns. Here, he carries the dead body of his youngest brother, played by Dean Stockwell.*

memories of working on *Gun for a Coward*, "I was so impressed with his (Fred's) total professionalism. He truly was the ultimate professional actor. He, at the time, was having a little trouble remembering his lines and I did not know if he was ill or truly had a bad memory. But he took it all very seriously and never got flustered in any way. He was a true star. I was fortunate to not be working myself and I was able to just watch him perform. Great memories."

In *Day of the Bad Man* Fred plays a judge whose duty it is to carry out the execution of a condemned man, but has to contend with the attempts of the man's brothers to set him free. Fred's leading lady in the film is Joan Weldon, who is best known to filmgoers today for her role in the 1954 sci-fi classic *Them!* Miss Weldon recalled *Day of the Bad Man* as a "fun movie to make" and recalls that the she and co-stars Robert Middleton and Skip Homeier played a great deal of gin on the set between scenes. As for Fred,

Weldon recalls him as a "very nice man. Very private. He comes oı set, he shoots, he's there, he gives as an actor, but 'Cut!,' and he's off." also recalls him as an "intense man" both personally and in his work. Fred's director on both *Day of the Bad Man* and *Quantez* was a man named Harry Keller, who was best known as a film editor before being becoming a B film director mostly at Republic and then later at Universal. It was at Universal

Fred with Jeffrey Hunter in **Gun for a Coward.**

in 1958 that Keller was called in to direct retakes and two additional scenes of the Orson Welles classic *Touch of Evil* after Welles had, in effect, been banned from the Universal lot. Welles even thought that Keller had done a good job in matching Welles' very distinctive style. Unfortunately, there was little very distinctive or stylish about Keller's own films.

Good Day for a Hanging boasted a strong supporting cast (including Robert Vaughn, Maggie Hayes, Denver Pyle, Howard McNair, James Drury and Joan Blackman) with a fairly intelligent story featuring Fred as a man who brings a sheriff's killer to justice only to find the townspeople don't seem to care if the killer is punished or not. *Face of a Fugitive* cast Fred as a man wrongly accused of murder that escapes to a new town and assumes a new identity only to find his past catch up with him. The film features James Coburn in one of his earliest roles. Probably the least effective of the seven Westerns made between 1955 and 1959 is *The Oregon Trail*, which cast Fred as an Eastern reporter investigating Indian attacks. The film, in the words of *New York Times* critic Howard Thompson, "manages to include most of the standard wagon-train clichés of the last twenty-five years." While these sagebrush epics were usually ignored by critics and urban markets, they did fairly well in smaller communities and recouped back to the studios their modest investments at the box office, without ever being among the top hits of the years they were released. By 1959, Fred had become so identified with the Western film that he was invited to Reno, Nevada to accept the "Silver Spurs" award at their tenth annual ceremony. Each year an actor received the award that best portrayed "the courage, fortitude and bravery of the pioneer." Past recipients included John Wayne, Gregory Peck, James Stewart, Gary Cooper and Glenn Ford. Still, Fred was telling anybody within listening distance that he was beginning to get a "little saddle sore" and was looking for a comedy role as a change of pace. He also said he got tired of people coming up to him and asking, "Why don't you get back into the movies?"

In between Fred did manage one interesting little film which reunited him with Barbara Stanwyck and Joan Bennett, Universal's *There's Always Tomorrow*, which was directed by Douglas Sirk. Sirk had been a German filmmaker who fled to Hollywood shortly after Hitler came to power. During the 1950s he was Universal's top contract director and the one they usually assigned to their more prestigious films, usually in collaboration with producer Ross Hunter. That they were usually melodramatic soap operas or "women pictures" didn't seem to matter because they made a bundle of loot at the box office. The Hunter-Sirk films also helped to establish one bona-fide star, Rock Hudson, who performed with increasing confidence in several of their films. (1954's *Magnificent Obsession* was the film that firmly established Hudson as a top box office matinee star.) Among the best films in the Hunter-Sirk canon are *All That Heaven Allows, Written on the Wind, The Tarnished Angels* and *Imitation of Life* (Sirk's final film before retiring to Switzerland in 1959). Not quite up to their standard, visually or commercially, is *There's Always Tomorrow*, but thanks to a first-rate script, solid direction and the strong cast it's probably Fred's best film of the decade with the exception of *The Caine Mutiny*. The film is not well known today and Adrian Danks, President of the Melbourne Cinematheque, in a wonderful essay on the film, accurately calls it, "one of the least discussed of Sirk's great melodramas of the 1950's."

There's Always Tomorrow features Fred as Clifford Groves, a successful toy manufacturer, working on his latest project, "Rex, the walky, talky robot man." (The robot is often used in the picture as an analogy with Clifford; the robot representing the stiff, mechanical man that Clifford has become.) He lives in a seemingly ideal upper-middle-class Los Angeles suburb and has a wife (Joan Bennett) and three children. He should be a happy man but is not, something is lacking in his life. His wife and children take him for granted. The children are often insensitive to Clifford and monopolize the time of their mother, not that she seems to mind. Cliff often feels like a man looking from the outside in on the life of "his" family. Into this picture comes Norma Vale (Barbara Stanwyck), an ex-flame of Clifford's. She is a successful dress designer who used to work for Cliff years ago when he was just starting out. She left his employment when she realized the love

Fred and Barbara Stanwyck in their fourth and final film, the underrated **There's Always Tomorrow.**

she felt for him wasn't returned. She returns to town on a short-term assignment and decides to look Clifford up. After years of being in a rut and feeling unappreciated, Clifford sees Norma as his way of escaping to a more
exciting and useful life — in contemporary terms the man wants his mojo
back. Norma, who has never married, still carries a torch for Clifford, and
they make plans to go off to New York together. The Groves' children are
much more suspecting of what is happening between their dad and Norma
than the mother, who lives in a kind of *Donna Reed*-type glaze, not wanting
to see anything which will disrupt her assumed suburban bliss. The children
go and see Norma and she comes to realize that a man like Clifford will
always live with guilt if he abandoned his family and ruin any kind of happiness they might have together. She leaves for New York without him.

The film is very dark in tone and full of symbolic shadows — a kind of
domestic *film noir* — no bad woman trying to get some sap to kill her husband in this one, but a man slowly dying from boredom and neglect trying to rekindle passion in his life. In the book *Sirk on Sirk* Douglas Sirk,
who considered Fred a "very good actor," summed up the plot of the film
this way, "… a successful man, but a failure in his own house." While Sirk
would say that he didn't have "an entirely bad feeling" about the film, he still
thought it came up lacking. "I think I became the victim of an unfinished
thought … which I tried to continue, but it didn't work out." Sirk thought
that "both MacMurray and Stanwyck were excellent," but he had reservations about the casting of Joan Bennett.

William Reynolds, who played the eldest son, had this to say about working with MacMurray and Stanwyck: "MacMurray was a nice guy. People
said that he still had the first nickel he ever earned and I believe it. He had
tape holding together both his glasses and his pipe. But he was just a really
nice guy, and what a professional. They both were professional. Barbara
Stanwyck was the epitome of a professional actress and Fred was the quintessential professional actor. Always knew their lines; always well prepared;
always on time. I can remember that one time I was a little late on the set
for some reason or another. I thought I had a good excuse at the time, but
Stanwyck indicated that she wasn't pleased! She reminded me that professional actors were always on time. Point taken!"

The film, when released in January 1956, received mixed reviews and
didn't generate the kind of box office interest that other Sirk films of this
period did, which may be one of the reasons why the director himself seemed
to gloss over it when discussing his own work.

III

Even though Fred's professional career was lean, his family life was happy
and stable. June, at just 28, was adjusting to being the stepmother of eleven-
year-old Bobby and fourteen-year-old Sue. "It should have frightened me,

but it didn't," recalled June. "And of course I made the inevitable mistakes: I tried being their pal. They don't want a pal. More than anything they want to call someone mother." She admitted that it wasn't easy taking another woman's children on as her own, given the attachment they had to their deceased mother, but with time, understanding and loving concern the children eventually came to accept her — and she them. "And I learned to love

Fred and June with the Van Heflins at a Judy Garland concert in mid-'50s.

them because of love of my husband," explained June. June decided that the children should not have to share Fred with her. She wanted to make sure that they had their time with him — exclusively — along with periods of time with all of them — together — as a family. According to one account, "June saw to it that Sue was left alone with her father from time to time and that he took her shopping too. She'd insist that he go off only with his son to hunt and fish, though she loves both sports too." Her strategy apparently worked and the kids did come to accept her. June later recalled that Bobby was always looking forward to the day when he would be taller than his 5'2" stepmother. When the day finally came, and he was about a half-inch taller, he stood next to her and said, "Hello down there, Mom."

June had also determined not to return to work. Since coming out of the convent, and even before marrying Fred, she had not accepted any of the many offers she had received to do films or television programs. She was content with this new phase of her life, being a wife and mother. Fred also didn't make any bones that he preferred to be the sole breadwinner of the family, but he wouldn't pressure June, it had to be her decision. She was tempted only once when she was offered a role in the film version of *Guys and Dolls*, but ultimately she turned it down. "No, I do not feel I submerged a career," June said at the time. "I had ten good years in the movies. I'm here now. I do the marketing and worry about the laundry, and got calluses on my hands sewing camp tags on their clothes until Fred bought me a sewing machine. I'm a mother. I'm needed."

June found that even though she had come to love both Sue and Bobby, she had a natural desire to want children of her own. But she discovered that she could not conceive, which naturally disappointed her, but June was always somebody who rebounded quickly from disappointments, it was part of her nature. If she couldn't conceive, perhaps they could adopt? June approached Fred to discuss adopting a baby. Starting a second family was, frankly, an option that Fred had not given much thought to. "Here I am in the twilight of my life!" Fred told June. "We should be traveling; we should do all the things we've never had a chance to do." Fred had forgotten that June was eighteen years younger than he was. In another account of his objections to second-time-around fatherhood Fred told Hollywood columnist Louella Parsons, "I said 'No. I want you to be free to go hunting and fishing and on vacations with me.' I told June. 'I don't want you tied down.'"

Shortly afterward, Fred and June went to a party where in attendance were several doctors, including an OB man that June knew from volunteer work at St. John's Hospital in Santa Monica. The doctor was telling a story about a baby he had just arranged to have adopted by friends of the MacMurrays. June couldn't resist saying, "I wish you'd thought of us," to which Fred raised his eyebrow and cleared his throat. "I wish I'd known you were in the market," the doctor told June. Fred tried to change the subject, but June was having none of it. "We're in the market," she replied. Later that night Fred told June he would "think about it," but made no promises.

It was just a week later that June was at the beauty parlor and under a dryer when she was called to the phone. She didn't know what to expect when she heard Fred's voice telling her to "sit down." When she was sitting and expecting the worse, he told her, "What are we going to do with twins that were born yesterday?" She was so excited she didn't even bother finishing her drying job but "flew all the way to the hospital." At the hospital June found two red-headed baby girls who had been born prematurely. She put a mask on and saw them for the first time in their incubators. "So beautiful!" she thought, and then rushed home to be there when Fred got home from the studio. When Fred arrived, according to June, he telephoned their friends Jimmy and Gloria Stewart, who had also recently had twin girls, and asked Jimmy, "What do we do? They're twins!" to which Stewart replied, "Buy two of everything." They named the girls Laurie and Katie. June would later say, "It was lucky they were 'preemies' as it gave us a little time to shop. We bought out the stores. And you should have seen Fred when all the things came in. He worked like a frenzied boy putting up the bassinets, the bathinettes. A few more days and the babies arrived. He had the camera ready and started taking pictures. He even helped with the night feedings; he was just marvelous." His friends thought they had never seen Fred so happy. His pal Claude Binyon would later say, "Ever since those little girls arrived, Mr. Nice Guy has become even nicer — not only that but also younger, busier, bigger and better than ever."

Only once in the years after June married Fred did she return to acting, and briefly, in December 1957, when Fred was working with Lucille Ball and Desi Arnaz on one of the hour-long specials that the couple did after ending their half-hour sitcom. "Lucy Hunts Uranium" found the Ricardos and Merzes (William Frawley and Vivian Vance) traveling by train to Las Vegas where Ricky is performing at the Sands Hotel. On board they meet Fred MacMurray. While in Las Vegas Fred, the Ricardos and Mertzes join forces to hunt for quick riches when uranium is discovered in the nearby desert. Of course, ultimately, they all learn to distrust each other in a comical takeoff on *The Treasure of the Sierra Madre,* culminating with a slapstick car chase between the actors (Fred in one car, Lucy and Desi in another and Bill and Viv in a third) which was filmed on location. Fred was finding that the comedy roles he wanted were not in the movies, but on television, and he eagerly accepted them. There is a scene in the script which called on Fred to call June (who is not seen or heard in the scene). "I had a scene where I called June on the phone to tell her that I'd lost my $100 allowance and I was supposed to be scared. Desi said, 'Gee, wouldn't it be great if we could get June to come in on the last part?' I told Desi to call her and talk to her. It wasn't up to me." The show was sponsored by the Ford Motor Company, and to entice June to do it, Desi offered her a free station wagon for one day's work. June thought it over and decided that with their growing family they could use a new car and agreed to do it. She got up early and went into the studio and didn't get home until late that night. Fred recalls her telling him, "You know, that's the end of this. I haven't seen the babies all day; they were asleep when I left and they were asleep when I got back. No more of that." (Interestingly, Lucille Ball didn't enjoy working with Fred. "Fred MacMurray was a nice enough guy," she was later quoted as saying, "but a complete square to work with. I didn't think he was funny, and kept working with him on that telephone scene to his wife. He just couldn't get it. I guess I was wrong, though. He was on for eleven seasons with his own show. But not my kind of comedy.") June allowed her blonde hair to go to her natural brunette coloring and never looked back, enjoying her new calling as a wife and mother. (Fred and June did actually team up once more on screen in a television commercial in 1959 for which they received two electric ranges, one for their Brentwood home and the other for the ranch. "And now I won't use a cook," June told columnist Sheilah Graham, "I do it myself and with Fred who's a wonderful cook.")

IV

In 1958 Fred was finally able to climb off the saddle and sink his teeth into a comedy role in a major motion picture, and in doing so he began an association with Walt Disney Productions, which would rejuvenate his career and bring him an international stardom which was even greater than in his days as a romantic leading man at Paramount. He also found a new generation of fans which would come to consider Fred as a kind of uncle or surrogate dad. According to author Richard Schickel, Fred became to the Disney Studios of the '50s and '60s, "what Mickey Mouse was to it in the 30's," and Schickel would add that Disney was devoted to Fred "as to no other actor since The Mouse."

June recalled that Fred came home with a "smile on his face" and waving a script like a "triumphant banner." Fred considered the script sent to him from Disney, "the funniest I've seen in a long time." He told her the plot, which must have made June feel that Fred had spent a little too much time in the California sun that day, in which he would play a "father of a dog who talks. Walt Disney is going to make it and he wants me for the part."

The film was *The Shaggy Dog*, a slapstick family comedy. The film was initially supposed to be a two-part story for Walt Disney's weekly television show, but eventually it was decided to turn it into the Disney Studio's first live-action comedy film. The film would largely define the type of story the studio would make over the next two decades. The story is simple: Teenager Wilby Daniels, who is always experimenting (and at the beginning of the film is making a rocket in the basement which, unfortunately, is so realistic that it flies through the roof just as "pop" is trying to enjoy his morning breakfast), makes a visit to a local museum with his hot shot best friend Buzz, and a French girl who has just moved into the neighborhood, and who both boys develop crushes on. While at the museum he accidentally takes home with him an ancient ring which magically transforms him into a large shaggy sheepdog (just like the one his French neighbor has). This is inconvenient for many reasons (obviously) but one reason is that "pop," a postal worker, who has had more than his share of run-ins with dogs, absolutely despises them and is even willing to go so far as to shoot at them, not to mention that he is also allergic to dogs. He wonders to his wife why

Fred, with Jean Hagen, returned to comedy in the 1959 Walt Disney classic, The Shaggy Dog. © *Walt Disney Productions.*

his allergies are acting up, had she allowed a dog into the house? Had their youngest son, who is always badgering him for a dog, brought one into the house? Nope! It's just his "Shaggy Dog" son. In the second half of the picture we find out that the French girl's father and his associates are Russian spies (remember this was made at the height of the Cold War) and Wilby discovers the nefarious plot that they are working on and needs to enlist "pop" to help stop them, which culminates with a slapstick car chase through town and all the way to the waterfront.

When Walt Disney told the outline of this story to his brother Roy and his sister-in-law Edna at their house over dinner one evening the outspoken Edna didn't hold back her opinion. Edna held "strong opinions and often vented them" and was also one of the few people who could make Walt

Much of the focus of The Shaggy Dog *was on (from left to right) Tommy Kirk, Tim Considine and Roberta Shore. © Walt Disney Productions.*

"shut-up." It seems that Edna had known Walt since he was a ten-year-old newsboy and wasn't overly awed by his success since then. According to Roy and Edna's son, "Walt was still preparing the script for *The Shaggy Dog*. It was one of the early 'Let's do a black-and-white comedy with some special effects and not much money ' approach to the question, 'What else do you do besides animation?' There must have been ten-twelve people sitting around the table enjoying fried chicken and corn on the cob when Walt began his I'll-take-over-this-meeting thing, so he started: 'We're working on this wonderful story about a kid who turns into a dog.' He usually could keep people enthralled with his storytelling. He got a little bit into it, and Mother says, 'That sounds kinda dumb.' He went further on, and mother says, 'That really sounds like an awful stupid picture, Walt.' Every time she said something, Walt's distraction got a little bit worse. He got to the halfway point in the story and just gave up on it." That is gave up on trying to explain it to an audience which included Edna, but he still knew it was a good story and was intent on making it and making it for under a million dollars.

In addition to Fred, the cast included Jean Hagen (her most famous role being that of Lina Lamont in the film *Singin' in the Rain)* as his wife. Cast as the sons, Wilby and his younger brother Moochie, were Tommy Kirk and Kevin Corchoran (who had scored a hit as the brothers in the Disney classic *Old Yeller* two years earlier). Rounding out the cast was Mousketeer and Disney girl-next-door Annette Funicello (in her film debut) as the pretty neighbor girl ignored by Wilby and his friend Buzz (Tim Considine) when they are dazzled by the French teenage beauty Franceska (played by Roberta Shore).

Tom Kirk was a kid from Kentucky who came to Southern California when his dad got a job at an aviation plant. His father moved his family to the Los Angeles suburb of Downey. Tom's brother, like many kids who lived near Hollywood, wanted to become an actor and went to audition for a part in the play *Ah! Wilderness* that was being presented by the prestigious Pasadena Playhouse. Tom accompanied his brother and their mother to the audition. His brother lost out on the part he was going for, but the producers saw something in Tom that they liked and he read for and was given the part of the younger brother in the play. By the second week of that production he had an agent and began to audition for and win several appearances on television programs. Ultimately, Tom (or Tommy at that time) was signed to a contract by the Walt Disney Studios, where he was under contract from 1956 to 1964. His big break at the studio was appearing opposite Tim Considine in *The Hardy Boys*, which appeared as part of *The Mickey Mouse Club*. But it was his role as Travis in *Old Yeller* which led to Tom becoming the leading male juvenile actor at the studio for the next eight years. In that time he would work with Fred in four of the seven films that Fred made under the Disney banner.

Kevin Corchoran's "Moochie" is the typical kid brother, always trying to get involved in his big brother's projects, such as helping Wilby with his rocket. But he is also very protective when Wilby is transformed into the sheep dog of the title, not wanting him to be discovered by his dad, in part because Moochie has always wanted a dog of his own and his father won't get him one, and so now Wilby is not only his brother but his "best friend," his pet. Kirk and Corchoran have the same easy chemistry that they enjoyed together in *Old Yeller* and, according to Corchoran, when they did joint personal appearances many people really did believe that they were "real-life" brothers. "I love him. I still love him," Tom Kirk later said of Corchoran. "He was very dear to me. But we did have a falling out, where he said something to me and I said something back. There was some personality conflict." Happily, Kirk says that in 2004, when the two were reunited to do audio commentary for the DVD release of *The Shaggy Dog*, they had put their differences behind them and apologized to each other and had a "great time" working together again. Corchoran played Fred's son in two films (the other being *Bon Voyage!*), and would recall Fred as helpful to him without "talking down" to him because he was a child. In a Disney DVD tribute to Fred, Corchoran would call Fred, "one of the most underestimated actors of all time."

Of *The Shaggy Dog*, Kirk has mixed feelings. "In a way I thought it was stupid! And embarrassing in some ways," he recalled years later. "I hated to have to call Fred MacMurray 'pop.' I never had to call my dad 'pop.' But then I thought too that it was so crazy it might be entertaining." Not that Kirk had much choice. As a contract player he had to do the films he was assigned or he could be put on suspension and even fired.

Tom was excited to be working with Fred MacMurray, who he had seen and admired on the screen. "I recall meeting him for the first time on the set," said Kirk. "Of course, I knew who he was because I had seen *The Caine Mutiny* and a film called *Pushover* and I was very excited and liked him as an actor. I thought he was a wonderful and extremely sensitive actor. I perceived that he was an extremely sensitive person. He was not a glad hander or backslapper. We didn't have too much in common because he was fifty and I was still a teenager, but I did try to open lines of communication with him. He was polite and somewhat reserved. Between scenes he would sit in a chair and smoke his pipe and often be reading something."

The director of *The Shaggy Dog* was the veteran Charles Barton, who had many television and film credits (usually B films) on his resume. Kirk recalls Barton with affection. "I loved him! He was a little man, a pudgy little man, probably about 5' tall, but he was the kindest, nicest man and his forte was directing child actors." Barton brought the film in under schedule and under budget producing a film that, in the words of Disney historian Leonard Maltin, "... is a curious film. By rights, it should be fast-paced, broad entertainment, but, instead it takes its own sweet time, never pushing for laughs, and ambling through 104 minutes of running time."

Fred is wonderful as Wilson Daniels, proving that he was still an expert screen comedian. A highlight is the opening scene where Fred and his wife are at the breakfast table and suddenly, because Wilby is experimenting with his homemade rocket, they feel the whole house shaking — what is going on? The wife begins to grab the silver, to save from what they feel may be an impending explosion, and she urges Wilson to save something too and he grabs the coffee pot! Tim Considine would later say that he saw, for the first time, Fred do things which he would "marvel at" for years to come when they worked together on *My Three Sons*. He was particularly impressed by Fred's ability to do take after take of a scene the exact same way. Considine also got his first initiation to the patented MacMurray double-take which he described as being "a double take with 3 or 4 little takes in between." Tom Kirk found Considine "hard to get to know," but praised him as a "consummate professional and as smart as they come." But, overall, they were different personality types. "His thing was racing cars, which didn't interest me in the least. I'd rather read a book."

The film became, unexpectedly, a huge hit when released and was the third biggest grossing film of 1959, earning $12.3 million at the box office, to become Fred's second biggest grossing film up to that time (only *The Caine Mutiny* did better). The film out grossed such popular 1959 releases as *North by Northwest, Some Like It Hot* and *Pillow Talk*. Fred couldn't have been more delighted since the film put him back on the map as a comedy and box office star. *Variety* said in its review, "It's a pleasure to see such a master of timing and emphasize as Fred MacMurray back in comedy again … where he has a good line, he shows that he has few peers in this special field of comedy." When asked about his part in the film, he quipped, "It's an interesting role; just as well I'm not a method actor."

Annette Funicello (described by Tom Kirk as "Disney's fair-haired girl … she was strictly professional and had no temperament"), whose first film this was, later described as her "biggest thrill … meeting and working with such established Hollywood stars as Jean Hagen and Fred MacMurray. For both of them, the film represented a return to comedy, and for Mr. MacMurray, it solidified his image as the genial though sometimes bumbling father." Like Tom Kirk, Annette also "greatly admired" Fred and while finding him friendly he "mainly kept to himself" and during much of the filming she decided not to invade his space. But on the final day of shooting, "I mustered the courage to request his autograph," she later wrote, "… he kindly consented, writing, 'I worked with Kim Novak in her first movie, and look what happened. I have no doubt the same will happen with you.'"

V

Fred was still flush by the success of *The Shaggy Dog* (with Walt Disney planning more film projects for him) when he got a call from an unexpected source, Billy Wilder. Billy was the toast of the town due to the critical and box office success of *Some Like It Hot* and was only weeks away from beginning principal filming on his newest picture titled *The Apartment* when tragedy struck. The burly and versatile character actor Paul Douglas suddenly died of a heart attack. Douglas had been cast by Billy in a pivotal role in his new film and Wilder needed to find a replacement — fast. He thought of Fred. Wilder called up Fred and told him, "Fred, I'm in trouble." Fred replied, "You only call me when you're in trouble." As usual, Fred was dismayed by the assignment that Billy had in mind for him, according to author Ed Sikov, "Fred MacMurray... was fresh from Disney's *The Shaggy Dog* and was therefore a downright appalling choice for J.D. Sheldrake— insurance executive, Westchester dad, philanderer, swine. Brought to life by MacMurray, Sheldrake is the very essence of magnetic, every day rottenness, the kind of man who could drive a woman like Fran Kubelik to suicide." Fred protested to Billy that he and Disney were going to make more pictures together and it would go against his image to play a part like Sheldrake. Billy finally convinced Fred that the reason he wanted him for the part was because he could demonstrate the shades of gray in the Sheldrake role, an attractive man on the surface and a scheming philanderer on the inside. Fred could pull it off just as he had pulled off "heavy" roles in *The Caine Mutiny* and *Pushover.*

The Apartment, unlike *Some Like It Hot,* is not a farce, but a comedy-drama with equal amounts of both in its story of immorality in the corporate world. Jack Lemmon had so captivated Billy on *Some Like It Hot* that he immediately wanted to do another story with the talented actor. He cast Lemmon as C.C. (Bud) Baxter, one of many faceless workers at an insurance company in New York City. Bud works diligently and stays late at the office in a bid to impress his superiors and begin moving ahead. His hard work does get him attention, but he soon finds out that it takes more than hard work to get ahead in the corporate world. The insurance company hierarchy is made up of middle-aged married men who enjoy that old-fashioned American pastime of screwing the secretaries. The only problem they have is finding a place to hold their clandestine rendezvous. When Bud agrees to let one executive use his small bachelor apartment (no frills but it does have the required bed) as a love nest, soon other executives are asking for its use too, and Bud (or "Buddy-boy") soon has to juggle his own sleep with the appointments of these executives. In the meanwhile, Bud's own love life is non-existent, though he does take a liking to a young elevator operator, Fran Kubelik (Shirley MacLaine), who likes him too, but seems to be involved with another man. Into this mix comes Mr. Sheldrake, the director of personnel, who commends Bud on his work, and with Sheldrake's help Bud will begin to go places — but it comes with a price. With the promise of a promotion, and two tickets to *The Music Man,* Sheldrake is asking for exclusive use of the apartment (along with his own key) — in other words, you play ball with me and I'll play ball with you. Bud takes the bait and with the tickets to a big Broadway show in his hands he finds the courage to ask Fran to go to the theatre with him that night. She finally agrees and they make plans to meet in the lobby of the theater. She never shows up. It turns out that she had been having an affair with Sheldrake, a married man with children, who she had finally found the courage to break up with. But

Jack Lemmon, Shirley MacLaine and Fred in 1960's classic Billy Wilder comedy-drama, The Apartment.

Sheldrake wins her back with the promise (he has no intention of keeping) of divorcing his wife. After an office party, Fran meets with Sheldrake at the apartment, where she comes to the realization that he has no intention of leaving his wife. After Sheldrake leaves to spend the holidays with his family, Fran takes an overdose of sleeping pills. When Bud comes home and discovers her he gets his next door neighbor, Dr. Dreyfuss (Jack Kruschen), to save her. Dreyfuss already thinks of Bud as a Lothario because of the girls who come in and out of the apartment, but now he thinks he is a louse because he thinks Fran tried to kill herself over him. Bud falls in love with Fran during the two days they spend together at the apartment (platonically) while she recovers. Eventually, Sheldrake's wife finds out of the affair and initiates divorce proceedings and Sheldrake again gives Fran hopes that he will marry her now that he is a free man, but in the meanwhile Bud declares his declaration of independence to Sheldrake by resigning (by this time Bud had been promoted all the way up to being Sheldrake's assistant). When Fran finds out what Bud did she realizes that he really does love her and leaves the stunned Sheldrake sitting alone in a restaurant while she runs off to the apartment to profess her own love for him through a game of gin-rummy. Fade-out. The End.

Fred ultimately understood why Billy wanted him. "I played a real stinker in it," he later declared, "which is kind of fun to do, as an actor; but you knew the guy had to be an attractive, nice looking fellow for Shirley MacLaine to have fallen in love with — and then try and kill herself over him." Sheldrake is what would have become of Walter Neff had he not become involved with Phyllis Dietrichson. He would have gotten ahead at the Insurance Company, married and probably had a couple of kids, but still be the same smooth-talking sharpie on the lookout for a little tail on the side. Wilder summed up the character of Sheldrake by stating that Sheldrake "is such an effective liar because he chooses women who want to believe him. He's a perfect cad. Well, maybe not perfect. Nobody's perfect."

Jack Lemmon thought that Fred was "perfect" as Sheldrake. He also understood what Billy was doing by casting an actor who was not only attractive but had a reputation for all-American geniality. "There was a great deal of Fred and his persona in each of the characters he played," Lemmon later said. "I think that's why he was so attractive to people on the screen — and why he was able to play with so many of the top leading ladies over a period of decades. I felt he knew precisely what he was doing. He was injecting a great deal of his own persona into this part ... and it was pre-cisely what Billy wanted him to do — because he wanted him [Sheldrake] to be attractive on the surface."

Lemmon found Fred a "true professional" who went along with an unplanned bit of business which Lemmon sprung on him during the actual filming of a scene. In the film Bud suffers from a cold because he is always left out in the cold while some executive is using his apartment for their dal-liances. One of the props which Lemmon used was a nose spray he used for the sniffles. "I was playing around with it in my dressing room," Lemmon recalled, "and discovered that if I gave it a sharp squeeze the stuff would squirt ten feet. I filled it with milk to make it visible, and when the boss, Fred MacMurray, is crewing out this kid (me), who is very nervous, I used it. I didn't tell anybody, not even Billy, and when Fred said something like, 'Baxter, I hope we're not going to have this problem again,' I said, 'Oh, no sir!' and squeezed in nervous reaction. That milk shot out and sailed right by under MacMurray's nose. He was beautiful; didn't' say a word, just gave me a look and went right on with the scene. And Billy left it in."

There was an amusing incident during the filming of the picture which brought home Fred's alleged "frugality" with a dollar. "I'll tell you a very funny story about him," Billy Wilder told film director Cameron Crowe. "The last story that I tell you with Mr. Fred MacMurray, who was a very stingy man. I loved it. I loved the man and I loved his stinginess too. It amused me. There was a scene [in *The Apartment*] ... he has his shoes shined by a black man. And then, from his suit, he gets out a quarter and flips a tip to the shoe shine guy. And now we're shooting it, and we're shooting it, and he can't do it. And I say, 'That's all right, it's too small — let's do it with a fifty-cent piece, it's bigger.' And MacMurray says, 'I would never give him fifty-cents. I can't play this scene.'" But, of course he did.

Wilder would also tell the story of a prank he pulled on Fred when shooting *The Apartment*. There is a scene set on Christmas Eve where Fran Kubelik and Sheldrake are having a rendezvous at the apartment. Fran gives Sheldrake a present, a record album. Naturally, the self-absorbed Sheldrake didn't get anything for her, so he pulls a hundred-dollar bill from his wallet, which causes Fran to feel cheap and used and is the catalyst for her upcoming suicide attempt. Fred had a bit of trouble, according to Wilder, doing this scene. "Wilder hates stage money. He peeled off a genuine century note from this thick bankroll and gave it to MacMurray to use in the scene. After the take, the actor, lovingly caressing the bill, returned it to Wilder. At the end of the day Billy, having conspired with the crew and the cast— demanded his money back. MacMurray said he had returned it. Wilder argued so persuasively that MacMurray finally became uncertain and, beads of sweat breaking out on his face, he slowly opened his wallet and took out a hundred-dollar bill. Everybody on the set swore they had not seen him return Wilder's bill. So he handed it over. Only then did Billy reveal the prank."

Filming went very smoothly between October and late December of 1959 and Wilder was justly proud of the film. "Some people say it's my best comedy, but with 'The Apartment,' I never set out to make a comedy. But when they laugh I don't argue ... one of the few I wouldn't go back and change." Fred was so convincing as the philandering Sheldrake that it became the basis of a story that he would tell for the rest of his life. Shortly after the film had been released, Fred took his family to Disneyland. As he was standing in line a lady came up to him and introduced herself as a long time fan and then told him, "I saw *The Apartment* last night. How could you? You spoiled the Disney image!" And at that point, according to Fred, she took a whack at him with her purse.

Shortly after finishing up on *The Apartment* Fred and June, along with their close friends Dave and Maud Chasen (owners of the famous Hollywood eatery), took a trip to Europe which included a stop in Copenhagen for the opening of *The Shaggy Dog*. Fred recalled that "a man in a dog suit met us at the airport and escorted us to the theater. We went to a matinee and the people seemed to love it and laughed as much as our audiences here."

Astonishingly, this was to be Fred's first extended trip to Europe. "I was in Paris once before, for 24 hours," he recalled. "I'd done a show in London and had one day before going home, so several of us decided to fly to Paris. We dined at Maxim's and, since none of us spoke French, we wound up with roast beef, mashed potatoes and apple pie. Next morning we took a fast tour of Versailles before heading for home."

The Apartment was destined to be a big box office and critical success (*Time* declared, "*The Apartment* is the funniest movie made in Hollywood since *Some Like It Hot* ... serious about nothing but fun, much too shrewd to lecture to grown-ups") and was to be the last time that Fred would enact such a complex characterization, away from his established persona. In part this was because of the roles that he was playing, or planning on playing, for Walt Disney, but also because he would ultimately be persuaded to do something he never expected to do and in doing so became the representative father figure for a new generation of kids.

CHAPTER EIGHT

"The MacMurray System"

My Three Sons, Part One (1960-1965)

By 1960 Fred's movie career was back in high gear. He was in his best position in the industry in fifteen years. *The Shaggy Dog*, to the surprise of many, was one of the biggest box office hits of 1959. Fred had just completed filming one of the leading roles in Billy Wilder's *The Apartment* and expectations for the Wilder film were high. Walt Disney was waiting in the wings with yet another family comedy for Fred to star in. After a quarter of a century of moviemaking, Fred was enjoying a professional resurgence.

Over the years Fred had appeared in guest appearances on many television programs, most notably with George Gobel as Gobel's "good luck charm," opening and closing each segment of Gobel's variety show every season. He was also pursued to headline his own series. He was briefly considered for the part of Marshal Matt Dillon on TV's *Gunsmoke* before John Wayne recommended his protégé, young James Arness. There was more serious interest in Fred to play Perry Mason and Elliot Ness in *The Untouchables*. He and June had even been approached to do a husband-wife sitcom together. "Those husband-wife TV series are for the birds," Fred complained at the time. "They work miserably hard all day and come home at night too tired to talk to one another." In the end Fred just didn't want to be stuck in the grind of doing a weekly television series.

In early 1959 Fred and Randolph Scott were playing golf one day when the subject of doing a series came up. "I was shooting the breeze with Randy Scott and a few others," Fred later recalled, "and we just happened to mention the idea of doing a TV series, nothing more than speculative conversation, you know what I mean? Anyway, then next thing I knew everybody was real hot on it. The lawyers, the agents, everybody, they were all discussing terms. I have to admit, it was a helluva good deal. It was to be a western, with Randy and me, real elaborate."

As it turned out, both Scott and Fred got cold feet. "Yessir," recalled Fred. "We were almost hooked. We were at the starting gate, but we chickened out. I don't know, I guess it's because neither one of us wants to work that hard. Don't kid yourself, a TV series means lots of sweat, and three-quarters of your time ... Give me hunting and fishing anytime, and above all, just being with June and the kids."

In early 1960, Fred appeared on a well-received TV special spoofing cowboys and the American Western titled *The American Cowboy*. It featured a series of sketches and Fred worked with Wally Cox, Edie Adams, Carol Burnett and Hans Conried. The sketches include Fred, Cox and Conried buying guns in much the same manner as a woman would buy a dress, Fred and Carol Burnett in a sketch about a cowboy's domestic life, and Edie Adams joined Fred and Conried in a sketch about improbable happenings on a wagon train as it moved west. The special was produced by Max Liebman, the same man who produced the uniquely funny and often satirical *Your Show of Shows* featuring Sid Caesar in the 1950s. One joke Fred told on the show went like this: "A cowboy must have gotten off his horse once in a while—otherwise there wouldn't have been all those little cowboys." Even though Fred had made a breakthrough at the box office with *The Shaggy Dog* and the upcoming *The Apartment* was promising, in press interviews he wanted to make sure the special didn't offend Western fans because he fully expected he would be doing more of them. "I've played a lot of cowboys," he said, "and I'm still playing them. I don't think it would be very becoming of me to make too much fun of them. I wouldn't want to offend anybody, but I guess this doesn't. It's just a little joke." He still insisted that a TV series was not in his future.

In 1960 just as Fred's film career was on the upswing, producer Don Fedderson was intent on signing Fred for a new television series, a family comedy, and he won't take "No" for an answer.

My Three Sons tells the story of Steve Douglas, a widower who is left to bring up his sons, Mike, 17, Robbie, 14 and Chip, 9. With the help of his crusty father-in-law, they all live in a typical Midwestern town called Bryant Park, where Steve works as an Aeronautical engineer. What makes the show unique is that it consists of a household of males with Steve acting as father and mother with his father-in-law's, called "Bub," assistance. While Steve is out earning a living, Bub keeps up the house: washing, cleaning and preparing meals. It's not that Steve wouldn't have any female interests, there would be plenty, but they usually were fleeting and perhaps were scared away by the prospect of becoming an instant parent to three boys, or have some type of flaw which precludes her from being the next Mrs. Steve Douglas. Fred once put it this way, "One of our problems in *My Three Sons* is I'm not allowed to meet a girl who's too attractive."

Interestingly, it was the part of Bub which was filled first, by the character actor William Frawley, fresh from playing grouchy yet lovable Fred Mertz on *I Love Lucy*. The 73-year-old show business veteran was a perfect fit for the grouchy yet lovable Bub. In fact, if Fedderson was unsuccessful in signing Fred he was contemplating Frawley starring in a series titled *My Three Grandsons,* with the focus being on a grandfather raising his grandchildren after their parents are killed. (Fedderson later did a variation of this when he produced the mid-'60s comedy *Family Affair* and instead of a grandfather raising his grandchildren it is an uncle raising his two nieces and nephew after their parents are killed in an accident.)

Fedderson was prepared to approach Fred with as attractive a deal as any ever presented to an actor for his services in a television series up to that time. Not only would Fred get a large sum of money per episode, but he would also own 50 percent of the show, with Fedderson owning the other half. In effect, Fred would become Don Fedderson's "silent partner." This meant that Fred would receive 50 percent of any profits, if the show did prove profitable. As *My Three Sons* production manager John Stephens would later point out, 50 percent ownership of the series extended to everything connected to the show. "Now 50% of the profits meant not only the profits from the show itself, but all the publishing rights and everything, and you know that theme song, written by Frank DeVol, did very well, and there were an awful lot of ancillary rights to that, and Fred, as I used to tease him, probably made more money per minute than anyone that has ever acted in television; at least up to that time, he did."

When approached by Fedderson, Fred thought the financial arrangements were excellent, he could find no fault. But the real issue for Fred was his work schedule; he just didn't like the grind of weekly television, especially if it interfered with his family and recreational life. Fred would later tell Fedderson, "A lot of people enjoy working until their rumps drag. I don't." Fred then consulted with his friend Robert Young, who was just coming off of a six-season run on *Father Knows Best.* Young confirmed the worst to Fred about the long hours and rigors of doing a weekly television series.

But Fedderson, who had already produced such hits as *The Millionaire, The Lawrence Welk Show* and *Liberace,* wasn't backing off that easily. He continued to pursue Fred. Fred later wrote of the wooing in a 1962 article published in *The Saturday Evening Post:* "A couple of days later Fedderson sent me a story outline in the mail. Going over my agency's head was kind of sneaky, but I liked the fact that the script was comedy. I was also very much interested to hear that Fedderson had Bill Frawley signed as a supporting actor. But the thing that interested me most was an accompanying note in which Fedderson explained he had it figured so I wouldn't have to work every week. He named a hefty salary and said that he was willing to declare me in on a partnership deal. I called my agents, MCA, and said I thought we'd better have lunch with this man. At lunch I was told that Pete Tewksbury, who'd directed *Father Knows Best,* was to direct our script.

I began to have a boxed in feeling. It was going to be hard to say 'No' now. But after lunch when I went home and saw my wife June and the kids, I thought about how much time a TV show would mean away from them. I called MCA and said, 'I'm sorry, I just can't.' A week later I got another envelope from Fedderson. Inside was a promise, 'You will appear in all the shows, some more than others, but you will work only three months a year.' I thought if I only have to work three months a year for that kind of money plus a partnership percentage, I'd be a chowderhead to duck it ..."

Fedderson offered Fred a unique shooting schedule which would provide the star with the leisure time he demanded. With a deal like Fred got there could be no doubt about how serious Don Fedderson was about signing him for the show. Fedderson would shoot *My Three Sons* like it was one big "mega film." "Why not think of a television series - 39 half hour scripts as one giant movie scenario," Fedderson later explained. "It would be a movie five times as long as *Ben-Hur*, but just one movie. Shoot a scene here, a scene there, until all the scenes from this giant movie are shot, and then snip them apart and paste them together, until you have your original 39 shows. Why not, for instance, shoot a whole batch of scenes with Fred MacMurray, and then, while he's making a Disney movie or out fishing, shoot a whole bunch of scenes without MacMurray?"

So, in a nutshell, Fred signed an agreement which allowed him to work only 65 days each year. During those 65 days the production crew would shoot all of Fred's scenes, master shots, long shots, close ups, etc., for each episode. Those 65 days were exclusively for Fred's scenes and nothing else. When his 65 days were up the cast would reassemble, guest stars included, and shoot the rest of each episode. Furthermore, even when he was working those 65 (non-consecutive) days, he would work reasonable hours, 8:30 A.M. until 6:00 P.M. This was too good for Fred to throw away, but first he wanted to check with somebody whose opinion he respected more than any other in the business, Walt Disney. "I told Walt about the television show," Fred later recalled, "and he was a little concerned about my being over-exposed; he said if the series was a success it would help, but if it wasn't it would be harmful, I was lucky ..." This was good enough for Fred and he was prepared to sign when Fedderson came at him with an idea to re-title the show "The Fred MacMurray Show." Since he had a big star for a TV series, Fedderson figured, why not name the show after the star whose name had been posted on so many movie marques for 25 years? Fred was adamant in dismissing this idea, figuring that if his name were used in the title people would tune in expecting him to be the main focus in every episode rather than the center of an ensemble cast. The title remained *My Three Sons*.

The way *My Three Sons* was filmed ultimately became known as "The MacMurray System." As time went on, some rules were devised as to how to work within this method. One rule was to never show Fred with teenagers other than the actors who played his sons. "If we shoot MacMurray together with five kids in a master scene, and then have to pick up the action later," recalls production manager Stephens, "who knows whether we'll find all five kids again? If one quits acting and MacMurray is fishing in Colorado, that master scene kills us. So when you see on your screen Fred saying, 'Hi, Kids,' and the boys answering, what really happens is Fred looks down where the kids would be if they were there, and says his line. Later the dialog coach stands on a soapbox until she is 6'2" off the ground and the kids look up and say, 'Hello, Mr. Douglas.'" Many times when Fred shot these scenes, no other actors were actually there. Hank Jones recalls the "MacMurray System" first hand. "Any scene any of the other actors had with Fred MacMurray was usually filmed with the script girl, Adele Sliff, saying Mr. M's lines to us to which we then would react. By carefully splicing the scenes together with skillful editing, it appeared that Mr. M. was actually there in the scene with us, but most often he was not, just carefully inserted in post-production editing. What a gig for him! To paraphrase Mel Brooks, 'It's good to be 'da star.'" When Fedderson later offered Phil Harris a television series and promised to allow him to film it according to "The MacMurray System," Harris begged off, explaining, "I'm not a good enough actor to say my lines to furniture."

Another rule was to shoot scenes for several episodes, which utilizes the same set on the same day. For instance, one day the actors might shoot scenes which take place exclusively in the dining room or the upstairs hallway for five or six different scripts. Obviously the writers had quite a burden because under the "MacMurray System" they didn't have to start the season off with maybe 13 scripts ready to go, but really needed at least 26 scripts ready to shoot while having outlines of the 13 others which would comprise the season's output.

Tim Considine, the actor ultimately hired to play eldest son Mike, offered this recollection of "The MacMurray System": "It impacted everybody. I mean, people always say, 'God, it must have been really hard,' and all that. And it was. But it was hard for everybody. It was hard for the prop department. It was hard for the camera crew, and the guys who lit everything, because ... I mean everything had to match, you know. The light had to be coming from the same direction. Everything. The props had to be in the same place." Still, Considine doesn't fault Fred, who he calls "smart enough" to get such a cushy deal.

II

My Three Sons was different from the other family shows on television at that time because of its concept of an untraditional family. Instead, we have a family headed by a father with no mother and instead of a grandmother who would help out in the kitchen it was the crusty old grandfather. Ed

Hartmann, who produced the series for ten of its twelve seasons, called the show a "wonderful idea" for television because "you had three young fellows, each one at a different age, and you create stories about them at each level of their growing up. So you had a constant play of change. You weren't dealing with something that was static, where you had to improvise or bring people in from outside - all the things that create failure in television."

As noted, Fred was not the first actor cast for *My Three Sons*, William Frawley, the 73-year-old curmudgeon best known as blustery yet lovable Fred Mertz, was cast as the grandfather on the show, Michael Francis O'Casey, or, as the family would affectionately call him, "Bub." Frawley later described his character as the "den mother of the Douglas family ... He's an irascible, gruff-voiced old badger, with a vaudeville background, a some-times-too-vivid imagination, and a bark much worse than his bite," much like the man who portrayed him.

Of course, Frawley and Fred went way back, having appeared together in two 1930s films, *Car 99* and *The Princess Comes Across*, when Frawley was one of the most sought after character actors in films and Fred was just becoming one of its leading stars. Then, years later, they were together again on *The Lucy-Desi Comedy Hour*. Fred was delighted to work with Frawley, even though he did occasionally worry about his health and hard-drinking reputation. Fred went so far as to inquire about Frawley's drinking with Desi Arnaz, at whose studio (Desilu) the show would be shot and who worked with Frawley for nine years. Arnaz, who was, himself, descending into alcoholism at the time, reassured him that Frawley was a heavy drinker on his own time but a complete professional when working.

Frawley became a favorite of most everybody on the show. Production manager Stephens recalls him as a "great guy, they don't make people like him anymore. When Bill took a liking to you, you couldn't shake him." Frawley took a liking to Stephens, probably due to Stephens' love of base-ball, a sport which Frawley had been a life-long enthusiast.

Frawley always had an eye for young, pretty women and took an instant liking to blonde Cynthia Pepper, who was cast in the recurring role of the girl-friend of the show's eldest son Mike. Pepper would later recall that she would go to lunch with Frawley practically every day that she worked on the show. "He would have a couple of nips with his lunch, but when we got back to the set he was very professional and nobody could tell he had been drinking. He could be cantankerous and would occasionally use some salty language, but he was never bawdy, at least when I was around. I liked him a lot."

One day Frawley was eyeing a beautiful redhead on the set who was working as a guest star for that week. He summoned John Stephens over to him and pointed her out and said with gruff relish, "Boy, would I like to fuck her." Stephens was slightly jarred since the beautiful redhead was his wife, Joan. "Oh," an apologetic Frawley replied to Stephens. "Forget I said that."

Hank Jones, a young actor who made several guest appearances over the years on *My Three Sons*, would recall that "the real treat for me on the early black-and-white *My Three Sons* was working with a genuine show business legend, William Frawley ... Bill was a superlative character actor and a real character himself." Jones recalls that Frawley had an "active libido" and that "no young starlet's backside was safe from a Frawley pinch when she wasn't looking ... but no malice was meant by it." Jones also recalls how "fondly" the cast and crew would look at Frawley whenever he arrived on the set and that despite his age and infirmities when the cameras rolled, "he would gather his strength and growl out his lines like he did fifty years before."

Don Grady, cast as the middle son, Robbie, would recall Frawley as "one of the funniest people I've ever known. He loved to make people laugh, and I was an easy target for him, because he could make me laugh so easily." Stanley Livingston, cast as the youngest son, Chip, got his initiation to salty language hanging around Frawley. He would recall a Thanksgiving episode where Frawley is in the backyard attempting to carve a turkey and having considerable difficulty in doing so. "He couldn't get this line he had to say out, and all of a sudden he started stabbing the turkey and yelling, 'Goddamn, fuck! Who wrote this shit,'" which convulsed the boys into fits of laughter. According to Gene Reynolds, who would direct the third and fourth seasons, "Who wrote this shit" became a common Frawley utterance when Frawley, increasingly, had problems remembering his lines.

The first of the "sons" to be cast was nine-year-old Stanley Livingston. Stanley was the son of an appliance store owner and had spent a considerable amount of his childhood as an actor, along with his younger brother Barry. The two Livingston boys were discovered at a swim club in Hollywood and cast on *The Adventures of Ozzie and Harriet* as neighborhood kids. Stanley also appeared in such films a *Rally 'Round the Flag, Boys!* with Paul Newman and *Please Don't Eat the Daisies* with Doris Day.

According to John Stephens, Livingston confidently came into his audition and announced, "My name is Stanley Livingston and no cracks!" With that first utterance they were sure they had found their "Chip." Stephens went through the ritual of interviewing some other actors for the part but his own mind was made up and in the end Livingston was the only one he brought in to meet with Don Fedderson, who came away equally impressed. He was cute but not too cute, with tousled blond hair and a boyish devil-may-care attitude. He could also capture the pathos of the character, the only one that seemed to openly grieve the loss of his mother in many of those early shows.

Ryan O'Neal was originally signed to play the eldest son, Mike, but the director, Peter Tewksbury, who had guided *Father Knows Best* through its long run, had worked with O'Neal on an episode of that show and didn't like him. Just before shooting on the first episode of *My Three Sons* was to begin Tewksbury gave the producers an ultimatum: pay off O'Neal and recast the role or it was implied that Tewksbury would walk. According to Stephens, Tewksbury was "showing his authority," but Fedderson admired him and felt that the show needed him more than it needed Ryan O'Neal and O'Neal was let go. That was only the beginning. On the second day of rehearsals the actor hired to play the middle son, Robbie, Billy Chapin, brother of Lauren Chapin who played "Kitten" on *Father Knows Best*, was also let go. According to Don Grady, "The director, Peter Tewkesbury, had just come from directing *Father Knows Best*, and I guess it was his idea to bring Billy on the show. But he was a little too rebellious, and MacMurray wouldn't have that."

At the start of the second day of rehearsals, nineteen-year-old Tim Considine was signed to play the assertive oldest son Mike. Considine was born to parents in the industry and had been acting since he was 12. His best-known work was for the Disney studios on their *Mickey Mouse Club*, appearing in the *Spin and Marty* programs with Tommy Kirk. He had also recently appeared in *The Shaggy Dog* with Fred. Mike was a leader (by example) of his younger siblings and, when necessary, would attempt to "boss them around."

Considine respected Fred and thought he was an "amazing actor," but Considine had already spent several years in the industry and, at 19, he had formed some definite opinions of his own regarding characterization. He would later remember that he "almost got off on the wrong foot" with Fred. "I know we had a kind of confrontation early on," Considine would recall, "where both of us went away … huffed. It had been in front of the crew. A creative difference was what it was. And I was very strong defending my position, and when I got back in my dressing room, I was sort of going over it and grousing, and saying, 'By God, I think that this is the way it should have been done' and dad a dad a, you know, and I'm not gonna back off of it because of Fred MacMurray or anybody else,'… and I got to thinking about it, it seemed, 'Whoops. I think he is right. Wait a minute.' And I gritted my teeth and went and apologized to him, and I believe, I'm pretty sure I said something about it on the set as well when we next went on."

By lunchtime on the second day of rehearsals they still didn't have an actor to play Robbie, the middle son. Robbie was to be the heartthrob and "wild-child," or as wild as early 1960s television would permit. He was also to be the one who would exhibit his creativity through his music and Robbie was always in a band. Sixteen-year-old Don Grady was yet another veteran who had spent much of his childhood in front of the cameras. He also had a history with the Disney Studios, appearing as a Mousketeer on *The Mickey Mouse Club*, but more recently Grady had achieved a reputation within the business as a dependable young dramatic actor and really hadn't done much, if any, comedy up to this point in time.

Grady was called out of school at lunchtime and his mother took him to Desilu (the studio where the show was filmed) to meet the producers. He recalls the interview lasting only around twenty minutes. In that time he did a reading which John Stephens would later call "sensational." Following his reading, Don returned to school and, by the time he got home (and much to his astonishment), he found out that he had the part. Grady would

The original cast of **My Three Sons**: *Stanley Livingston, William Frawley, Fred, Tim Considine and Don Grady.*

later recall that one of the reasons he may have landed the role was because he had a dimple in his chin "just like MacMurray's." Hank Jones, who worked most frequently with Grady on the show, offered his perspective of Grady. "Don … was an extremely likable young man, also easy to work with and just as laid-back as Fred MacMurray in his own way. Their quiet attitudes were so similar that they really could have been father and son."

Because *My Three Sons* was Don Grady's first comedy, he was too preoccupied early on to take much notice of Fred. "I was really concentrating on who this 'Robbie' character was." But when he did, his first impression was of the man's physicality. "He was huge! Very tall. And very quiet most of the time. The best way to describe Fred is that he was primarily a shy person. Really very polite, proper, and considerate. I think that's where his humor came from." He would add that Fred's "timing was perfect. He was this big, proper man and his reactions to the improprieties around him were hilarious." Grady hastened to add that "he could be an excellent cad too" and pointed out Fred's performance in *The Caine Mutiny*. "You'll hate him."

The "MacMurray System" of filming didn't really matter to Don. "… I was feeling that the show was something special … What did I care! We were changing clothes 4-13 times a day, doing all the kitchen scenes for days in a row, until we couldn't eat anymore; I was just starting to get the comedy thing down, and I was doing whatever they told me regarding the wardrobe and makeup. If they had said, I needed to fly to New Jersey to get dressed, I would've done it. It wasn't till several years later that I noticed the hair being sandpapered off my legs from the constant change of pants!"

Finally, with the casting of Livingston, Considine, and Grady — along with Fred and Frawley — the core cast of *My Three Sons* was set. Even though Fred was part owner of the show, he really had nothing to do with their casting. Those matters, with rare exception, were left to the producers.

On the set Fred was low-key and didn't put on the airs of a star. He arrived on the set at 8:30 in the morning, sharp, knowing his lines and ready to go. By the time he had arrived, the set had been lit and the other actors were assembled and in their make up and ready to go, because, with Fred's limited schedule, it was imperative that they begin right away and film as much as possible while they had him. In between scenes, Fred usually retreated to his dressing room trailer. When asked if Fred ever "hung out" on the set, Don Grady replied, "Never! Fred did not hang. He was a private person, and sometimes I felt it took some effort for him to be sociable … although he was excellent at it! We rarely saw him at the commissary for lunch. Maybe twice. He brown-bagged his lunch and ate by himself in his dressing room. When he was done with the day's shooting, he would jaunt quickly toward the exit … he was happy to go home … Fred did not hang."

In a nutshell, the crew had to shoot all of Fred's scenes, master shots, long shots, close-ups, for every episode over the course of 65 days, and so when he was on the set this had priority over anything else. Furthermore, the writers had to begin the season with at least 26 ready and completed scripts to begin shooting. So that during those 65 days when he was available, everything revolved around Fred, every scene favored and involved him. When his 65 days were up, the rest of the cast, crew and guest stars would reassemble the body of each episode and if their characters had to react to Fred in some way they would actually be responding to the script girl or somebody, often holding up a mop so that the actors could have a proximity of eye contact with "Fred," the mop ultimately earned the nickname "Fred MacMop." Beverly Garland, who joined the cast in its tenth season, would call *My Three Sons* the "strangest show" she had ever been involved in because the star was never there.

If Fred felt any guilt over his unique shooting schedule, he never exhibited it. He later wrote, "I do all my work in about three months. This calls for great precision on the part of Don Fedderson ... but it leaves me free to make a movie ... and still recharge the batteries with at least five months of glorious, do-nothing leisure." The rest of the cast didn't really seem to mind either. According to Hank Jones, the cast was just happy to be gainfully employed and understood that without Fred there would probably be no show.

Fred's parental wisdom as Steve Douglas was imparted both on-screen and occasionally off. John Stephens would recall that "a lot of the kids ... were dating at the time (well, not Stanley yet)... Don and Tim would come in with stories of their escapades from the night before. And Fred would be sitting there, 'you shouldn't have done that. You shouldn't have done that.' And it was so funny to hear him, 'Oh, no. I'd never do that. No, no. Never do that. Watch out, watch out. You never can tell what they're after. Watch out.'"

Don Grady recalls Fred as a "no-nonsense guy, kind of like your parent ... he really was that way and he did expect us to react like stars. When we got on the set it was like, 'You better know your lines.' It wasn't like a dictator, but it was a fatherly kind of 'know your stuff.' We obviously respected him, and of course he had a sense of humor." But like so many others, Grady also recalled Fred as basically "shy, introverted and keep to yourself." Considine would recall Fred as "A class act. Wonderful guy. Very fatherly. A real straight-shooter. Bashful. People used to mistake his reserved behavior for aloofness. It wasn't aloofness. He was just a very private man, and a bit timid in social conditions."

Fred did occasionally try to council his young co-stars regarding acting techniques. "Fred was not a proponent of 'method' acting, and made no bones about it," according to Don Grady. "It was one area in which he advised us a number of times. Fred felt the actor didn't need to 'feel' the emotion ... and with TV sometimes there wasn't enough time anyway. As long as the actor got the audience to feel the emotion, that was the goal. We all learned the double-take with the raised eyebrow from him. Stanley got it down the best." Around this time Fred explained his acting "philosophy" to Hollywood columnist Vernon Scott, "I have no theories. When the cameras are turning I simply listen to what the other guy is saying and react as I might under real life circumstances." One visitor to the set of *My Three*

Sons would later write that "the three sons on the show — Tim Considine, Don Grady and Stanley Livingston — are smart enough to know when they are in the company of a professional actor, and on the set, they watch their 'father.' After a scene, they talk it over with him, listen to his suggestions, and ask questions. With the show going into its fourth season, there's little doubt that Fred's three 'sons' have learned from his experience as an actor."

Stanley Livingston was then (and still today) impressed by the fact that he was working with Fred MacMurray in a television series. "It's very hard for people today," he later told *Television Chronicles Magazine*, "our generation and people that are younger than us - they look, and Fred MacMurray's just some old geezer, but at the point in time when he came on TV he was, I mean, a major movie star." Livingston would later liken Fred's turning up in a television series akin to Robert Redford doing a series. Despite this, Livingston was more impressed working with Frawley than with Fred. "I didn't even realize until the day we started shooting that William Frawley was going to be the grandfather ... to be honest, I probably knew less about Fred MacMurray than Bill Frawley. Being the age I was, TV was the medium I was a little more familiar with, and I already was watching Bill on *I Love Lucy* for two or three years."

Cynthia Pepper recalls her character on the show, Jean Pearson, as the "girl next door" type that she almost always played at that point in her career. *My Three Sons* was Pepper's first big break in the business and she would recall Fred as being "very nice, a generous actor to work with and patient with the other actors. He was a very private person and when he wasn't on the set he would often spend his time in his dressing room, but he was never unpleasant." Pepper also came away impressed that Fred, one of the wealthiest actors in the business, would brown bag it for lunch most days when he was on the show.

Hank Jones affirms these impressions of Fred. "I remember Mr. M being very quiet and reserved and smoking his pipe a lot, just a nice laid-back guy."

Fred occasionally used his star prerogative in shaping the scripts, but frequently it was just when the scene was about to be filmed rather than before. "Everything had to be completely accurate, or he didn't want to do it," recalled John Stephens. "In one episode, the eldest son, Mike, has a girlfriend. The girlfriend has a crush on Mike's father. Mike and the girl are driving to some lover's lane type of place for youngsters, and the girl is asking all of these questions about Mr. Douglas. The next day, Mr. Douglas is in his office and gets a phone call from the girl. Immediately, Fred MacMurray shouts, 'Stop! Get John Stephens down here!'... I rush down to the set. 'John, this scene here - how did this girl get my phone number? How can there be a scene where she calls me up? Don't tell me she got my number out of the phone book because she doesn't know where I work.'" Stephens explained to Fred that because he isn't there for the filming of every scene it was assumed that she asked Mike where his father works and that is how she knew where to call him. This usually satisfied Fred, if a logical explanation was provided, but he always had to make sure each script had logic behind it or he would feel the show would lose credibility with the audience if the situation was absurd.

A TV magazine touting the new series, September 1960.

American television viewers were introduced to the Douglas family on September 29, 1960 in an episode titled "Chip off the Old Block" about father and son both having female problems. Director Peter Tewksbury, who helmed the entire first season, would sum up Fred's character, Steve Douglas, this way: "Steve ... has an alert agile mind, a sharp tongue and an ultimate sense of the ridiculous ... as head of a household he tries to sustain a role of propriety, often to his own acute embarrassment." *Variety* reviewed the new show in its October 5, 1960 issue, "*My Three Sons,* the new Fred MacMurray-Bill Frawley comedy of Don Fedderson's packaging outfit, shapes up as an amiable, leisurely family comedy ... MacMurray was excellent in his quiet comedy style, and Frawley was perfectly cast as his wry father-in-law who acted as chief cook and bottle-washier. Tewksbury got a very good performance out of young Livingston ... and Tim Considine and Don Grady as the other boys, though with little to do in the opener, looked as if they fit in right." Fred, June and the girls watched the opening show at home and, as June would later recall, the girls began a ritual, which would last for many years to come. They would see Fred's image on the television, run to the screen and kiss it, and then run back to the easy chair in which Fred was comfortably seated, watching the program, and kiss the real him. (Fred, who began losing his hair during the mid-'40s, had worn a toupee on screen and at important industry events for many years. But away from the studios and in his personal life he rarely wore it. When the twins would see one of his early films on television they would call to him, "Quick, daddy, come and look at yourself when you had hair!")

The *Variety* critic found the show to his liking, but still thought that it might lose the competitive wars to NBC's *Bachelor Father*, which starred John Forsythe and had a similar theme with a motherless household. However, *Sons* won its timeslot and went on to be the 13th highest rated series for the entire season and ABC's second best performing series (after *The Real McCoys*). The average rating for *My Three Sons* during its freshman season was 25.8; meanwhile, *Bachelor Father* didn't even crack the top 20. In 1960, Fred was not only featured in one of the most acclaimed movies of the year (*The Apartment*) but also starring in the second highest rated new series on television (only *The Andy Griffith Show* on CBS was rated higher). Fred had accomplished what very few major film stars had ever done before or since, he proved that his durability as an actor reached beyond the big screen to the far more intimate small screen. Fred's laid-back, easygoing, pipe-smoking style was a perfect fit. With the success of *My Three Sons*, Fred had found his 1960s' niche and he would never turn back. From this point forward, in the words of Don Grady, he would fully embrace "cardigan sweater roles."

III

When the show returned for its second season, changes were made. The biggest by far, though perhaps unnoticed by viewers, was the change in directors. Peter Tewksbury was a very creative director. Fred liked Tewksbury and admired the way he came to the show "armed with a detailed description of our TV family. He listed our street address, even our telephone number. Pete was convinced that all this was necessary to build the kind of show we wanted. To Pete those pages of family description, even the name of my youngest TV son's school teacher, were important in building our TV family as believable, living individuals." Tewksbury's dedication to the show was rewarded in another way; he became one of the few people associated with the show to be nominated by the industry for an Emmy Award. He didn't win but it was a measure of his esteem among his fellow directors. Fred was himself never nominated for an Emmy for his work on *My Three Sons*. Like his being overlooked for an Oscar nomination, he never let it bother him, at least not publicly. "My wife June was upset about it," he commented after being overlooked for the Emmy for the 1968-1969 season. "But I remained calm. I told her if they gave an award for durability I might get it some day." Don Grady would later say, "It bothered Fred, it bothered the producers ... of which Fred was one. It never occurred to me or the other sons, as far as I know, that there could be anything better than what we already had! I remember Ed Hartmann, one of our key producers, and some of the writers kvetching about it on the set one time. The show was very well written, and funny, and had an impact on its audience, yet the critics were overlooking it." Grady believed that Fred's skills as a comedic actor were "underestimated."

However, at Fedderson productions, Peter Tewksbury was becoming a liability. He was perceived as too much of a perfectionist and insisting on too many retakes, and, with Fred's limited availability, speed was of the essence. The first season Fred ended up working twenty-five days over the 65 specified in his contract, and in doing so he collected a cool $125,000 (a clause in his contract paid Fred $5,000 for every day he worked over the contracted 65). According to John Stephens, Don Fedderson wasn't used to losing money on a show, and so they held a meeting to determine why; the eventual consensus being that it was mainly Tewksbury's fault and so he wasn't invited back to direct the second season.

When he heard that there was an opening on the directing staff of *My Three Sons,* Mitchell Leisen, who guided Fred through so many films during the '30s and '40s and had been asked by Fred to direct his television debut in 1953 as a personal favor, sent Fred a telegram asking for the directing job on his show. Leisen had fallen on hard times. He had directed his last film in 1957 and had done some television since then but was earning most of his income through interior decorating and doing staging work for friends like Dorothy Lamour. When Fred received the telegram from Leisen he hesitated and wondered how he would respond. "I know Leisen's passes [at other men] troubled Fred MacMurray a great deal," Leisen biographer David Chierichetti would later say. Ultimately, Fred decided not to respond. "He sent me a telegram asking for the job," Fred recalled to Chierichetti. "He was, well, you know, a homosexual and he had gotten into some trouble on a picture he was making in Europe. With the young boys we had working on the show; I just didn't think it was right. So I never answered the telegram." Richard Whorf, a former stage and film actor turned director, was hired by Fedderson to direct the second season.

Whorf did a commendable job directing the second season, but in production manager Stephens' mind he was too much of a yes man to Fred to be effective. "Fred was right about things a lot of the times," Stephens says. "A lot of times he wasn't." Whorf was also not well physically and the demands of the "MacMurray System" began to take a toll on his health. There was one week when he took ill midway through the filming, so Stephens took over for him. When Fred found out, he let Stephens know that he would help him. This made Stephens apprehensive. "Please, Fred," Stephens recalls telling his star, "don't be rewriting the script as we go along. If you have any changes, give them to me tonight." Fred assured Stephens he had no problem with the script. The next day Fred was rehearsing a scene with guest-star Joan Blondell. The rehearsal went well and Stephens called for the scene to be filmed. As Fred and Blondell were shooting the scene Fred suddenly stopped the action to tell Stephens that he had a good idea which would improve the scene comically. Stephens had to painstakingly explain to Fred that the idea he had would add considerable time to the scene and something else would need to be cut if they did it that way. Fred gave in, but he had many more suggestions for Stephens as the day continued, driving Stephens crazy. Later that night when Stephens was at home pouring

Fred as Steve Douglas on **My Three Sons.**

himself a drink to unwind from a very exacting day, Fred called him. "John, did I give you any trouble?" he asked. Despite this, Stephens would say that Fred was "the best actor and star I ever had the pleasure of working with."

John Stephens' contribution as production manager was immeasurable. He worked with the director and producer to make sure the show (which was already very difficult to shoot) ran as smoothly as possible and, when need be, he could be intimidating. "John Stephens used to scare the bejesus out of me," Don Grady recalls. "He would show up on the set and take a stance, thumbs hooked into his pants pockets, elbows straight out, feet wide apart, and glare at me as though I were the cause of all of his problems. He actually brought me to tears once … But John Stephens has turned out to be probably the biggest reason for the show's continued success. He steered the corporate decisions with a firm and intuitive wisdom, and kept peace on the set with an iron hand, especially difficult to do with the rotating casts and the insane way we shot the show. With all the comings and goings of writers, actors and directors, John was the glue that held it together. And to think he did it for 12 years!"

My Three Sons was still strong in the weekly ratings during its second season, jumping from 13th place in the weekly Nielsen ratings to 11th, the highest ranking it would hold during its 12 years. ABC definitely wanted the show back for a third season, but an unexpected problem came up: Fred MacMurray wasn't sure he wanted to return for another season.

Fred still enjoyed doing the show and enjoyed working with "his boys." He said in one interview that most child actors could be "monsters, but not these boys." But he still thought he was working too much, with an annual movie commitment included. He also worried about over-exposure. But the main reason he gave was to spend more time with his twin daughters. "I want to start spending more time with them while they're young and what with more pictures coming up all the time, I find myself working all year." Some felt that this was just a renegotiating ploy, but Fred did re-sign for a third season and he did get some improvements in his contract. Instead of being required to work until 6:30 P.M., he could now leave at 5:00 P.M. Instead of a five-day work week he would work four days and have long weekends. When the announcement was made that Fred was coming back Daniel Melnick of ABC enthused that Fred "richly deserved the designation he won a few years back as Television Father of the Year, and as far as the public is concerned, he has been the Television Father of every year since."

Another reason Fred always returned was that he genuinely liked the show and the character of Steve Douglas. "The father in our show isn't a dope," he said. "He can handle things better than I can at home. Then, too, we don't have any big messages. No dramatic problems. I play myself. Most actors do. Maybe I happen to be the kind of fellow I'm playing. I don't tell jokes. I react to the jokes. I'm not really a very funny fellow."

IV

The third season (1962-1963) ushered in yet another director, Gene Reynolds, who began his career as an actor and then, with the assistance of his friend Jackie Cooper, was launched as a television director on Cooper's television show *Hennesey*. From there, Reynolds went on to direct such series as *Hogan's Heroes*, *The Ghost and Mrs. Muir*, *Room 222* and, most memorably, as producer and director on *M*A*S*H**. Of his two seasons directing *My Three Sons* Reynolds would later state, "One year would have been enough. I had exhausted all I could do." He blamed his agent of the time for being too lazy and allowing him to be committed to the show for two years rather than lining up other opportunities.

Still, Reynolds adapted well to the "MacMurray System" of shooting the show; he was younger and more vigorous than his predecessor, Richard

Whorf. But the process was as demanding as ever. "Because of the shooting schedule we had to match every shot so we had a photographer on the set who would take pictures so we could match clothes and hair styles. The prop man had a big job too and he was given this little closet and it's amazing all he put in that closet, it was like Fibber McGee's closet!"

Matching the hair styles was probably the most common problem on the set. Tim Considine would later say, "My hair had to be the same six months from now in a close-up as it was ... it was a real pain in the ass ... When I left *My Three Sons* I vowed that I would never do that again, and I grew my hair down to my ass. Tied it back and never messed with it."

John Stephens would recall an instance when Vera Miles made a guest appearance on the show. She came in early and shot all the scenes which involved her with other cast members but not Fred, who was still away shooting a movie. Several months then passed and Miles was required to return to shoot her scenes with Fred. In the meanwhile, she had also done a film. Before she was set to return, she called John Stephens and said, "John, I've got to tell you something. My hair is shorter." Stephens didn't think that would be much of a problem, "Ah, no one'll notice that," he replied. "Well," said Miles, "it's also a different color." "Oh," Stephens gulped. (In fact, many guest-stars never worked with Fred. Rose Marie would recall that she did the show "a couple of times" but that she never shared a scene with Fred. Hank Jones, who appeared several times and seemed to share several scenes with Fred, actually recalls working with him once; otherwise, it was saying "Hi" to Adele the script girl saying Fred's lines.)

Gene Reynolds also experienced what the other directors had with Fred: his tendency, just prior to shooting a scene, to offer a suggestion or request a change. "Fred never was involved with scripts or story conferences," Reynolds recalls, "but when it came time to shoot a scene he often made a suggestion or found some kind of problem which we needed to resolve." Reynolds recalls that on his first show with Fred he found fault with how Reynolds was shooting a scene and called out for the producer Ed Hartmann to come down to the set. "I took him aside," Reynolds recalls, "and explained to him why the scene was written the way it was, we discussed it and when Ed arrived on the set, Fred called out to him, 'That's OK we don't need you.' From that point forward he trusted me and we worked extremely well together." Reynolds found that while Fred got along with the kids it was his observation that there was a "certain separation" between them, "there were no hugs, but no hostility either."

As for the kids they were very fond of Reynolds. John Stephens would later write in his memoirs, "The kids just adored him ... He really understood acting and understood the kids ... The shows ran very smoothly with him." Hank Jones sensed that, as a former child actor himself, Reynolds "had great empathy for the pressure we were under to deliver a good performance. He was patient and kind and made it easy." And for his part, Reynolds was fond of the kids, on the most part. He found Grady and the Livingston brothers to be "exceptionally sweet guys." His feelings for Considine, the oldest, were a little more ambiguous. "He is very bright, but he could be difficult."

One of the changes made during the third season of *My Three Sons* was to bring in a permanent girlfriend for oldest sibling Mike. Meredith MacRae, the pretty daughter of Gordon and Sheila MacRae, was hired to play Sally. She would recall what an "honor" it was for her, a novice in the business, to have her initiation in show business working with veterans like Fred and Bill Frawley. "I really consider myself very blessed and lucky because they were just both such consummate professionals. They were wonderful actors, and delightful people as well off-camera. You couldn't imagine or fantasize a better first job, to suddenly come into this family that had already been together for several years and be made to feel welcome." John Stephens would tell authors Rob Edelman and Audrey Kupferberg that this feeling of being welcome was due to Fred. "It was a great cast. Everybody got along. That's because Fred MacMurray, I think, set the pace."

One of the highlights of the third season was an episode which featured perhaps the most famous of the many guest stars that appeared on *My Three Sons*, and a good friend of Fred's, Jimmy Stewart, and they got him at a premium price and with a resulting controversy. The storyline dealt with Robbie getting a reputation for being an "egg-head" in school by getting A's on his exams and getting teased by the other kids because of it. The script called for somebody to come into Robbie's class and give an inspirational speech to the class about the importance of working hard and getting good grades. They didn't want a fictional character but a real-life hero. Their first choice was John Glenn, who had just orbited around Earth, but he proved unavailable, as did many other astronauts.

At the time, and for many years to come, Stewart gave two weeks per year to the United States Air force as a Major-General. According to John Stephens, the head of the Hollywood film office for the Air Force suggested Stewart. "We'd like Jimmy Stewart," Stephens replied, "but we're not going to get him," expecting that Stewart would be much too expensive for their budget. The Air Force representative replied that Stewart was at that time their property and he could order him to appear as part of his two-week commitment to them. Furthermore, they could order Stewart to appear without receiving any fee. This was just a little too much for Stephens, who worked out a deal paying Stewart scale, $70 per day. Stewart reported to the set and was letter-perfect performing his scenes in one take.

After the Stewart segment aired, Stewart's agent, who had no idea that all of this had transpired, called up Stephens. "He's flipping out to put it mildly." The agent told Stephens that Stewart recalled that Stephens had mentioned something about donating $20,000 in Stewart's name to the Air Force Academy. Stephens told him that was never discussed and it was news to him. But the agent was adamant and so a meeting was arranged between Don Fedderson, the Air Force's representative to Hollywood, Stewart and his agent. The Air Force backed Stephens' interpretation that no mention was made of a donation to the Academy in Stewart's name. Stewart replied that he "took it for granted" it would be done. Since the Air Force backed up Stephens, Stewart and his agent "stormed out" of the office.

When it had been proposed that Stewart would be a guest-star, Fred was a little "dubious," according to Stephens, and it's not known if the controversy hurt his friendship with Stewart or not (Fred didn't appear in any scenes with Stewart, nor was he present when Stewart filmed his scenes), but Stephens guessed that it might have cost him a job several years later as production manager on Stewart's own television series.

The work on *My Three Sons* was hard, especially with scenes from multiple episodes being shot at the same time. But there was a sense of fun too, and occasionally Fred would even get involved. Don Grady tells the following story: "Fred occasionally liked to send a laugh up to the execs watching the dailies. There was a scene where Sally, Mike's girlfriend, was spending the night in the Douglases' guest room. Steve, Mike and Sally were saying goodnight to each other in the hallway. They then each walked off to their separate rooms and closed the doors. On the aired version, that's where the scene ended. But for the dailies, after a few moments, Mike came out of his bedroom and stealthfully snuck down the hallway toward the guest room, where Sally was staying. Just before he put his hand on the doorknob, Steve abruptly opened his door, stuck his head into the scene, and barked, 'MIKE!' Mike, of course, scurries back to his room, tail between his legs."

Hank Jones also recalls a funny incident on the set. "We had a scene in a schoolroom on one of the episodes. Just before the cameras rolled, the assistant director noted that the blackboard was empty, with no writing on it. So he asked one of the extras to hurriedly go up and just write some gibberish on the board to make it look like a real schoolroom blackboard. She did. We started filming a few takes until there was this big yell from behind the camera. On the blackboard, the extra had written 'What was the Mann Act?' [The Mann Act was a law that promised punishment for anyone taking a girl over a state line for immoral purposes.] We had to film everything again from the top, with muttered curses from the assistant director, but smiles and winks from the cast and crew."

Jones also recalls a scene when Heinz Ketchup was sponsoring the show. "I remember that we had a scene in a malt shop … Somebody had to say 'Pass the catsup …' We had to stop filming until they checked with the sponsor to see how to pronounce the word (ketchup or catsup). The world stopped for at least a half hour until the clarification came thru."

One of the fringe benefits for the cast when Chevrolet was sponsoring the show (during its first three seasons) was the presentation of a brand-new car each year to each cast member. The company also sponsored an annual party for the cast and crew of the shows that they sponsored. Tim Considine later recalled one party, which included one of his favorite memories of Fred. "I remember dancing at this party that was given by the advertising agency, and I was dancing away and looked over and there was Fred playing saxophone with the band. [He was] just lost in it. It was wonderful. Absolutely wonderful."

V

By the fifth season Bill Frawley was slowing down. He continued to go across the street every day to his favorite restaurant, Nickodell's, for lunch. He was drinking more than he was eating and finally it was catching up with him. John Stephens would later state, "Bill Frawley, of all the drinkers I've been around in my life, I've never been around one that could hold more than Bill Frawley could." Each year the actors had to have a physical for insurance purposes. According to Stephens, the company had a doctor who "would pass anybody" and Frawley had always been insured, but this time the doctor told Stephens he couldn't pass him, "He should have been dead two years ago." Stephens didn't tell Frawley what the doctor told him, but instead gave a report of the situation to Don Fedderson and they decided to gamble on keeping Frawley alive for the first thirteen episodes of the fifth season and then take it from there.

According to Gene Reynolds, Fred began to worry about Frawley. "Fred would come up to me and say he was worried that Bill was having a series of small strokes, because as time went on he had a harder time recalling his lines." Reynolds says he tried to make it easier for him, "sometimes I succeeded and sometimes I didn't." It got to be that Frawley would be "so bombed" after lunch that John Stephens would have to put him in a master shot next to Tim Considine who "had to stand next to him with his arm around him, and when it was time for Bill Frawley to give a line, Tim had to hit him to wake him up. He'd fall asleep standing up."

When the first 13 episodes of the season were completed, the decision was made; they couldn't risk continuing with Frawley on the show without insurance. Frawley was informed of this and, according to Stephens, "he didn't take it well." Fedderson decided that Frawley was too beloved in the role of Bub for another actor to take over the part. So, instead they wrote a story where Bub goes off to visit his mother (!) in Ireland, and, while he is gone, his brother, another salty, gruff character with a heart of mush, takes his place, Uncle Charley O'Casey, an ex-merchant marine. To play him they cast another veteran character actor, William Demarest, who, like Frawley, had also worked with Fred in several films, most recently in Disney's *Son of Flubber*.

On the show the transition from Grandpa "Bub" to Uncle Charley was seamless, but on the set, less so. Frawley came to the studio to pack up some of his belongings and Demarest was there, having arrived a day earlier than expected for wardrobe fittings. According to John Stephens, "It was a rather ugly scene on the set." Apparently, Frawley complained bitterly about having been forced to leave and the fact that Demarest was the one replacing him, because they had been competitors in the past for many of the same roles. "They had a few words which don't bear repeating," according to Stephens. (In the book *Meet The Mertzes*, a duel biography of William Frawley and Vivian Vance, it is indicated that Frawley would occasionally come back to the *Sons* set after leaving the show but inevitably would let his frustration show and criticize Demarest's reading of a line. After doing this a few times, Frawley was told he wouldn't be welcome back on the set any longer.)

After leaving the show Bill Frawley lived on for another year or so. His last acting job was filmed shortly before his death in March 1966. It was essentially a walk-on arranged by Lucille Ball for her *The Lucy Show*. On March 3, 1966, Frawley was walking on Hollywood Boulevard when he suddenly collapsed and died of a heart attack. The years of hard drinking had finally caught up with him. When informed of his death, Fred called Frawley's passing, "a great loss ... I'm terribly sad." His funeral was held at Good Samaritan Catholic Church in Hollywood. "Fred MacMurray and I were paired as pallbearers at the front of the coffin," recalled Desi Arnaz in his autobiography. "It was a very heavy coffin and a very hot day. Both of us were really sweating and struggling. I looked across at MacMurray and said, 'I know Bill is up there, looking down at us struggling with this goddamn coffin, sweating, breaking our backs, and I'll bet you he's laughing like hell.'"

The kids were close to Frawley and would accept Demarest, but not with the same warmth. Stanley Livingston was especially close to Frawley, who had become a kind of surrogate grandfather for him. "I was pretty upset ... the fact that he wasn't coming back. Until my brother came aboard, he probably was the person I was closest to." Livingston came to like Demarest too, though "probably not as close as with Bill [Frawley]..." Frawley and Demarest were roughly the same age, but Demarest was in much better mental and physical condition. "I'll never forget the time," Tim Considine would recall, "he did one of his patented pratfalls. It was frightening; it was so good, and hysterically funny. I mean, it was really funny. Oh, yeah. He was a great faller. By God, his feet went up in the air and it looked like he landed on his ass. He was funny as hell."

Demarest was more distant with the kids, unlike the beloved Frawley. "Frawley may have been a cantankerous old guy," according to Stephens, "but he loved kids and got along great with them. Bill Demarest was much more of a professional, and he was a lot tougher on the kids." Hank Jones recalls one encounter with Demarest. "I once inquired about the health of his friend Spencer Tracy (with whom I once nearly collided on the MGM lot when Tracy was wobbling along on his bicycle, and neither of us was looking where he was going). Taciturn Demarest wasn't about to share his feelings with any young kid actor like me, so it was a pretty brief conversation and ended before it started."

As for Demarest, he conceded that when he joined the show he had landed in a "soft spot" due to the work Frawley had done in defining the part, but he quickly added, "I intend to make the part mine."

As the fifth season was coming to a close, other changes were in store. For one thing, Tim Considine didn't want to continue on the show. He increasingly had found that his character was more observing the action than participating in it. For the past two seasons he had steady girlfriend (Sally, played by Meredith MacRae), to whom he eventually got engaged. So he was no longer playing the field and the storylines involving girl problems had switched from his character to Don Grady's character of Robbie. He told *People* Magazine in 1992, "I got tired of playing clean-cut, boy-next-door types."

He was allowed in the last couple of years to write and even direct a couple of shows. One of his writing efforts was a memorable episode called "Goodbye Again," which aired during the fifth season and one which Considine would later call "revolutionary" because of the use of extensive flashbacks (the episode brought back Cynthia Pepper, his girlfriend from the first season, in a story in which they looked back in time).

But the most important decision was Fred's who, according to Stephens, had ended the season not really knowing if he was going to return for a sixth year, and ABC was anxious to renew the show, not for only one more season but for two seasons. But Fred kept hemming and hawing and finally, despite the ratings, ABC decided to take a pass on the show. Fred may have been distracted in making up his mind because shortly after the end of the fifth season, his mother, who had been in failing health for some time, died in early August at the age of 84. While funeral rites were conducted at Forest Lawn's Church of the Recessional, Maleta was buried in Beaver Dam.

Fred finally made up his mind on the future of the show and told Fedderson, "You know, I think I want to do the show again." Only thing, the network had already passed, but then CBS came to the rescue, decided to pick the show up for their network and, according to John Stephens, "the deal with CBS was unbelievable. They paid a goodly amount of money."

The show would begin its sixth season on a new network with one son leaving, Tim Considine, which made it imperative that another son be found, after all it was called *My Three Sons* not *My Two Sons*.

Fred in My Three Sons.

CHAPTER NINE

The Disney Years

The 1960s Disney Films

It has been suggested that the characters Fred played in many of the films he made for the Disney Studios were extensions of Walt Disney himself. Ned Brainard, the character Fred played in two highly popular Disney films, *The Absent Minded Professor* (1961) and its sequel *Son of Flubber* (1963), was a college professor who was always tinkering around experimenting and creating. According to Disney's house composer Richard Sherman, "Walt Disney identified with the characters Fred played — he was the Absent Minded Professor... [Walt] was always experimenting." It's also easy to see Disney in Lem Siddons, the community-minded man that Fred played in *Follow Me, Boys!* (1966). Lem is a man of small-town Midwestern values who wants to give back to his community and his way of giving back means giving the boys in his community a sense of purpose by organizing a boy scout troop. Tom Kirk, who appeared in more than twenty Disney films between 1957 and 1965, put it well. "Fred could express the things which Disney felt but couldn't articulate, so he did it through Fred." Leonard Maltin called Fred a "perfect fit" for the Disney studios due to his family-friendly image, which was reinforced by the television success of *My Three Sons.*

Many actors who worked at the Disney studios have fond memories of the experience. "The Disney studios were one of the best studios to work at," recalled Karl Malden. "It was like a college campus. Between shots people would play volleyball, shoot baskets. It was a relaxed atmosphere. Disney didn't ask for much. He trusted filmmakers and the actors. He tried to get the best and, when he did, he let them do their work without much interference."

Hank Jones, who appeared in several Disney films of the '60s and '70s, likened the experience to attending summer camp. "Everyone smiled, really, because everyone was just plain glad to be working there," Jones later recalled. "There was a sense of pride in what we were doing in all of us at Disney that

I never felt before or since. The boss set the tone of the team atmosphere: he would get angry if someone ever called him 'Mr. Disney' instead of 'Walt.' Everybody got into the act. On my first day there, I noticed that the security guard at the gate looked familiar, kind of like a sad-faced basset hound. Later on I realized why I thought I knew him. The Disney animators had used his unique visage as a model for one of the characters in their *Lady and the Tramp* film, and here he was making sure I had a studio pass to get on the lot." Elliott Reid, who appeared opposite Fred in three Disney films, also confirmed that Disney insisted on being called "Walt." "He [Disney] was a charming man and very friendly," Reid recalls. "One day I ran into him and said, 'Hi, Mr. Disney,' and he told me to call him Walt." Dick Van Dyke recalled his first meeting with Disney, "I was called to meet him about *Mary Poppins* and found out why everybody called him Uncle Walt. He was the most old shoe guy I met in my life. He was comfortable to be around. An avuncular personality is what he was."

Tom Kirk was 14 when he began working at Disney. His recollections are more ambiguous. "When Disney was still alive, it was very clean, very wholesome — squeaky clean — and we had to walk on egg shells ... it was very Victorian." Kirk recalled that like any other studio in Hollywood the actors had a morals clause in their contracts and could be let go if they did something which the studio considered morally objectionable. He recalled that just prior to his arriving at Disney the young star of such Disney films as *Song of the South, Treasure Island* and the voice of *Peter Pan*, Bobby Driscoll, had been let go due to drug problems. "There was no Betty Ford Clinic back then." Walt Disney's nephew Roy E. Disney recalled Walt as "Victorian, prudish — that whole generation of our family was because that's the era they were from." For his part Fred liked the atmosphere around the Disney Studios. "There's a lack of tremendous pressure in the Disney studios," Fred said. "It's a pleasant place to be." He also was happy to make pictures he felt comfortable having his daughters see and associate their father with.

Between 1961 and 1967 Fred starred in five major Disney films (he also did one outside film project, but without the Disney name attached that film, *Kisses for My President* [1964], which did not succeed at the box office), which collectively grossed over 80 million dollars at the box office; two of the films, *The Absent Minded Professor* and *Son of Flubber,* were (like *The Shaggy Dog* before it) among the top box office successes of their release years. Walt Disney did not pay his actors top dollar, but the films were efficiently made and had a built-in audience which guaranteed wide exposure for the actors who appeared in them. Increasingly in the film industry stars were being given a percentage of the profits that the movies earned at the box office. This, however, was not the practice at the Disney Studios, which Fred later came to regret. "Nowadays everybody gets percentage deals," Fred said. "Disney doesn't go for percentages. But he does make successful movies and what is good about owning 100 percent of a movie that's a flop? However, I must admit that I would like to have a few percent of *The Professor* or *The Shaggy Dog*." Fred MacMurray was one of two actors who became the face of the Disney Studios in the early to mid-1960s, the other would have to be young Hayley Mills, the only other Disney actor of the time, other than Fred, who had films built around her. "Disney liked Fred enormously," recalled Tom Kirk, who very quickly added, "For one thing, Fred's movies were money in the bank." Disney himself put it this way, "He's a down-to-earth, practical actor. He has no temperament. He's considerate of everybody's problems and comes on understanding his lines. He has a way of handling comedy that nobody else can compare with. I've got a lot of respect for Fred and, besides, he's a wonderful fellow, I dunno, I just like him."

The Disney films, along with his father role on *My Three Sons*, would do much to lengthen Fred's career. He would find a new generation of fans who only a few years earlier probably had no idea who he was. "Suddenly the youngsters began to associate me with Flubber and with being a television father," Fred would later say. "Three years ago kids never knew who I was. Now my wife says appearing with me in public is like going out with Elvis Presley — so many kids want to say hello." A case in point would be an appearance he made at a commemorative parade at Black Lake, Colorado in the summer of 1961. He found himself surrounded by kids who wanted his autograph. "What d'you know? I've got a new audience," he said.

Just before starting production on *My Three Sons* Fred returned to the Disney Studios to begin shooting his second feature for them, a black-and-white slapstick comedy titled *The Absent Minded Professor*. The film offered some of the same elements as *The Shaggy Dog*; slapstick antics, a scientific potion which causes chaos, and even some of the same actors, but *Professor* also benefits from a higher budget and a wittier script and presents Fred in a somewhat more positive light than his harried dog-hating mailman from the earlier film. Also, unlike *The Shaggy Dog*, Fred's character dominates this film and has the audience's sympathies from beginning to end. It was near the end of filming on *The Shaggy Dog* that Walt Disney approached Fred with another idea for a comedy teaming. Fred was used to producers saying things like this to actors and then not following up, so he took Disney's comments in stride. "I didn't know Walt very well then. I went home and told my wife June about it, but added that I'd probably never hear about it again." He soon learned differently when Disney sent the completed script of *The Absent Minded Professor* to his attention. Fred read it and pronounced it a "wild one" and enthusiastically agreed to do it.

The movie opens with Professor Ned Brainard (Fred) conducting an experiment before his science class at Medfield College (no city or state given, but one gets the feeling that it's situated in a nice middle-class Midwestern city). An explosion occurs and the credits follow. Professor Brainard is certainly an intelligent instructor, but he is, as the title points out, absent minded. He suddenly recalls that he is to be married to his long-time fiancée, Betsy Carlisle (Nancy Olson), that very night. They had planned to be married twice before but each time absent-minded Ned, caught up in some scientific experiment, missed his own wedding. This time if he misses, it's

Professor Ned Brainard and wife drive into Disney Studios to film The Absent Minded Professor, *1961.*

three strikes and he's out. Still, the professor, being the man of science he is, can't resist, and is working on an experiment in his garage/lab, when an explosion occurs which knocks Ned out cold. When he awakens, he discovers that a gooey substance inside a heavy metal container is causing the container to rise up into the air. He comes up with a name for the substance called "Flubber," which is short for flying rubber. He also discovers that he was out so long that he once again missed the wedding, but is convinced that when Betsy hears about this discovery she will — once again — forgive him. He also believes that the substance could be used to save Medfield College, which has serious financial debts. But that isn't the case. In a wonderfully played scene between MacMurray and Olson, Betsy (who is also

Fred vs. the space age in The Absent Minded Professor. *©Walt Disney Productions.*

the Dean's secretary) is trying to take dictation from the Dean (veteran actor Leon Ames) when Brainard appears in the doorway and tries to whisper his reasons for missing the wedding to Betsy, and explain his discovery. But she will have no time for him or his explanations; besides, Brainard's arch-rival Professor Shelby Ashton (Elliott Reid) is now pursuing her. Brainard also has to contend with a corrupt businessman, Alonzo P. Hawk (Keenan Wynn), and his son Biff (Tommy Kirk), who discover Ned's formula and try to steal it for nefarious reasons.

Walt Disney had to believe in a story if he was to produce it, and so he actually came to feel it might be possible to actually concoct such a substance as "Flubber." "We had a technical adviser on *The Absent Minded Professor*," recalled producer Winston Hiber. "And after a while, Walt half-seriously thought it might be possible to actually develop something like Flubber. In other words, to Walt there had to be credibility. The audience had to be able to say, 'yes, even in a wild crazy way that could be true.'"

The film has several highlights: A basketball game between Medfield and its arch-rival, where Medfield is being slaughtered on the court until Ned applies Flubber to the soles of the players' shoes causing the much shorter Medfield players to suddenly leap above the opposition and make a stunning comeback; Ned using Flubber on the soles of his own shoes at the Homecoming Dance, impressing all with his acrobatics on the dance

Fred and Nancy Olson. © Walt Disney Productions.

floor; and Hawk, with Flubber on his shoes, becoming a human yo-yo. But the most enduring image of all is the one of Fred riding through the air in his Flubber-propelled Model T jalopy, almost colliding with space age jets. The Disney publicity department came up with a catchy tagline used in ads: "It's all about a wacky prof who invents an anti-gravity goo that flew!" "Ned the Nut," as Professor Brainard is dubbed by the students, is an endearing character and the film is one of Fred's career highlights — and he makes the most of it.

This was Nancy Olson's first film with Fred. (Had Fred accepted the role of Joe Gillis in *Sunset Blvd.*, he would have worked with Miss Olson a decade sooner since she played Gillis' young love interest in that classic film.) Olson enjoyed working with Fred and found that even though Fred was a total professional on the set he didn't take acting "too seriously," to Fred acting was a job, and not his all consuming passion. Personally, she found Fred to be easygoing and friendly, yet like most people who worked with Fred she came to realize that she couldn't get too close to him. "If there was pain in his life — tragedy — he didn't reveal that." She found Fred "self contained," which she felt was "highly unusual for an actor," noting that when he finished a scene he didn't seek approval from others for what he had just done because "he knew exactly what he was doing — all the time — and he did it so effortlessly." Olson believed that many people in the industry didn't take Fred seriously as an actor because he was essentially playing himself, but Olson found Fred's performance as Brainard, "so real and yet with extraordinary humor," an observation backed up by Leonard Maltin, who wrote in his essential book *The Disney Films*, "The most important casting of all … was that of Fred MacMurray, and he is inspired in the lead role. He plays his part with such utter conviction that you believe him completely — his naiveté, his absent-mindedness, his determination and even his occasional stupidity." Maltin believes that, in less skillful hands, the Brainard character could have been a "boob or a caricature." The Brainard-Betsy romance works well, despite the fact that Miss Olson was nearly twenty years younger than Fred, in part because Fred looks at least a decade younger than his fifty-odd years.

The Absent Minded Professor marked a reunion between Fred and character actor Elliott Reid, who had worked together on *Woman's World* several years before. While Reid didn't really get to know Fred on the earlier film, they developed a very easy working relationship on *Professor* which would endure through two more films with Reid cast, inevitably, as Fred's rival for the affections of the girl. In *Professor* where Fred is absent-minded, the Reid character, which would be the basic characterization for the films to follow, was stuffy and arrogant. Reid considered his Professor Shelby Ashton, "a miserable, condescending person — the man you love to hate. Shelby was convinced that he would get the girl and that Fred was a nothing … but I had a great time playing Shelby, he was a fun character to play." Reid recalled Fred as a "reticent person of Scottish background," and because he had a strong understanding of the Scottish people, Reid knew, instinctively, that Fred's shy nature would balk at being directly engaged in conversation. He would recall a young actor on the set who would "pull his chair up" to

Fred's and try to engage him in a conversation and the "pain" on Fred's face when this happened.

It is perhaps because Reid gave Fred the space he needed and respected his inwardness that they did begin to gravitate toward one another. "We both sensed that we were comfortable with each other, you can tell if you hit it off and we did, we just did." With Reid, Fred did what he seldom did with anybody, invited him to his dressing room, where he showed Reid trout flies he had made himself in his workshop at home. Reid found the flies to be well constructed and colorful and told Fred, who appreciated the compliment. From that point on Reid believes that Fred accepted him. Reid was impressed by Fred's ability as an actor, "he definitely was a good actor. The thing about his acting is that you weren't conscious of the fact that he was acting, which is a trait all the great actors possessed." Despite this warming up to each other on the set, they didn't become off-set friends. "He invited me to dinner at his house once and for some reason it was cancelled and it was never rescheduled."

One of the reasons Reid found *The Absent Minded Professor* a treat to make was because he was working with the English director Robert Stevenson, who had directed several well-made films from the late 1930s onward, including *Tom Brown's School Days* and *Jane Eyre*, which starred Orson Welles and Joan Fontaine. From the late 1950s until the mid-1970s Stevenson became the Disney studio's most prolific and celebrated director, helming such memorable films as *Old Yeller, Mary Poppins* (for which Stevenson was nominated for an Academy Award as Best Director), and the two *Flubber* films which starred Fred MacMurray. Reid would recall Stevenson as "wonderful" to work with and that he seemed to "guide" the actors more than direct them. Hank Jones, who also worked under Stevenson more than once, remembers the director as a "very proper" Englishman, "somewhat reserved, but with a noticeable twinkle in his eye. Robert worked almost always from illustrated storyboards made in conjunction with the Disney sketch artists which detailed each and every shot he would eventually make … Robert constantly referred to those storyboards as his prime 'bible.'" Tom Kirk came to "love" and respect Stevenson. "As much as I wanted Fred's friendship and approval, I wanted Robert's more," Kirk states. "I needed somebody strong in my life. I looked up to Robert Stevenson immeasurably. He was very easy to work with. I never saw him in a hurry. He was always patient and always relaxed. He said everything with a smile. I never had a cross word with him and he always treated me with kindness and respect, which I didn't always get from others at the studio."

Stevenson was a generous man who went out of his way to help actors whose careers had peaked and had been down on their luck. Such is the story of Ed Wynn's casting in *The Absent Minded Professor*, and two other films which were directed by Stevenson. "Wynn's memory was failing, and he

had difficulty memorizing dialogue. But his wit was sharp and so he improvised his lines to wonderful effect as the camera rolled. Stevenson, a stickler
for the script, said nothing, merely smiled encouragingly from the sidelines.
'I wouldn't let anyone interrupt him,' Stevenson remembered. 'I just let him
go on and on. You see, he had the most wonderful imagination.'"

When *The Absent Minded Professor* made its New York premiere police
estimated that 10,000 fans stood in line, some for up to five hours. In Los
Angeles, the film caused traffic jams when it played at a local drive-in theater. One woman later wrote of the experience, "We left home before 7 and
didn't get home until after 9. We didn't' see the movie, but we saw a mon-
umental traffic jam. There were literally hundreds of cars waiting in line
to get into the theater. I have no idea how many were turned away." Walt
Disney said at the time that he thought that the film could be the biggest
moneymaker in the studio's history. "I'm glad to be in a picture," Fred said,
"that people come out feeling good, rather than these pictures with a lot of
problems."

The Absent Minded Professor was released on March 16, 1961 and while
it didn't quite make as much money as *The Shaggy Dog*, it was still among
the ten top grossing films of the year (earning $11.42 million and rank-
ing #5 at the box office, out grossing *The Parent Trap*, *Lover Come Back*,
King of Kings and *Breakfast at Tiffany's*), and its reviews, on the whole, were
much more satisfying than *The Shaggy Dog* had received. *Time* magazine
proclaimed the film "the season's kookiest science fiction farce" and that
"*Flubber* provides the fuel for a very funny piece of hyperbolic humor in the

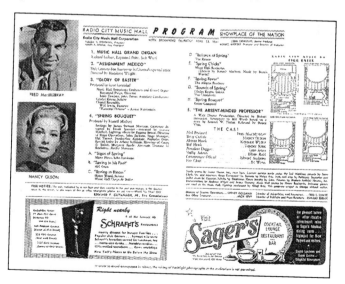

The Absent Minded Professor *program during its engagement at Radio City*
Music Hall.

grand American tradition." *The New York Times'* stuffy Bosley Crowther points out in his review that "the children should have a fine time ... and the grown ups should find it entertaining for the silly shenanigans it contains and for the simple satisfaction of noting the pleasure it gives the kids." He offered Fred a back-handed compliment: "At the center of the farcical confusions, Fred MacMurray does a fair enough job for an actor not equipped with the talent and physical grotesquery of one of the old time silent comedians — who were deft at this sort of sport." *Variety* offered one of the more perceptive reviews: "Enjoyable as an absurd, uncomplicated comedy-fantasy, but discerning film-goers may discovered deeper, more significant humorous nuances ... for beneath the preposterous veneer lurks a comment on our times, a reflection on the plight of the average man haplessly confronted with the complexities of a jet age civilization burdened with fear, red-tape, official mumble jumble and anxiety ... a subtle protest against the detached, impersonal machinery of modern times." They also gave Fred his due. "MacMurray, a seasoned film comedian, is ideally cast as the car-hopping professor, and plays the role with warmth and gusto."

The picture got generally good reviews, but the occasional poor one caused Walt Disney some trepidation, he just couldn't understand why. "A critic had written a snide article in some high-profile news magazine about *The Absent Minded Professor*," recalled composer Richard Sherman. "Other critics had also taken it the wrong way. Walt just couldn't understand the response to this film. *The Absent Minded Professor* was such a funny idea. Walt sucked on his tooth, which he always did, looked out his window at the studio and said, 'You know, I've got all those mouths to feed ... Well, I still think the majority of people are gonna like that picture.' Don't let anybody ever tell you Walt was immune to a bad review. It bothered him! The good reviews never went to his head, but the bad reviews went to his heart."

Just prior to the film's opening, the Academy of Motion Picture Arts and Sciences announced their Oscar nominations for the year 1960. To nobody's surprise *The Apartment* led the way with the most nominations (10) and was nominated in nearly every category: Best Picture, Wilder for Best Director (as well as Best Original Screenplay with his collaborator I.A.L. Diamond), Jack Lemmon for Best Actor, Shirley MacLaine for Best Actress and Jack Kruschen as Best Supporting Actor. Once again the Academy overlooked Fred's very important contributions to this picture. As good as Kruschen is, Fred's pivotal role as the philandering Sheldrake is the catalyst of the film, and he manages to make this scoundrel both attractive and despicable. If any performance deserved a supporting nomination in that film, it's Fred's. Fred's billing is third behind both Lemmon and MacLaine, but still above the title. In those days it was less common for established stars to be nominated in the supporting category (though Judy Garland and Montgomery Clift would be the next year in *Judgment at Nuremberg*, but their roles were clearly limited and in support while it could be argued that Fred was one of the leads). True to form, Fred did nothing to promote himself. In the end, *The Apartment* earned four statuettes, including Best Picture, Best Director and Best Screenplay.

Bon Voyage! is the first film that Fred made after he began *My Three Sons.* By the time production began in the fall of 1961 Fred had already completed filming portions of 22 episodes of *Sons* for the series' second season. When completing the Disney film he would return to shoot his scenes for another dozen or so episodes to finish out that season.

Bon Voyage! tells the story of the Willards, a middle-class, middle-western family (from Ohio), and their misadventures on their first vacation abroad, and is based on a best-selling novel. The Willards are Dad (Fred) and Mom (Jane Wyman) and their three children: a daughter (Deborah Walley), who finds love with a self-absorbed playboy, a son (Tommy Kirk — in his third film with Fred), absorbed by the Parisian women, and younger brother (Kevin Corcoran). What makes this film different from other Disney films of the time is that the plot doesn't just focus on the younger generation but the parents are also exposed to l'amour, including a Hungarian playboy who attempts to court the mother and in the end succeeds in making the father jealous enough to fight for her. For a Disney film there are even some mildly risqué things which occur, such as the scene in the film when Dad innocently has contact with a prostitute. Richard Schickel, in his book *The Disney Version*, wrote, "Somehow Disney let the sequence pass, but it was a disaster: his audience couldn't understand what was happening, he later claimed, and neither could he. The shock to their expectation was simply too rude, and Disney vowed never again to deal in such racy material."

Disney spared no expense on this film. Rather than shoot the shipboard scenes at the studio, Disney hired the passenger ship *SS United States* and had those scenes shot on board. Location scenes were also shot on the French Riviera and in Paris. Continuing with his tradition of appearing with some of the great leading ladies of the screen, Jane Wyman was cast opposite Fred, in their only film together (though Miss Wyman would later appear on a 1970 episode of *My Three Sons),* and although in "real life" Wyman and her then-husband Fred Karger did a great deal of socializing with Fred and June. Hedda Hopper tells a story of the MacMurrays and Kargers on a fishing trip to Black Lake, Colorado in 1958. According to Hopper, Wyman was fishing on a small skiff about a mile off of shore when a heavy wind began to blow. Fred thought that she needed to be rescued and jumped into a speedboat to pick her up. Halfway to the destination, the speed-boat ran out of gas. Fred also discovered that the boat had no oars. It turned out that it was Fred who needed rescuing while a cool-as-a-cucumber Wyman went on fishing. Wyman biographer Lawrence Quirk later wrote that Jane accepted the part in *Bon Voyage!* because she "admired MacMurray's talents, respected the Disney studio for trying to keep its entertainment clean and sensible and also because it was the best thing offered to her at the time." Wyman later said the film was "no great shake but it was clean" and that she "always liked Fred. He was a master of underplaying and just an absolute joy to work with." When asked why so many of the great actresses of the movies liked working with him, Miss Wyman did not hesitate, "Many peo-

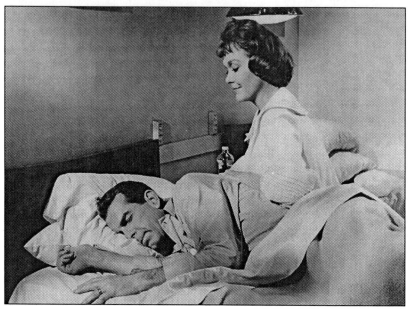

Fred and Jane Wyman in 1962's Bon Voyage! ©*Walt Disney Productions.*

ple assume that the prima-donnas of films are actresses, but, honey, the truth is that the prima donnas are the men, Fred was one of the exceptions!"

When Tom Kirk began production on *Bon Voyage!* he was twenty years old, and been in over a dozen films, and was the leading male juvenile actor at the Disney studio. Even though the films he appeared in were, on the whole, quite successful, he had no real choice of what films he acted in. Like Fred in the '30s at Paramount, Tom was a contract actor and he did the films he was assigned to without complaint, as he would later say, "I knew who buttered my bread." He was also coming to terms with his sexuality while working at a studio which was the very essence of family values. He was and still is a sensitive man who has been hurt by others whose friendship he had sought. He told of an actor he worked with in more than one film who he considered a friend, but only "wanted to get me into bed" when this actor invited him to his home and forced himself on him. He sought the approval and friendship of others, including director Robert Stevenson, who, in his own quiet way, did respond positively to Tom, and he also sought it in Fred — who didn't.

The filming of *Bon Voyage!* was a very difficult one for Tom Kirk. For one thing he disliked the character he played, the son Elliot, who he called "an asshole and the butt of the movie. The character was such a dick!" He also had no rapport with the director James Neilson. "I couldn't stand him. He was a pipe-smoking stiff shirt who acted like it was all rather distaste-

Tommy Kirk, Jane Wyman, Kevin Corcoran and Fred in **Bon Voyage!** *© Walt Disney Productions.*

ful." He went into the film excited to be working with an Academy Award-winning actress like Jane Wyman, but came away disillusioned by her. "She was very mean to me. She went out of her way to be shitty ... but she was a total bitch and I think she was homophobic." He had worked on two previous films with Fred and knew enough about him to know that it was near impossible to forge the kind of friendship he wished to have with him, but on the other hand he and Fred had always had a perfectly proper and correct relationship, though one lacking in warmth, so it was shattering when on this film he had what he would later term as "one of the worst experiences of my professional life" with Fred.

A little background. Tom had known and worked with Elliott Reid (Shelby in the *Flubber* films), and Reid had a habit of doing a Groucho Marx impression ("Say the secret word ...") which Tom and others found hilarious. Tom began copying this impersonation and began doing it with some regularity on his own. One day after the *Bon Voyage!* company returned from France, and was doing some interior shooting at the Disney Studio in Burbank, Kirk was rehearsing a scene involving Fred and himself, and the director was about to shoot the scene when Fred suddenly interrupted to say, "I feel funny standing here. Can I face that way?" The director approved the move. "So now it was Fred instead of me facing the camera," recalled Kirk, "and for some stupid reason I said, using my Groucho Marx impres-

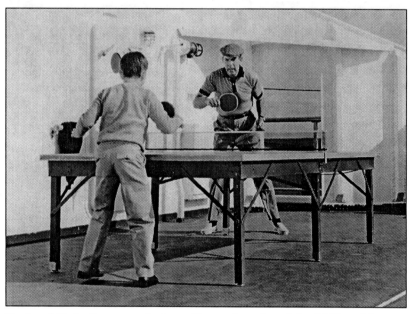

Fred and Kevin Corcoran playing table tennis on board the SS United States in Bon Voyage! © *Walt Disney Productions.*

sion, 'Oh! So now you get the close up.' Well, he just began to tremble, he was shaking and turning red, he was bristling mad; I really thought he was going to hit me. He thought I was trying to accuse him of upstaging me. He called out, 'Did you hear that?' To no one in particular he just said, 'Did you hear that?' And then he waved his finger at me, it was as if I accused him of being a pick pocket, and he said, 'When you've been in this business as long as I have, 30 years, to say something like that to me! You're full of shit!' It was a terrible experience for me because I'm a very sensitive person."

The confrontation was very upsetting for Kirk, who truly believed that Fred was mad enough to sock him. "Fred had a very definite temper, he could get mad. He looked like a boxer. He was very tall and very muscular and could be very frightening when he got mad." He couldn't sleep that night. Instead, he composed a letter of apology to Fred, explaining that he was trying to be funny but instead he said something very stupid. He went to the studio messenger office to have it delivered to Fred. A couple of days later he arrived on the set to shoot a scene with Fred. When Fred arrived on the set, he greeted Kirk with a "Good morning, Tom" as if nothing ever happened. It was also on this film that Fred did something which "really impressed" Kirk. There is a scene in the film where the characters played by Fred and Jane Wyman perhaps had a little too much to drink. There was a follow-up scene involving Fred, which Kirk says "really offended him," and he refused to do it. It had to do with the implication by someone else that his character was a drunk, but Fred refused to do the scene. "Fred very quietly told the director James Neilson and the producer Ron Miller, who was Walt Disney's son-in-law, that 'I'm not going to do it,'" Kirk recalled. "And he didn't. I was very impressed because I had never seen an actor do that before."

During the making of this film Fred held an on-set interview, and took the time to deny that he felt he was being over-exposed by being seen each week by millions of people on *My Three Sons* and in his annual films for Disney. "Over-exposure?" Fred asked. "No, I wouldn't say that I think the same people who go to see my movies also watch *My Three Sons*. But if a series is good I think it helps the movie and vice-versa." Fred also denied that he was really working more than he had a decade or so earlier. "I'm just doing pictures that more people see."

When the film was released in June 1962, it didn't equal the success of Fred's first two Disney films, but it still grossed a healthy $5 million at the box office, and out-grossed such films as *Days of Wine and Roses, What Ever Happened to Baby Jane?* and *Lolita*. Still, Disney had higher expectations for it, and even though its gross looked good on paper it had also been a more expensive picture to make, and so its profit margins were meager. Disney

Radio City Music Hall Program for **Bon Voyage!**

historian Leonard Maltin believes that the film "didn't appeal to a wide audience" due to its subject matter, despite the same promotional push that Disney used for all of his pictures which were released during this time. In his book *The Disney Films* Maltin writes, "*Bon Voyage!* is a hackneyed and tremendously overlong film (its run time is 132 minutes) ... Even the expertise of Fred MacMurray could not save some scenes." Maltin believes that the film "is aimed at the wrong audience" since it concentrated more on the parents than on the kids. However, the *New York Post* called the film "competent, super clean and efficient. Performances are all ingratiating." Hardly a rave, but better than most reviews that the picture received.

After the relative box office disappointment of *Bon Voyage!* it was back to the basics for Disney and Fred with a tried-and-true formula, a sequel to *The Absent Minded Professor, Son of Flubber.* The entire cast returns, along with a couple of new faces including Paul Lynde as an exasperated sportscaster. If you thought that Professor Brainard's money problems were over with the discovery of Flubber you are decidedly wrong. The government has taken control of Flubber out of Ned's hands, and, like many newly married couples, Ned and Betsy have money problems which culminate in Betsy's leaving Ned and contemplating divorce, with smug Shelby Ashton again attempting to steal Betsy away from her absent-minded husband. Also back in action is Alonzo P. Hawk, who is threatening to bulldozer Medfield College down unless his loan isn't paid back, and soon. This causes dissention in the Hawk family with son Biff opposing his old man, and even teaming up with "Ned the Nut" and his flying Model-T to stop his father. Ned also experiments with the remnants of Flubber, and invents a device which controls the weather called "dry rain."

If the film seems very familiar, it is because it follows the storyline of the original pretty well. For instance, there is even a climatic sporting event but this time, instead of a basketball game it's a football game. Fred thought this idea worked better and was funnier than the basketball game in the original film. "We can't lose the ball with an incomplete forward pass because we pass the ball AND the player." Disney, who didn't want the scene to seem too unbelievable, questioned the notion of throwing a player along with the ball and consulted a rule book. "I could find no law against it," said Disney. Once again Brainard attacks his arch-rival Shelby as the smug-minded professor is driving home, this time causing it to rain on the inside of Ashton's car causing Shelby to once again run into a police squad car, spilling coffee on the unsuspecting officers. When Elliott Reid was asked about the sequel he replied, "I think it's pretty good" and added, "Some people think it was the most enjoyable of the pictures, I love both the *Flubber* films."

Son of Flubber was welcomed by Tom Kirk after the experiences of *Bon Voyage!* Unlike the character he played in *Bon Voyage!* he enjoyed playing "Biff." He found the role less irritating and more realistic. He enjoyed working with many in the cast and crew again, including his favorite director, Robert Stevenson. Nancy Olson was "very sweet" to Kirk and he especially enjoyed working with Keenan Wynn ("Very nice guy! He went out of his way to be nice to me, very respectful and treated me as an equal") and his legendary father Ed Wynn ("A beautiful man"). As for Fred, their relationship was back to usual, polite but without warmth. But this time the MacMurray

Fred and Nancy Olson reunited in Son of Flubber *(1963) © Walt Disney Productions.*

Scottish temper didn't flare up at Tom, but at a visiting reporter on the set. As Kirk recalls it, he, Fred and other cast members were being interviewed when the reporter asked what Kirk thought was a relatively innocent question, to which, once again, Fred turned red-faced and snapped, "That's the kind of question I hate!" and abruptly ended the interview.

Son of Flubber was the final film that Tom Kirk appeared in with Fred and he still considers the two *Flubber* films among his favorites. He is reconciled to the fact that he was never able to develop the kind of relationship he hoped for with Fred, an actor he continues to admire, "as a light comedian he was as good as it gets, like Cary Grant at his best." He considers Fred "a fascinating subject," but he had a "wall around him" which Kirk couldn't get around. It hurt him, a few years later, when he heard that Fred, when asked about working with Kirk, allegedly said, "He's such a kook." This was after Kirk himself had left the Disney Studios, his contract not renewed because of fear that his sexuality would become public knowledge. When asked if he believed that Fred was aware of his sexuality and perhaps that this is one reason for the wall between them, Kirk replied, "I think he was aware of my sexuality. To some people if you know somebody is gay and you approach them, and try to be friendly, they think you are coming on to them ... it is very ignorant."

Son of Flubber is the first sequel that the Disney studios ever produced and it was very successful, earning almost as much money as the original film. *Variety* believed that the sequel didn't quite "match the comic quotient of the original," but that Fred, with his "knack for perfect reactions," gives a "winning performance." *The New York Times* critic Bosley Crowther seemed to like this film more than the original, calling it "crazy ... in the spirit of old-fashioned sight gag slapstick farce, but it is fun — and, indeed, a bit of a satire on the weird inventions of the new atomic age." The film grossed $10.45 million and ranked number 7 at the box office for the year, outgrossing such films as *Dr. No, Charade, The Great Escape* and *The Birds.*

It should be emphasized that *Kisses for My President* is not a Disney film. It is the last film Fred would star in that wasn't released by the Disney studios and the only film he made during the 1960s, with the exception of *The Apartment,* that wasn't a Disney film. It is a film which today may seem ahead of its time because of its story — of the first woman president and the comical and embarrassing situations which the nation's "First Man" endures. Polly Bergen was cast as the president. While the plot is ahead of its time, its execution is very much of its era.

According to the film's director, the veteran Curtis Bernhardt (*A Stolen Life, Processed*), Fred wasn't even interested in reading the script. "I knew his agent, Arthur Parks," Bernhardt recalled. "I called Arthur and told him I had a script for his client which I thought would make a good movie. Two days later we got the answer from Fred MacMurray. He would star in *Kisses* on the condition that I directed and produced." Given that the film was written by Fred's friend Claude Binyon, who had written many of Fred's best comedies from the '30s and '40s, it doesn't seem conceivable that Fred would have ever refused to read a Binyon script. If anything, it seems more likely that Fred committed to this, the only non-Disney film he would appear in for 18 years, out of his friendship for Binyon.

While everybody was happy to have Fred on this film, especially given his box office track record of the past few years, not everybody wanted Polly Bergen. Jack Warner wanted Maureen O'Hara, but she was in turn vetoed by Bernhardt, not because he didn't think she would have done a fine job, but because he was feuding with Warner and anybody Warner wanted, Bernhardt turned thumbs down on. Bergen became a kind of compromise, which Bernhardt felt weakened the picture. "I felt the worst problem with the film was the casting of Polly Bergen. She just was not interesting enough to play the lead." The singer and actress had just scored in Universal's *Cape Fear* and Fox's *Move Over, Darling* and was considered a hot property. Still, Bernhardt did tip his hat in Bergen's favor in one area, her personal appearance. "What I did appreciate about Polly Bergen is that she has such a convincing Kennedy-era look. Her chicness is quite convincing and makes her look like a president, even if she doesn't know how to act like one."

Warner Brothers, in their advertising for Kisses for My President, *reminded moviegoers of two of Fred's biggest '60s hits:* The Absent Minded Professor *and* Son of Flubber.

June very rarely visited Fred on the set, but one day while Fred was filming a love scene with his co-star, the beautiful red-headed Arlene Dahl, June decided to pay a visit, without Fred's knowledge, and taking his mother along to boot. When June and Maleta arrived on the set, the director, Curtis Bernhardt, was shooting a scene where Arlene Dahl's character attempts to seduce Fred. It happened to be a hot day and with the heavy lights used on a film it was a very stuffy, very hot set. While Fred was performing the scene with Dahl, she suddenly broke out with a nose bleed, probably due to the heat. The scene was halted while Arlene cleaned herself up and the crew kidded Fred about being a great lover when he looked up and noticed June and his mother. Fred got flustered, but the entire crew, including Fred, broke up when June shouted, "You never gave me a nose bleed!"

This was the second film that Arlene Dahl made with Fred (the first being *Woman's World* a decade earlier) and she recalls Fred on the set of this film as being "a little looser, more affable, I'm sure the change came through his marriage to June, but otherwise he was the same very professional person he had been on *Woman's World.*" On the set Dahl would recall that Fred would occasionally offer Bernhardt "suggestions, and most directors would just let him alone, they understood that he knew what he was doing." She also recalls that Fred had the habit of getting together with the person he was working with in a scene and together they would go over the upcoming scene and "work out pieces of business." Dahl calls Fred a "meticulous" actor because "he knew exactly what the character was about and knew the business he wanted to do in each scene, I think if he wanted to be he could have been a very fine director." When asked why so many great actresses wanted Fred as their leading man Dahl replied, "Because he was a fine actor and was tall! Most actresses were 5'7" or more and wanted a tall leading man rather than one who had to stand on a box or something and beside that Fred gave as good as he got. Acting is like tennis, you want a good rally."

The film does contain some funny sequences, including one in which Fred, wearing his pajamas, gets lost in the White House and keeps running into a tour group. But all in all, Bernhardt was disappointed in the film and the "concessions" he had to make including the finale. "There were a lot of reasons I made concessions and compromises. The less said about this movie — the better."

Released in the year of the Johnson-Goldwater election, the film failed to catch on at the box office. Bosley Crowther review in *The New York Times* raked the film over the coals from its first paragraph: "Corn is a basic commodity that bounds in several forms in Washington ... but even the corniest congressman would hardly dare shovel it out as obviously as it is shoveled in *Kisses for My President.*" He put much of the blame on the director: "Curtis Bernhardt ... evidently takes a dim view of the prospect of a woman president. It wouldn't be funny! That's what the picture says." He didn't spare Fred: "And since it is cornily reckoned that he would be a typical middle-class American spouse — the sort of ad-copy Mr. Good-Guy that only Fred MacMurray could portray — it not only makes sure that these involvements are tediously obvious and banal but it also has none other than Mr. MacMurray to throw his dead weight into the role." He was kinder to Bergen: "Polly Bergen is attractive as Madame President, but she has a thankless job."

Curtis Bernhardt offered a perceptive view into why the film failed. "You know the bad luck with *Kisses?* It came out right after Kennedy was murdered. After such a tragedy, no one was in the mood to see a comedy about the presidency."

Follow Me, Boys! is the first and only dramatic motion picture that Fred would make for Walt Disney. Well, the film is basically a drama with some comedic undertones. It was a serious project by Walt Disney to pay homage to the Boy Scouts of America and based on a popular novel *God and My Country* by MacKinlay Kantor. Kantor was a prolific author who had published the novel *Glory for Me* in 1945 which became the highly acclaimed film *The Best Years of Our Lives* in 1946 (the very film which Fred turned down because he didn't think his role was substantial enough). He later won the Pulitzer Prize for the Civil War novel *Andersonville.* Walt Disney fell in love with the novel *God and My Country* when it was published in 1954 and optioned it early, and went through several script drafts until Louis Pelletier produced one to his liking in 1964 with the working title of "On My Honor." The hero of the film is Lemuel ("Lem") Siddons and Disney had nobody else in mind for this role other than Fred MacMurray, despite the fact that Fred, at 57 years of age, is at least 20 years too old. But it was a tribute to Fred's still youthful looks that he gets away with it and the film does allow the character to age over a period of years.

Fred starred in Disney's 1966 heartwarming or over the top (you pick) Follow Me, Boys!

Lem has been a member of a jazz band for more years than he likes to think about when the band stops in the small Midwestern town of Hickory. He realizes that this is what he has been looking for all his life, a place to set down roots. He quits the band on the spot and almost immediately gets a job as a candy store clerk. He also finds himself attracted to Vida Downey (played by Vera Miles) who works as a bank teller where she is the girlfriend of the son of the president of the bank (Elliott Reid, once again cast as Fred's stuffy romantic rival). Partially to impress Vida and because of his own willingness to be give the boys in town a sense of purpose, Lem takes on the responsibility of scout master. Eventually, Lem and Vida marry, but she will always share her husband with "his boys," especially when she cannot conceive children of her own. The film's conclusion includes a sentimental scene where the now elderly Lem is honored by the town for his work with the Boy Scouts over the years and many of the boys whose lives he influenced come back to pay tribute to him.

To make the small town of Hickory (population 4,951) the studio back lot provided the basics, but a major expansion had to be made to meet the demands called for by the script. New exterior buildings were erected "to give the picture an authentic feeling of the thirties," among these were an ice cream parlor, general store, bank, pool hall, livery stable, newspaper and even an old-fashioned Bijou Theater. Outdoor scenes involving the scouts were filmed at Disney's Golden Oak Ranch, which was situated thirty-five miles from the studio. The camping and war games scenes were all shot at Golden Oak as well as the scene involving Fred and Vera Miles in a leaking canoe with Fred proposing to Miles while they are both sinking into the waist-deep waters.

Like Disney, Fred MacMurray was attracted to the story for its old-fashioned values, in a day when many believed those values were becoming a thing of the past. It was the ultimate film to strike the chord of Richard Nixon's so-called "silent majority." Fred could certainly relate to a story set in a town not unlike his own Beaver Dam, Wisconsin. Elliott Reid later recalled that Fred was, "very much in tune with this film and his character and really enjoyed playing him." Fred felt that this film would be easier to make than the gadget-filled *Flubber* films. "I play a scoutmaster in the movie," Fred said at the time. "One of the scouts becomes governor. It's not a tough role, not like 'Flubber,' which took a lot out of me physically. I have signed to spend 12 weeks on the movie. I hope it won't take that long, but you can bet it will."

Reid, who would call this film, "Disney's tribute to the Boy Scouts," recalls that his character wasn't originally part of the conception of the film. "Originally there was no real villain in the piece," remembers Reid, "and Disney said, 'We need a villain,' and of course he thought of me because of the chemistry that Fred and I had in the other pictures. So Disney said, 'Get Reid!' and they had to rewrite it."

Also cast in the film, as Reid's sympathetic rich aunt, is screen legend Lillian Gish. "When I got the picture and found out Lillian Gish was in it," Reid recalled with the ring of excitement still in his voice, "I was awestruck and tremendously excited to work with her, and I got the opportunity to tell her so. She was marvelous." In his first film appearance with Fred since

Exclusive nearly thirty years earlier Charlie Ruggles is cast as the proprietor of the drugstore where Lem gets his first job in town. Fifteen-year-old Kurt Russell is cast in the first of ten Disney films he would appear in over the next decade as "Whitey," a boy from a broken home who is abused by his drunken father and is ultimately taken in by Lem and Vida and treated as their own son. Reid would recall it as a "happy set on a happy film."

Kurt Russell recalls that Walt Disney would occasionally come down to the set and engage him in conversation, to get a child's point of view. "Sometimes he'd come down to the set and ask, 'Do you want to see part of a movie that's being put together?'" Russell recalled. "So I'd watch a movie or parts of a movie with him and we'd talk about it and he'd ask questions. What was interesting about Walt, as I look back on it now, is that he was picking the mind of an uninhibited 13-year-old ... I think he was finding out how a young mind worked."

When the film premiered on December 1, 1966 (only weeks before Walt Disney's death) many critics didn't doubt the sincerity of the filmmakers, but they also found the film overly sentimental and clichéd. Judith Crist of the *New York Journal Tribune* called the film a "two-hour commercial for the Boy Scouts of America." Richard Schickel calls the film an "orgy of sentiment unparalleled in our day and age" in his 1967 book *The Disney Version.* He goes on to write, "The plot is no more than a loose string of incidents; the characters, so bland as to be fully explained the minute they appear on screen ... What might have been barely bearable at the length of an hour and a half was simply excruciating when spread over better than two hours."

Leonard Maltin, in his book *The Disney Movies,* praised MacMurray's performance. "As always, Fred MacMurray's simple, honest approach to his role breathes life into lifeless dialogue and enables one to believe the hokiest lines." He also gives his due to Miles, who "does nicely as his sympathetic wife." Maltin also concedes that there is sentimentality to spare in *Follow Me, Boys!,* calling it the "biggest barrel of corn ever put together by the Disney studio," but he adds that "if one is sentimental and willing to let the movie work on one's emotions, it's possible to be taken in, so that even the clichés serve their purposes — and when aging Lem Siddons looks around him at the end of the film and sees a throng of happy grateful people, one can be genuinely moved."

Variety raved about the film, calling it a "top-notch Walt Disney drama with heavy family and general audience appeal ... blending comedy, drama and romance in build-up towards an emotionally charged climax ... *Follow Me, Boys!* is Disney at his best." The entertainment newspaper also gave Fred one of the best reviews he ever received during his entire career: "MacMurray scores heavily as the scoutmaster ... he plays part with a light approach while basically underscoring its dramatic elements and comes up ith one of the best performances of his long career." The film was Disney's major release of Christmas, 1966, where it played Radio City Music Hall, breaking records. In the end, *Follow Me, Boys!* was an unqualified success at the box office, grossing $7.3 million, and it was the second highest grossing Disney film of the year (only Dick Van Dyke's *Lt. Robin Crusoe, USN* was more successful) and was the thirteenth most popular film of the year, ranking ahead of such contemporary films of the era as *Our Man Flint, The Wild Angels, Murderers' Row, Blowup* and taking in just a little less than *Alfie* and *Georgy Girl.* It was clear that in the "Swingin'·'60s" there was still room for the kind of wholesome family entertainment that *Follow Me, Boys!* represented.

The Happiest Millionaire is the final live-action film that Walt Disney personally supervised before his death in December 1966. Disney had hoped that this film, his third live-action musical, would be the next *Mary Poppins* in terms of both box office and prestige. It wouldn't even come close. It is also the least appreciated film that Fred made for the Disney Studios, though when it was restored to its original theatrical release length it had more charm than I had originally recalled when I first saw the film many years ago, as well as a more cohesive storyline. (It was originally 164 minutes long for its road-show presentations, which would include a short intermission in between, but when the film was roasted by the critics, and audiences were not willing to pay road show prices, 46 minutes were cut to make room for more daily showings at local theaters.)

The film is based on a successful Broadway musical which starred Walter Pidgeon as Boston blue-blooded millionaire Anthony J. Drexel Biddle, an unorthodox and eccentric millionaire, who heads a household into which John Lawless (Tommy Steele), a young recent immigrant from Ireland, is hired on as a butler. Cast as his Biddle's wife is Greer Garson, in her only film appearance for Disney. The rest of the cast is equally distinguished: Geraldine Page, Gladys Cooper, and Hermione Baddeley, with John Davidson and Lesley Ann Warren as the young lovers in their feature film debuts. The film, directed by Norman Tokar, might have been in better creative hands (for this type of material) had Robert Stevenson (the director of *Mary Poppins)* been assigned to direct.

Pidgeon very much wanted to recreate his Broadway role in the film, and had already made one previous Disney film (also directed by Tokar), *Big Red,* but it was nowhere near as successful at the box office as the films Fred was turning out for the studio. It might have been tempting for Disney to cast Pidgeon in the Biddle role because of the publicity value of reuniting him with Greer Garson, they had been a top film team at MGM during the '40s, appearing in such box office and critical hits as *Mrs. Miniver* and *Mrs. Parkington.* A film reunion between the two of them would have generated a great deal of publicity. Others at the studio had their own personal favorites for the role of Biddle. Among the candidates were Burt Lancaster and Brian Keith. Richard and Robert Sherman, the composers of the score, favored Rex Harrison, who would have made an excellent Biddle, given his starchy and unorthodox screen persona, but, in the end, "Walt Disney chose his favorite, Fred MacMurray, whom he had wanted from the beginning." Filming began in May 1966, inauspiciously, when Fred suffered a

Fred as Biddle in 1967's **The Happiest Millionaire.** © *Walt Disney Productions.*

sprained ankle rehearsing the "I'll always be Irish" number. But he managed to film around that injury. Lesley Ann Warren considered herself fortunate to be cast in her first film, opposite such veteran stars as Fred and Greer Garson. She recalled Fred as "patient" with her regarding the many questions she asked as a new film actress. She felt that Fred was very much like the father figure he played in the film, a tower of strength. Warren also discovered some of the do's and don'ts of the Disney Studios. She found out, according to one article at the time, that the studio frowned on their stars wearing low-cut dresses, form-fitting slacks and bikinis. She also discovered that swearing on the set was taboo. "We did a scene that I didn't think was particularly good the other day and I swore," Warren recalled at the time. "There was a deathlike silence on the set. And I was told not to do that again. A girl must be a lady at all times here. They even told me not to drink — which I don't do anyhow." To John Davidson, Fred was "the most laid back guy — the most un-theatrical guy I've ever met." He recalls Fred telling him that basically he was just a saxophone player and was the "least likely guy" to be found acting in the movies. Years later when Davidson was invited to guest-host *The Tonight Show* he was asked who he wanted as a guest and replied without hesitation, "Fred MacMurray." The talent bookers on *The Tonight Show* invited Fred to be on the show and he declined, but Davidson didn't take his initial denial sitting down and personally phoned Fred only to have him politely decline the invitation saying, "I just don't do talk shows well," and that he was basically "not interesting." Fred honestly thought he wasn't colorful enough or interesting enough to be a good interview subject, which is why he did so few talk shows or even newspaper interviews over the course of his long career.

Despite the fact that her good friend Walter Pidgeon had been overlooked for the film it seems that Greer Garson and Fred got along well. "I always hoped Mr. Disney would invite me to come to his studio," Garson told a reporter. "And this is a delightful *Life with Father* kind of picture. I really don't have all that much to do, but I love working with Fred MacMurray." One of the reasons why they seemed to have hit it off so well was because they each owned a ranch. "Fred and I have something in common," she said to another reporter. "Cows." Garson and her husband Buddy Fogelson owned a cattle ranch in New Mexico. They got along so well that it was reported that once filming was completed on *The Happiest Millionaire* the Folgelsons invited Fred, June and the girls to visit them on their ranch.

Fred, basically a shy man, didn't like his sets open for visitors, but during the making of *The Happiest Millionaire* members of the press were invited one day to watch a scene being shot to be followed by interviews with some of the actors on the set. "We were filming the big dinner scene," Fred recalled of the incident. "All day long we were doing close-ups of the different actors in the scene. Then came mine, just as some visitors came on the set, Well, I lost the dialogue and it ended with the director saying, 'Why not go outside and take a walk around' ... If I go bad in a scene, I think they're thinking, 'He gets paid all that money and he blows his lines.'"

The film had its Hollywood premiere on June 23, 1967 at the Pantages Theater on Hollywood Boulevard. It was fitting that the theater served this purpose since Walt Disney had been awarded fifteen of his Academy Awards at ceremonies held there. The Pantages was decorated to resemble the Biddle estate and the cast arrived in a vintage automobile from the era the film represented. The premier benefited one of Walt Disney's favorite charities, The California Institute of the Arts. (So dedicated to Cal-Arts was Disney that when Dick Van Dyke offered to play the role of the old, decrepit banker in *Mary Poppins* for free, Disney, realizing how much Van Dyke wanted to play the role, and ok'd it on condition that Van Dyke donate $4,000 to Cal-Arts. "You didn't get anything for nothing from old Walt," Van Dyke would recall.) Among the stars (other than the cast) who attended the premiere were Joan Crawford, Helen Hayes, Agnes Moorehead, Bob Hope, Irene Dunne, Milton Berle, Jane Wyman and Annette Funicello. A huge buffet dinner was served afterwards. "I have rarely attended premieres of my films or any other films for that matter," Fred said. "But this was something special being the last picture that Walt produced and it was done in the old Hollywood style." According to press accounts of the premiere when Fred, along with June and his two twin daughters, emerged from their car, Fred drew the loudest and most prolonged cheers of the night from those assembled in the bleachers.

Fred's performance as Biddle is certainly enthusiastic, but the character itself is contrary to the type of endearing persona that he utilized in his other Disney films, the easygoing, honest and paternal persona he had developed through the Disney films and *My Three Sons*. Biddle comes off as "eccentric," according to *Time Magazine*, "but not lovable." For one thing Biddle is highly competitive and always challenging someone to a fight. In some respects, Biddle is as stuffy as the characters Elliott Reid played in the

The Hollywood premiere of The Happiest Millionaire *was Disney's biggest premiere since* **Mary Poppins.**

Flubber films. "My personal theory about *The Happiest Millionaire,*" says Leonard Maltin, "is that the average moviegoer didn't really want to see a movie about a millionaire, happy or otherwise. Biddle certainly was an unusual - perhaps even unique -choice for the protagonist of a Walt Disney film." Richard Schickel had little (if any) good to write about the film or Fred's performance. "Fred MacMurray, a modestly gifted farceur in the romantic comedies of his youth, an amiable enough presence in more middle-class surroundings, was unable to capture the Wodehousian nuttiness of an aristocratic eccentric and received precious little help in the attempt from either direction or script." Still, the film did give Fred the chance to do a little light singing, such as in the patter song, "What's Wrong With That?" which Maltin says, "must have come as quite a surprise to many viewers that he could sing at all; in fact he has a very pleasant singing voice." Bosley Crowther of *The New York Times* dismissed the whole film as "vulgar."

Still, the film did get a few good reviews along the way, including the local Hollywood trade papers. *The Hollywood Reporter* called it a "bounding, joyous hit in the happy tradition of *Mary Poppins.*" *Variety* called the film "outstanding," with Fred delivering an "excellent characterization." When the film opened at the Radio City Music Hall in late November 1967, as the Music Hall's Christmas season movie event, Ann Guarino of *The New York Daily News* wrote, "Radio City Music Hall unwrapped a festive holiday package yesterday with a gay musical on screen and the traditional religious pageant and lively variety show on stage. The combination makes top entertainment for the entire family."

The film itself cost $5 million to produce, which was a high budget by the standards of those days. Perhaps because it was drastically cut from 159 minutes to 118 minutes, and because the more sophisticated newspapers and journals panned the film (plus Walt Disney's own high expectations for the film's success), an idea has fostered over the years that *The Happiest Millionaire* was a box office flop. This is not the case. According to *Variety,* the picture grossed $12,979,877 during its initial run, but, unlike other Disney films, it was never reissued until it came out in home video. It was nowhere near what *Mary Poppins* grossed, and without *Poppins* critical raves, but hardly a flop.

By the time *The Happiest Millionaire* was released Walt Disney had been dead for several months. He had been incredibly active almost up to the very end not only in supervising his studio and the films and television shows it produced, but he was also deep into plans for what would eventually become Walt Disney World in Florida. In November 1966, only a month before the release of *Follow Me, Boys!,* he entered the hospital where it was discovered that Disney, a heavy smoker, had a cancerous lesion on his lung. A portion of his left lung was removed. In fact, while he was hospitalized for this operation, Walt Disney was still taking calls and holding conferences on the editing of *The Happiest Millionaire* from his hospital bed. He was released and seemed to rally, but then on December 5, his sixty-fifth birthday, he was readmitted, where he died ten days later. Upon hearing of the death of Walt Disney, Fred issued a statement: "There can be no bigger loss to people all over the world than that of Walt Disney … None of us who knew Walt and worked with him can ever forget him."

The Happiest Millionaire was Fred's final film for five years. Could it be that those in charge of the studio after Walt died decided that Fred was old hat and a remnant of the studios past, despite his strong box office record? Not so, according to Disney archivist and historian Dave Smith. "I haven't heard any reason why there was the four-year gap in the films that Fred made for us, unless, of course, there were no projects which could make use of his talents." Smith added that he is unaware of any other Disney films made from 1968-1972 for which he was considered, adding, "We were making few films during that era, generally only three or four a year." They also had a new male lead that represented the new generation at the studio, Dean Jones. Jones' vehicles for the studio (including *That Darn Cat!*, *The Horse in the Gray Flannel Suit, Blackbeard's Ghost* and especially *The Love Bug)* proved almost as strong at the box office as the films Fred did, but mostly without the same magic. But most of these films, in particular *The Love Bug,* include many of the same elements of whimsy and fantasy that are a part of Fred's Disney films. In the days before home video Disney often reissued its older films so that they could find new generations of fans. When such MacMurray films as *The Shaggy Dog* and *The Absent Minded Professor* were re-released in the late '60s and mid-'70s they out-grossed many newer films.

CHAPTER TEN

My Three Sons, Part Two

1966-1972

Entering its sixth season, *My Three Sons* was still one of the most popular shows on television. In its final season on ABC the series ranked number thirteen overall, an improvement over the prior two seasons when it had dropped out of the top twenty all together (but still performing quite solidly in the top thirty). When ABC took a pass on the series because of uncertainty about whether Fred was going to return, CBS happily picked the show up.

The sixth season brought a big change in its premier episode with the wedding of Mike and Sally, and then saw them drive off, never to be seen and seldom heard from again, almost as if they had never existed. This left two sons, Robbie and Chip, but the series was titled *My Three Sons*. The producers came up with a way to deal with this.

For the past couple of seasons Stanley Livingston's brother Barry had been making frequent guest-appearances on the show as Chip's friend Ernie Thompson. In the premier episode of the season Ernie's parents are killed leaving the little boy orphaned. Because Ernie has no close relatives to take care of him, Steve takes him in until a decision on guardianship is determined. Vera Miles (who had just finished working with Fred in *Follow Me, Boys!* for Disney) is cast as an attractive adoption specialist who Steve becomes romantically involved with. The second part of the three-part trilogy involves Ernie trying to ingratiate himself with the family, pretty easy except for one member, cantankerous old Uncle Charley, but by episode's end the old sea salt had warmed up to the little fella. The final part of the trilogy has Steve passing all the tests to adopt Ernie, except one: a mother in the household. But when the adoption people see Uncle Charley in action, keeping the house and the kids in line with love and understanding beneath the crusty exterior, the old sea dog is considered better than a woman and the adoption goes through and Ernie is made to feel like every bit a Douglas as the other boys. In fact, John Stephens would recall in *Television Chronicles,* "one year later, there was never any talk of an adoption. He was always there and he was always one of the sons. We did those things. Mike simply got married and then was gone, and he was never mentioned again."

Another change which occurred as the sixth season began was the transition of the show from being broadcast in black and white, as it had been

Fred, Meredith MacRae and Tim Considine in the episode which launched the sixth season of **My Three Sons.**

during the ABC run, to color when it moved to CBS. "Color won't change the show very much," Fred said, "except that we'll have to be more careful about what we wear. In black and white, I could wear a green tie and a blue suit." Demarest made light of it. "We'll be in color next season. They think I look so young they may change the title to 'My Four Sons.'"

Despite these changes the premise of the show (a male-dominated household coping without a female presence) continued along for the next couple of seasons in much the same way as it always had. The next major change came at the start of the ninth season (1967-1968) when the Douglas family is moved from fictional Bryant Park to North Hollywood, California due to Steve being transferred with his job. CBS, which had allowed the show to be filmed at Desilu, where it had been since its inception, now wanted the show to be filmed at the CBS Studio complex in Studio City because it would cost less money rather than having to rent space at another studio. With a change in studios would come a change in sets and so it was written into the storyline that the Douglas family moved. (When *Leave It to Beaver* moved from CBS to ABC during its third season the Cleaver family also moved to a different house.)

But there was more to it now than physically moving from one studio to another. CBS now wanted to insert other control mechanisms on the show. They could do it because they had bought out Fred and Fedderson for the sum of $15 million (which the two split). Fedderson continued on as executive producer of the show, but, according to John Stephens, when CBS told Fedderson that they now wanted to call the shots on the show, Fedderson told CBS, "Let us just do what we can do and let Fred and John run the show, and if you don't like what they're doing after two or three months, then by all means, then step in." CBS agreed to this and because the show was functioning effortlessly and performing well in the ratings they finally let well enough alone. "They just totally left us alone. It was a great, great lot to work in. We had our own company entirely, and they didn't bother us. We had everybody. Every department, we had ourselves, and they were all on Don Fedderson's payroll, not on CBS's. It was kind of unique in that respect."

With the change in venue came a change in directors. Fred de Cordova, who would later become famous for producing *The Tonight Show*, starring Johnny Carson, from the '70s through the '90s, was brought in. De Cordova was well known as a television director and producer (including *The Jack Benny Program)* and on a personal level was known as one of the all-time great storytellers in Hollywood and on virtually everybody's A-party list as a guest. John Stephens would later tell *Television Chronicles*, "He just revitalized the whole show, 'cause when he came in, he brought energy to it that'd been kind of missing for a few years." In his own autobiography John Stephens tells the following story regarding Fred de Cordova: "De Cordova was a unique man. He not only energized me, but the entire cast and crew as well. Fred came to Hollywood in the 1930's and should be in the *Guinness Book of World Records* for drawing continuous weekly salary checks from the East Coast to Hollywood, receiving them until his death in 2001. Fred had a sharp wit and was very clever. He was the only director we ever had who could talk so fast that after we did a shot with MacMurray, while Fred was wondering about it, de Cordova was already set up for the next shot. De Cordova was actually able to convince MacMurray that the shot was absolutely perfect and go on to the next one."

Barry Livingston was especially enchanted by de Cordova, according to comments he made in *Television Chronicles.* "I absolutely idolized him when

The Livingston brothers, Barry and Stanley, with Fred on My Three Sons.

I was on the show," Livingston recalled. "To the point that I think I was becoming Fred de Cordova to a degree. And Fred de Cordova's known for being one of the wittiest, most acerbic wits that you'll ever encounter … And I wanted to be him. I wanted to be like him." De Cordova was also well known as a prankster and he was secure enough to even rib Fred. "Fred de Cordova loved to kid people, including Fred MacMurray," recalls Beverly Garland, who would later join the *My Three Sons* cast. "I remember that he would constantly ask Fred [MacMurray] all these crazy questions which Fred didn't want to answer and tried to avoid answering and I began to go along with this act, and the two of us were just plying Fred with these terrible questions which MacMurray would be so shocked about, it was hilarious." De Cordova worked well within the "MacMurray System," but he wrote later in his autobiography, "The devil himself must have negoti-ated Fred's contract." He quickly added, in a typical, de Cordova touch,

"Unfortunately, all those days off didn't help MacMurray's golf swing."

One of the changes made that season was to give Robbie a regular girl-friend rather than having him play the field. At college Robbie meets sweet, perky and California blonde Katie Miller. Several young actresses vied for the part and after a day of watching some of the auditions somebody said, "Hey, who was that girl who went out with Robbie last season?" Don Fedderson recalled the episode in mind and had it run for himself, Fred and June Haver, who happened to be at the studio. After watching the tape of 24-year-old, pretty, blonde Tina Cole, a member of the King Family Singers, Fedderson, Fred and June all agreed that she was the right girl for the part. The audience accepted her readily. "I think they wanted to get Robbie married quickly," Don Grady later told *Television Chronicles*, "to bring new interest to the show. And they had already made up their minds that Robbie and Katie were going to get married and have triplets … I actually welcomed the change, and I thought Robbie had played a teenager for long enough."

While Grady welcomed the change, he wasn't sure if Tina Cole represented the kind of girl that Rob would be interested in. "I opposed Tina Cole playing the role." He felt that Ronne Troup, daughter of singer Julie London and Jazz pianist/composer Bobby Troup, who had already made some guest appearances on *My Three Sons*, would make a better type for Robbie. (Troup would eventually join the cast in the final two seasons as Chip's girlfriend and eventual wife.) Grady also concedes that, "I had a crush on Ronne Troup!," which was the primary reason why he favored her for the role of Rob's love interest. Tina Cole found that being the first woman cast as a regular on the show proved difficult for the formerly all-male cast. "It was difficult for the others to realize that a woman takes much longer to get ready. Your hair, your lipsticks not quite right. Now they're used to me, but I'm still the biggest calamity on the show."

When Rob and Katie did get married another problem arose, sleeping arrangements. By now it was the late 1960s and Don Grady was aghast when he was told that Rob and Katie would sleep in separate beds. "A lot was happening in the world, civil rights, free love, new attitudes, and in my early twenties I was in the middle of most of it," Grady recalls. "The idea that Robbie and Katie would sleep in separate beds was not even a consideration from me. At this point in the show, if I had something to say, the producers were willing to listen. I remember saying we shouldn't have any bedroom scenes at all if Rob and Katie were going to be in separate beds. Did any newlyweds sleep in separate beds anymore? I couldn't even believe the writers had suggested that! Jokingly, I insisted that the only way I would do a scene with separate beds is if they zoomed in on a well-worn carpet path between them! They finally agreed I was right, but did not want to be the first show on the air to set the precedent and risk the consequences. I looked at every show on the air, and when I finally found a married couple in one bed on *Bewitched*, we got our big bed. Imagine having this kind of controversy on *Desperate Housewives!*"

II

As *My Three Sons* began its ninth season, it had one of its most formidable challenges in the ratings when NBC placed its supernatural comedy *The Ghost & Mrs. Muir*, which starred Hope Lange and Edward Mulhare, opposite it. At first the ploy seemed to be paying off and *Ghost* was besting the long-time favorite in its timeslot. But slowly but surely the powerhouse known as *My Three Sons* made a comeback due in part to a storyline which had Katie getting pregnant. "I thought this might have been our last year," Fred commented at the time. "NBC put *The Ghost and Mrs. Muir* opposite us, and their ratings were good in the beginning. I thought to myself, Dammit, maybe we should have quit while we were ahead instead of going down with a losing season." Fred went so far as to write a letter to CBS executive Tom Dawson in which he noted that the show had apparently run its course (at the time he wrote the letter the show was ranked 45th) and suggested to Dawson that the "game was up." For some reason the letter never reached Dawson, his guardian angel must have been looking down on him, because the letter was returned to Fred unopened. But in the end while *Mrs. Muir* was nominated, and won, a bunch of Emmys, *My Three Sons* won the ratings war, ending the season ranked number fourteen, while NBC cancelled *The Ghost & Mrs. Muir* (though ABC would pick it up for one last season). At the end of the ninth season of *My Three Sons*, Rob and Katie have triplets (named Steve Jr., Robbie and Charley), and so we are full circle with Robbie having three sons. (It makes one wonder if poor Mike had girls and that was the reason he was never heard from again.) The biggest change the show encountered came about at the start of the tenth season and affected Fred's character directly.

Over the years the producers had always cautioned that Steve Douglas could never get too emotionally involved with any female because there was really nowhere for such a storyline to go, if he married it would alter the premise of the show which got much of its humor from observing an all-male household. However, with the introduction of Katie, the landscape had already been altered to a degree. She was now a member of the household and the mother of Steve's grandchildren. With the show still popular but aging many thought it needed a shot in the arm to revitalize it, and one such suggestion was to marry the happy widower off. "That was probably, in the entire 12 years … the biggest argument that we all had going," John Stephens would later recall about the fateful decision to alter the show and bring in a wife for Steve. Don Grady concedes that with the addition of Tina Cole and then a wife for Steve, "the writers were running out of ideas for the male household ... they were redoing themes they'd already done, twice before. Marriage for Robbie, and Steve, opened up new literary territories for the *Sons'* writing team, and probably bought them another 3-5 years of audience interest." As for himself, Grady, "missed the rough-edged male brouhaha that had been our signature for so long."

It wasn't an easy sell for Fred, either, who had always credited the show's

The cast of My Three Sons, *circa 1967.*

success to the male-dominated household. "If there is an explanation, it is the all-male, motherless family that Don Fedderson ... devised. Five men without a woman lend themselves to a lot of funny things." But even Fred could see the writing on the wall. "It was time for the characters to move on."

But who would they cast as the ideal TV wife for the ideal TV dad? According to one source, June Haver was suggested, but Fred vetoed that almost immediately. He wanted and enjoyed a separation of work and home life. A *TV Guide* story later indicated that Rhonda Fleming, Joanne Dru, Joan Caulfield, Pippa Scott and Mala Powers were all under consideration. When the trade papers announced that the producers were seeking a wife for Fred MacMurray on *My Three Sons,* one of the actresses who read the story was a friend of Beverly Garland's and called Garland with the news. Garland was a highly recognizable face on television having guest-starred on numerous series over the years. She was also a pioneer, portraying a police woman on television as the star of *Decoy* more than fifteen years before Angie Dickinson. She was not altogether recognizable as the ideal TV wife because her forte was playing what she called "tough broads." When she told her agent that she wanted him to get her an audition for the part on *My Three Sons,* even he was dubious. "No! No!, Beverly," he told her, "you're a police woman, a murderess, a seductress, you're not Fred MacMurray's wife!" But she wanted to be Fred MacMurray's television wife and kept pestering him to get her a script, which he finally, reluctantly did. It's not like she never had played a wife and mother on television before; she spent one season as Bing Crosby's TV wife on *The Bing Crosby Show* a few years earlier.

Beverly would later recall the meeting which led to her being offered the part of Barbara Harper on *My Three Sons.* "There was a meeting between me and three others, Fred, Don Fedderson and Fred de Cordova, but really it was a chance for Fred to see me and evaluate me because ultimately the decision was his. That morning my husband (who I rarely listen to!) was telling me something he read in the sports page of the newspaper. Well, at this meeting we were just talking and somewhere along the way Fred MacMurray mentions the very thing that my husband had told me that morning, and so I think I surprised Fred by being able to talk sports with him and all of a sudden it just clicked between the two of us, it was very spontaneous, and I got a call from Don a couple of days later telling me I got the part, and offering me $1,500 per episode. Well, that took me aback because that was what I had gotten on my last series a few years earlier, so I said, 'Don, you're not really going to pay me that?' and he said, 'I'm sorry, Beverly, take it or leave it, there are 1,500 actresses who would kill for this part.' So I took it." Fred later commented that if Garland "was good enough for good 'ol Bing, she was certainly good enough for good 'ol Steve Douglas." But he quickly added, "I felt comfortable with Bev Garland."

That was not all; the idea early on, according to Garland, was to have Fred's character get married again, and then have a baby! "Fred put his foot down on that," recalls Garland. "He said, 'No, we've done every baby joke before this and I don't want to start repeating the same jokes.'" So the alternate idea was to have Beverly's character be a widow with a little girl, "and that pleased him a great deal to add a little girl, probably because he had two little girls at home."

So, while they were casting Barbara Cooper they were simultaneously looking for a little girl to play Barbara's daughter, Dodie. Around this time *Nanny and the Professor* was also casting for its pilot, and five-year-old actress Dawn Lyn tested for and won the part of Prudence. Lyn shot the pilot only to be told that the network had turned it down. She was now available when the producers of *My Three Sons* were casting the role of Dodie. (ABC later changed its mind about *Nanny and the Professor* and picked the show up. The producers then wanted Dawn for their show and attempted to stop her from working on *My Three Sons*, but they had legally released her from her obligation with that show and so Dawn was free to do *My Three Sons.*)

Fred and Beverly Garland on **My Three Sons.**

Both Beverly Garland and Dawn Lyn came to the show as the new kids on the block. Garland felt right at home on the set from the very beginning. She would later recall that one day, early on, Don Grady told her, "You act like you belong here."

The storyline which launched the tenth season and introduces Steve to Barbara is fairly simple: Ernie is having trouble with his new teacher, Mrs. Harper. He makes her out to be an uncompromising old bitty, and his description of her is enough to warrant Steve to pay her a visit, where sparks fly between the two and a dinner invitation is extended. Eventually this leads to romance and marriage, complete with Acapulco honeymoon.

Garland was excited to play the role of Barbara and envisioned her television wife as akin to Laura Petrie on *The Dick Van Dyke Show*. "I saw Barbara as not afraid to speak up, she had spunk." She was disappointed, when, early in the filming, she was doing a scene with Fred where Steve is teaching Barbara how to use a golf club and she keeps messing up and Steve has to keep showing her the correct way to use it. "And Barbara's saying to him," Garland later recalled, "'c'mon, didn't you just tell me! Didn't you just show me?' with some exasperation. Well, the next day I arrive on the set and six black suits walk in and say, 'Beverly, there is no way that Barbara would talk that way to Fred, she is sweet and kind and gentle and would never talk like that.' Well, there went my idea for the character."

Beverly had never worked with Fred prior to *My Three Sons* but admired the fact that this major star was doing a television series. "How wonderful and how successful he had been, you know, he was one of the first major stars to successfully make the transition to television. Henry Fonda had a show where he was a police detective and had a family, but it didn't make it. Jimmy Stewart also didn't for some reason click on television, but Fred did." She was also welcomed by the cast as an equal despite the years the other actors had worked together. "They couldn't have been nicer to me." She enjoyed working with Fred. "He was easygoing. He was a conservative man, not shy, just conservative, but he was just a sweetheart to work with and easy with all of us. We worked very hard since we had a tough schedule. We had laughs, but we were there to work and we did, especially because Fred was only contracted to work three months a year when the average series took eight months to shoot."

Five-year-old Dawn Lyn recalled Fred as being "very quiet and formal. He kept to himself. I only saw him when we were actually filming." (In an interview with *Television Chronicles* Dawn mentions that MacMurray didn't like her "precociousness ... I wanted to look at the camera and see how it worked and I wanted to be up on the catwalks where the lighting is. You know, I was a very curious child.") The "MacMurray System" didn't faze the young actress. "I was so young at the time, and it was my first series, that I didn't know any different so I had no trouble adapting." Despite only forging a "professional" relationship with Fred, Dawn came to adore Beverly Garland.

"I love her dearly, and she is a second mom to me." The feeling is mutual, with Garland referring to Lyn as "a real sweetie … just a little pumpkin."

Both newcomers loved working with William Demarest. "Demarest was great fun and very sweet. He would do a wonderful Turkey impression for me, shaking his head and gobbling," recalled Dawn Lyn. Beverly Garland recalled that Demarest "had been in nearly every movie ever made and he worked with everybody and he loved to tell stories and he never shut up!" she laughed. "But he was a sweet man and had been in show business all of his life so nothing fazed him. He was a real pro."

When asked which was the easiest, being the TV wife of Bing Crosby or Fred MacMurray, Beverly picked MacMurray without hesitation. "Bing was often in his own little world, Fred was not. Bing's persona is very easygoing and so natural, you never see any tension, but in actuality Bing was full of tension in his real life. When I was hired for Bing's show I was told, 'Bing isn't going to give you anything,' meaning he wouldn't show any tenderness to show that he was in love with my character. So I was told it was up to me to do it, so I would do things like always touching him, hugging him and it worked and it worked because I had to make it work. With Fred, I didn't have to, he was there and he didn't put it all on my shoulders, and people really believed that Steve and Barbara were a happily married couple." When she worked on the Crosby show the dictates of the times called for their characters to sleep in separate beds, but, perhaps because of Don Grady's battle for Robbie and Katie to sleep in the same bed, as well as the changing times, the producers gave Steve and Barbara a king-sized bed. "I told Fred we were going to sleep spoon style," Garland recalls, "and he said, 'What?' and I explained to him that we were going to sleep spoon style because we had just gotten married and we were supposed to be in love and we needed to show that to the audience, and Fred was fine with it."

III

Fred liked, and was proud of, all the boys who played his sons on the show. Beverly Garland observed, "He just adored all the boys and they adored him, after all they had been working together for so long and they used to go to Fred about their problems and he was like a dad to them and he would offer advice and he seemed to have a father-son relationship with the boys." Stanley Livingston would recall that when he got married to a "go-go dancer," at the tender age of 18, Fred "spoke to me about it a couple of times. You could tell he didn't approve." But it was also Garland's observation that Don Grady may have been first among the equals, an observation that Dawn Lyn backs up.

When Don began the show in 1960 he would recall that he was 15 years old and his own parents had just divorced. "You might say that Fred sort of became a replacement dad for me, or at least an older male figure to whom

I looked for approval." Don would recall that even though Fred "had a certain formality about him," and wasn't a "cuddly person," he did have a certain "warmth that made children feel comfortable around him. Now that I think about it there wasn't much about Fred that was kid-like, or child-like. He had a very adult persona. I think that's what made his reactions to children so comical, as though they were sometimes from another planet."

Don Grady played the character of "Robbie" on the show, which was also the name of Fred's own real-life son from his first marriage. Rob MacMurray was coming of age during the 1960s and a certain generation gap had erupted between father and son. In a 1968 cover story on Fred *TV Guide* would write that Fred "watched his own real-life son go the hippie route via the South Seas to 'find himself'" and quotes Fred as saying, "He's at an age where it's hard to communicate. I guess it's a rough time to be a kid. We didn't have the problems of whether to smoke marijuana; the worst we ever did was that eight of us would get together and buy a pint of wine. I've always said I just wish the problems we have in real life were as simple as those we have on the show. But it doesn't always work out that way." Don Grady says that Fred's son was "attempting to distance himself from his father and create his own identity. This caused Fred a lot of distress, and I think it left a soft spot in him for me. We were very close for the first several years; there were many things that Fred shared with me, and I shared with him."

Despite this Don says that he and Fred didn't socialize outside of the studio setting. "I was invited to his home once. It was the beginning of the 3rd or 4th season and I had been accepted at Michigan State U for pre-med. I wanted to be a doctor. The trimester conflicted with my shooting schedule. So I called Don Fedderson to see if it was all right to push my schedule back a little. Don said it was really up to Fred."

So Don went for the first and only time to Fred's house. "It was a cozy house in Brentwood, and it seemed smaller than the house I thought he would be living in. But there were a lot of warm little nick-knacks and a lot of wood, especially in the living room. Not coincidentally, I'm sure, it had sort of an Irish feel to it ... I think it was even in a glen! I felt very comfortable during the visit, and I remember Fred sitting in his chair by the fireplace as we talked. It was not too different than being on the set! But I do remember he smiled and glowed more, there in his home."

Don isn't clear about how the conversation went, could he push his schedule back so that he could go to Michigan State for pre-med, but he does recall Fred's advice. "... Fred, very warmly and gently, convinced me to push back my plans to be a doctor." It was advice that Grady would later come to appreciate more than he ever thought. "As I sit here with my family and my musical life [today Don Grady is a very successful musician], knowing what I do about the medical profession, it may be the best ting that Fred ever did for me."

Don and Fred continued to have a close relationship but as the decade continued some strain began to set in. "Then the '60s hit with a vengeance!" Grady recalls. "My politics started to differ from his and I went off to march for civil rights in Selma, Alabama. He didn't feel an actor's place was in politics, basically. There were lines you didn't cross with Fred, but you can say that about anybody, can't you?"

Fred and Don Grady on the **My Three Sons** *set.*

As the show was starting its eleventh season in 1970, Fred was telling the press that he was "semi-retired" despite starring in a television series. If it had been any lead actor in a television series other than Fred, the press might have laughed their heads off over that statement, but with Fred it was literally the truth. He was done with his *Sons* duties within three months and unlike the early years of the series he wasn't even making any movies in between. Most of his time was spent with his family at his ranch or on a golf course. "Every year I think we ought to quit while we're ahead," he said. "But at the end of the season when the ratings come out, we stand very high. So we just carry on another year."

At the end of the eleventh season Don Grady's contract was up and he made the difficult decision to move on. "It was a very emotional experience, leaving that family [his TV family], but I really wanted to move on, and, my gosh, the show looked like it could go on another ten years, but I wanted to start doing music professionally." CBS and Fedderson didn't want to lose Grady, so it was suggested that Don and Tina Cole do a spin-off series called *After the Honeymoon,* but Don was ready to put Rob Douglas behind him once and for all. In retrospect, Grady says, "I tearfully and happily bid goodbye to that wonderful experience, to see what life had in store for me. If I'd known, I probably would've stayed on and hoped the show went another twelve years! It took me ten years to get credibility as a composer. Looking back, I'm glad I did what I did."

The next season would be the show's 12th and final one, and the first without Don Grady. However, unlike Tim Considine's leaving in 1965, the producers didn't bring in another character to play a third son. Robbie was so popular with fans that his character couldn't just be written out or forgotten. Instead, Robbie is sent away to Peru on a work assignment while Katie and his three infant sons stay home. In the meanwhile, "Robbie" is mentioned from time to time in the form of letters. But it appears that the producers toyed with the idea of actually killing off Robbie. The reason? To allow Katie the chance to date. "Well, the network didn't like that," Fred said in an interview prior to the start of the '71-'72 season. This time, unlike a few years earlier when Don wanted to go to pre-med school, Fred didn't try and persuade Grady to stay, "he wished me well." Fred said in an interview at around the time of Grady's departure, "I can understand why he wanted to leave. He's a clever boy with lots of talent and direction and he has been in the series a long time." He must also have realized that Don had put a lot of thought into his decision and at age twenty-seven, having done the show for eleven years, he was entitled to try other things. Still, Grady does recall "everybody being sad I was leaving. It was a difficult thing for me to do."

Just as *My Three Sons* was preparing for its 12th season, Fred's buddy Jimmy Stewart was being wooed to lend his easygoing screen persona to a new series to be called *The Jimmy Stewart Show* in which he would play a small city college professor with a family. Fred advised to Stewart to go for it, telling Jimmy that doing *My Three Sons* was the "easiest thing" he had ever done. The producers of *The Jimmy Stewart Show* were even willing to allow Stewart to film the show according to the rules of "The MacMurray System," but Stewart decided that he preferred to interact more with his fellow actors than "The MacMurray System" allowed and turned it down, experiencing the long hours, eight months per year that shooting a weekly television series usually involved. Stewart came to regret that decision as well as coming to loath the series. It folded after one season.

The season began with a trilogy featuring Fred MacMurray playing Steve's cousin Fergus from Scotland who comes to America in search of a wife and falls for a waitress (played by Anne Francis). Miss Francis recalls Fred as "charming" and like all guest-stars got caught up in the bedlam of the "MacMurray System." "They lined up the close-ups and medium shots on him for many of the shows in a lump group and he would change his wardrobe and do them all in one day," Francis recalls of the experience. "In other words, he did the scenes with us, but his coverage was done separately. That way, he had more time off." Perhaps due to being an aging show or because the loss of Don Grady was acutely felt or because times were changing and gentle family comedies such as *My Three Sons* were falling out of favor and more "relevant" social comedies like *All in the Family* gaining favor (or all three combined), the show began a serious fall off in its ratings during this season.

Beverly Garland recalls that CBS was also trying to kill the show. "The thing is that Fred Silverman took over at CBS and wanted every show to be his, to have his imprint, so he cancelled many of the so-called 'rural comedies' that were on the schedule, but it wasn't so easy to cancel *My Three Sons*, it was still a very popular show and everybody loved Fred." So, Silverman, according to Garland, decided to "slowly bleed us to death. He scheduled our show late in the evening when many of our viewers were already in bed. It began to affect the ratings." In short, *My Three Sons* was killed off because it had the wrong demographics. Silverman wanted CBS to have the demographics of younger, hipper urbanites rather than the older viewers and young children who still enjoyed *My Three Sons*.

Garland recalls that Fred was "absolutely livid" about the way the network was treating the show. He went to Silverman, who explained to MacMurray that "your ratings are slipping." Fred replied that it was due to being moved out of their timeslot. When CBS finally did cancel *My Three Sons* at the end of the season Fred was "really upset," according to Garland. "He loved the show and wanted to continue to do it, it was his thing, and I don't think he ever forgave CBS or Silverman." CBS made the official announcement that they were dropping *My Three Sons* after twelve seasons on April 4, 1972, the same day that ABC announced that their long-time ratings hit *Bewitched* was also leaving network television after eight seasons.

When asked if he felt the show had run its course a season or two earlier, and perhaps had overstayed its welcome, Don Grady replied, "If you're an actor, you most likely want the show to run as long as possible. From the perspective of what was happening in the TV landscape at the time, *All in the Family* changed everything ... making it obvious that shows like *Sons* had seen their day. So *Sons* may have enjoyed a little more dignified ending if it had bowed a few years earlier."

My Three Sons aired its final episode on August 24, 1972, without fanfare.

CHAPTER ELEVEN

Twilight of a Saxophone Player

1973-1991

Following the cancellation of *My Three Sons* in 1972, Fred went directly into his first film in almost six years. *Charley and the Angel* was his seventh and final Disney film over a span of fourteen years. It would also be his final starring role in a major theatrical picture after nearly forty years as a leading actor in Hollywood.

Charley and the Angel tells the story of Charley Appelby (Fred), a miserly sporting goods store owner in the 1930s, who learns that he only has a short time to live from his guardian angel (Harry Morgan). Charley realizes that he spent his life nickel and diming himself and the family he's shown little warmth for. In the remaining time he has left Charley decides to redeem himself and show the family the love he really always felt for them, but rarely demonstrated. Cloris Leachman, eighteen years younger than Fred, and the winner of the Academy Award for her performance in the previous years *The Last Picture Show*, plays Fred's long suffering wife. Kurt Russell, Vincent Van Patten, Scott Kolden and Kathleen Cody also appear.

George Lindsey, best known for his role as Goober on *The Andy Griffith Show*, also appears in the film, and recalls that he was "thrilled" to work with Fred, somebody he found "very easy to act with." Though they didn't share many scenes together, and he didn't get to know him well, Fred did, for many years, accept Lindsey's invitation to play in his celebrity golf tournament benefiting the Special Olympics in Montgomery, Alabama. When he came to the tournaments, Lindsey recalls that the crowds would become very excited because "everybody just loved him and June." Lindsey recalls Fred as, "a great movie star, but more than that he was a good guy and easy to talk to. I liked him."

In an interview on the *Charley and the Angel* set, the 64-year-old Fred, reflected on his career and stated, "It's a miracle to me that I ever got into pictures. I'm a very dull person — I don't know how I've lasted as long as I have." Luckily, his red-headed, curly-haired daughter Katie was seated nearby during the interview and interjected, "He's not dull at all. He is just a very modest man. He loves his family and his close friends and is a wonderful father." In an interview with writer Margaret Rau, at around this same time, Katie put it this way: "You know, Daddy's always calling himself dull, but that's because he's got an inferiority complex. Really he's a modest, very private sort of man."

Harry Morgan, Cloris Leachman and Fred in his final leading role in a major Hollywood film, **Charley and the Angel.** © *Walt Disney Productions.*

The twins were now sixteen years old, but to some they seemed from a different generation. Dawn Lyn recalled that when they visited Fred on the *My Three Sons* set that even at her young age she was surprised to see the girls in starched dresses and wearing white gloves, rather than the hipper clothing of the early '70s. They were an incredibly close-knit family. Katie MacMurray sat in on another interview on the set of *Charley and the Angel* and spoke of the simpler times that the film's era represented. "All the kids at school like the old clothes and music of the '30s. I think we've become much more sophisticated. Kids today miss the past when everyone seemed to have a lot more fun." Katie spoke proudly of her mother. "She's the president of the mother's club at Marymount High School. Laurie and I act as go-betweens for the other girls when they want something special. We get them together with mother and she takes it to the principal and it works out."

According to Katie, the more outgoing and public of the twins, there was no generation gap in the MacMurray household. "We can talk to our parents where a lot of kids can't, but it's not all one way. It helps if parents are willing to listen too. But modern parents seem to be afraid of their kids because of the way they dress, things like that. They don't know what to say so they just keep their mouths shut." According to Fred, the girls could, and did, talk to them about all subjects from sex to drugs. "I'm sure we've talked with them about everything, so they know just about everything that goes on and can go on, that way nothing is a shock to them ... kids today are more aware than when I was growing up. Television has done it." Fred added that weddings used to be a big thing with people, but that "today a lot of people don't believe in getting married." While he said he wouldn't judge such unions he hoped that the children of these unions would "grow up in a world where they'll be accepted."

The family bonding continued on the road when Fred purchased a camper. The camper weighed a ton and had a special 40-gallon gas tank put in it instead of the usual 20-gallon tank. Furthermore, Fred had a custom-made 7' bunk installed to fit his 6'3 frame and then some. They took many trips across the country over the years in their camper. Fred's cousin Lester Martin recalls that when his daughter got married (they were now living in Washington State) the entire family, Fred, June and the twins, got in their camper and drove all the way up from California to both attend the wedding and to help with the decorations. Martin recalls the twins as "great girls and they loved Fred very much." The family took trips in their camper visiting places like Yosemite or Yellowstone, and above all they went to the ranch where they could indulge themselves in such mutual pleasures as horseback riding and bicycling. They also worked together in the kitchen making homemade bread and jelly and jam for themselves and their friends.

The ranch held special memories for the MacMurray children. Kate MacMurray would remember that the first time she was ever put on a horse was by Fred, at the ranch when she was about three years old. "Dad put me on a saddle in front of him," Kate recalled. "His big hands covered mine with the reins and he made a clicking sound to make Candy, a beautiful quarter horse, step forward. I still recall the smell of the horse and of my

Dad's leather chaps; that's a great memory." Kate would recall that when the family escaped to the ranch they left many modern conveniences behind. "First of all, we never had television out here," Kate recalled years later. "If we wanted to see a ball game, golf game or some favorite TV show, we had to go to our aunt and uncle's house in Sebastopol. Dad wanted us to read, hike and to have a relationship with nature. We had our horses here; we worked the cattle, milked cows at 4 a.m. and gathered the eggs. This wasn't something we were playing at; this was our life. This was what was important to us as a family." After the chores were done, the girls (by this time the older MacMurray kids were off on their own) would be off to play, explore, ride or fish, whatever they wanted to do, within reason. "Dad would let us out in the morning and we'd be gone all day. He'd ring this big bell and we'd come in at night. We were just roaming around the ranch all over the place. It was a great, a wonderful way to grow up." On the ranch Fred also invested a great deal of time in his garden and the family often grew their own vegetables. One of Fred's favorites was tomatoes. Fred took so much pride in his ability to grow tomatoes that when the crop was first picked he would sit the family at the dining room table and then blindfold them. He would then quiz each one on what type of tomato they were eating: red, yellow or green. In fact, food was a big part of life at the ranch and the relationship between Fred and June. "Mom and Dad worked hard for us all to have dinner together every night," Kate MacMurray recalled. "They each cooked, but they had different styles and they had heated debates. Stir or fold? Mom thin-sliced, Dad thick-sliced. Dad drank red wine, Mom drank white. Mom said she needed two stoves to prepare Thanksgiving dinner and Dad thought one was just fine. Finally he gave in and put in a second stove." According to Kate, "being in Los Angeles was work; meaning daddy was in a film. When we were back in Sonoma (on the ranch), as a family, we were home."

The ranch became a home away from home for visiting friends of Fred and June's. Among the famous guests were Henry Fonda, John Wayne (Fred even named one of the cottages on the ranch "The John Wayne House" in honor of his good friend) and Jimmy Stewart. Stewart, in fact, stayed at the ranch while filming the 1978 film *The Magic of Lassie* at a nearby location. But mainly the family enjoyed the company of each other at their true home, the home that Fred loved the most. "The fog rolling in and out of the redwoods reminded Daddy of Scotland and Beaver Dam, Wisconsin," recalled Kate.

When he wasn't at the ranch, Fred's favorite form of recreation continued to be golf. He played in many celebrity/charity golf tournaments over the years, as well as just for fun on a Saturday morning with one of his buddies. Tom Poston tells the following amusing story in the book *Who's Your Caddy:* "I remember the first time I played Bel-Air. I didn't know anybody yet, so they sent me off No. 10 by myself. When I got to 11, there were four guys standing there, asking me if I wanted to join them. It was Fred MacMurray, Fred Astaire, Randolph Scott, and Ray Milland. I was struck dumb, frozen. I couldn't say a thing. So they played on without me." One of Fred's most publicized rounds of golf had him partnered with Jimmy Stewart against Bob Hope and President Richard Nixon at a charity event in 1971. According to Bob Hope, Stewart and Fred "almost changed the course of history" when they almost ran Nixon down with a runaway electric golf cart. "It was a very close thing and would have been very nasty indeed — especially for the President!" Lester Martin later commented that "Fred played golf with presidents, but that didn't phase him. He'd play golf with anybody!"

When Fred wasn't at the ranch or on the golf course he liked to play handyman around the house, sometimes with less than favorable results. When leaky pipes began dripping away in an upstairs bathroom at his home in Brentwood, Fred decided to attack the problem himself rather than call in a plumber. "I'm pretty good at plumbing and things like that," he said. "So I was all set to fix it when June told me that the water heater had quit. She won the argument about calling in a plumber." When the plumber arrived Fred told the man that he would work on the leaky faucet if the plumber wanted to tackle the water heater. Two hours later, Fred thought the job was all done and was sitting enjoying lunch when he heard water pouring into the living room. "I rushed into the living room, all beautifully paneled, you know, and I was sick. Water was pouring in from the ceiling. I'd left the hot water faucet on in the bathtub. The plumber had turned off the water into the house while working on the heater. When he finished, he had turned the water back on, with that faucet wide open. It was my fault, really."

When *Charley and the Angel* was released in the summer of 1973, it proved escapist fare for a country engulfed by strife, war and a presidency hanging in the balance. It was paired with a reissue of *Cinderella* and was moderately successful despite lukewarm reviews. Howard Thompson opined in the *New York Times*, "*Cinderella*, the cartoon-revival half of a current Walt Disney package, is far and away the better part of yesterday's double bill at the Guild and Quad I Theaters. Wise parents will time it so that the youngsters see this treat first. The new live-action comedy, *Charley and the Angel*, can be taken as a tame, friendly caboose … The picture set in the depression years, has a mildly diverting façade of nostalgia in costumes, tunes and those fine, tacky old cars. Mr. MacMurray, by now a Disney veteran, is front and center, unremittingly wide-eyed."

Of course during the last six years it wasn't as if Fred wasn't offered any movie opportunities. He was seriously considered to play the husband of Lucille Ball in the family comedy *Yours, Mine and Ours* in 1968. It would have been a natural role for Fred with its story of a widow with a large fam-

ily who marries a widower with an even larger family and the problems created by mixing the two families together. Director Mel Shavelson admits
that Fred "would have done very well," but that when Henry Fonda became
interested all bets were off. "Fonda gave reality to a naval officer after *Mister
Roberts*," says Shavelson, who also says that Fonda's navy connections were
useful in getting naval cooperation for location filming aboard an aircraft
carrier. The film became a big box office hit in 1968 and went on to inspire
the television series *The Brady Bunch*.

That Fred wasn't ready to retire is evident by his next project, a made-for-
television movie for ABC which served as a pilot for a series which didn't
pan out, *The Chadwick Family*. Fred is cast as the patriarch of a large family
in Coronado, California who is also the editor-publisher of a small newspaper. Fred said he "identified" with the character of Ned Chadwick. "I grew
up in a small town. You learn down to earth values in a small town — hon-
esty, love, and the importance of the simple laws of nature. Most of all you
learn how to live as a family." Had the pilot film been accepted as a series,
Fred wouldn't have had to do much more work than he did on *My Three
Sons*. The cast was a large ensemble, and stories would have reflected more
on the younger generation than the older, with Fred kind of overlooking the
action and offering a few words of advice here and there.

At this point in his career Fred was pretty much doing one big project
per year coupled with one or two television guest appearances as a means
of keeping his name before the public. For instance, in 1973, he appeared
in the Disney film *Charley and the Angel* as well as appearing on a television
special, *Walt Disney: A Golden Anniversary Salute*. Dean Jones, his successor as perennial Disney leading man, served as host with Fred appearing as
a special guest star along with Julie Andrews, Buddy Ebsen, and Annette
Funicello, among others. In 1974 his big project was *The Chadwick Family*,
but he also appeared in another Disney television special, *Herbie Day at
Disneyland*, this one hosted by Bob Crane, who was then appearing in the
Disney film *Superdad*.

In 1975 Fred starred in another television movie, *Beyond the Bermuda
Triangle*. Fred plays Harry Ballinger, a man who loses his brother in the
infamous Bermuda Triangle. He decides to find out as much as he can about
the Triangle and goes about seeking out and interviewing people who've
either had a strange experience in the Triangle themselves and survived, or
are friends and relatives of people who have been lost in the Triangle. Harry
slowly becomes obsessed with his investigation, even as others try to pull
him back before he himself gets lost in the Triangle. The film had a good
cast, including perennial '70s TV-movie stalwart Donna Mills, Sam Groom
and Dana (*Diff'rent Strokes*) Plato as a young girl who joins Harry in trying to find her mother. At the time interest in the Bermuda Triangle was
high with several best-selling books and documentaries, and this film per-

formed well in the ratings. As it turned out, this would be Fred's final role as a leading actor.

In 1976 producer Irwin Allen (*The Towering Inferno, The Poseidon Adventure*) had asked Fred to star in a made-for-television movie for NBC called *Fire!* Allen, the king of disaster films, invited Fred to play the pivotal role of Sam Brisbane in a film which would also feature Vera Miles, Patty

A dapper Fred and Ginger Rogers at an Academy Awards ceremony.

Duke, Alex Cord, Donna Mills, Lloyd Nolan, Neville Brand and Ty Hardin. The plan was to show it on television in the United States and then theatrically abroad. The story concerned a rampaging fire that threatens to overrun a lumber community. The film began shooting on location in Silverton,

Oregon in December 1976. While he was shooting a scene involving a fire, Fred became short of breath and was rushed to a hospital in Portland. Tests were performed and it was found that Fred was suffering from acute bronchitis and he was admitted to the hospital. Rather than delay the film, Fred decided to back out of his role and Allen hired Ernest Borgnine to replace him, but Allen promised Fred a role for him in his next picture.

It was while in the hospital that doctors found a far more serious problem than bronchitis; they discovered that Fred was also suffering from cancer of the throat, situated just behind the tongue. Years of pipe and cigarette smoking had certainly not helped. The cancer had been detected early and Fred went through a series of radiation treatment until it went into remission. Fred also went to Germany in 1977 for Laetrile treatments to help prevent the disease from reappearing. Laetrile is a compound which was used world-wide as an anti-cancer treatment, but had not been approved by the FDA in the United States, which is why Fred went to Germany for treatment. The FDA found that there was not enough evidence that Laetrile was effective against cancer. The drug was commonly given intravenously over a period of time and then orally for maintenance therapy. In an interview Fred wanted it clearly known that he had not depended solely on Laetrile. "I'm going through all the standard treatment."

With Fred's throat cancer in remission, Allen was as good as his word and offered him a role in his next project, the big-screen, all-star *The Swarm*, another disaster film, this one about invading killer bees. Fred was cast as the mayor of the small town where the killer bees are heading toward. The all-star cast included headliners Michael Caine and Katherine Ross, but also included such golden-age favorites as Henry Fonda, Richard Widmark, Ben Johnson and Olivia de Havilland. In fact, Fred and Johnson have a subplot where they both romance de Havilland. Unfortunately, the film, which turned out to be Fred's final big-screen acting role, offered little for him, or any of the other great stars, to do except die an agonizing death at the hands of killer bees. It's a shame that Fred didn't get his chance to go out with a little more style, like John Wayne in *The Shootist* or Henry Fonda in *On Golden Pond*. In fact, Fred would later tell a reporter that he thought he was retired until Allen called him up for a part in this film. Fred would say of his role in his final film, "It's not a big part, but it's a good part in a big motion picture. That's important." The lead actor in the film, Michael Caine, would later recall his delight, when at a get-acquainted party just prior to the beginning of principal photography, he entered the room and "there staring at me were Fred MacMurray, Henry Fonda, Olivia de Havilland and Richard Widmark. And I became the kid from the Elephant here with all these stars and I thought to myself, 'My God, what am I doing here?' And I dried up. When I was a boy, these people weren't real — they were myths and legends. And here I was talking with them. It's the only time I've ever dried up on a film set." Several years later (after the critical roasting and box office disappointment that *The Swarm* became) when asked about the film Fred replied, "We don't talk about that one." A few years later, director Ron Howard asked Fred to play the leading role in a film about senior citizens who find the fountain of youth when they take a swim in a pool containing alien cocoons. Fred turned the role down and it went to Don Ameche, who scored a big hit and an Oscar for the film, *Cocoon*.

From here on out Fred would limit his appearances to occasional television guest shots honoring friends and collaborators in the industry (*The American Film Institute Salute to Henry Fonda, The American Film Institute Salute to Billy Wilder* and *An All-Star Tribute to Jimmy Stewart*, which at least gave Fred the opportunity to play the sax while Stewart played the piano and sang "Ragtime Cowboy Joe") or an occasional entertainment special or television program (*Tony Orlando and Dawn* and a couple of Bob Hope specials). He also participated in events not televised, such as a Lincoln Center Salute to one of his favorite leading ladies, Claudette Colbert.

In May 1977 Fred received one of his first awards from the industry he had served for so long when he received the "Artistry in Cinema" award by the National Film Society. The ever unassuming Fred told the audience, "I was never a Gable, or a Cooper, by any means; I'm a personality - rather than an actor." Yet Gable and Cooper were certainly two of the biggest "personality-actors" in cinema history and Fred certainly belongs in their company, and in fact, probably showed more range during his career than either of those movie titans. Could you imagine either Gable or Cooper as Walter Neff in *Double Indemnity* or Lt. Keefer in *The Caine Mutiny*?

In November 1977, just after filming *The Swarm*, he participated in a special on ABC which saluted both *My Three Sons* and *The Partridge Family* and was hosted by Fred and Shirley Jones. Casts from both shows were reunited, with Shirley and Fred both reminiscing together, and then separately, with their individual TV families as they viewed some of their favorite clips. In an interview promoting the special both Fred and Shirley took a strong pro-family values/conservative stand. "Homosexuality, drugs, violence - they don't belong in our TV entertainment," Jones told *The New York Daily News*, to which Fred added, "I'm no prude, but I think today's shows can have an awful effect on children … Our show, in comparison to today's comedies, was more tame. The worst thing we ever said was that one of the neighbors was on pot. I don't think you have to get dirty or smutty to attract an audience." The special titled *Thanksgiving Reunion with the Partridge Family and My Three Sons* was telecast the day after Thanksgiving to decent, if unspectacular ratings.

But by the late '70s, and after his cancer scare, Fred was content to just enjoy his family life with June and his children and grandchildren. "I don't really miss it," Fred said when asked about his relative idleness. "A lot of actors go crazy if they're not working, but I guess I'm a little lazy."

In June of 1977 Fred traveled to Milwaukee to participate in the Vince Lombardi Golf Tournament to raise funds to combat cancer. Following the tournament he made his first trip to Beaver Dam since 1956, again staying with his boyhood friend Randall McKinstry and his family. Fred and June arrived on a Sunday morning and spent the afternoon at the cabin of McKinstry's son John, which is situated on Beaver Dam Lake. Fred was eager to show June how to catch bullhead fish, according to John McKinstry. Using bamboo fishing poles and worms dug up from the ground Fred, June and the McKinstrys went fishing and it was later reported that Fred caught two bullheads and June eight! McKinstry would tell the *Beaver Dam Daily Citizen,* "Bud didn't forget how to take bullheads off the hook." The MacMurrays spent the night and then on Monday took a drive around town and visited McKinstry's Hardware store, one of the oldest businesses in town, the YMCA Community Center and Oakwood Cemetery, where Fred visited his mother's grave. Despite it being more than twenty years since Fred had visited Beaver Dam he and the McKinstry family had stayed in contact through telephone calls and letters.

Two years later Fred again returned to his Beaver Dam roots, along with June and his daughter Kate, again staying with the McKinstrys. During his stay in July of 1979 Fred visited with students at Wilson Elementary School, where he had attended a creative drama class, and took questions from the students. Later, he spent time signing autographs. According to an article in the *Beaver Dam Daily Citizen,* the kids were delighted and impressed by meeting Fred. According student Mark Kornley, Fred would make a good father "because he doesn't yell at his kids on TV." Amy Verhulst agreed adding, "He really knows how to handle kids." According to the article many of the kids interviewed were nervous meeting Fred because, "he's so big and a movie star and everything." But when they did meet him he was as "calm and easygoing" as he was often depicted on the screen. Fred's favorite compliment came from student John Stellpflug, who couldn't believe that Fred was 71. "His hair isn't grey enough. I'd say he's about in his 40's."

The 100 or so students who Fred visited with that day asked him a wide range of questions, including "how he came to be called 'Bud,'" and even asked if the rumors were true that he was the richest man in Hollywood, to which Fred replied that it was a story started by Bob Hope. "It's not true. I wouldn't want all that money." He told his favorite story about the woman who belts him with a purse at Disneyland for having starred in *The Apartment.* He spoke fondly of *My Three Sons.* "It helped an awful lot of fathers communicate with their children, including me. There was a lot of love in the family." He spoke about how, now that he was "semi-retired," he played golf and also spent time in his garden and worked around the house.

"I don't spend time painting anymore. I have the studio, beautiful watercolor paints and paper. I've got everything but the talent. I know what a good watercolor is and that's not what I see."

In 1981 Fred's name was involved in a bizarre scheme where three men were accused of trying to defraud him. It involved the creation of phony title documents in which an "experienced land investor" nearly paid $675,000 to the three men who he thought were representing Fred in the selling of 131.5 acres of underdeveloped land. Even though the phony documents misspelled Fred's last name as "McMurray" in two places and "McUrry" in another the plot didn't really become unraveled until the buyer called Fred's representatives about removing a deed restriction on the land. The would-be buyer said, "I've been in the business since 1976 and have handled hundreds of land deals, but this is the first time I've run into a phony deed. This looked legal and even had the tax stamps of the Riverside County Recorders office on it." Fred's only public comment was that he was "quite surprised" that such a hoax could go as far as it did.

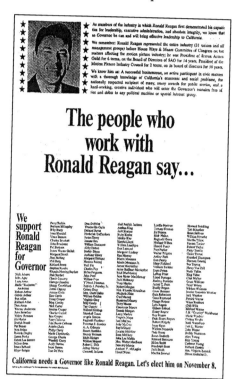

Fred rarely got publicly involved in politics but was generally a conservative Republican. In 1966 he added his name to those in the industry who supported Ronald Reagan for governor.

Fred was basically a conservative politically and supported Republican causes. He supported his friend Ronald Reagan when he ran for governor and later when he ran for president. But unlike Charlton Heston or Jane Fonda he wasn't outspoken about his politics. "I feel very often I'm a bad citizen not to get involved in things more than I do," Fred once explained. "But just because I happen to be an actor I shouldn't get up and say 'vote for this man,' knowing as little as I know about him. I'm not saying other actors shouldn't do it, that's up to them. But I'm no good at speech making; when people ask me I always say 'No' and finally they learn that you're going to sit there. I'm a family man and that's about it." He expanded on his family man activities: "On weekends I work in the yard, prop the trees up a little bit ... I'm a family man. I just die when I have an interview because I don't seem to feel strongly about anything. You read these other interviews — Kirk Douglas is involved in a lot of things — you wish you were that kind of guy. I always feel like a pretty dull, uninteresting character."

By the 1980s Fred's semi-retirement was by and large a total retirement. The only appearances he made were at industry functions (with the exception of an NBC TV special hosted by Bob Hope in 1984 titled *Unrehearsed Antics of the Stars)*, but there were no more motion pictures or television roles, if he made an appearance now it was as Fred MacMurray, beloved television and film star.

Fred continued to turn up at industry events in his tux (Beverly Garland said that June wouldn't allow Fred to become a "hermit ... she made him get out and put on a tux and be seen around town so people would know he was still alive"), paying tribute to Jimmy Stewart, Henry Fonda, Billy Wilder, and Barbara Stanwyck, among others. (He paid tribute to Stanwyck by saying, "I was lucky enough to make four pictures with Barbara. In the first I turned her in, in the second I killed her, in the third I left her for another woman, and in the fourth I pushed her over a waterfall. The one thing all these pictures had in common was that I fell in love with Barbara Stanwyck, and I did too.") Tributes the industry wouldn't pay him. He was overlooked for such honors as *The American Film Institute Life Achievement Award, The Kennedy Center Honors* and even a special Academy Award for a lifetime of achievement in motion pictures (both Fonda and Stewart had received late career honorary Oscars from the Academy). But it didn't seem to bother him. "Fred didn't need honors from the industry to sustain him," June once observed. "The fan mail he continued to receive even after he retired from young and old alike meant more to him than some statue or plaque." Fred joked with writer Jay Navarro that he had received "one of my finest awards — the Popscar," given to him by the Popcorn Growers Institute of America because his film *The Shaggy Dog* had sold the most popcorn in movie theaters when it was released. They awarded him a year's supply of popcorn!

June and Fred turned up at Hollywood parties too, sometimes with diverse guest lists. Sammy Davis, Jr. loved old Hollywood and his parties usually included a mix of the old Hollywood with the new Hollywood and even underground Hollywood. "In the spring of 1980 Sammy and Altovise [Mrs. Davis] threw a party," wrote Sammy's biographer. "There was no special occasion; it was just a party. Some tents on the lawn; a catered affair; the usual. The guest list, showing Sammy's taste, was as always eclectic: Fred MacMurray and his wife, June Haver, Jack Haley, Jr.; and his wife, Liza Minnelli; Edmund O'Brien; Loretta Young; porn star Marilyn Chambers —

and an assortment of 'obscure white and black actors,' as Sammy put it. Altovise looked ravishing, gliding about the festivities in a Galanos gown. In one corner, there stood MacMurray and Marilyn Chambers, chatting away. The avuncular father of television's *My Three Sons* and the porn starlet."

Fred was genuinely gratified when the Walt Disney Company honored him in 1987 with an award which honored his "body of work [which] epitomizes the Disney product." "Fred was the first person presented with the Disney Legends award on October 13, 1987," Disney historian and archivist Dave Smith recalled. "He arrived for a low-key ceremony attended by Disney employees in front of the Disney Studio Theater in an open car accompanied by a large Shaggy Dog. He placed his handprints and signature in wet cement, and received a plaque from Disney chairman and CEO Michael Eisner." In 1988 there was no Disney Legends award presented, but by the time of the 1989 ceremony a special bronze figurine which depicted Mickey Mouse holding a star-tipped wand was presented to several of the studio's animators (both living and deceased) and, according to Smith, "in addition to the awards presented at that year's ceremony, one was made for Fred. Jeff Hoffman, head of our Legends Committee, personally took the figurine to Fred's house, and presented it to him, as June looked on. By that time, Fred was in poor health."

Fred and June out on the town.

That same year his home state of Wisconsin also honored Fred. The then 78-year-old actor, who had aged considerably over the last few years due to continuing health problems, appeared in Milwaukee to be inducted into the Wisconsin Performing Artists Hall of Fame. June, as usual, accompanied Fred to the event. Fred was awarded a clay plaque of his likeness and his name was added to those of other Wisconsin film and stage luminaries who had received the award, such as Orson Welles, Fredric March, Dennis Morgan, Jack Carson, Spencer Tracy, Colleen Dewhurst and stage legends Alfred Lunt and Lynn Fontanne. Among those who spoke that night was June, who recited a Father's Day Poem she had written for Fred which concluded, "From Beaver Dam, here is a man, not a mouse ... I'm glad to have this man around my house." The evening also included an anthology of clips from Fred's body of work, including scenes from *Double Indemnity, The*

Caine Mutiny, The Apartment and many of his popular Disney films. But the audience applauded most heartily when scenes of Fred appeared as everybody's favorite dad, Steve Douglas, in *My Three Sons*. The climax of the evening came when the previous year's recipient, David Zucker (of *Airplane!* fame), introduced Fred. Fred was assisted to the podium where he said little, but what he did came from the heart: "Gee, I'm glad I came ... I'm honored ... I'm just glad to be from Wisconsin." He also invited the more than 30 residents from Beaver Dam who attended the ceremony, and who might find themselves in Hollywood, to just knock on his door and say "Beaver Dam" and they would be welcomed into his home.

His health problems were catching up with him. Shortly before Thanksgiving in 1987 his throat cancer reappeared and he underwent surgery for removal of a tumor, a surgery which the doctors initially believed to be successful. "The fact that the tumor - which turned out to be malignant," Fred recalled in an interview shortly after the surgery, "was totally contained meant that the entire cancerous growth could be removed without fear of it spreading ... the doctors assured me, thank God, they got it all and I was just to rest now and regain my strength." Just weeks prior to this Fred had hip surgery and initially when the cancer reappeared Fred and June didn't want the public to know that he was being operated on for cancer, so they told the press that he was being readmitted to the hospital for follow-up work on his hip. But when he got a clean bill of health from the doctors Fred and June decided to be up front with his many fans and he took pride in saying, "I beat the cancer." But he continued to have radiation treatments, which gave his entire system a beating and left him terribly fatigued.

His health worries were not over. On December 27, while at home watching a football game, he complained that he was feeling ill and began to have trouble speaking clearly. His doctor was called and when Fred's problems were described to him he thought, perhaps, the radiation treatments were causing some problems with his voice and he made plans for Fred to report to the hospital the next morning for tests. The next morning Fred couldn't get out of bed by himself and found he couldn't speak at all. When he was helped out of bed, his right leg caved in under his weight. Paramedics were called, who rushed him to St. John Hospital in Santa Monica. He was placed in the intensive care unit, but made such an impressive recovery that on December 30 he was moved to a private room. Doctors believed he would eventually recover "at least 90 percent from the stroke." June stayed with him almost constantly during his hospitalization. By the end of the month he was at home but undergoing rigorous physical therapy. By April of 1988 told a reporter, "Each day I'm feeling stronger ... I know that in no time at all I'll be back on the golf course." He went on to say, "Until you get hit with the sort of things I've been hit with lately, you don't realize how good life is ... I'm grateful that I'm still around, and have my wonderful wife and family." According to June, "He's doing incredibly well. He undergoes physical therapy every day."

In August of 1988, Fred turned 80. He was still recovering from his stroke and the celebration was to be family only and very low-key. A reporter called the MacMurray home in Brentwood to get a comment from Fred on this milestone and found that he was taking a nap. Instead, he spoke with June. "We are just going to have the family here," June told him. "We will have a special cake, but we hope we don't burn the house down with all the candles!" She added, "He's very happy to be 80 years old. Many of his friends are older, you know. He looks at George Burns and Bob Hope and he says, 'Gee, I feel like a kid.'"

Over the next couple of years Fred did improve, but he never entirely shook the effects of the stroke. He also had a recurrence of cancer, developing Leukemia. All of this kept him weak and generally away from the activities he enjoyed most, such as golf and enjoying the pleasures of his ranch (though he still did occasionally go as much as his health permitted). He was also, for all intent, truly retired from the industry and rarely made any personal or public appearances. He was often bedridden in his final months. Shortly before Fred died, June shared a limousine to the American Cinema Awards with Jane Greer, Ann Rutherford and Fred's old friend Macdonald Carey. Carey later said of that trip, "I could see that it was painful for her to talk about him, and by the time we dropped her at home afterwards, Fred's name had barely been mentioned."

Fred did his best to keep his spirits, and the spirits of others, up. Don Grady stayed in touch with him over the years, and once he heard that Fred was getting seriously ill he would occasionally call him, just to let him know that he was there and that he cared. "I would call the house and talk to him. Not frequently, but every so often. Even a few weeks before he passed he was making jokes on the phone with me." The final time Grady spoke with Fred he would recall, "He couldn't make it down the stairs to the phone. He kept his sense of humor, though. He always had that." Grady was full of praise for June who he called "the light of Fred's life" and recalled that whenever June would visit the *My Three Sons* set "Fred would light up like a Christmas tree! He would laugh and enjoy himself like no other time ... she had this loosening up power over him. And why wouldn't she! She was always beaming herself! What a beautiful woman, and what a magnificent personality she had." Tim Considine backs this up, recalling Fred and June at a tribute a few years before Fred died. "She took wonderful care of him," Considine recalled. "He wasn't physically strong at the time. She made sure everything was right for him without being intrusive or overly protective."

By early November 1991, Fred's health had taken a turn for the worst. He developed a Urinary Tract Infection, which quickly turned into a very serious blood infection, Sepsis Syndrome. By the fourth of November he was admitted to St. John's Hospital in Santa Monica, suffering from, as if that weren't enough, pneumonia. June again stayed almost constantly with him, as did his daughter Kate. The other kids were contacted, Susan in Arkansas, Rob in Hawaii and Laurie in Arizona, when Fred died on November 5. He was 83 years old. Lester Martin, who was informed of his cousin's death by Fred's daughter Laurie, recalled that "I knew Fred was ill, but I didn't think anybody believed it was terminal—at least I didn't."

Not surprisingly, given the longevity of his career and the affection felt toward him, his passing made front page news all over the world and led television newscasts. Obituaries in several papers mourned his loss. Perhaps the most heartfelt was in the *Beaver Dam Daily Citizen,* which headlined: BD LOSES ITS 'FAVORITE SON.' Other papers in the days following his death played to his versatility as an actor. *The Salt Lake Tribune* headlined FRED MACMURRAY: WHEN HE WAS GOOD, HE WAS BLAND, BUT WHEN HE WAS BAD, HE WAS REALLY GOOD. *The Vancouver* (Canada) *Sun* headlined GOOD GUY OR BAD GUY, FRED ALWAYS FIT THE BILL.

His colleagues and friends in the industry expressed their sadness and admiration:

James Stewart: "He was a fine gentleman and a wonderful actor. He was adept at both comedy and drama with a style all his own."

Claudette Colbert: "Fred was one of my favorites; it was always a joy to work with him and to know him."

Jane Wyman: "I'm deeply saddened by the loss of this wonderful man, devoted husband and father, good friend and fine actor."

Billy Wilder: "He always resisted doing a movie with me because he thought I would destroy his image — but he always did — and he was always wonderful — I'll miss him."

Barry Livingston: "He wasn't your glamour-boy type of star ... he was very humble, down to earth man who felt extremely uncomfortable with his celebrity. There was a real sweetness about the man, but he wasn't anybody's fool either."

Disney Studios CEO Michael Eisner issued a statement: "At Disney, he will always be remembered as a fine actor and a true gentleman."

Beverly Garland learned of Fred's passing when a reporter called asking her for a comment. She said that the phone didn't stop ringing all day. "All I could think of was 'how sad,'" recalled Garland, "he was such a wonderful guy and I was heartbroken not only to have lost a friend, but of course, for June and the family. But Fred had been ill for some time." Beverly's official quote carried nationwide by the Associated Press was, "Such a lovely, shy, funny, wonderful man. I'll miss him." Elliott Reid had seldom seen Fred in the twenty-five years since they had last worked together in the film *Follow Me, Boys!* but upon learning of Fred's death he wrote a heartfelt letter of sympathy to June and was overjoyed when she later responded back to him, assuring Reid that Fred had liked and enjoyed working with him. "To know this," he later said, "meant a great deal to me." To this day he treasures that letter from June. (June, who never remarried, would pass away in 2005, of respiratory failure.)

Two days following Fred's death, the *Los Angeles Times* critic Charles Champlin wrote an appreciation: "The movie camera, with its undeniable capacity to see past the characterization to the player's soul, saw the nice guy that MacMurray really was. Later and not without anxiety attacks, MacMurray let himself play against the nice guy image, creating that small but indelible gallery of bad guys, such as in *Double Indemnity*. The villains seemed more villainous, or more smarmy, as in the philandering boss in *The Apartment,* because it was Fred MacMurray, for crying out loud ... MacMurray knew, better than anyone, his strengths and limits as a performer. The stage and the sound stage were his acting schools and he was a quick study. Naturalness on camera -which is as much an illusion as tears or rage - seemed easy for him, and from early days he was a good actor (as the nervous suitor in *Alice Adams,* for example) and he turned out to be one of Hollywood's most expert light comedians. The miracle of Hollywood in its early days was that it kept finding the men and women who could help to define the movies' possibilities. Fred MacMurray was one of the men."

One week following Fred's passing *People* had a cover story on Fred titled "A Dad for All Seasons." In it Don Grady recalled appearing several years earlier at a Hollywood Bowl reunion of the Disney Mouseketeers, with various celebrities in the audience. The celebrities were introduced, one by one, to "polite applause," but when they came to Fred, "You suddenly heard the whole bowl go 'Ahhhh!' and this warm gush came out of everyone. I never realized until then what an effect he had on people. What we've lost is that warm gush."

Kate MacMurray, in her travels on business or pleasure, still encounters people who would fondly recall her dad. "He had an endearing nature that people were very drawn to," she said. "I ran into someone the other day ... and he said, 'you know, I didn't have a dad. Your father raised me for 12 years and I hope I can raise my boys that way.' That was the most beautiful compliment. I'm not sure Daddy was aware of the effect that he had on so many generations of children."

In 1986 Fred, in his own understated and humble way, summed up his career this way: "Well, I've done pretty good for a guy who plays saxophone." Two years later, on his 80th birthday, when asked how he wanted to be remembered, he replied, "Fondly." He got his wish.

Fred MacMurray, as we remember him.

Feature Films of Fred MacMurray

Fred appeared as an "extra" in three films shot in 1929:
Girls Gone Wild
Why Leave Home?
Tiger Rose

Friends of Mr. Sweeney (1934, Warner Brothers) *D:* Edward Ludwig.
Cast: Charlie Ruggles, Ann Dvorak, Eugene Pallette, Robert Barrat, Burton Churchill, Dorothy Burgess, Dorothy Tree, Mike Tyler. 68 mins. B&W.
Plot: Ruggles plays his usual hen-pecked and mild-mannered character (from this period) in a story about a reporter learning to stand up for himself.
Trivia: Fred has a small walk-on appearance.

Grand Old Girl (1935, RKO) *D:* John Robertson.
Cast: May Robson, Mary Carlisle, Fred MacMurray, Alan Hale, Hale Hamilton, William Burress, Edward Van Sloan, Fred Kohler, Jr., Ben Alexander, Gavin Gordon.
Plot: May Robson is the "Grand Old Girl" of the title, a high school teacher who is let go after 38 years of dedicated service. Fred plays a truck driver who becomes smitten by Mary Carlisle, a young girl who befriends Robson.
Trivia: One of the working titles of this film was "Woman Aroused," which didn't seem to fit a film which was being hyped for family audiences.
Reviews: "If you dislike *Grand Old Girl,* you are likely a beast and derive your major satisfaction from hurling stones through the windows at the old ladies' home." *New York Times,* 2/26/35. "*Grand Old Girl* is a home spun, likable little family picture." *Variety,* 3/6/35.

The Gilded Lily (1935, Paramount) *D:* Wesley Ruggles.
Cast: Claudette Colbert, Fred MacMurray, Ray Milland, C. Aubrey Smith, Edward Craven, Luis Alberni, Grace Bradley. 80 mins. B&W.
Plot: Claudette must choose between rich international playboy Milland

and the down-to-earth working stiff played by Fred.
Trivia: The first of seven screen teamings between Fred MacMurray and Claudette Colbert. The working title of this film was "One Night Like This."
Reviews: "A new leading man, Fred MacMurray, makes himself felt in the role of the brash but likeable newspaperman." *Chicago Herald & Examiner*
"Fred MacMurray, a tall regular-looking fellow, makes his debut here. Taken from leading a jazz orchestra, the pleasant and unactorish MacMurray had the girls ga-ga at the preview." *Los Angeles Examiner,* 1/6/35.
"Breezy romance with plenty of entertainment ... Picture will attract plenty of attention for two young leading men — Fred MacMurray and Ray Milland." *Variety,* 3/12/35.
"... a fresh and engaging screen comedy." *New York Times,* 2/9/35.

Car 99 (1935, Paramount) *D:* Charles Barton.
Cast: Fred MacMurray, Ann Sheridan, Sir Guy Standing, Frank Craven, William Frawley, Martina Schubert [Koshetz], Dean Jagger, John Howard, Robert Kent, Del Cambre [Alfred Delcambre], Nora Cecil. 67 mins. B&W.
Plot: In this programmer, Fred plays a green Michigan State Policeman who wins the day and the girl when he captures some mobsters.
Trivia: The director, Charles Barton, later directed Fred in *The Shaggy Dog,* a film which resurrected Fred's career and led to his long association with Walt Disney Productions. This is the first of two films that Fred made with William Frawley, who later played "Bub" on *My Three Sons* (1960-1964).
Reviews: "MacMurray's personality and talent flicks into prominence from the start of the fable." *Variety,* 2/27/35.
"I should not say that Mr. MacMurray's performance was distinguished, but he does add to the good first impression registered in *The Gilded Lily.*" *Syracuse Herald,* 7/5/35.

Men Without Names (1935, Paramount) *D:* Ralph Murphy.
Cast: Fred MacMurray, Madge Evans, Lynne Overman, David Holt, J.C. Nugent, Leslie Fenton, Dean Jagger, Elizabeth Patterson. 66 mins. B&W.
Plot: Another programmer, with Fred playing a G-Man who goes undercover in a Kansas town which serves as headquarters to a criminal organization.
Trivia: Leslie Fenton, who plays Monk in this film, later turned director and directed Fred in two mid-40s films, *Pardon My Past* and *On Our Merry Way.*
Reviews: "MacMurray breezes through his assignment as the top boy, being completely believable and acceptable with the exception of the few moments when he's asked to get romantic." *Variety,* 7/35/35.

Men Without Names, *1935*.

Alice Adams (1935, RKO) *D:* George Stevens.
Cast: Katharine Hepburn, Fred MacMurray, Fred Stone, Evelyn Venable, Frank Albertson, Hattie McDaniel. 99 mins. B&W.
Plot: Booth Tarkington's novel becomes an excellent Hepburn vehicle in this story of a girl falling in love with an unpretentious man (Fred) whose social status she has always wanted to attain.
Trivia: RKO wanted Randolph Scott for the role played by Fred, but Hepburn and director George Stevens held out for Fred.
Reviews: "Up to its last five mins 'Alice Adams' is all that a film should be. Its acting, its photography, its telling of the story and the story itself are all fascinating." *Commonweal,* 8/30/35.
"Hollywood bestows a garland on the languishing summer cinema in the splendid screen version of *Alice Adams.*" *New York Times,* 8/16/35.
"*Alice Adams* is sturdy cinematic substance, and virtually audience proof." *Variety,* 8/21/35.

Hands Across the Table (1935, Paramount). *D:* Mitchell Leisen.
Cast: Carole Lombard, Fred MacMurray, Ralph Bellamy, Astrid Allwyn, Marie Prevost. 80 mins. B&W.
Plot: The story is similar to *The Gilded Lily* as career girl Lombard must choose between two suitors, Fred and Ralph Bellamy. Bellamy plays a more

textured part than his usual chump characterization and as such gives Fred a run for his money.

Trivia: Samuel Goldwyn optioned the story as a film for Miriam Hopkins, but let the option lapse, allowing Paramount to pick it up. William Demarest, who later played "Uncle Charley" on *My Three Sons,* is cast as Natty. One of several screen appearances he would make with Fred over the next thirty years.

Reviews: "Of all the numerous efforts to recapture the mood of *It Happened One Night,* the new photoplay at the Paramount is easily the most successful." *New York Times,* 11/2/35.

"In its appeal to a U.S. box office which rarely resists the situation of two young people living together and not making love, *Hands Across the Table* should do well." *Time,* 10/28/35.

"First rate entertainment results from this blending of substantial material, good playing and clever direction." *Variety,* 11/6/35.

"A laugh riot from start to finish." *The Galveston Daily News,* 1/19/36.

The Bride Comes Home (1935, Paramount) *D:* Wesley Ruggles.
Cast: Claudette Colbert, Fred MacMurray, Robert Young, William Collier, Sr. Edgar Kennedy. 82 Mins. B&W.

Plot: Paramount certainly struck a formula with Fred in yet another love triangle romantic comedy. Colbert again must choose between working-class Fred and rich Young. Hmm, who will she choose?

Trivia: Robert Young, like Fred, became one of television's most famous dads due to his starring role on *Father Knows Best,* which ended its run the year that Fred began *My Three Sons.*

Reviews: "Deft Comedy and light romance flow merrily at a dark tempo, directing attention (together with the expertise of the performances) away from the slightness of the plot." *Commonweal,* 12/27/35.

"*The Bride Comes Home* is pleasurably performed and shrewdly directed and gives every appearance of being an excellent motion picture in search of a plot." *New York Times,* 12/25/35.

"A crisp, invigorating picture." *The Galveston Daily News,* 1/19/36.

The Trail of the Lonesome Pine (1936, Paramount). *D:* Henry Hathaway.
Cast: Sylvia Sidney, Henry Fonda, Fred MacMurray, Fred Stone, Fuzzy Knight, Beulah Bondi, Spanky McFarland, Nigel Bruce. 102 mins. Color.

Plot: Story of feuding families eventually coming together when a railroad is built on their land.

Trivia: This film had been filmed three times before, all in silent films, the second version by Cecil B. DeMille.

Reviews: "As a demonstration of outdoor photography in color — it is an

outstanding achievement." *New York Journal*
"*Trail of the Lonesome Pine* should blaze a new trail to the box office for new records. It is an outstanding triumph in the field of natural color, portrayed by an excellent cast, and the last word in scenic beauty." *Box Office* "*The Trail of the Lonesome Pine* is a film of dramatic and artistic magnificence, a great piece of entertainment for all classes and a box office smash by every sign." *Daily Variety*.

Thirteen Hours by Air (1936, Paramount) *D:* Mitchell Leisen. *Cast:* Fred MacMurray, Joan Bennett, ZaSu Pitts, John Howard, Bennie Bartlett, Grace Bradley, Alan Baxter, Ruth Donnelly, Dean Jagger. 80 mins. B&W.
Plot: Murder mystery with comedy undertones set on a transcontinental flight.
Trivia: This would be the first of two films which Fred made with Joan Bennett. The second one was filmed twenty-years later, *There's Always Tomorrow*.
Reviews: "Fred MacMurray has one of those hero parts which permits doing all a hero could ask for … on top of this MacMurray has the best of the comedy lines, including a couple of corkers." *Variety*, 5/6/36

Ad for **Thirteen Hours by Air**, *1936*.

"… shrewd sense of pace, with a purposeful preservation of suspense and a knack for comic interlude." *New York Times*, 4/30/36.

The Princess Comes Across (1936, Paramount) *D:* William K. Howard.
Cast: Carole Lombard, Fred MacMurray, Douglass Dumbrille, Alison Skipworth, William Frawley, Porter Hall, George Barbier, Lumsden Hare, Siegfried Ruman, Mischa Auer. 76 mins. B&W.
Plot: Lombard impersonates a princess on an ocean voyage who gets romantically involved with a bandleader (Fred) and together they solve a mystery.
Trivia: George Raft was originally cast in the role Fred played, but dropped out due to his lack of comedic ability.
Reviews: "*The Princess Comes Across* just about gets across as a mild-to-boresome comedy." *New York Times*, 6/4/36.

"Slick piece of satire and whodunit ... MacMurray blends in smoothly with the Lombard style and leaves nothing wanting ... William Frawley contributes a goodly share of the film's wealth of comedy moments." *Variety*, 6/10/36.

The Texas Rangers *(1936, Paramount) D:* King Vidor.
Cast: Fred MacMurray, Jack Oakie, Jean Parker, Lloyd Nolan, Edward Ellis. 95 mins. B&W.
Plot: Fred, Oakie and Nolan are friends who eventually split up. Fred and Oakie become Texas Rangers while Nolan becomes an outlaw who they inevitably have to go after.
Trivia: The film did well enough to spawn a remake in 1949, *Streets of Laredo*.
Reviews: "MacMurray shows up very favorable as a straight-shooting bronc rider ... What appears to have been intended as an epic of the southwest is just a fancy horse opry. It holds more entertainment than the average western." *Variety*, 9/30/36.

"Except for a bright characterization by Jack Oakie and an equally pleasing sinister one by Lloyd Nolan, 'The Texas Rangers' is simply a revival of a decadent cinema form, generically referred to as 'cops and robbers.'" *New York Times*, 9/24/36.

Champagne Waltz (1937, Paramount) *D:* A. Edward Sutherland.
Cast: Gladys Swarthout, Fred MacMurray, Jack Oakie, Herman Bing, Vivienne Osborne. 87 mins. B&W.
Plot: Gladys' father operates a Vienna waltz palace which is situated next to a club where Fred's American jazz band has set up shop. As they say, opposites attract.
Trivia: This film launched Paramount's 25th anniversary and was selected, according to *Time* magazine, because Paramount chairman Adolph Zukor believed it to be the "most festive of Paramount's present crop." Paramount launched the film simultaneously with showings in 80 theaters "all over the globe."

Ad for **Champagne Waltz**, *1937.*

Reviews: "The perennial and expensive effort to make a Grace Moore out of Gladys Swarthout … This version of the endeavor is a heavy-footed musical naively designed to combine the best features of jazz with those of the Viennese waltz." *Time,* 1/25/37.

"*Champagne Waltz* is Gladys Swarthout's third picture for Paramount and her best to date … Some driving power is realized by the presence in the cast of Fred MacMurray." *Variety,* 2/10/37.

Maid of Salem (1937, Paramount). *D:* Frank Lloyd.
Cast: Claudette Colbert, Fred MacMurray, Louise Dresser, Gale Sondergaard, Beulah Bondi, Bonita Granville, Virginia Weidler, Donald Meek, Harvey Stephens, Edward Ellis, Mme. Sul-Te-Wan. 86 mins. B&W.
Plot: Set in Salem during the witch trials, Claudette is accused of being a witch and Fred stands up for her.
Trivia: Production was halted on this film for several days when director Frank Lloyd (*Mutiny on the Bounty*) battled the flu. Colbert was out of the production for nearly a month following a car accident. Fred wasn't immune. According to press reports, on September 14, 1936, while this film was in production, Fred was knocked unconscious on the set when a "passing workman dropped a heavy metal tripod on his head." The report indicates he was treated at a Hollywood hospital for a "slight" concussion and then returned to the set two hours later.
Reviews: "*Maid of Salem* is slow starting — gets a little exciting and then drags badly again to its ending … Neither Miss Colbert nor MacMurray are favored by the script." *Variety,* 3/10/37.
"MacMurray, here to fore a trade emblem of flip 20th century youth, invents a kind of brogue which fails to transport him back two centuries and a half." *Time,* 3/8/37.

Swing High, Swing Low (1937, Paramount). *D:* Mitchell Leisen.
Cast: Carole Lombard, Fred MacMurray, Charles Butterworth, Jean Dixon, Dorothy Lamour, Harvey Stephens, Anthony Quinn. 95 mins. B&W.
Plot: Fred plays an arrogant musician, with Carole as the woman who tries to humanize him. Featuring future stars Quinn and Lamour in supporting roles.
Trivia: Fred's trumpet playing was provided by two members of the Victor Young band, Frank Zinziv and William Candreva.
Reviews: Swing High, Swing Low, like most Ferris wheels, doesn't go anywhere — at least, nowhere that you have not been. Its players really are worthy of better treatment." *New York Times,* 4/15/37.
"Vastly over-ballyhooed by Paramount the pictures' chief virtues are providing pretty Carole Lombard with a few good comedy lines almost up to the standards she had in *My Man Godfrey,* and reminding cinemaddicts that

Fred MacMurray ... got his start in cinema after a five-year career as a member of the California Collegians." *Time,* 3/22/37.

"*Swing High, Swing Low* has already proved itself in some of the key cities as strong box office with Carole Lombard and Fred MacMurray topping a strong cast, plus basic entertainment ingredients, no reason to believe that *Swing High* will not jam 'em at the gate." *Variety,* 4/21/37.

Ad for Exclusive, *1937.*

Exclusive (1937, Paramount). *D:* Alexander Hall.
Cast: Fred MacMurray, Frances Farmer, Charlie Ruggles, Lloyd Nolan, Fay Holden, Ralph Morgan, Horace McMahon. 85 mins. B&W.
Plot: Newspaper comedy-drama dealing with Farmer joining a tabloid which competes with the paper her father runs and that her boyfriend (Fred) is the editor of.
Trivia: Up-and-coming Paramount actress Frances Farmer got the leading female role after Carole Lombard rejected it.
Reviews: "Uneasy mix of comedy, romance, and melodrama." Leonard Maltin, *Movie and Video Guide.*
"Alexander Hall has directed without assurance, and his film lacks conviction at any point. Production is on a big scale, but the story misses completely." *Variety,* 7/21/37.
"Ruggles plays one of his finest roles. Miss Farmer is charming as his wisecracking peppery newspaperman, and MacMurray is excellent as the city editor." *The Burlington (NC) Daily Times-News,* 8/21/37.

True Confession (1937, Paramount). *D:* Wesley Ruggles.
Cast: Carole Lombard, Fred MacMurray, John Barrymore, Una Merkel, Porter Hall, Edgar Kennedy, Lynne Overman, Irving Bacon, Fitz Feld. 85 mins. B&W.
Plot: Great cast saddled with a so-so script about a woman who confesses to a murder she didn't commit. Fred plays her lawyer-husband who defends her and tries to find the real murderer.
Trivia: This film was remade by Paramount in 1946 as *Cross My Heart* and starred Betty Hutton and Sonny Tufts.
Reviews: "Although *True Confession* had a pulpwood sound, it proved yesterday to be a highly polished, smoothly grained Yule log which deserves to crackle right merrily at the Paramount from now until well after Christmas." *New York Times,* 12/16/37.
"Miss Lombard handles herself well ... MacMurray is as good as she is in developing suitable background for the somewhat goofy yarn. MacMurray's work is not his best, however." *Variety,* 11/24/37.
"*True Confession* is skillfully played and paced, keyed up to the pitch of the dizziest haywire skit. Yet what makes *True Confession* funnier than most haywire comedies is that as melodrama it could be just as effective." *Time,* 12/27/37.

Cocoanut Grove (1938, Paramount). *D:* Alfred Santell.
Cast: Fred MacMurray, Harriet Hilliard, Yacht Club Boys, Ben Blue, Rufe Davis, Billy Lee, Eve Arden. 85 mins. B&W.
Plot: Fred is cast in yet another musical as a bandleader who appears at the famous Hollywood club of the title. Harriet Hilliard is best known as Harriet Nelson of *Ozzie and Harriet* fame.
Trivia: Harriet Hilliard had worked with Fred years earlier when she was a girl singer with the California Collegiates. Harriet had a top-selling song with the Frank Loesser and Burton Lane tune "Says My Heart." Fred sings "You Leave Me Breathless."
Reviews: "Pleasant musical, more or less familiarly patterned." *Variety,* 5/18/38.
"Tuneful music, a story that's a pip, fine performances ..." *The Hollywood Reporter*
"Flimsy musical, with nine songs you'll never hear again." Leonard Maltin, *Movie and Video Guide.*

Fred and Louise Campbell in **Men With Wings,** *1938.*

Men with Wings (1938, Paramount). *D:* William Wellman.
Cast: Fred MacMurray, Louise Campbell, Ray Milland, Andy Devine, Walter Abel, Virginia Weidler. 105 mins. Color.
Plot: Good aviation scenes can't redeem lackluster story of rival pilots (Fred and Ray) competing not only in the air but for the love of Campbell.
Trivia: Budgeted at over $2 million this was one of the most expensive films produced by Paramount up to that time.
Reviews: "For its intention and for its photographic content the picture deserves to rank as one of the year's most important productions. Were the narrative, the writing and the acting ... up to the same standard, it would rank as one of the best pictures ever made. Unfortunately, they are not." *Time,* 11/7/38.
"*Men With Wings* is a giant bomber from the Paramount hangar. Designed on a lavish scale by the skilled air picture mechanic, William A. Wellman, and polished off beautifully in Technicolor. *Variety,* 10/26/38.

Sing, You Sinners (1938, Paramount). *D:* Wesley Ruggles.
Cast: Bing Crosby, Fred MacMurray, Donald O'Connor, Elizabeth Patterson, Ellen Drew, John Gallaudet. 88 mins. B&W.
Plot: Bing and Fred play brothers — one irresponsible (Bing) and the other trying to prod him into facing his responsibilities. Good songs.

Trivia: This was the second film that young Donald O'Connor appeared in with Fred. In *Men with Wings*, O'Connor played Fred's role as a teenager.
Reviews: "Crosby plays his part strongly, but with restraint. He doesn't hog anything from MacMurray nor moppet O'Connor ... MacMurray makes a strong impression." *Variety*, 8/17/38.

Café Society (1938, Paramount). *D:* Edward H. Griffith. *Cast:* Madeleine Carroll, Fred MacMurray, Shirley Ross, Jessie Ralph, Claude Gillingwater. 83 mins. B&W.
Plot: Okay musical-comedy with heiress Carroll making a bet that she can make Fred her husband.
Trivia: This was the first of five films over the next decade to feature Fred and Madeleine Carroll.
Reviews: "On the whole, *Café Society* makes a pretty good picture, thanks to Virginia Van Upp's script, Edward H. Griffith's direction, and a cast who present this society without overacting." *Commonweal*, 3/3/39.
"... production is nicely paced ... Edward H. Griffith has merged all the ingredients skillfully." *Variety*, 2/8/39.

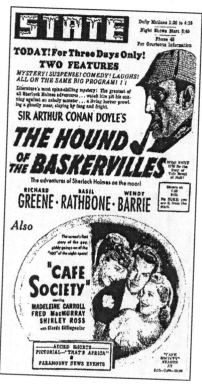

Ad for Café Society, *1938.*

Invitation to Happiness (1939, RKO) *D:* Wesley Ruggles.
Cast: Irene Dunne, Fred MacMurray, Charlie Ruggles, William Collier, Sr., Eddie Hogan. 95 mins. B&W.
Plot: Irene plays a socialite who marries a boxer and the problems they endure when he wants to continues his career in the ring over her objections.
Trivia: According to one Paramount press release, 1,357 extras were used in the prize-fighting scene.
Reviews: "There is the most terrifying and agonizing prize fight you ever saw on screen, and fine, glib dramatic performances by MacMurray and Irene Dunne." *Stage*, 5/15/39.
"Picture is an emotional drama with plenty of heart tugs." *Variety*, 5/10/39.

Fred and Madeleine Carroll in Honeymoon in Bali, *1939.*

Honeymoon in Bali (1939, RKO) *D:* Edward H. Griffith.
Cast: Fred MacMurray, Madeleine Carroll, Allan Jones, Osa Massen, Helen Broderick, Akim Tamiroff, Carolyn Lee, Monty Woolley. 95 mins. B&W.
Plot: This time around Fred chases Carroll with Jones as the third wheel of the triangle. Good romantic comedy, better than *Café Society* with same leads and director from 1938.
Trivia: Little Carolyn Lee, who plays Rosie in this film, would later work again with Fred in 1941's *Virginia.*
Reviews: "*Honeymoon in Bali* is an infectiously sparkling comedy-drama." *Variety,* 9/13/39.
"*Honeymoon in Bali* is bright, clever, romantic and uneven." New *York Times,* 9/21/39.
"*Honeymoon in Bali* is one of those over-jaunty comedies that have too good a time the first part of the evening, suddenly begin to stagger around, then fold up for the night. The rest is hang-over." *Time,* 10/29/39.

Remember the Night (1940, Paramount) *D:* Mitchell Leisen.
Cast: Barbara Stanwyck, Fred MacMurray, Beulah Bondi, Elizabeth Patterson, Willard Robertson, Sterling Holloway, Charles Waldron, Paul Guilfoyle, Fred "Snowflake" Toones, Georgia Caine. 94 mins. B&W.
Plot: During the Christmas season Stanwyck plays a woman who is arrested

for shoplifting and Fred is the D.A. who prosecutes her. When the trial is stayed until after the holidays, Fred arranges bail for Stanwyck so she won't have to spend the holidays in jail. When he finds out her mother lives in Indiana he invites her to drive with him (since his family lives in Indiana as well). He witnesses her mother heartlessly rejecting her and invites her to spend an old-fashioned Christmas with his family. They fall in love.

Trivia: Marjorie (Ma Kettle) Main was the first choice to play Stanwyck's hardened mother, but, according to David Chierichetti's study of director Mitchell Leisen, Main played the role "like a crazy woman" and "lost all control." Leisen replaced her with Georgia Caine.

Reviews: "Story basically, is of familiar pattern, but is dressed most presentably with much sparkling dialog. Carries added advantages of excellent direction by Mitchell Leisen, and impressive performances by Barbara Stanwyck, Fred MacMurray and all members of the supporting cast." *Variety,* 1/10/40.

"After dallying too long with the leftovers of 1939, the screen has awakened finally to a new year and new entertainment responsibilities. 'Remember the Night' presented at the Paramount yesterday, is the real curtain-raiser for 1940, the first word of reassurance Hollywood has offered since '39 went into the past. It is a memorable film, in title and in quality, blessed with an honest script, good direction and sound performance. Perhaps this is a bit too early in the season to be talking of the best pictures of 1940; it is not too early to say that Paramount's nomination is worth considering." *New York Times,* 1/18/40.

"Mitchell Leisen's brisk directing keeps the disjointed story rolling, makes a rather enjoyable, sometimes moving film out of what is essentially an implausible, episodic, mushy tale replete with stock characters and situations." *Time,* 1/29/40.

Little Old New York (1940, Twentieth Century-Fox) *D:* Henry King.
Cast: Alice Faye, Fred MacMurray, Richard Greene, Brenda Joyce, Andy Devine, Henry Stephenson, Fritz Feld, Ward Bond, Clarence Hummel. 100 mins. B&W.
Plot: Fictionalized biography of Robert Fulton (Greene) and his steamboat. Fred plays the builder of

Ad for **Little Old New York,** *1940.*

the boat and both vie for the love of Faye.

Trivia: Marion Davies had starred in an earlier 1923 version of this film with the same title. The head of Twentieth Century-Fox, Darryl Zanuck, initially wanted his contract player, Henry Fonda, to play the role Fred ended up playing.

Reviews: "... difficult to reconcile this edition of *Little Old New York* with the fact that *Grapes of Wrath*, a masterpiece ... came from the same studio at about the same time." *Variety*, 2/7/40.

Too Many Husbands (1940, Columbia) *D:* Wesley Ruggles.
Cast: Jean Arthur, Fred MacMurray, Melvyn Douglas, Harry Davenport, Dorothy Peterson, Melville Cooper, Edgar Buchanan. 84 mins. B&W.
Plot: Fred has been lost at sea for seven years. Declared legally dead, he comes back to discover that his wife has remarried.
Trivia: Director Wesley Ruggles filmed two endings to this film, one where Jean Arthur takes Melvyn Douglas and the other where she takes Fred MacMurray. The MacMurray ending was the top choice of preview audiences. This film was based on a Somerset Maugham stage play *Home and Beauty*, although its basic premise is similar to the same year's *My Favorite Wife*.
Reviews: "It takes direction like Wesley Ruggles and a good cast to make a gay movie like *Too Many Husbands* out of a thin, modern Enoch Arden story. The author's witty lines and music, used sparingly, but well, help the humor along." *Commonweal*, 3/22/40.
"Light, fluffy and amusing." *Variety*, 3/6/40.
"Brilliant and sophisticated comedy which vacillates between farce and screwball variety, with a dash of slapstick for garnishment, but well qualified to keep all audiences uproariously entertained for its entire length." *Boxoffice*.
"This sort of fluff is perfectly suited to the talents of the players, all of whom — especially Melvyn Douglas, have themselves a high old time. There is little reason why audiences should not emulate them." *Time*, 3/25/40.

Rangers of Fortune (1940, Paramount) *D:* Sam Wood.
Cast: Fred MacMurray, Albert Dekker, Gilbert Roland, Patricia Morison, Joseph Schildkraut, Dick Foran, Betty Brewer, Arthur Allen, Brandon Tynan, Minor Watson. 80 mins. B&W.
Plot: A trio fleeing Mexican bandits stops off in a bordertown and offers their assistance in cleansing it of bandits and other assorted villains.
Trivia: Parts of this film were filmed in the Mojave Desert and Victorville, California.
Reviews: "Lusty and adventurous western." *Variety*, 3/11/40.
"Seasoned director Sam Wood turns tail on his recent fragile work (*Goodbye,*

Rangers of Fortune, *1940*.

Mr. Chips, Our Town) to make of *Rangers of Fortune* the most thrilling and funny movie brawl of the current western craze." *Time,* 9/30/40.

Virginia (1941, Paramount) *D:* Edward H. Griffith.
Cast: Madeleine Carroll, Fred MacMurray, Sterling Hayden, Helen Broderick, Carolyn Lee, Marie Wilson, Paul Hurst, Tom Rutherford, Louise Beavers. 110 mins. Color.
Plot: Carroll, born and bred in Virginia, but having lived in the North for many years, returns home where she must choose between her Yankee beau (Hayden) and her courtly southern aristocratic neighbor (Fred).
Trivia: Carroll and Sterling Hayden met and fell in love on this film and married in 1942.
Fred told reporters that, like his friend Clark Gable in *Gone with the Wind,* he would not even attempt a southern

Ad for **Virginia,** *1941.*

accent: "I'm not going to try to talk like a southerner. I think if you don't have the real accent, it's best not to pretend you have and make a mess of things. So many of them do."

Reviews: "In spite of its story's inconsistencies and tricky ending *Virginia* makes good entertainment." *Commonweal,* 2/7/41.

"Well mounted but tedious film." Leonard Maltin, *Movie and Video Guide.*

"Fred MacMurray, as the noble Virginian, is substantial but somewhat smug." *New York Times,* 1/29/41.

One Night in Lisbon (1941, Paramount) *D:* Edward H. Griffith.

Cast: Fred MacMurray, Madeleine Carroll, Patricia Morison, Billie Burke, John Loder, Dame May Whitty, Edmund Gwenn, Reginald Denny, Billy Gilbert. 97 mins. B&W.

Plot: English Carroll and American flyer Fred meet in the Lisbon and fall in love despite the interference of his ex (Morison).

Trivia: Billie Burke's best-known role was that of the "Good Witch of the West" in *The Wizard of Oz.*

Reviews: "*One Night in Lisbon* over does its boy meets girl theme, exaggerates its characters until they become types, substitutes risqué lines and situations for plot until it loses its modern significance and becomes any cliché-ridden comedy." *Commonweal,* 6/20/41.

"An effervescing romantic comedy ... MacMurray surprises with the excellence of his performance in a light role as the continually aggressive suitor." *Variety,* 5/14/41.

New York Town (1941, Paramount) *D:* Charles Vidor.

Cast: Fred MacMurray, Mary Martin, Robert Preston, Lynne Overman, Eric Blore, Fuzzy Knight, Cecil Kellaway, Edward McNamara. 75 mins. B&W.

Plot: Martin plays a Vermont girl who must choose between a photographer (Fred) and a rich playboy (Preston).

Trivia: Mitchell Leisen was originally assigned to direct this film, but when he was reassigned to direct *I Wanted Wings,* Charles Vidor was assigned as his replacement.

Reviews: "There's little to anybody's credit in this film." *Variety,* 7/30/41.

"Routine boy-meets-girl comedy." *New York Times,* 11/13/41.

Dive Bomber (1941, Warner Brothers) *D:* Michael Curtiz.

Cast: Errol Flynn, Fred MacMurray, Ralph Bellamy, Alexis Smith, Regis Toomey, Robert Armstrong, Allen Jenkins, Craig Stevens, Herbert Anderson, Moroni Olsen. 133 mins. Color.

Plot: Flynn and Bellamy play doctors trying to find a cure to high altitude pilot blackout, with Fred as a stern Navy flier who's at first skeptical of their work but then becomes a willing guinea pig.

Trivia: Future stars Gig Young, Alan Hale, Jr. (The Skipper on *Gilligan's Island*) and William Hopper (the son of gossip columnist Hedda and later detective Paul Drake on the long-running *Perry Mason)* all have small roles as pilots.

Reviews: "If you want to see some first rate Technicolor and outstanding shots of flying *Dive Bomber* is your picture." *Commonweal*, 9/12/41.

"MacMurray, as the flight commander, considerably overshadows Flynn in the acting line." *Variety*, 8/13/41.

"For its oddly dramatic subject and its most extraordinarily colorful contents, *Dive Bomber* takes the palm as the best of the new service films to date." *New York Times*, 8/31/41.

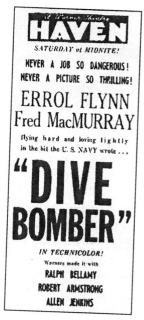

Ad for **Dive Bomber**, *1941.*

The Lady is Willing (1942, Columbia) *D:* Mitchell Leisen.

Cast: Marlene Dietrich, Fred MacMurray, Aline MacMahon, Stanley Ridges, Arline Judge, Roger Clark, Sterling Holloway, Harvey Stephens. 92 mins. B&W.

Plot: Marlene plays a stage star who finds a baby she wants to adopt but can't unless she is wed, so she asks pediatrician Fred to marry her so she can give the baby a home.

Trivia: A radio version of this film was presented on *Lux Radio Theatre* with Kay Francis in the Dietrich part.

Reviews: "Racy and sophisticated marital comedy ... strong performances by both principles under fine direction of Mitchell Leisen." *Variety*, 1/28/42.

"The lady is too willing and not sufficiently sincere." *New York Times*, 4/24/42.

Take a Letter, Darling (1942, Paramount) *D:* Mitchell Leisen.

Cast: Rosalind Russell, Fred MacMurray, Macdonald Carey, Constance Moore, Robert Benchley, Cecil Kellaway, Kathleen Howard, Margaret Seddon, Dooley Wilson. 93 mins. B&W.

Plot: In this battle of the sexes comedy Russell is a tough female executive who hires Fred on as her secretary.

Trivia: In addition to Claudette Colbert, Katharine Hepburn was initially considered for the role which went to Rosalind Russell.

Ad for Take a Letter, Darling, *1942.*

Reviews: "*Take a Letter, Darling* is one of those unimportant but witty movies full of gay situations and wisecracks … Miss Russell and Mr. MacMurray play their roles for all that's in 'em without overdoing." *Commonweal,* 7/3/42.
"Glistening dialog and … laughable bits of business." *Variety,* 5/6/42.
"One of those rare sophisticated romantic comedies that entertains without talking its head off." *Hollywood Motion Picture Review,* 5/9/42.

The Forest Rangers (1942, Paramount) *D:* George Marshall. *Cast:* Fred MacMurray, Paulette Goddard, Susan Hayward, Lynne Overman, Albert Dekker, Eugene Pallette, Regis Toomey, Rod Cameron, Clem Bevans, James Brown. 87 mins. Color.
Plot: Fred plays a forest ranger with a wife who loves the city (Goddard) and an ex-girlfriend (Hayward) who wants him back. Naturally, there is a climactic forest fire which traps them all.
Trivia: Madeleine Carroll was originally cast in the Goddard part, but

Ad for The Forest Rangers, *1942.*

withdrew from the film.

Reviews: "You will see some very beautiful tall trees and scenic spots, but you will also get large doses of Hollywoodian forest fires and an unbelievably fishy story … You're not sure whether you're laughing with or at it." *Commonweal,* 10/9/42.

"The human drama is less searing … in a spectacle of this sort one doesn't quibble about silly characters; one asks 'Where's the fire?'" *New York Times,* 10/22/42.

Star Spangled Rhythm (1942, Paramount) *D:* George Marshall. *Cast:* Betty Hutton, Eddie Bracken, Victor Moore, Anne Revere, Walter Abel, Cass Daley, Macdonald Carey, Gil Lamb. Guest Stars: Bob Hope, Fred MacMurray, Franchot Tone, Ray Milland, Lynne Overman, Paulette Goddard, Veronica Lake, Dorothy Lamour, Alan Ladd, Dick Powell, Mary Martin. 99 mins. B&W.

Plot: Nearly every contract actor on the Paramount lot participates in this patriotic talent show. Fred, Ray Milland, Franchot Tone and Lynne Overman participate in a sketch showing what it would be like if men played cards like women.

Trivia: This film received an Academy Award nomination for best song for "That Old Black Magic," which was introduced by Johnnie Johnston in the movie.

Reviews: "Only trouble exhibits will have in selling *Star Spangled Rhythm* will be finding a marquee big enough to hold all the names." *Variety,* 12/30/42.

Flight for Freedom (1943, RKO) *D:* Lothar Mendes. *Cast:* Rosalind Russell, Fred MacMurray, Herbert Marshall, Eduardo Ciannelli, Walter Kingsford, Damian O'Flynn, Jack Carr, Matt McHugh, Hugh Beaumont. 101 mins. B&W.

Plot: Russell plays an Amelia Earhart-type female aviator, with Fred cast as her navigator. He loves her and she thinks she loves Herbert

Ad for **Flight For Freedom,** *1943.*

Marshall. Russell and Fred are then recruited by the US Navy for a spy mission over the Pacific.

Trivia: The proceeds from the premier of this film went to various war charities.

Reviews: "Rosalind Russell plays the lady with an excess of stars in her eyes and Fred MacMurray plays the gentleman with almost painful noncha-lance." *New York Times,* 4/16/43.

Ad for Above Suspicion, *1943.*

Above Suspicion (1943, MGM) *D:* Richard Thorpe.

Cast: Joan Crawford, Fred MacMurray, Conrad Veidt, Basil Rathbone, Reginald Owens, Richard Ainley, Ann Shoemaker, Sara Haden, Felix Bressart. 93 mins. B&W.

Plot: Fred and Crawford play newlyweds who become English spies when they make their way through pre-war Germany on their honeymoon.

Trivia: The final film of Crawford's 18-year contract with MGM. She felt that MGM was no longer tailoring good roles for her and soon signed with Warner Brothers, where she would become the chief rival of Bette Davis thanks to the success of *Mildred Pierce,* a film Davis turned down.

Reviews: "Above Suspicion has been made into a curiously uneven movie. Some of it is thrilling, and the suspense is swell … but the whole is unsat-isfying, because the theme is as dated as the plot … Fred plays the whole thing in an off-hand manner that is almost too carefree." *Commonweal,* 9/10/43.

"Above Suspicion is something new in Joan Crawford pictures. Instead of

setting a special table for her saucer-eyed talents, it all but relegates Miss Crawford to playing stooge to pouty Fred MacMurray. Still worse, Joan's endless array of hats is reduced to a bare subsistence level." *Time,* 8/23/43.

No Time for Love (1943, Paramount) *D:* Mitchell Leisen.
Cast: Claudette Colbert, Fred MacMurray, Ilka Chase, June Havoc, Richard Haydn, Paul McGrath, Marjorie Gateson, Bill Goodwin. 83 mins. B&W.
Plot: Claudette is a fashion photographer and Fred is the muscle-bound foreman of a crew digging a tunnel under the Hudson River. They are opposites who attract.
Trivia: Fred, said to have been the model for "Captain Marvel," dons a cape and plays a Superman-like character in a dream sequence within this film.
Reviews: "Since war times seem to call for escapist pictures, a brittle adult comedy like *No Time for Love* might be just the answer … the film aims to be a humorous study in pink icing and mud, and as such it succeeds beautifully." *Commonweal,* 12/17/43.
"Claudette Colbert and Fred MacMurray are the clashing girl and boy in the case, and it is largely through their crisp playing that the chemical elements finally jell." *New York Times,* 12/2/43.
"The principals … paste each other pleasantly with verbal custard pies. But the freewheeling foolishness leaves little time or energy for acting." *Time,* 1/3/44.

Fred and Claudette Colbert in **No Time for Love,** *1943.*

Standing Room Only (1944, Paramount) *D:* Sidney Lanfield.
Cast: Paulette Goddard, Fred MacMurray, Edward Arnold, Roland Young, Hillary Brooke, Porter Hall, Clarence Kolb, Anne Revere, Marie McDonald. 83 mins. B&W.
Plot: Fred is a businessman with Paulette as his secretary in this comedy about the wartime housing shortage in Washington. They can't find rooms to stay on so they become servants for a wealthy couple (Young, Revere) in exchange for lodging.
Trivia: Rosalind Russell had originally been announced as Fred's leading lady but eventually Goddard got the role.
Reviews: "This is a picture for all the family. All problems are dealt with in the light vein used by most predecessors based on similar themes ... the film is escapist entertainment with many amusing sequences." *Variety,* 1/5/44.

And the Angels Sing (1944, Paramount) *D:* Claude Binyon.
Cast: Fred MacMurray, Dorothy Lamour, Betty Hutton, Diana Lynn, Mimi Chandler, Raymond Walburn, Eddie Foy, Jr., Frank Albertson. 96 mins. B&W.
Plot: When bandleader Fred fleeces the "Angel Sisters" of $190 so to bring his band to New York, the sisters pursue him. Eventually, sisters Lamour and Hutton both fall in love with the louse, who ultimately is redeemed.
Trivia: This film is a partial remake of Fred's 1938 film *Sing, You Sinners,* which had been written by this film's director, Claude Binyon.
Reviews: "Ace romantic comedy packed with laughs and the power to pull and please fans everywhere." *Film Daily*
"The best to be said ... is that it tickles a few witless laughs." *New York Times,* 7/13/44.

Double Indemnity (1944, Paramount) *D:* Billy Wilder.
Cast: Fred MacMurray, Barbara Stanwyck, Edward G. Robinson, Porter Hall, Jean Heather, Tom Powers, Byron Barr, Richard Gaines. 107 mins. B&W.
Plot: Glib insurance salesman Walter Neff's life is forever changed when he arrives at the home of Mr. Dietrichson to renew a policy and finds that Dietrichson isn't home but his sultry and dangerous wife is — and it's lust at first sight. She knows a sucker when she sees one and seduces him into a plan to murder her husband.
Trivia: *The Hollywood Reporter* reported that Susan Hayward was initially cast as Stanwyck's stepdaughter "Lola."
Reviews: "While one might question the point of telling such an unsavory story, *Double Indemnity* justifies itself in the high quality of its cinema technique, the sincere acting, its objective tone and crime doesn't pay conclusion." *Commonweal,* 5/26/44.

"Double Indemnity is the season's nattiest, nastiest, most satisfying melodrama." *Time,* 7/10/44.

"MacMurray has seldom given a better performance. It is somewhat different from his usually light roles, but is always plausible and played with considerable restraint." *Variety.*

"Miss Stanwyck gives a good surface performance of a destructively lurid female, but Mr. MacMurray is a bit too ingenuous as the gent who falls precipitately under her spell. And the ease of his fall is also questionable. One look at the lady's ankles and he's cooked." *New York Times,* 9/7/44.

Practically Yours (1944, Paramount) *D:* Mitchell Leisen.
Cast: Claudette Colbert, Fred MacMurray, Gil Lamb, Cecil Kellaway, Robert Benchley, Tom Powers, Jane Frazee, Rosemary DeCamp, Isabel Randolph. 90 mins. B&W.
Plot: Fred plays a World War II pilot who thinks he is on a suicide mission. In a radio communication to his buddies, which is picked up by the nation's

Fred in a coffee ad which also advertises **Practically Yours,** *1944.*

media, he says goodbye to "piggy" his dog, but it is reported to be "Peggy," a girl he worked with as a civilian. He survives the mission and comes home a hero, with Peggy believing that his "last communication" was about her.
Trivia: This was Colbert's final film of her Paramount contract. In 1945 she would appear in an adaptation of this film on the *Lux Radio Theatre* with Ray Milland in Fred's role.
Reviews: "Fred MacMurray and Claudette Colbert play the chance-mated couple in this piece, which follows the pattern for comedies of mistaken identity. And they play them with all the hectic humor of actors experienced in light comedy." *New York Times,* 3/29/45
"Though it recalls the brilliant *Hail the Conquering Hero,* the picture is in many respects just the sort of smoothly routine, over-contrived comedy that Colbert and MacMurray team so crisply in. Yet its artificial flowers turn out also to be a nest for some surprisingly virulent vipers; and much of their venom is good for what's wrong with the American soul." *Time,* 4/9/45.
"Pic is a deft combination of chuckles and heart-throbs, plus a sock patriotic theme that can't miss." *Variety,* 12/20/44.

Murder, He Says (1945, Paramount) *D:* George Marshall.
Cast: Fred MacMurray, Helen Walker, Marjorie Main, Jean Heather, Porter Hall, Peter Whitney, Mabel Paige, Barbara Pepper. 91 mins. B&W.
Plot: Wacky comedy about a pollster who has a run-in with a hillbilly family reminds one of Frank Capra's *Arsenic and Old Lace,* except that it is funnier. Fred's characterization in this film set the stage for his Disney comedies of the '60s.
Trivia: The working title of this film was "Murder Farm."
Reviews: "Murder and good gags combine to provide an amusing light two hours in the theatre." *Motion Picture.*
"For this offering ... mixes mayhem and clowning with the happy abandon of a drunk suffering from dementia praecox. As a result, this caricature of a hillbilly family, who combine the seamier attributes of the Jukes and the Jeeter Lesters, dilutes the effects of numerous laughs with an always incredible plot." *New York Times,* 6/25/45
"Though it is easily the season's craziest show, and probably the funniest, *Murder, He Says* lacks much of the ticklish wit and lightness of *Arsenic and Old Lace;* it lays most of its laughs on with a shovel. But by and large it is a rare old romp, played in specially fine style by ... MacMurray, Hall and Whitney and the incredibly ferocious Marjorie Main." *Time,* 6/18/45.

Where Do We Go From Here?
(1945, Twentieth Century-Fox) *D:*
Gregory Ratoff.
Cast: Fred MacMurray, Joan Leslie,
June Haver, Anthony Quinn, Gene
Sheldon, Carlos Ramirez, Alan
Mowbray, Fortunio Bonanova, Herman
Bing, Otto Preminger. 77 mins.
Color.
Plot: Fred plays a 4-F salvage yard
security agent who finds a lamp which
contains a genie who grants him three
wishes.
Trivia: Fred co-stars with June Haver,
then a Twentieth Century-Fox con-
tract player, but within the decade
following the death of Fred's first
wife would become the second Mrs.
MacMurray.
Reviews: "Mr. MacMurray sort of
sing-talks his way through the picture.

Ad for **Where Do We Go
From Here?**, *1945.*

At times he is quite good, really capturing the wondrous spirit of the character, but at other times he looks very much ill at ease." *New York Times.*
"Doesn't quite ring the bell all the way." *Variety,* 5/23/45.

Captain Eddie (1945, Twentieth Century-Fox) *D:* Lloyd Bacon.
Cast: Fred MacMurray, Lynn Bari, Charles Bickford, Thomas Mitchell,
Lloyd Nolan, James Gleason, Mary Philips, Darryl Hickman, Spring
Byington, Richard Conte. 107 mins. B&W.
Plot: Bio-pic of famed pilot Captain Eddie Rickenbacker is told in flash-
back by Rickenbacker while floating the Pacific after his plane is downed.
Trivia: David O. Selznick had at one point expressed interest in filming
Rickenbacker's story, but like many of the projects he attempted post-*Gone
with the Wind,* it fell through.
Reviews: "Fred MacMurray without his usual flippant mannerisms portrays
the persistent and strong-willed hero ... more of an assembly line than a
flesh and blood man." *Commonweal,* 8/17/45.
"If you want straight romantic entertainment, with familiar family comedy
and sentiment, you will get it in this picture. All the stock ingredients are
here. And the performers do very nicely - in everything but those scenes on
the rafts." *New York Times,* 8/9/45.

Pardon My Past (1946, Columbia) *D:* Leslie Fenton.
Cast: Fred MacMurray, Marguerite Chapman, Akim Tamiroff, William Demarest, Rita Johnson, Harry Davenport, Douglass Dumbrille. 87 mins. B&W.
Plot: Fred plays dual role as a no-good playboy and a decent man (not unlike the real MacMurray) who is often mistaken for the playboy.
Trivia: Director Leslie Fenton, a former actor himself, played the role of the captain of the torpedo boat. In the film, Fred and Demarest are on their way to Beaver Dam, Wisconsin, Fred's real-life hometown. This is also the only film that Fred ever produced.
Reviews: "The ingredients were of a sufficient quality but - for us, anyhow - they didn't jell." *New York Times,* 1/28/46.
"MacMurray's dual role is deftly handled ... actor contributes an ace performance in his best style." *Variety,* 9/12/45.

Smoky (1946, Twentieth Century-Fox) *D:* Louis King.
Cast: Fred MacMurray, Anne Baxter, Burl Ives, Bruce Cabot, Esther Dale, Roy Roberts, J. Farrell MacDonald, Max Wagner, Guy Beach. 87 mins. Color.
Plot: Will James' popular novel of a rancher who tames and befriends a wild stallion.
Trivia: This was Burl Ives' first film. A popular folk singer, Ives went on to act in several films and won an Academy Award for his performance in *The Big Country* (1958). He is best known for playing "Big Daddy" in the 1958 film *Cat on the Hot Tin Roof.*
Reviews: "Based on Will James'

Fred in a publicity photo from **Smoky***, 1946.*

popular story about a horse, really concentrates on its hero and succeeds in keeping the eccentricities of people in second place. Fred MacMurray as Smoky's special friend, Anne Baxter as the ranch owner with a yen for Fred and Bruce Cabot as Fred's mean brother with no heart of gold are good actors and not afraid to let a horse star." *Commonweal,* 7/26/46.
"*Smoky* is the story of a long, beautiful, rather intense friendship between Fred MacMurray and a horse. An expert Technicolor treatment of Will

James's famed, 20-year-old novel, the picture is a big-budget Western designed to delight small boys of all ages." *Time*, 7/8/46.

Suddenly, It's Spring (1947, Paramount) *D:* Mitchell Leisen.
Cast: Paulette Goddard, Fred MacMurray, Macdonald Carey, Arleen Whelan, Lillian Fontaine, Frank Faylen, Frances Robinson, Georgia Backus, Victoria Horne. 87 mins. B&W.
Plot: Goddard and Fred play a married couple who after being separated during the war contemplate divorce.
Trivia: Claudette Colbert was originally cast as Fred's leading lady but had to back out at the last minute.
Reviews: "Suddenly It's Spring is one of those plump, shiny comedies that director Mitchell Leisen can pack — and Paramount can crank out — like so many frankfurters." *Time*, 3/17/47.
"Here is one of those extraordinary pictures that turns out just as funny as its makers hoped it would. Paramount hasn't had as gay and riotous a farce to release in many moons ... MacMurray ... plays his farcical dodges for their full worth." *The Hollywood Reporter*, 2/10/47.

The Egg and I (1947, Universal) *D:* Chester Erskine.
Cast: Claudette Colbert, Fred MacMurray, Marjorie Main, Louise Allbritton, Percy Kilbride, Richard Long, Billy House, Ida Moore, Donald MacBride. 108 mins. B&W.
Plot: Adaptation of best-selling novel about a city couple who buys a chicken farm, predating *Green Acres*. Introduces Marjorie Main and Percy Kilbride, as "Ma and Pa Kettle," who steal the picture from leads Colbert and MacMurray.
Trivia: Marjorie Main, under contract to MGM, was borrowed by Universal and attained her greatest success playing Ma Kettle. She was nominated for a Best Supporting Actress Oscar for her performance in this film.
Reviews: "The Egg and I, an adaptation of Betty MacDonald's cackle-happy best seller about a city couple who learn to run a poultry farm, will probably be as popular as the book. Fred MacMurray and Claudette Colbert, who pretend to be the distraught pioneers, are sure-fire box office comedians." *Time*, 4/28/47.
"In this reviewer's opinion, a good opportunity was here lost to do a delightful satire upon the movement back to the farm - or, at least, a witty dissertation upon the dirt-road bucolic life. But to judge by the girlish squeals and giggles which were heard in the audience yesterday, there are some who will find the picture adequate." *New York Times*, 4/25/47.

Singapore (1947, Universal) *D:* John Brahm.
Cast: Fred MacMurray, Ava Gardner, Roland Culver, Richard Haydn, Thomas Gomez, Spring Byington, Porter Hall, George Lloyd, Maylia. 79 mins. B&W.
Plot: Fred returns to Singapore, where, prior to the war, he had hid a fortune in jewels, and runs into his ex-wife who doesn't remember him.
Trivia: This film was remade by Universal as *Istanbul,* which starred Errol Flynn, in 1957.
Reviews: "*Singapore* is a pretty poor excuse for an entertainment, even as minor league jewel smuggling fare." *New York Times,* 9/17/47.
"MacMurray walks through his paces in standard okay form. Miss Gardner, miscast as sweet, young item, has no chance to display her sultry charms." *Variety,* 8/6/47.

On Our Merry Way (1948, United Artists) *D:* King Vidor, Leslie Fenton, George Stevens
Cast: Paulette Goddard, James Stewart, Henry Fonda, Fred MacMurray, Burgess Meredith, William Demarest, Hugh Herbert, Eduardo Ciannelli. 107 mins. B&W.
Plot: In this episodic film, Fred and William Demarest play gangsters who regret a run-in with a child.
Trivia: The Fonda-Stewart episode was originally going to be directed by John Huston, who backed out unexpectedly, and producer Burgess Meredith brought in George Stevens.
Reviews: "A million dollar cast in a ten-cent film." *New York Daily News,* 2/3/48.
"Least interesting is the episode involving Fred MacMurray and William Demarest in their encounter with a brat during their itinerant travels as con-men." *Variety,* 2/4/48.

The Miracle of the Bells (1948, RKO) *D:* Irving Pichel.
Cast: Fred MacMurray, Valli, Frank Sinatra, Lee J. Cobb, Harold Vermilyea, Charles Meredith, Jim Nolan, Veronica Pataky, Philip Ahn. 120 mins. B&W.
Plot: Fred plays a press agent who visits a Pennsylvania mining community where an actress friend (Valli) had been born and is now to be laid to rest. He arranges with the local priest (Frank Sinatra) to ring the church bells for four days, which produces an unexpected miracle.
Trivia: John Cromwell, one of David O. Selznick's favored directors (*The Prisoner of Zenda, Since You Went Away*), was originally announced as the director of this film, but was replaced by Pichel. Producer Jesse Lasky asked the advice of various members of the Catholic Church before casting Frank Sinatra as a priest in this film due to unsavory gossip regarding Sinatra and

his mob ties at the time.

Reviews: "A weak story, first, and heavy scoring in the direction of Irving Pichel have not made the jobs of the actors either simple or promising. Fred MacMurray has the air of an embalmer in even the least fatalistic scenes as he gives a representation of the press agent with a load of woe. And Alida Valli is evidently burdened with the notion that she is playing Camille … Frank Sinatra acts with formal piety and gives of himself with obvious caution in the singing of one grave folk-song." *New York Times,* 3/17/48.

"*Miracle of the Bells* comes to the screen as a tremendously moving drama told with compelling simplicity and great heart …" *Variety,* 3/3/48.

Don't Trust Your Husband (1948, United Artists) *D:* Lloyd Bacon.
Cast: Fred MacMurray, Madeleine Carroll, Charles "Buddy" Rogers, Rita Johnson, Louise Allbritton, Alan Mowbray, Mike Romanoff. 90 mins. B&W.
Plot: Fred and Madeleine are a married couple, with she suspecting him of having an affair. Fifth and final screen teaming of Carroll and MacMurray.
Trivia: This was Carroll's first American film since 1942. This film is also known as "An Innocent Affair."
Reviews: "Since all the performers are agreeable and competent it seems reasonable to conclude that the director and the authors are responsible for the routine quality of the presentation." *New York Times,* 9/29/48.

Family Honeymoon (1949, Universal) *D:* Claude Binyon.
Cast: Claudette Colbert, Fred MacMurray, Rita Johnson, Gigi Perreau, Jimmy Hunt, Peter Miles, Lillian Bronson, Hattie McDaniel, Chill Wills. 80 mins. B&W.
Plot: Fred teams with Colbert in a comedy about a professor and a widow who marry and end up taking their honeymoon with her three children.
Trivia: The last of seven films to team Colbert and MacMurray, though they would work together two more times after this on the radio show *Lux Radio Theatre,* performing adaptations of *Family Honeymoon.*

Ad for Family Honeymoon, 1948.

Reviews: "It is true that the joke grows weary and a little forced towards the end of the film. But it gets off to such a fast and smooth start that some coasting can easily be allowed." *New York Times,* 2/25/49.

"... one of those pleasant family comedies, as the title indicates, which represents no extraordinary talent expenditure, save for the co-stars, resolves no major issues, but emerges as a wholesome hour-and-a-half film divertissement." *Variety,* 12/8/48.

Father Was a Fullback (1949, Twentieth Century-Fox) *D:* John M. Stahl.
Cast: Fred MacMurray, Maureen O'Hara, Betty Lynn, Rudy Vallee, Thelma Ritter, Natalie Wood, Richard Tyler, Buddy Martin. 84 mins. B&W.
Plot: Fred is a college football coach who finds troubles on the field and at home with his daughters (Lynn and Wood) and his acerbic maid (who else but Thelma Ritter). O'Hara plays Fred's understanding wife.
Trivia: The original director, Elliott Nugent, withdrew after three days of filming due to a then undiagnosed bout of depression. O'Hara and Wood were so effective as mother and daughter in *Miracle on 34th Street* that they were reunited as such on this film.
Reviews: "*Father Was a Fullback* may be short on football but it is satisfyingly long on laughs." *New York Times,* 10/13/49.
"MacMurray and Miss O'Hara team delightfully, responding expertly to Stahl's understanding direction." *Variety,* 8/7/49.

Borderline (1950, Universal) *D:* William A. Seiter.
Cast: Fred MacMurray, Claire Trevor, Raymond Burr, Roy Roberts, Jose Torvay, Morris Ankrum, Charles Lane, Don Diamond, Pepe Hern, Richard Irving. 88 mins. B&W.
Plot: Uneasy mixture of *film noir* and comedy with Trevor as a Los Angeles police woman who goes undercover to Mexico to bust drug lord (Burr). Fred plays a federal narcotics agent unaware that Trevor is a policewoman and thinks that she is Burr's moll.
Trivia: This film was produced by Borderline Pictures, Inc., which was formed by producer Milton Bren (the husband of Claire Trevor), William Seiter and Fred. Bren, Seiter, Fred and Trevor all deferred their salaries to produce this film.
Reviews: "Spotty entertainment values in this picture stem from its indecisive treatment as either a straight comedy or a serious meller ... performances are handicapped by the uneven scripting but Miss Trevor and MacMurray team nicely in the light romantic repartee." *Variety,* 1/11/50.
"No matter what one calls *Borderline,* it cannot be termed a misnomer. For the newcomer, who began a stand at the Criterion on Saturday, skips back and forth across the borderline between melodrama and comedy with a curious indecision. As a result, this yarn about dope smugglers is neither

exciting cops-and-robbers fare nor a rib-tickling travesty of same." *New York Times*, 3/6/50.

Never a Dull Moment (1950, RKO) *D:* George Marshall.
Cast: Irene Dunne, Fred MacMurray, William Demarest, Andy Devine, Gigi Perreau, Natalie Wood, Philip Ober, Jack Kirkwood, Ann Doran, Margaret Gibson, Lela Bliss, Irving Bacon. 89 mins. B&W.
Plot: A worldly city woman marries Wyoming rancher and has to learn to adjust to new surroundings.
Trivia: In 1945 Myrna Loy was announced as the leading lady in an adaptation of this film. When she dropped out, the project was put on hold until 1949 when RKO was working on a deal to loan out Ann Sothern from MGM. MGM decided not to loan Sothern out, and the part went to Irene Dunne.
Reviews: "This amiable light-hearted comedy does not always live up to its title." *Library Journal*, 12/1/50.
"Presentation of Irene Dunne in a series of rustic encounters that are about as funny as stepping on a nail." *New York Times*, 11/22/50.
"*Never a Dull Moment* tries to hatch another *Egg and I*, merely lays an egg." *Time*, 12/4/50.

A Millionaire for Christy (1951, Twentieth Century-Fox) *D:* George Marshall.
Cast: Fred MacMurray, Eleanor Parker, Richard Carlson, Kay Buckley, Una Merkel, Douglass Dumbrille, Raymond Greenleaf, Nestor Paiva, Chris-Pin Martin, Julian Rivero, Everett Glass. 91 mins. B&W.
Plot: Parker, in a rare comedic role, plays a legal secretary who falls in love with a millionaire.
Trivia: This is the fifth and final film that Fred made with director George Marshall.
Reviews: "Miss Parker and MacMurray are an excellent team and pull all stops in selling their goofy characters ... Picture reaches its hilarity high mark about midway, and that pace continues to the end under the broad directorial handling of George Marshall." *Variety*, 8/1/51.
"Moviegoers are likely to get a fair share of laughs." New York Times, 10/5/51.

Callaway Went Thataway (1951, MGM) *D:* Norman Panama and Melvin Frank.
Cast: Fred MacMurray, Dorothy McGuire, Howard Keel, Jesse White, Fay Roope, Natalie Schafer, Douglas Kennedy, Elisabeth Fraser, Johnny Indrisano, Stan Freberg, Don Haggerty. Guest Stars: Clark Gable, Elizabeth Taylor, Esther Williams. 81 mins. B&W.

Plot: Satire on early television about an old-time cowboy actor whose films find a new audience thanks to their showings on television. When his new fans want to see him in person, he is nowhere to be found. Enter Fred and McGuire as partners in an advertising firm who find a lookalike for the elusive Callaway (Keel).

Trivia: Calloway may have been loosely based on "Hopalong Cassidy," which was enjoying renewed popularity in the early '50s when Hoppy's old films were shown on television.

Reviews: "The satire doesn't bite; being all in fun ... Nonsense is ably paced by the star trio of Fred MacMurray, Dorothy McGuire, and Howard Keel." *Variety,* 11/14/51.

"It might be wished, too, that Fred MacMurray and Dorothy McGuire didn't so mouth their words that some of their conversation can barely be understood, for their acting as the advertising agents is amusingly arch and harassed, and it is plain that some clever dialogue has been written by Panama and Frank." *New York Times,* 12/6/51.

"*Callaway Went Thataway* holds out great promise from its very first scene, which is a parody on the climaxes in ancient horse operas. But the dashing spirit of the film soon eludes those who are pursuing it, disappearing from sight over thataway and leaving Panama and Frank milling around in circles thisaway with a tired posse of forced attitudes and conventional dilemmas." *New York Herald Tribune,* 12/6/51.

Fair Wind to Java (1953, Republic) *D:* Joseph Kane.
Cast: Fred MacMurray, Vera Ralston, Robert Douglas, Victor McLaglen, John Russell, Buddy Baer, Claude Jarman, Jr., Grant Withers, Howard Petrie, Paul Fix, Keye Luke. 92 mins. Color.
Plot: Fred plays a sea captain in Java who has to contend with volcanoes, pirates and Vera Ralston, playing a sarong girl named Kim-Kim.
Trivia: Vera Ralston was the top leading lady at Republic in no small part to the fact that she was married to Herbert J. Yates, the president of Republic Pictures.
Reviews: "General market will find this Republic adventure feature equipped with all the necessary ingredients to enjoy an ok box office response." *Variety,* 4/29/53.
"Even the most ardent champions of the comic book spirit should find *Fair Wind to Java*, which blew into the Holiday yesterday, heavy weather indeed." *New York Times,* 8/28/53.

The Moonlighter (1953, Warner Brothers) *D:* Roy Rowland.
Cast: Barbara Stanwyck, Fred MacMurray, Ward Bond, William Ching, John Dierkes, Morris Ankrum, Jack Elam, Charles Halton. 77 mins. B&W.
Plot: A "Moonlighter" is a cattle rustler and Fred plays one who returns to

his hometown where he meets up with an old flame (Stanwyck) and finds redemption.

Trivia: In October 1952 the *Los Angeles Times* announced that Jennifer Jones and director King Vidor were going to make *The Moonlighter* as a follow up to the film *Ruby Gentry* which they had just completed.

Reviews: "The stars do their work well." *Variety,* 9/9/53.

"Exactly why the protagonists of 'Double Indemnity' should have elected to participate in such cowtown petty larceny is a mystery." *The New York Times.*

Ad for The Caine Mutiny, 1954.

The Caine Mutiny (1954, Columbia) *D:* Edward Dmytryk.

Cast: Humphrey Bogart, Jose Ferrer, Van Johnson, Fred MacMurray, Robert Francis, May Wynn, Tom Tully, E.G. Marshall, Arthur Franz, Lee Marvin, Claude Akins, Jerry Paris, Steve Brodie, Whit Bissell, James Best. 125 mins. Color.

Plot: Film based on Herman Wouk's novel about the mutiny committed aboard a navy ship whose captain (Bogart) suffers from combat fatigue. Fred plays Lt. Keefer, who both encourages and condones the mutiny and then denies it in open court.

Trivia: Young Robert Francis, who plays Ensign Keith in *The Caine Mutiny,* died in 1955 shortly after completing John Ford's *The Long Gray Line.* Keith, who was only 25, perished in a plane crash.

Reviews: "The Caine Mutiny is a highly recommendable motion picture drama, told on the screen as forcefully as it was in the Herman Wouk best selling novel ... One of 'Caines' strongest points is its casting. While there are four stars named, actually it's an all-star cast right down to the small-

est bit … Fred MacMurray, fourth top liner, also has a chance, and makes much of it, to sock over the character of Lt. Tom Keefer, the ship's intellect. Brilliant on the surface, a coward underneath." *Variety,* 6/9/54.
"*The Caine Mutiny* has plenty of what it takes to bring people into the theaters — a famous title, Technicolor and four famous names … But it has less of what it takes to make a first-class film." *Time,* 6/28/54.
"Van Johnson as the blunt executive officer who commits the so-called act of mutiny does an excellent job of revealing the distress and resolution of this man, and Fred MacMurray is likewise fascinating as the modern "sea lawyer" who eggs him on. Humphrey Bogart's twitchy performance of the 'by the book' Captain Queeg is a bit in the usual Bogart manner but, by and large, it is sound." *New York Times,* 6/25/54.

Pushover (1954, Columbia) *D:* Richard Quine.
Cast: Fred MacMurray, Kim Novak, Phil Carey, Dorothy Malone, E.G. Marshall, Allen Nourse, Phil Chambers, Alan Dexter, Robert Forrest. 88 mins B&W.
Plot: Basically good cop Fred turns bad because of a woman (Novak). Fred is in *Double Indemnity* mode again.
Trivia: This film had three working titles: "The Killer Wore a Badge," "322 French Street" and "The Night Watch."
Reviews: "Suspense holds up nicely despite its mite too long 88 mins. MacMurray portrays the cop who goes wrong in a low key, moody delineation in keeping with the character of the role … Kim Novak, who reportedly is being groomed by Columbia as a possible rival to Marilyn Monroe, shows possibilities." *Variety,* 7/28/54.
"Fred MacMurray is going through the motions of his *Double Indemnity* role in a mild facsimile of that ice-cold masterpiece called *Pushover* … again as a solid citizen who abruptly murders for money and a sultry blonde." *New York Times,* 7/31/54.
"*Pushover* is a better than workmanlike melodrama, but it is all as predictable as the force of gravity." *New York Herald Tribune,* 7/31/54.

Woman's World (1954, Twentieth Century-Fox) *D:* Jean Negulesco.
Cast: Clifton Webb, June Allyson, Van Heflin, Lauren Bacall, Fred MacMurray, Arlene Dahl, Cornel Wilde, Elliott Reid, Margalo Gillmore, Alan Reed. 94 mins. Color.
Plot: Corporate president Clifton Webb bases his choice for the new general manager on the qualities of the wives of the candidates. The candidates and their wives are invited to a stormy weekend at Webb's estate. Bacall plays Fred's wife.
Trivia: According to the *New York Times* (2/14/54), Eleanor Parker, Glenn Ford and Charlton Heston were announced to appear with June Allyson,

Lauren Bacall and Fred in this film. Parker, Ford and Heston backed out to be replaced by Dahl, Heflin and Wilde. During the filming of *Women's World,* Fred brought a thermometer to the set one day when the cast was shooting a dinner scene. With twelve people gathered around the table the thermometer registered 115 degrees. Fred wanted to make the point that it was just too darn hot on that set.

Reviews: "Too many cinematic cooks spoil the celluloid broth." *Cue,* 10/9/54.

"Five or six writers are responsible for the sum total of this exercise, and the best to be said for their invention is that they manage an occasional brittle joke." *New York Times,* 9/29/54.

Ad for **Woman's World,** *1954.*

The Far Horizons (1955, Paramount) *D:* Rudolph Mate.
Cast: Fred MacMurray, Charlton Heston, Donna Reed, Barbara Hale, William Demarest, Alan Reed, Eduardo Noriega, Larry Pennell, Argentina Brunetti, Herbert Heyes. 108 Mins. Color.
Plot: Fred and Heston play explorers Lewis and Clark in this fictionalized account of their expedition. Reed plays the Indian guide Sacajawea.
Trivia: The producers of this film initially wanted Leslie Caron to play Sacajawea, but when negotiations with MGM (where she was under contract) fell through they hired Donna Reed, who had just recently won the Academy Award for best supporting actress for her part in *From Here to Eternity.*
Reviews: "Aside from nature and a consistently winning performance by Miss Reed, as the Indian guide, Sacajawea, this slow and unimaginative safari seldom suggests either history or life. In some respects it is absurd." *New York Times,* 5/21/55.
"Overlong, spottily-paced … scenically … has magnificent values." *Variety,* 5/25/55.

The Rains of Ranchipur (1955, Twentieth Century-Fox) *D:* Jean Negulesco.
Cast: Lana Turner, Richard Burton, Fred MacMurray, Joan Caulfield, Michael Rennie, Eugenie Leontovich, Gladys Hurlbut, Madge Kennedy, Carlo Rizzo, Beatrice Kraft, Paul H. Frees. 104 mins. Color.
Plot: Remake of the 1939 film *The Rains Came,* with Lana playing the wife of an English nobleman (Rennie) who falls in love with Burton, playing

Fred in The Rains of Ranchipur, *1955.*

the wise and noble Indian physician. Into this story comes alcoholic Tom Ransome (Fred), a one-time lover of Turner's.
Trivia: This film was originally budgeted at $3.5 million, and ended up costing more than $4.5 million, losing money when its box office receipts topped only $2.0 million.
Reviews: "Fred MacMurray is just plain miscast as the disillusioned drunkard." *Variety,* 12/14/55.
"Fred MacMurray as an expatriate American engineer, who is finding surcease in alcohol, seems out of place in Ranchipur." *New York Times,* 12/16/55.

At Gunpoint (1955, Allied Artists) *D:* Alfred Werker.
Cast: Fred MacMurray, Dorothy Malone, Walter Brennan, Tommy Rettig, Skip Homeier, John Qualen, Harry Shannon, Whit Bissell, Irving Bacon, Jack Lambert, Frank Ferguson. 81 mins. Color.
Plot: Fred plays a storekeeper who can barely shoot a gun, but gets off a lucky shot which kills an outlaw. Now the dead man's gang is out to take revenge on MacMurray and the town he lives in.
Trivia: Joel McCrea had been the original choice for the part ultimately played by Fred. This film was shot in about three weeks, from May 6, 1955 to roughly the end of May.

Reviews: "MacMurray's gun-shy hero is his best in some time." *Variety,* 12/7/55.
"Mr. MacMurray is pretty much a dud." *New York Times.*
"MacMurray who bears most of the burden of the Daniel M. Ullman script gives a noteworthy, quiet, convincing performance." *Oakland Tribune,* 1/21/56.

There's Always Tomorrow (1956, Universal) *D:* Douglas Sirk.
Cast: Barbara Stanwyck, Fred MacMurray, Joan Bennett, Pat Crowley, William Reynolds, Gigi Perreau, Race Gentry, Myrna Hansen, Judy Nugent, Jane Howard. 84 mins. B&W.
Plot: Fred plays the unappreciated husband and father who finds himself tempted by an old flame (Stanwyck).
Trivia: Robert Young and Melvyn Douglas were considered for the part of Clifford Groves which Fred ultimately was signed to play.
Reviews: "Married man falls for the other woman, and somebody has to suffer. The same formula has been selling soap for years." *New York Herald Tribune.*
"... the moral (if not the picture) is worth broadcasting: For Pete's sake, have mercy on dad -especially if you are contemplating taking him to see this film." *New York Times,* 1/21/56.
"The even-paced, almost placid scripting ... gives the Douglas Sirk direction very little on which to hang some dramatic punch." *Variety,* 1/15/56.

Gun for a Coward (1957, Universal) *D:* Abner Biberman.
Cast: Fred MacMurray, Jeffrey Hunter, Janice Rule, Chill Wills, Dean Stockwell, Josephine Hutchinson, Betty Lynn, Iron Eyes Cody. 88 mins. Color.
Plot: Fred is the older brother of troublemaker Stockwell and sensitive Hunter and runs the family spread after the death of their father in this character-driven Western, one of Fred's better horse operas of the late '50s.
Trivia: Originally, Warner Brothers had an option on this story with the intention of casting James Dean in the part ultimately played by Jeffrey Hunter. However, after Dean's death, the studio let the option pass and it was picked up by Universal.
Reviews: "Mr. MacMurray adds a serious and solid characterization as the harried brother who finally finds surcease when relieved of his responsibilities." *New York Times,* 1/31/57.
"Story and characterization values makes this above-average western." *Variety,* 1/16/57.

Quantez (1957, Universal) *D:* Harry Keller.
Cast: Fred MacMurray, Dorothy Malone, James Barton, Sydney Chaplin, John Gavin, John Larch, Michael Ansara. 80 mins. Color.
Plot: When outlaws invade a small border town they hold out in a saloon which holds, among others, Fred and Malone.
Trivia: Low-budget Western was second-billed to the Debbie Reynolds' *Tammy and the Bachelor.*
Reviews: "Why, a regular moviegoer might wonder, would a star like Fred MacMurray, or a recent Oscar winner like Dorothy Malone become involved in something like this? Well, they are ... Mr. MacMurray looks downright embarrassed as a philosophical Easterner ... This one bites the dust long before Indians converge." *New York Times,* 9/7/57.
"MacMurray, a smooth and capable actor, delivers the competent performance to be expected." *Variety,* 8/28/57.

Day of the Bad Man (1958, Universal) *D:* Harry Keller.
Cast: Fred MacMurray, Joan Weldon, John Ericson, Robert Middleton, Marie Windsor, Edgar Buchanan, Skip Homeier, Eduard Franz. 82 mins. Color
Plot: Fred plays a traveling judge whose duty it is to make sure that a convicted murderer is duly hanged and must contend with the condemned man's kin, who are out to save him.
Trivia: This film had three working titles: "Decision at Durango," "Law of the Trigger" and "Point of Decision."
Reviews: "In MacMurray's capable playing the story-line gets some interest and substance where as in less experienced hands the whole thing would have bordered on the ridiculous." *Variety,* 1/15/58.

Good Day for a Hanging (1958, Columbia) *D:* Nathan Juran.
Cast: Fred MacMurray, Maggie Hayes, Robert Vaughn, Joan Blackman, James Drury, Edmon Ryan, Wendell Holmes, Kathryn Card, Bing Russell. 85 mins. Color.
Plot: Fred plays an ex-lawman who captures a charming killer (Vaughn) and must contend with a town which doesn't care if he is convicted of the crime.
Trivia: Vaughn would go on within two years to greater Western fame in the classic film *The Magnificent Seven.* Meanwhile, Drury would spend nine years playing *The Virginian* on NBC. Bing Russell is the father of Kurt Russell, who would later appear with Fred in two Disney films, *Follow Me, Boys!* and *Charley and the Angel.*
Reviews: "MacMurray has a rather solid role but invests it with authority and interest ... not altogether successful, but it is several notches above its modest budget class." *Variety,* 12/24/58.

The Shaggy Dog (1959, Buena Vista) *D:* Charles Barton.
Cast: Fred MacMurray, Jean Hagen, Tommy Kirk, Annette Funicello, Tim Considine, Kevin Corcoran, Cecil Kellaway, Roberta Shore, Alexander Scourby, Strother Martin. 104 mins. Buena Vista.
Plot: Fred is a postman who is allergic to dogs which doesn't help matters when his teenage son, Wilby (Kirk), is magically transformed into an English sheepdog and gets his father and younger brother (Corcoran) involved in cloak-and-dagger dealings with spies.
Trivia: This film was Disney's biggest box office hit up to that time, grossing $8 million during its initial release. It was later re-released in 1967 (on a bill with 1961's *The Absent Minded Professor)* and 1976.
Reviews: "Producer Walt Disney tells his Shaggy Dog story so doggedly that he soon runs it into the pound." *Time,* 4/20/59.
"Walt Disney has taken a brisk but unrewarding plunge in a new direction with *The Shaggy Dog." New York Times,* 3/20/59.
"Pleasant Disney comedy, attractive to family or youngster audiences." *Variety,* 2/25/59.
"Walt Disney's studio, which likes to make pictures that win the young but isn't averse to attracting adults, has come up with a modern fantasy that may very well satisfy both groups. *The Shaggy Dog* tells the story of a teenager who turns into an Old English sheep dog; and some of this skittish plot is very amusing thanks to the lively script and pleasing cast." *Commonweal,* 4/10/59.

Face of a Fugitive (1959, Columbia) *D:* Paul Wendkos.
Cast: Fred MacMurray, Lin McCarthy, Dorothy Green, Alan Baxter, Myrna Fahey, James Coburn, Francis De Sales, Gina Gillespie, Ron Hayes. 81 mins. Color.
Plot: Fred plays a man wrongly accused of murder that escapes and starts a new life in a new town, but finds that his past can't escape him.
Trivia: The working title of this picture was "Justice Ends with a Gun."
Reviews: "Columbia's *Face of a Fugitive* is a fair program western which attempts to be off-beat and succeeds at being down-beat." *Variety,* 4/29/59.

The Oregon Trail (1959, Twentieth Century-Fox) *D:* Gene Fowler, Jr.
Cast: Fred MacMurray, William Bishop, Nina Shipman, Gloria Talbott, Henry Hull, John Carradine, John Dierkes, Elizabeth Patterson, James Bell. 82 mins. Color.
Plot: Fred plays an Eastern newsman sent west to report on Indian attacks.
Trivia: This would be Fred's last Western, although he was considered for one of the all-star roles in MGM's mammoth *How the West Was Won* in 1961.
Reviews: "... manages to include most of the standard wagon-train clichés of the last twenty-five years." *New York Times.*

The Apartment (1960, United Artists) *D:* Billy Wilder.
Cast: Jack Lemmon, Shirley MacLaine, Fred MacMurray, Ray Walston, Edie Adams, Hope Holiday, Jack Kruschen, Joan Shawlee, Naomi Stevens, Willard Waterman. 125 mins. B&W.
Plot: Insurance numbers man Lemmon tries to get ahead by loaning out his apartment to executives who use it as a love nest, not realizing that the elevator girl he is in love with (MacLaine) is the mistress of the married head of the companies human resources department (Fred).
Trivia: The Broadway musical *Promises, Promises,* by Neil Simon, was based on this film.
Reviews: "Billy Wilder has furnished *The Apartment* with a one-hook plot that comes out high in comedy, wide in warmth and long in running time ... MacMurray is strong as the two-way player." *Variety,* 5/18/60.
"*The Apartment* is a very funny movie that can take its place among the finest comedies Hollywood has turned out." *Newsweek,* 6/20/60.
"There is a telephone conversation between lovers MacMurray and mistress MacLaine (she has tried to commit suicide, he couldn't care less about her condition — or more about possible scandal) that makes a rarely profound and ignoble vignette." *Time,* 6/6/60.
"You might not think a movie about a fellow who lends his rooms to the married executives of his office as a place for their secret love affairs would make a particularly funny or morally presentable show ... But under the clever supervision of Billy Wilder ... the idea is run into a gleeful, tender and even sentimental film." *New York Times,* 6/16/60.
"While much of *The Apartment* is clever satire, much of it is also disturbingly sad; and the total effect is as if Wilder were to burlesque *Room at the Top.* Even though *The Apartment* has a so-called happy ending when the worm turns, the putative hero and adulterous heroine hardly endear themselves. The film does convey that Jack and Shirley, in spite of all the temptations around them, are winners in the rat race; or, as the script says, 'That's the way it crumbles, cookiewise.'" *Commonweal,* 7/8/60.

Ad for The Apartment, *1960.*

Fred, Keenan Wynn and Nancy Olson in The Absent Minded Professor, *1961.*

The Absent Minded Professor (1961, Buena Vista) *D:* Robert Stevenson.
Cast: Fred MacMurray, Nancy Olson, Keenan Wynn, Tommy Kirk, Elliott
Reid, Leon Ames, Ed Wynn, Edward Andrews. 97 mins. B&W.
Plot: Fred plays Professor Ned Brainard who comes up with a concoction
which causes rubber to levitate which he calls "flubber." Olson is his long-
time fiancée who decides to dump the professor when he misses their wedding, setting the stage for Brainard's rival, Prof. Shelby Ashton (Reid), to
move in. Meanwhile, Keenan Wynn plays an unscrupulous businessman
who tries to steal Brainard's formula.
Trivia: Director Robert Stevenson was Walt Disney's most talented house
director and his most famous and most popular film is 1964's *Mary Poppins*,
for which Stevenson was nominated for the first and only time for an
Academy Award as Best Director of the year.
Reviews: "The season's kookiest science fiction farce." *Time*, 3/10/61.
"The comedy is deftly and expertly handled by director Robert Stevenson."
Variety, 2/22/61.

"MacMurray deserves much of the credit for the comedy's success. He has just the right fidgety archness to make the absurdities credible." *New York Herald-Tribune,* 3/17/61.

"As the center of the farcical confusions, Fred MacMurray does a fair enough job for an actor not equipped with the talent and the physical grotesquery of one of the old time silent comedians who were deft at this sort of sport." *New York Times,* 3/17/61.

Fred and Deborah Walley in Bon Voyage!, *1962.*

Bon Voyage! (1962, Buena Vista) *D:* James Neilson.

Cast: Fred MacMurray, Jane Wyman, Michael Callan, Deborah Walley, Tommy Kirk, Kevin Corcoran, Jessie Royce Landis, Georgette Anys, Ivan Desny, Francoise Prevost, Carol White. 130 mins. Color.

Plot: A Midwestern family's first trip to Europe and their misadventures along the way.

Trivia: This film was nominated for two Academy Awards, best sound and costume design.

Reviews: "People who fondly remember the old Hardy Family films notice a slight resemblance in this one to some of them. Tommy Kirk's callow performance of the older son may not be quite as bright as Mickey Rooney's of Andy, but it is the same brash and bumptious vein. And while Mr. MacMurray's father is not as dignified as Lewis Stone's, it is a whole lot livelier and cornier. That, indeed is the characteristic of the whole film." *New York Times,* 5/18/62.

"Walt Disney dishes up another comedy blockbuster in this rollicking tour de force." *Variety,* 5/9/62.

"Apart from an innocently comic passage when Pop is trying to signal for help in the sewers by waving his index finger through a slit in the pavement, the film is not very entertaining for anyone over 10. But it is tremendously good hearted, and in an odd way rather jolly and endearing." *The (London) Observer,* 6/17/62.

"... Still, the picture is fairly effective ... mainly because MacMurray has a basic and ineradicable masculinity that diverts any feeling of bathos in moments of bumbling defeat and never lets you feel embarrassed for him in cornier passages. All in all, I feel *Bon Voyage* is a family picture and would be seen to best advantage in a family group." *New York Herald Tribune,* 6/18/62.

Son of Flubber (1963, Buena Vista) *D:* Robert Stevenson.
Cast: Fred MacMurray, Nancy Olson, Keenan Wynn, Tommy Kirk, Elliott Reid, Joanna Moore, Leon Ames, Ed Wynn, Ken Murray, Charlie Ruggles, William Demarest, Bob Sweeney, Paul Lynde, Alan Hewitt. 100 mins. B&W.
Plot: The further misadventures of Prof. Ned Brainard who, this time, comes up with "flubber gas."
Trivia: Fred actually is playing the sax during the film's party scene.
Reviews: "*Son of Flubber.* It's that man again — Neddie the Nut, that is. Remember him? In *The Absent Minded Professor* the nuttiest science fiction farce of recent years. Neddie (Fred MacMurray) invented 'flubber' — lab gab for flying rubber. In Professor the professor put flubber in a flivver and flew. In this picture he turns flubber slubber into flubbergas and starts blowing flubbles. Infantile? Absolutely. But fun." *Time,* 2/22/63.

"A studious repeat, or rebound, of a good entertainment formula." *New York Times,* 2/9/63.

"Like most sequels *Son of Flubber* (now there's an original title) works to the strict theory that what was funny the first time out must be just as funny the second. And like most too-deliberate sequels, the film falls a victim to its own making. For whereas the first piece had a charm of sorts, indeed its mixture of fantasy and fooling was very well done, this one has none." *Films and Filming,* March 1963.

"Walt Disney's *Son of Flubber* is not a horse, a dog nor even a 40-pound tyke. I'll tell you what it is — it's hilarious." *Washington Post,* 2/16/63.

"Call it corn, which it is, *Son of Flubber* is good corn and more fun than its title suggests." *Boston Herald,* 2/18/63.

Kisses for My President (1964, Warner Brothers) *D:* Curtis Bernhardt.
Cast: Fred MacMurray, Polly Bergen, Arlene Dahl, Edward Andrews, Eli Wallach, Donald May, Bill Richards, Anna Capri, Ronnie Dapo, Bill Walker. 113 mins. B&W.
Plot: Fred plays the "first husband" to the first woman elected president of the United States.
Trivia: Jack Warner originally wanted Maureen O'Hara for the Polly Bergen role.

Ad for **Kisses for My President,** *1964.*

Reviews: "Sappy little election year comedy." *Time,* 9/4/64.
"Essentially a one-joke idea that telegraphs plot lines, gags and obvious sightlines most of the way." *Variety,* 8/19/64.
"The plots and characterizations could be easily overdone in this Warner Brothers film but they are not. If you want to forget about politics for an evening, this will do it." *Oakland Tribune,* 10/10/64.

Follow Me, Boys! (1966, Buena Vista) *D:* Norman Tokar.
Cast: Fred MacMurray, Vera Miles, Charlie Ruggles, Elliott Reid, Lillian Gish, Kurt Russell, Luana Patten, Ken Murray, Donald May, William Reynolds. 131 mins. Color.
Plot: Fred plays a saxophone player with a band which stops off in a small town. Thinking he has found the hometown he has always searched for, he leaves the band and gets a job in a grocery store and eventually gets married. He and his wife (Miles) can't conceive a child of their own but become the surrogate parents of a generation of the boys he is the scoutmaster to.
Trivia: This was Kurt Russell's first film for the Disney Studios, where he would appear in ten films over the next ten years.
Reviews: "Walt Disney, who sometimes likes to represent America as a giant niceberg floating in an ocean of nostalgia, has now represented the model American male as a simpering scoutmaster." *Time,* 12/16/66
"*Follow Me, Boys!* is Disney at his best." *Variety,* 10/12/66.
"Scoutmaster Lem … is played with warmth and nice comedy touches by Fred MacMurray … My greatest row … is its 131-minute running time, which is an awful lot of mins devoted to surface Americana and cloying wholesomeness." *Commonweal,* 12/9/66.
"*Follow Me, Boys!* is just too sweet for words — but millions of movie fans will drool over this entertaining, saccharine depiction of small-town

America." *West Virginia Sunday Gazette Mail*, 12/25/66.
"*Follow Me, Boys!* is an occasionally droll, hugely sentimental film whose issuance at this particular time is a fresh reminder of Walt Disney's dedication to family entertainment." *Christian Science Monitor*, 1/14/67.

The Happiest Millionaire (1967, Buena Vista) *D:* Norman Tokar. *Cast:* Fred MacMurray, Greer Garson, Tommy Steele, Geraldine Page, Lesley Ann Warren, John Davidson, Gladys Cooper, Hermione Baddeley, Paul Peterson, Eddie Hodges, Joyce Bulifant. 164 mins. Color. *Plot:* Disney musical about the family life of an eccentric Philadelphia millionaire (played by Fred).
Trivia: This is the last live-action film which Walt Disney person-

Ad for The Happiest Millionaire, *1967.*

ally supervised and it was his hope that this film would be his most successful since *Mary Poppins*, which it proved not to be.
Reviews: "Brooks Atkinson said in 1956 (of Walter Pidgeon's stage performance as Biddle) that 'Mr. Pidgeon gave a wonderful performance … that could be a bore if acting did not have style.' Mr. MacMurray manages to avoid that essential element." *New York Times*, 12/1/67.
"Outstanding Walt Disney film version of book and play, with original new music. Handsome production, excellent cast." *Variety*, 6/28/67.
"Fred MacMurray copes well with the part of Biddle, though the script shackles any real development of character or personality." *Films and Filming*, June 1968.
"*The Happiest Millionaire* is obviously aimed at the family market, but the adults may find it oversimplified and youngsters may find it overlong." *Christian Science Monitor*, 10/9/67.

Charley and the Angel (1973, Buena Vista) *D:* Vincent McEveety. *Cast:* Fred MacMurray, Cloris Leachman, Harry Morgan, Kurt Russell, Kathleen Cody, Vincent Van Patten, Scott Kolden, Edward Andrews, George Lindsey. 93 mins. Color.
Plot: Fred plays a dour storekeeper whose chief interest in life is making a living to the detriment of his family life and is given another chance by a banjo playing angel (played by Morgan) in this Disney comedy.
Trivia: Cloris Leachman had won an Academy Award for *The Last Picture*

Show just prior to beginning work on this film.

Reviews: "*Charley and the Angel* falls in line with past Disney comedy-type offering which should fare well in its intended market ... MacMurray enacts another of his bewildered characters with his usual aplomb and gets good mileage from role." *Variety,* April 1973.

"The picture, set in the Depression years, has a mildly diverting façade of nostalgia in costumes, tunes and those fine, tacky old cars. Mr. MacMurray, by now a Disney veteran, is front and center, unremittingly wide-eyed." *New York Times,* 6/28/73.

The Swarm (1978, Warner Brothers) *D:* Irwin Allen.

Cast: Michael Caine, Katharine Ross, Richard Widmark, Richard Chamberlain, Olivia de Havilland, Fred MacMurray, Ben Johnson, Henry Fonda, Lee Grant, Jose Ferrer, Patty Duke, Bradford Dillman, Cameron Mitchell. 116 mins. Color.

Plot: Killer bees from South America are breeding with gentler Northern bees and are moving northward rapidly spreading death and destruction along their path. In his final feature film performance, the 69-year-old Fred plays Clarence Tuttle, the mayor of a small town, who is vying with Ben Johnson for the attentions of Olivia de Havilland.

Trivia: So that the actors would be safe from the "killer" bees, the stingers had been clipped off the bees used.

Reviews: "Some day, African killer bees may wind up having the last buzz on us, but for the time being they simply aren't scary, at least not in Irwin Allen's *The Swarm.*" *New York Times,* 7/15/78.

"... It's the kind of screenplay where characters who supposedly are familiar with certain technical work spend most of their time explaining it to each other. Such corny exposition is but one lowlight. Then there's the sub-plot romance between school marm Olivia de Havilland (with the worst phony Southern accent imaginable) and either Fred MacMurray and Ben Johnson." *Variety,* 7/19/78.

Fred MacMurray on Radio

Fred had a fairly rich career on radio, making many guest appearances on anthology programs such as *The Lux Radio Theatre* and *Screen Director's Playhouse* recreating many of his performances from motion pictures. Radio also gave him the opportunity to work with some leading ladies he never had the opportunity to work with in films (yes, there were a few!) such as Bette Davis, Loretta Young, Joanne Dru, Ida Lupino, Ginger Rogers, Ann Sothern and Linda Darnell. And not every program he did was a recreation of one of his films. For instance, on *The Lux Radio Theatre*, he and Claudette Colbert got the opportunity to recreate the roles played by Cary Grant and Rosalind Russell in the film *His Girl Friday*. On *The Screen Guild Theatre* he took on Gary Cooper's role from the film *Bluebeard's Eighth Wife*, opposite Claudette Colbert.

He also had his own radio show, a newspaper drama called *Bright Star*, which lasted a year and starred him opposite Irene Dunne. The following list is by no means complete, but it gives a pretty good indication of Fred's long and varied career on radio.

Bright Star (a.k.a. *The Irene Dunne-Fred MacMurray Show*)
A newspaper comedy-drama stars Irene Dunne as Susan Armstrong, the glamorous and strong-willed editor of the struggling *Hillsdale Morning Star*, and Fred MacMurray as her ace reporter, George Harvey. In addition to being editor-reporter, the two share a thinly disguised infatuation with each other. The program was syndicated throughout the country and transcribed rather than performed live. The sponsor was the Frederic W. Ziv Company. According to the *Los Angeles Examiner* (8/14/51), both Dunne and MacMurray signed a contract worth $300,000 over three seasons (of which only one season worth of programs was fulfilled). Harry Von Zell was the announcer.

Episode Guide:
10/23/52: *Oil Swindle*
10/30/52: *Susan Runs for Mayor*

11/6/52: *Hillside Becomes Mom and Dad*
11/13/52: *Miss America Visits*
11/20/52: *George and the Informer*
11/27/52: *Crooked Carnival*
12/4/52: *George and the Chorus Girl*
12/11/52: *George and the Society Burglar*
12/25/52: *The Boxer*
1/1/53: *Dramatic Lessons*
1/8/53: *French Dress Designer*
2/12/53: *George Covers Hillsdale Fire*
2/19/53: *George Coaches Hillsdale High*
2/26/53: *The Haunted House*
3/5/53: *Rodeo Star*
3/12/53: *Scientific Living*
3/19/53: *New Homemaker Page Editor*
3/26/53: *Hotel Room Shortage*
4/2/53: *Aunt Sophia Plays Matchmaker*
4/9/53: *The Talking Parrot*
4/16/53: *The Patient's Aid*
4/23/53: *Sammy and Shirley*
4/30/53: *Beaver Park*
5/7/53: *Cousin Emily*
5/14/53: *Susan's Poetry*
5/21/53: *A Flower for Susan*
5/28/53: *Box Supper*
6/4/53: *Chorus Girl*
6/11/53: *The Society Burglar*
6/18/53: *One Word Cablegram*
6/25/53: *Missing Childhood Sweetheart*

The Charlie McCarthy Show
Broadcast: 9/15/46. Fred guest stars along with Ray Noble in the highly popular radio series starring Edgar Bergen with his "dummies," Charlie McCarthy and Mortimer Snerd.

The Chase and Sanborn Hour
Broadcast: 9/17/39. This musical variety show was hosted by Don Ameche and featured Edgar Bergen and Charlie McCarthy. Fred guest stars on this segment along with Nelson Eddy and Helen Broderick.

Command Performance
Broadcast: 5/29/46 for the Armed Forces Radio Service (AFRS) and hosted by Bob Hope with appearances by Fred MacMurray, The King

Sisters, Jerry Colonna, Kay Kyser, Mel Blanc, Edgar Bergen, Frances Langford, among others.

Four for the Fifth
Broadcast: June, 1944. The Treasury Department sponsored this half-hour variety show to raise funds for the Fifth War Bond drive. Fred appears with Bea Benaderet, Mercedes McCambridge, Lou Merrill, Verna Felton and Cathy Lewis.

G.I. Journal
Broadcast: 9/21/41 for the Armed Forces Radio Service (AFRS) and hosted by Bob Hope with his guests Fred MacMurray, Mel Blanc and Linda Darnell.

Hollywood Hotel
This 1930s anthology series was initially hosted by Dick Powell, but when he left the show in the spring of 1937, Fred took over the hosting chores for several weeks. He also appeared on the show as an actor. Famed Hollywood gossip columnist Louella Parsons often interviewed the actors who made guest appearances on the show.

> *Hands Across the Table* 9/20/35: Fred and Carole Lombard recreate their film roles.
> *Thirteen Hours by Air* 3/13/36: Fred and Joan Bennett recreate their film roles.
> *Swing High, Swing Low* 1/15/37: Fred and Carole Lombard recreate their film roles.
> *God's Country and the Woman* 1/22/37: Fred MacMurray hosts, with George Brent guest-starring.
> *Green Light* 1/29/37: Fred MacMurray hosts, with Errol Flynn guest-starring.
> *On the Avenue* 2/5/37: Fred MacMurray hosts, with Dick Powell and Madeleine Carroll guest-starring.
> *Sea Devils* 2/12/37: Fred MacMurray hosts, with Victor McLaglen and Ida Lupino guest-starring.
> *Black Legion* 2/19/37: Fred MacMurray hosts, with Humphrey Bogart guest-starring.
> *Interns Can't Take Money* 2/26/37: Fred MacMurray hosts, with Barbara Stanwyck and Joel McCrea guest-starring.
> *Nancy Steele is Missing* 3/5/37: Fred MacMurray hosts, with Victor McLaglen and Peter Lorre guest starring.
> *Love is News* 3/19/37: Fred MacMurray hosts, with Loretta Young and Tyrone Power guest-starring.

Top of the Town 3/19/37-Fred MacMurray hosts, with Gertrude Neisen and George Murphy guest-starring.
Call it a Day 3/26/37: Fred MacMurray hosts, with Olivia de Havilland and Roland Young guest: starring.
Maytime 4/2/37: Fred MacMurray hosts, with Jeanette MacDonald guest: starring.
The Woman I Love 4/9/37: Fred MacMurray hosts, with Miriam Hopkins guest: starring.
Marked Woman 4/16/37: Fred MacMurray hosts, with Humphrey Bogart and Bette Davis guest: starring.
Wake Up and Live 4/23/37: Fred MacMurray hosts, with Alice Faye guest: starring.
A Star is Born 4/30/37: Fred MacMurray hosts, with Fredric March and Janet Gaynor guest: starring. (This was Fred's final appearance as interim host of this show.)
Exclusive 7/23/37: Fred recreates his film role with Ida Lupino taking on the role played by Frances Farmer in the film.
True Confession 12/3/37: Fred and Carole Lombard recreate their film roles.

The Kate Smith Hour
Broadcast: March 3, 1944. Musical-variety series starring the popular singer. Fred guest-stars on this segment creating a scene from the film *Standing Room Only.*

Lux Radio Theatre
Fred appeared many times on this long-running radio anthology program (running from 1935-1955), which for many years had been hosted by director Cecil B. DeMille.

The Gilded Lily 1/11/37: Fred and Claudette Colbert recreate their film roles.
Another Language 5/17/37: Fred got the opportunity to work with Bette Davis, who must have been less than taken with him. She later described him as "personality-zero."
Up Pops the Devil 10/18/37 with Madge Evans.
Front Page Woman 1/16/39: This was the first time Fred worked with Paulette Goddard in a recreation of the film which had starred Bette Davis and George Brent.
Invitation to Happiness 10/23/39: with Madeleine Carroll in the role that Irene Dunne had played on screen.
Made For Each Other 2/19/40: Carole Lombard and Fred

star in this drama, which had been a 1939 film starring Lombard and James Stewart.

Remember the Night 3/25/40: Fred and Barbara Stanwyck recreate their roles from the popular film, which had just been released in January.

True Confession 5/13/40: Fred recreates his role from the 1937 film with the Carole Lombard role filled by Loretta Young.

His Girl Friday 9/30/40: Fred and Claudette Colbert recreate the roles played in the film by Cary Grant and Rosalind Russell of newspaper editor Walter Burns and his ace reporter Hildy Johnson

Standing Room Only 10/30/44: Pits Fred and Paulette Goddard in a recreation of their current film.

Pardon My Past 5/13/46: Featuring Fred with Marguerite Chapman.

The Egg and I 5/5/47: Claudette Colbert and Fred recreate their film roles.

Miracle of the Bells 5/31/48: Fred and Frank Sinatra reprise their film roles in this radio adaptation.

June Bride 12/28/53: Fred and Irene Dunne play the roles created by Bette Davis and Robert Montgomery in the 1948 film version.

Mail Call
Broadcast: September, 1942. The series was produced for the Armed Forces Radio Service (AFRS). This program was hosted by Loretta Young and featured Fred MacMurray, Bob Hope, Frances Langford, and Jerry Colonna. *Broadcast:* November 17, 1943. Fred makes another *Mail Call* appearance, this time with George Burns and Gracie Allen hosting and guest stars Dennis Day and Dorothy Lamour joining Fred.

Martin and Lewis Show
Broadcast: 5/19/53. Fred guest stars on this radio series starring the highly popular film and nightclub team, broadcast on NBC.

Screen Director's Playhouse
This series recreated, in a condensed form, movies on radio. The show gets its name because the director of the movie which is recreated introduces the show and often, but not always, the same stars of the film reenact their roles:

Suddenly It's Spring 3/27/49: Featuring Fred MacMurray, Virginia Gregg and Frank Lovejoy. Mitchell Leisen hosts.

Don't Trust Your Husband 9/23/49: Featuring Fred MacMurray.

Take a Letter, Darling 2/1/51: Featuring Fred MacMurray and Rosalind Russell. Mitchell Leisen hosts.

The Screen Guild Theatre

Another anthology series which ran for a number of years (1939-1952) and featured top name film stars in dramatic plays or radio recreations of popular films.

Vivacious Lady 4/7/40: Fred teams with Ginger Rogers (in their only time working together) in a recreation of her 1938 film. Fred plays the role played by Jimmy Stewart in that film.

Desire 12/1/40: Fred teams with his *The Lady is Willing* co: star, Marlene Dietrich, two years before they worked together on that film, in a recreation of Dietrich's 1936 film, which had co: starred Gary Cooper.

True Confessions 4/13/41: This would, sadly, be the last teaming of Fred and Carole Lombard, in a recreation of their 1937 film. Lombard would die in a plane crash in January 1942.

Bachelor Mother 11/23/42: Fred teams with Ann Sothern in a recreation of the 1939 film, which had starred Ginger Rogers and David Niven.

No Time for Love 6/19/44: Fred and Claudette Colbert recreate their roles from the 1943 film.

Double Indemnity 3/5/45: Fred and Barbara Stanwyck recreate their sensational performances from the 1944 Billy Wilder film. (In 1950, Stanwyck would again recreate her role from this film on this program, but with her then: husband Robert Taylor in the MacMurray role of Walter Neff.)

Guest Wife 5/20/46: Fred teams with Claudette Colbert in a recreation of her 1945 film which had co-starred Don Ameche.

The Moon Is Our Home 3/24/47: Fred teams with Robert Young in a recreation of the 1936 film which had starred Henry Fonda.

Bluebeard's Eighth Wife 4/14/47: Fred teams with Claudette Colbert in a recreation of her 1938 film which had co-starred Gary Cooper.

Take a Letter, Darling 11/4/48: Fred and Rosalind Russell

recreate their roles from the popular 1942 film.

Family Honeymoon 12/15/49: Fred and Claudette Colbert recreate their roles from the 1948 film.

Father Was a Fullback 11/16/50: Fred recreates his role from the 1949 film with Linda Darnell pinch: hitting for his film co-star Maureen O'Hara.

Suspense

Long-running anthology series featuring stories of horror and suspense. Broadcast on CBS radio network.

The Windy City Six 2/8/51: Fred stars in this story based during the Roaring Twenties.

The Flight of the Bumblebee 5/19/52: Fred stars in a story about the crew of a B-29 returning from a bombing mission over Korea.

The Great Train Robbery 4/13/53: Fred in a story about a man and his uncle who attempt to rob a mail train.

My Three Sons

EPISODE GUIDE

ABC September, 1960-September, 1963 *Thursday, 9:00-9:30*
September, 1963-September, 1965 *Thursday, 8:30-9:00*
CBS September, 1965-August, 1967 *Thursday, 8:30-9:00*
September, 1967-September, 1971 *Saturday, 8:30-9:00*
September, 1971-December,1971 *Monday, 10:00-10:30*
January, 1972-August, 1972 *Thursday, 8:30-9:00*

Season One

Chip Off the Old Block (9/29/60) *D:* Peter Tewksbury. Both Steve and eight-year-old Chip have unwelcome female problems.

The Little Ragpicker (10/6/60) *D:* Peter Tewksbury. Chip begins collecting for the annual school rag drive, which causes the Douglas' neighbor, Miss Pitts, to assume the worst about her neighbors. (Such as Bub waving a bottle that looks like a Whiskey bottle, causing her to think he is hitting the sauce.)

Bub in the Ointment (10/13/60) *D:* Peter Tewksbury. Poor Bub has to rebuke each of his grandsons, which cause them to give him the cold treatment.

Countdown (10/20/60) *D:* Peter Tewksbury. One of the most memorable episodes about a typical Monday morning of chaos in the Douglas household compared and contrasted with a missile launch at Cape Canaveral.

Brotherly Love (10/27/60) *D:* Peter Tewksbury. Mike and Robbie vie against one another over a girl.

Adjust or Bust (11/3/60) *D:* Peter Tewksbury. Steve must adjust when a series of catastrophes keeps him from an important meeting.

Lady Engineer (11/10/60) *D:* Peter Tewksbury. Steve is tempted to mix business with pleasure when he meets a beautiful new co-worker.

Chip's Harvest (11/17/60) *D:* Peter Tewksbury. It's Thanksgiving Day at the Douglas household. Cynthia Pepper marks her first appearance on the show as Jean Pearson, Mike's girlfriend from next door.

Raft on the River (11/24/60) *D:* Peter Tewksbury. When Mike and Robbie are away camping, Chip feels left out until he finds a makeshift raft in the backyard and he and Steve pretend they are floating down the Mississippi.

Lonesome George (12/1/60) *D:* Peter Tewksbury. George Gobel guest stars as himself, invited to dinner and to spend the night at the Douglas house. Steve is out of town, and when he arrives home late at night, he finds "Lonesome" George occupying his bed.

Spring Will Be a Little Late This Year (12/8/60) *D:* Peter Tewksbury. Robbie is having problems with his girlfriend. (Don Grady's Robbie gets his first on-screen kiss in this episode.)

My Three Strikers (12/15/60) *D:* Peter Tewksbury. The boys decide to go on strike when they don't get a raise in their allowances.

The Elopement (12/22/60) *D:* Peter Tewksbury. Steve and Bub get the idea that Mike and Jean might be preparing to elope.

Mike's Brother (12/29/60) *D:* Peter Tewksbury. Robbie is tired of always being compared to older brother Mike.

Domestic Trouble (1/5/61) *D:* Peter Tewksbury. Bub is called out of town and so Steve tries to arrange through an agency for domestic help while he is gone, unaware that he accidentally called up the agency "Domestic Bliss, Inc.," a matchmaking service.

Bub Leaves Home (1/12/61) *D:* Peter Tewksbury. Bub decides that he isn't needed any longer and gets a job as a movie theater manager.

Mike in a Rush (1/19/61) *D:* Peter Tewksbury. Mike begins making preparations toward going to college which also means joining a fraternity.

The Bully (1/26/61) *D:* Peter Tewksbury. Chip is having problems with the school bully, or is it the other way around?

Organization Woman (2/2/61) *D:* Peter Tewksbury. Steve's sister arrives and begins taking over the household. Director Peter Tewksbury's real-life sister, Joan, plays Steve's sibling.

Other People's Houses (2/9/61) *D:* Peter Tewksbury. Robbie visits the house of a school friend and is overcome by envy because of the opulence. On the other hand, his friend is taken with the more lived-in and relaxed atmosphere at the Douglas household. David White, who played Larry Tate on *Bewitched,* guest stars as the boy's father.

The Delinquent (2/16/61) *D:* Peter Tewksbury. Where are Mike and Tramp disappearing to every night?

Man in a Trench Coat (2/23/61) *D:* Peter Tewksbury. Robbie is avidly reading mystery novels when he suddenly sees a mysterious man in a trench coat. Is it his imagination?

Deadline (3/2/61) *D:* Peter Tewksbury. When Mike criticizes the sports page of his school newspaper, he is given the opportunity to reshape it.

The Lostling (3/9/61) *D:* Peter Tewksbury. Chip is tired of being the runt of the family and thinks it would be a blast to be an older brother.

Off Key (3/16/61) *D:* Peter Tewksbury. Trouble begins when Chip brags that Robbie can fix anything, he is given the job of repairing a grand piano.

Small Adventure (3/23/61) *D:* Peter Tewksbury. Tramp the dog somehow finds a WWII-era piece of dynamite which he brings home.

Soap Box Derby (3/30/61) *D:* Peter Tewksbury. In a variation of the first episode, sons have similar problems on different scales. Robbie has a deadline to construct a race car while Steve is working on trying to get a missile off the ground.

Unite or Sink (4/6/61) *D:* Peter Tewksbury. Robbie and Mike want some more pocket money but Steve won't give them a bigger allowance and tells them they should try and earn it the old-fashioned way, by getting jobs.

The Wiley Method (4/13/61) *D:* Peter Tewksbury. Robbie goes "theatrical" to get the attentions of a girl.

The National Pastime (4/27/61) *D:* Peter Tewksbury. Poor Chip is having a batting slump and quits the baseball team.

The Croaker (5/4/61) *D:* Peter Tewksbury. Bub thinks that Malcolm, a frog that Chip found, looks just like his Uncle Clancy.

The Musician (5/11/61) *D:* Peter Tewksbury. Robbie is into a girl with refined tastes and so he pretends to be someone he isn't.

The Horseless Saddle (5/18/61) *D:* Peter Tewksbury.

Trial by Separation (5/25/61) *D:* Peter Tewksbury. Mike and Jean decide to test their relationship by not seeing each other for the week before their graduation.

The Sunday Drive (6/1/61) *D:* Peter Tewksbury. The Douglases join their neighbors, the Pearsons, for a "nice quiet Sunday drive."

Fire Watch (6/8/61) *D:* Peter Tewksbury. Mike gets a summer job with the forest department. Peter Tewksbury's final episode as director.

Season Two

Birds and Bees (9/28/61) *D:* Richard Whorf. Tramp is going to have puppies, so Steve thinks it's about time to tell Chip about the "Birds and the Bees."

Instant Hate (10/5/61) *D:* Richard Whorf. Another classic early episode. A new family moves in across the street and it seems it is a case of "instant hate" on both sides.

The Crush (10/12/61) *D:* Richard Whorf. At college Mike thinks he finds a new girlfriend, but when he takes her home to meet the family, she finds herself attracted to Steve!

Tramp the Hero (10/26/61) *D:* Richard Whorf. Chip gets to think that his friend has the better bargain in dogs, an efficient German Shepard vs. old reliable but slow Tramp. Tramp will prove him wrong.

A Perfect Memory (11/2/61) *D:* Richard Whorf. A flashback episode as Steve wanders around town thinking about his old high school sweetheart.

Bub's Lodge (11/9/61) *D:* Richard Whorf. Both Bub and Mike are trying to get into exclusive clubs.

A Lesson in Any Language (11/16/61) *D:* Richard Whorf. Mike wants a skiing lesson but also needs to ace a test, so he comes up with a memory exercise which is supposed to work while he is sleeping. When Steve's room is painted, Steve uses Mike's bedroom and gets a crash course.

The Ugly Duckling (11/23/61) *D:* Richard Whorf. Robbie is getting an F in World Lit, so his teacher assigns a good-looking tutor, and now he can't stop thinking about the tutor.

Chip's Composition (11/30/61) *D:* Richard Whorf. Chip has to write a composition titled "What My Mother Means to Me" for school and the motherless boy decides to write it in honor of his grandfather, Bub.

Mike in Charge (12/7/61) *D:* Richard Whorf. When both Steve and Bub are called out of town, oldest sibling Mike takes charge.

Bub Goes to School (12/14/61) *D:* Richard Whorf. Bub decides to go to night school because he is finding it difficult to answer questions his grandchildren ask him.

Robbie's Band (12/21/61) *D:* Richard Whorf. The family gets more than it bargained for when Robbie's band begins rehearsing at their house.

Damon and Pythias (12/28/61) *D:* Richard Whorf. Robbie wants to join a club at school, but doesn't want to join the club Mike belonged to.

Chip Leaves Home (1/4/62) *D:* Richard Whorf. Feeling ignored by the family, Chip decides to run away.

The Romance of Silver Pines (1/11/62) *D:* Richard Whorf. Steve takes a week-long vacation from the family where he finds romance. Irene Ryan, "Granny" on *The Beverly Hillbillies*, has a guest appearance.

Blind Date (1/18/62) *D:* Richard Whorf. Both Mike and Robbie have blind dates, and somehow they end up with the other's date.

Second Time Around (1/25/62) *D:* Richard Whorf. The same female who gave Steve problems in the show's pilot is back trying to land the reluctant widower.

The Girls Next Door (2/1/62) *D:* Richard Whorf. Four airline stewardesses who move in next door prove a big distraction for Robbie.

Bub Gets a Job (2/8/62) *D:* Richard Whorf. Bub is bored and decides he needs a job outside of the home. Raymond Bailey, Mr. Drysdale on *The Beverly Hillbillies,* makes a guest appearance as his employer.

Le Petit Stowaway (2/15/62) *D:* Richard Whorf. Chip stows away when Steve takes a trip to Paris and is befriended by a little girl.

Robbie Valentino (2/22/62) *D:* Richard Whorf. Yet another castaway from *The Beverly Hillbillies* guest stars, Miss Jane herself, Nancy Kulp, who appears as Robbie's 9th grade physics teacher.

The Masterpiece (3/1/62) *D:* Richard Whorf. Chip enters an art contest with a drawing which was actually drawn by Bub.

A Holiday for Tramp (3/8/62) *D:* Richard Whorf. When the Douglas family goes to the train station to meet a returning Steve they take Tramp with them, then lose him to a woman who takes a shine to the shaggy dog. Eve Arden guest stars.

The Big Game (3/15/62) *D:* Richard Whorf. Nancy Kulp returns as Robbie's teacher in a story about Robbie not being able to play in a big game unless he passes a test.

Chip's Party (3/22/62) *D:* Richard Whorf. Chip's tenth birthday party becomes a bust when Steve catches the measles and concerned parents are concerned about sending their children into the sick house.

Casanova Trouble (3/29/62) *D:* Richard Whorf. A female friend of Steve's asks his advice of how to deal with an "older man" who is interested in her daughter. Steve thinks it is Mike, but it turns out to be Robbie! Linda Evans guest stars.

The Pencil Pusher (4/5/62) *D:* Richard Whorf. Chip thinks that Steve's job is unglamorous but then during a visit to an airport an emergency arises which redeems Steve in his son's eyes.

Innocents Abroad (4/12/62) *D:* Richard Whorf. When Robbie hears Steve and an old friend talking about the time they ran away to earn money as kids, Robbie and a friend decide to do the same thing.

Robbie the Caddy (4/19/62) *D:* Richard Whorf. Perpetually in need of money, Robbie gets a job as a caddy during a local golf tournament.

Coincidence (4/26/62) *D:* Richard Whorf. This episode is a fan-favorite. In a *Twilight Zone*-type twist the boys drive Steve to distraction when he is trying to work, causing him to wish he had had girls.

Air Derby (5/3/62) *D:* Richard Whorf. Robbie and another boy compete for a school scholarship in a model airplane contest. Butch Patrick (Eddie on *The Munsters)* has a small role.

Too Much in Common (5/10/62) *D:* Richard Whorf. Mike thinks he and his latest girlfriend are in a rut and thinks they need to see other people.

Chug and Robbie (5/17/62) *D:* Richard Whorf. On his first day at high school, Robbie is assigned a locker with the most popular kid in school, star athlete, Chug Williams. (Ryan O'Neal, who was the original choice to play Mike but vetoed by director Peter Tewksbury, guest stars as Chug.)

Good Influence (5/24/62) *D:* Richard Whorf. Steve wants Chip to go on a week-long vacation with a boy he doesn't like, who's shy and retiring, yet when Chip calls the boy a name he gives the Chipster a black-eye.

The Hippopotamus Foot (5/31/62) *D:* Richard Whorf. Mike and several other students pull a fraternity prank involving the foot prints of a hippopotamus.

The Kibitzer (6/7/62) *D:* Richard Whorf. Two old pals of Bub's try to solve the problems of the Douglas family as they see them.

Season Three

Weekend in Tokyo (9/20/62) *D:* Gene Reynolds. Steve takes the boys with him on a business trip to Japan where Mike falls in love. Ed Hartmann takes helm as the show's new producer and would stay with the show for the remainder of its run. Gene Reynolds, a former actor, takes over as the director and would stay on the show for two seasons before going on to other challenges, including producing and directing *M*A*S*H.*

Robbie's Employment Service (9/27/62) *D:* Gene Reynolds. Robbie and his friend Hank think they will impress the ladies by opening an employment service.

Tramp's First Bite (10/4/62) *D:* Gene Reynolds. Tramp is accused of viciously biting a rich kid (Tim Matheson). Robbie decides to do his own investigation to prove that it was only in self-defense.

Moment of Truth (10/11/62) *D:* Gene Reynolds. Mike invites two girls to the Saturday night dance, thinking that one of them will decline – boy, is he in for a surprise.

Daughter for a Day (10/18/62) *D:* Gene Reynolds. An old friend asks Steve to look after her daughter while she is out of town, but it turns out to be on a weekend where everybody else in the Douglas household is gone, leaving Steve with a "daughter for a day." The little girl, Suzanne Cupito, would go on to play adult roles under the name Morgan Brittany.

The Ghost Next Door (10/25/62) *D:* Richard Whorf. Chip and his friend Sudsy think the house next door to the Douglases is haunted when they see strange happenings on Halloween. (This episode was actually shot during the second season but held over, which is why Richard Whorf, who also co-wrote the story, is the credited director.)

Pretty as a Picture (11/1/62) *D:* Gene Reynolds. Robbie falls for a high school senior who doesn't give him the time of day.

What's Cooking? (11/8/62) *D:* Gene Reynolds. There is a cooking contest at school, and poor Chip is upset because he doesn't have a mother with a recipe to enter. Luckily, Steve does. Fred MacMurray actually enjoyed cooking and had a favorite stew recipe he enjoyed making.

Chip's Last Fight (11/15/62) *D:* Gene Reynolds. Chip is thrown out of the clubhouse because he won't fight an older kid. So he makes plans to fight another kid, which turns out to be the day he is going to have his tonsils taken out.

Steve Gets an 'A' (11/22/62) *D:* Gene Reynolds. Robbie uses an old school paper that Steve wrote that got an 'A' as his own paper, but gets an 'F' which confounds Steve.

Heat Wave (11/29/62) *D:* Gene Reynolds. There is a heat wave which has everyone grumpy except for Steve, until he can't find some plans he was working on and suspects that they may have been given to the kid collecting for a paper drive.

The Beauty Contest (12/6/62) *D:* Gene Reynolds. Mike is the only judge of a beauty contest, which makes tough going when his girlfriend is one of the contestants.

Doctor in the House (12/13/62) *D:* Gene Reynolds. Steve throws his back out and thinks that there is only one doctor who can possibly help him.

Going Steady (12/20/62) *D:* Gene Reynolds. Robbie wants to date a fifteen-year-old cutie, but his mother (played by Lola Albright) is opposed.

Mother Bub (12/27/62) *D:* Gene Reynolds. Bub wants his say when Chip wants to buy a model airplane.

Honorable Grandfather (1/3/63) *D:* Gene Reynolds. Chip gets to go to a party for a Steve's friend's "honorable grandfather." Benson Fong, who plays Steve's friend, would appear in several episodes to come.

How to Impress a Woman (1/10/63) *D:* Gene Reynolds. Mike has to recruit some women on the campus for a fashion show.

Roman Holiday (1/17/63) *D:* Gene Reynolds. Steve is supposed to go to Rome on a business trip and the family wants to come too, but Steve (unlike the trip to Tokyo) is reluctant to do so because, we learn later, it was a special place which he shared with his deceased wife. This is one of the few episodes which actually dealt with Steve's emotions regarding to loss of his wife.

Flashback (1/24/63) *D:* Gene Reynolds. Steve meets a sixteen-year-old girl (Joyce Bulifant) at a bus depot, who reminds him of a girl he had a crush on from his school days. But is she as sweet and wholesome as she seems?

The Dream Book (1/31/63) *D:* Gene Reynolds. Steve is pressured to join his company band as a saxophonist. Warner Klemperer, Col. Klink on *Hogan's Heroes*, appears.

Big Chief Bub (2/7/63) *D:* Gene Reynolds. Chip's Cub Scout den mother may be moving away, who can they get to take her place? Bub?

The Clunky Kid (2/14/63) *D:* Gene Reynolds. Chip's good friend Sudsy starts spending more time with another kid in the neighborhood, virtually ignoring Chip.

Caged Fury (2/21/63) *D:* Gene Reynolds. Robbie's wrestling team needs a tutor and Rob suggests Steve. Soon, the house is quarantined for Diphtheria, which means that Bub won't be able to get together with an old friend.

Make Way for Yesterday (2/28/63) *D:* Gene Reynolds. Robbie and his classmates are holding a carnival and Bub makes some suggestions which sound too old fashioned and corny for their tastes.

Robbie Wins His Letter (3/7/63) *D:* Gene Reynolds. Robbie receives a special achievement award which causes his friends to refer to him as an "egg head." The class gets a guest lecturer who teaches the class how important it is to do well in their studies. This episode guest starred James Stewart, then on reserve duty for the Air National Guard, which volunteered him for this show.

High on the Hog (3/14/63) *D:* Gene Reynolds. Robbie gets involved in yet another scheme to make money quickly without worrying about the consequences.

First Things First (3/28/63) *D:* Gene Reynolds. Poor Mike has an important Air Force Reserve maneuver scheduled on the same weekend as a big date and basketball game.

Bub's Butler (4/4/63) *D:* Gene Reynolds. Bub wins a contest and his prize is his own British butler! (This is the series' 100th episode; today, it would take five seasons for a show to reach this hallmark.)

Francesca (4/11/63) *D:* Gene Reynolds. Steve and Bub are both gone for the weekend and the boys think they are going to spend a carefree weekend until they find a poor little lost girl.

The Rug (4/18/63) *D:* Gene Reynolds. Chip has lost or broken somebody else's property once too often and Steve tells him he will be grounded for a month if he does so again.

The System (4/25/63) *D:* Gene Reynolds. Mike tries to put the principles he learns in his psychology class to work in this episode written by Tim Considine and his brother John.

Let's Take Stock (5/2/63) *D:* Gene Reynolds. Robbie and his classmates are given $10,000 (not real) for an economics project which they are supposed to invest.

Total Recall (5/9/63) *D:* Gene Reynolds. Bub hears that an old classmate, who went on to be a baseball manager, is getting an award. The two had been rivals in school and Bub thinks this classmate lived a more interesting life than he has.

When I Was Your Age (5/16/63) *D:* Gene Reynolds. The boys get sick of Bub telling about "when I was your age…" and how kids in his day had more responsibility than the youth of today; they set out to prove him wrong.

Chip's World (5/23/63) *D:* Gene Reynolds. Chip tries to help a runaway toddler, which means that he will have to leave his house against specific orders from Steve.

Evening with a Star (5/30/63) *D:* Gene Reynolds. Chip decides to offer a raffle for a date with a big star, Bub.

The Date Bureau (6/6/63) *D:* Gene Reynolds. Robbie and his friend Hank set up a match-making service which attempts to match people according to their interests.

Bub's Sacrifice (6/13/63) *D:* Gene Reynolds. Robbie has girl troubles again and Bub decides to help by giving Robbie two tickets to a sold out fight, with the stipulation that he also has to take an aunt to the movies, a chore Bub wants to avoid.

Found Money (6/20/63) *D:* Richard Whorf, Gene Reynolds. The family searches for a valuable but lost stamp. Flashback scenes were directed by Richard Whorf for an episode produced but not shown during the series' second season.

Season Four

Almost the Sound of Music (9/19/63) *D:* Gene Reynolds. Robbie writes a song to impress a girl.

Scotch Broth (9/26/63) *D:* Gene Reynolds. The Douglas inherit a castle in Scotland.

Didya Ever Have One of Those Days? (10/3/63) *D:* Gene Reynolds. It's one of those days where everything seems to be going wrong for Steve.

Dear Robbie (10/10/63) *D:* Gene Reynolds. Robbie writes an "advice to the lovelorn" column for his school's paper.

A Car of His Own (10/17/63) *D:* Gene Reynolds. Mike offers to give Robbie his old car, but Robbie isn't overly happy about it.

How Do You Know? (10/24/63) Mike meets a new girl who blows him away, while Steve tries to bring him down to earth. This episode introduces Meredith MacRae as Sally Morrison, who would become Mike's love interest (and eventually his wife) for the remainder of Tim Considine's time on the show.

My Friend Ernie (10/31/63) *D:* Gene Reynolds. Chip and his new friend Ernie Thompson go on a treasure hunt. This episode introduces Barry Livingston, Stanley's little brother, as "Ernie."

The End of the You-Know-What (11/7/63) *D:* Gene Reynolds. Chip and Ernie, who hear that the earth's days are numbered, decide what they will do with their remaining time left.

The Toupee (11/14/63) *D:* Gene Reynolds. When the sister of an old pal comes visiting, bald Bub buys a toupee which he uses a disagreeably foul-smelling tonic on.

The Ever-Popular Robbie Douglas (11/21/63) *D:* Gene Reynolds. Robbie and another boy who have crushes on the same girl campaign against one another for student council.

The Proposals (11/28/63) *D:* Gene Reynolds. Mike wants to propose to Sally and uses tips he hears from Steve and Bub (William Frawley in flashback wearing a toupee) in how to best propose to a girl. Tom Skerritt plays Steve in his flashback (his voice, however, is MacMurray's).

Steve and the Vikings (12/5/63) *D:* Gene Reynolds. Steve agrees to look after a friend's 17-year-old daughter, who ends up exhausting him.

Par for the Course (12/12/63) *D:* Gene Reynolds. To get on Steve's good side after getting in hot water, Robbie takes up golf, Steve's favorite recreational.

Windfall (12/19/63) *D:* Gene Reynolds. Chip rescues a trapped dog, which leads to his membership in a club.

My Three Sons.

Top Secret (12/26/63) *D:* Gene Reynolds. Steve flies to Washington on a top-secret mission, which everybody in the household wants to know about. Sandra Gould, the second Mrs. Kravitz on *Bewitched*, appears in this episode.

Will Success Spoil Chip Douglas? (1/2/64) *D:* Gene Reynolds. Chip is selected to play an Indian in a play about Christopher Columbus, which pleases that old vaudevillian Bub immensely.

Second Chorus (1/9/64) *D:* Gene Reynolds. Steve meets a cabaret singer and ends up hitting the nightspots with her. Mike and Robbie think they need to protect their old man. Singer Jaye P. Morgan, who went on to her biggest fame as one of the panelists on *The Gong Show*, plays the singer.

Never Look Back (1/16/64) *D:* Gene Reynolds. Steve is looking forward to his twenty-fifth high school reunion, but Bub cautions him that his classmates won't be quite as he remembers them.

Marriage by Proxy (1/23/64) *D:* Gene Reynolds. Mike and Sally decide to learn the truth about marriage by observing and talking to two recently married people.

The Chaperone (1/30/64) *D:* Gene Reynolds. Robbie has a party and Bub is the chaperone. This is the first episode to feature Hank Jones.

My Fair Chinese Lady (2/6/64) *D:* Gene Reynolds. Robbie tries to "Americanize" a traditional Chinese teenager.

House for Sale (2/13/64) *D:* Gene Reynolds. The family thinks they are about to move to Hawaii (where Steve is going on business) when a "For Sale" sign appears on their front yard. Tina Cole, who would join the cast during the series' seventh season as "Katie," makes an early guest appearance.

Stone Frog (2/20/64) *D:* Gene Reynolds. Chip is given a stone frog, which he feels is magical.

Stage Door Bub (2/27/64) *D:* Gene Reynolds. Bub wants to get back into show business, so he goes to work at a local playhouse while an actress at the playhouse takes over for him in the kitchen. Pert Kelton, the original Alice in *The Honeymooners*, guest-stars.

Fish Gotta Swim, Birds Gotta Fly (3/5/64) *D:* Gene Reynolds. Mike tries to teach Sally how to fish since she will be joining the family on a camping trip.

Cherry Blossoms in Bryant Park (3/12/64) *D:* Gene Reynolds. The girl that Mike fell for in Tokyo the previous season (Kimiko) comes to Bryant Park to see if she still loves Mike. She has to know before she gives her love to another man.

What's the Princess Really Like (3/19/64) *D:* Gene Reynolds. Steve's high school sweetheart is now a real-life princess.

The People's House (3/26/64) *D:* Gene Reynolds. Steve wants a date with an attractive magazine editor, so he submits an entry into beautiful home contest sponsored by the magazine. He ends up having to contend with the magazine's not so attractive and formal secretary instead. Jean Stapleton, who would go on to great fame as Edith Bunker on *All in the Family,* guest stars as the secretary.

The Tree (4/2/64) *D:* Gene Reynolds. The community is up in arms when an old tree which stands outside of Robbie's girlfriend's house is scheduled to be cut down.

The Substitute Teacher (4/9/64) *D:* Gene Reynolds. When Robbie's history teacher breaks her leg, the students expect somebody even crankier to substitute but they are in for an unexpected surprise.

Mike Wears the Pants (4/16/64) *D:* Gene Reynolds. Mike and Sally have different ideas about marriage. Beau Bridges guest stars.

The Guys and the Dolls (4/23/64) *D:* Gene Reynolds. Mike tries to raise money for a mute girl's operation, so why not put on a show? Martin Sheen guest stars.

The Ballad of Lissa Stratmeyer (4/30/64) *D:* Gene Reynolds. Talk about girl problems. Robbie's team is on a losing streak and the guys' girlfriends won't speak to them until they start to win!

Tramp Goes to Hollywood (5/7/64) *D:* Gene Reynolds. Tramp gets a Hollywood screen test, is he the new Rin-Tin-Tin?

Adventures in New York (5/14/64) *D:* Gene Reynolds. Mike and Robbie write a song and go to New York to get it published. Don Grady, along with Gary Abrams, wrote the song included in this episode, "A Broken Heart Gets Better."

Huckleberry Douglas (5/21/64) *D:* Gene Reynolds. Chip and Ernie get caught up in the adventures of Tom Sawyer, and try to emulate him.

Guest in the House (5/28/64) *D:* Gene Reynolds. The guest is a delinquent who Steve brings into the house; it will be a long week.

Season Five

Caribbean Cruise (9/17/64) *D:* James V. Kern. A new director joins the series. Steve and Robbie take a Caribbean cruise.

A Serious Girl (9/24/64) *D:* James V. Kern
Robbie, Bub and Ernie have girl problems. Hank Jones appears in this episode.

The Practical Shower (10/1/64) *D:* James V. Kern. Bub plans a bridal shower for Sally.

Dublin's Fair City (10/8/64) *D:* James V. Kern. Bub has a winning lottery ticket and takes the Douglas family on a trip to Ireland. Part one of two.

Dublin's Fair City (10/15/64) *D:* James V. Kern. Part two of two.

One of Our Moose is Missing (10/22/64) *D:* James V. Kern. Steve brings a business associate home for the weekend, forgetting that he has a prior commitment with Chip's Cub Scout troop.

Lady President (10/29/64) *D:* James V. Kern. Steve escorts a visiting congresswoman. (I wonder if this episode had anything to do with Fred's current film release that fall of '64, *Kisses for my President?*)

A Touch of Larceny (11/5/64) *D:* James V. Kern. The school bully gives Chip lessons.

Goodbye Again (11/12/64) *D:* James V. Kern. Cynthia Pepper makes a one-time guest appearance as Mike's old girlfriend who he has a hard time telling that he has a fiancée. John and Tim Considine co-wrote this episode.

The Coffeehouse Set (11/19/64) *D:* James V. Kern. Robbie gets a job as a singer-guitarist in a coffeehouse. Tina Cole, Hank Jones and Jamie Farr (Corporal Klinger on *M*A*S*H)*, guest star. Songs, "Where Did the Years Go?" and "Dodge City Walk," were written by Don Grady and Ed Hartmann

The Lotus Blossom (11/26/64) *D:* James V. Kern. Steve arranges a dinner party to help bring a pretty waitress out of her shell.

First You're a Tadpole (12/3/64) *D:* James V. Kern. Don Grady co-wrote this episode (with Gary Abrams) about Robbie seeking Sally's advice on his latest flame.

You're in My Power (12/10/64) *D:* James V. Kern. Robbie dabbles in hypnotism.

The In-Law Whammy (12/17/64) *D:* James V. Kern. Mike meets his future father-in-law, played by *Family Affair's* Sebastian (Mr. French) Cabot.

Robbie and the Nurse (12/24/64) *D:* James V. Kern. Robbie breaks his leg and at first it's a bummer to be in the hospital until he gets a look at his pretty nurse.

Divorce Bryant Park Style (12/31/64) *D:* James V. Kern. Mike and Sally get cold feet when their best friends get a divorce.

A Woman's Work (1/7/65) *D:* James V. Kern. Bub is on vacation, and so Steve pinch-hits for him, discovering that it isn't easy running a household.

Here Comes Charley (1/14/65) *D:* James V. Kern. This episode introduces William Demarest as "Uncle Charley," who arrives unexpectedly in the nick-of-time due to Bub leaving for Ireland.

Charley and the Kid (1/21/65) *D:* James V. Kern. A little girl becomes intrigued in Uncle Charley while staying with the Douglases.

He Wanted Wings (1/28/65) *D:* James V. Kern. Robbie buys an antique aircraft. Is the title a play on Fred's 1938 film *Men with Wings?*

Be My Guest (2/4/65) *D:* James V. Kern. The Douglases want to join a country club, but does the club want them?

Lady in the Air (2/11/65) *D:* James V. Kern. Steve is designing a plane for a woman aviator he finds attractive.

Hawaiian Cruise (2/18/65) *D:* James V. Kern. Steve had been planning a cruise to Hawaii, but has to cancel, so Charley and the boys plan a luau in the backyard.

The Teenagers (2/25/65) *D:* James V. Kern. Both Robbie and Chip face typical teenage problems involving girls.

Mexico Ole (3/4/65) *D:* James V. Kern. While on a family vacation in Mexico, Robbie (naturally) falls for a girl.

Fountain of Youth (3/11/65) *D:* James V. Kern. Charley and Robbie go to see an old vaudeville pal of Charlie's, but the old pal fails to recognize Charley.

It's a Dog's Life (3/18/65) *D:* James V. Kern. What happened to the blueprints that Steve was working on and Charley's chocolate chip cookies? Maybe Tramp knows?

The Sure Thing (3/25/65) *D:* James V. Kern. Can Robbie take the place of a race horse that loses his mascot?

Chip the Trapper (4/1/65) *D:* James V. Kern. Chip gets a job in the trapping business.

Steve and the Computer (4/8/65) *D:* James V. Kern. A computer selects different names for Mike and Sally.

Tamp and the Prince (4/15/65) *D:* James V. Kern. Tramp runs away from home rather than confront a cat. Co-written by Don Grady.

Chip O' The Island (4/22/65) *D:* James V. Kern. Charley, Robbie and Chip take a trip to the Fuji islands.

The Glass Sneaker (4/29/65) *D:* James V. Kern. A teenage boy's Cinderella story, featuring Chip.

All the Weddings (5/6/65) *D:* James V. Kern. Sally's mother decides to take over all arrangements for the upcoming wedding.

The Leopard's Spots (5/13/65) *D:* James V. Kern. Sally's beautiful but irresponsible cousin comes to visit.

Uncle Charley and the Redskins (5/20/65) *D:* James V. Kern. Charley allows an Indian family to hold a ceremony in the Douglas backyard, which at one time was an Indian tribal ground.

Season Six

The First Marriage (9/16/65) *D:* James V. Kern. Mike and Sally tie the knot and Steve begins to feel old. The final episode to feature Tim Considine and Meredith MacRae. Barry Livingston, as "Ernie," joins as a regular member of the cast.

Red Tape Romance (9/23/65) *D:* James V. Kern. Steve makes plans to adopt Ernie, who has lost his parents, and in the meanwhile is attracted to a beautiful adoption official (played by Vera Miles).

Brother Ernie (9/30/65) *D:* James V. Kern. One problem arises in the Douglas' efforts to adopt Ernie: there is no lady of the house.

Robbie and the Chorus Girl (10/16/65) *D:* James V. Kern. Is Robbie being corrupted by a chorus girl?

There's a What in the Attic? (10/21/65) *D:* James V. Kern. This episode is a fan favorite about Ernie reporting to a sleepy Steve that there is a lion loose in the house.

Office Mother (10/28/65) *D:* James V. Kern. Steve hires a new secretary (played by Joan Blondell), who runs the office like a kitchen.

Mary Lou (11/4/65) *D:* James V. Kern. Chip falls for an older woman who is in the 9th grade.

Monsters and Junk Like That (11/11/65) *D:* James V. Kern. Steve gets stuck in a robot suit and ends up having to wear it to a father-son event with Chip.

Charley and the Dancing Lesson (11/18/65) *D:* James V. Kern. Uncle Charley takes dance lessons with an alluring instructor (Joanna Moore).

My Son the Ballerina (11/25/65) *D:* James V. Kern. Robbie wants to join the track team. So, to gain better timing he takes ballet lessons.

The Ernie Report (12/2/65) *D:* James V. Kern. Robbie and Chip are spending more time with girls than Ernie, leaving the little guy feeling ignored.

The Hong Kong Story (12/9/65) *D:* James V. Kern. On a Hong Kong visit, Charley seeks out his girlfriend of 30 years ago.

Marriage and Stuff (12/16/65) *D:* James V. Kern. The family thinks that Steve is making secret plans of getting remarried

Douglas A Go-Go (12/23/65) *D:* James V. Kern. Chip plans his first "mixed" party, meaning including girls.

Charley the Pigeon (12/30/65) *D:* James V. Kern. When two girls take Robbie for $50 at pool, that old pool shark Charley plans to get even.

What About Harry? (1/6/66) *D:* James V. Kern. A "shaggy dog" stray takes to Steve, and howls every time Steve attempts to leave the house.

From Maggie With Love (1/13/66) *D:* James V. Kern. One of the richest women in the world falls for Steve!

Robbie and the Slave Girl (1/20/66) *D:* James V. Kern. Robbie saves a Chinese girl and she becomes his slave.

Steve and the Huntress (1/27/66) *D:* James V. Kern. Steve is invited on a safari by a beautiful female explorer (played by Terry Moore).

Robbie the College Man (2/3/66) *D:* James V. Kern. Robbie wants to live away from home while attending college so he takes on more than he can handle job-wise. Hank Jones guest-stars.

Whatever Happened to Baby Chip? (2/10/66) *D:* James V. Kern. Chip grows shoulder-length hair, so Steve thinks he needs to spend more time with him. Jay (Dennis the Menace) North guest stars.

Robbie and the Little Stranger (2/17/66) *D:* James V. Kern. Robbie has an argument with his girlfriend while babysitting and ends up taking the little baby home with him. Tina Cole guest-stars.

Call Her Max (2/24/66) *D:* James V. Kern. Steve and Chip fall for two "tomboy"-type females.

Kid Brother Blues (3/3/66) *D:* James V. Kern. Robbie has a date which Chip disrupts.

Robbie's Double Life (3/10/66) *D:* James V. Kern. Robbie dates two girls at one time. Is it too good to last? You bet.

Our Boy in Washington (3/17/66) *D:* James V. Kern. Ernie sends a thank you note to France for the Statue of Liberty and the French government invites the Douglases to Washington.

Ernie and that Woman (3/24/66) *D:* James V. Kern. Fourth-grader Ernie falls for a sixth grader.

The State vs. Chip Douglas (3/31/66) *D:* James V. Kern. Chip is accused of stealing a valuable penny from Ernie. Jimmy Mathers (the brother of Jerry Mathers) guest stars.

A Hunk of Hardware (4/7/66) *D:* James V. Kern. Ernie feels he has let the Douglas family down when he fails to win a trophy.

The Wrong Robbie (4/14/66) *D:* James V. Kern. A boy who looks like Robbie causes Robbie headaches on campus.

The Wheels (4/21/66) *D:* James V. Kern. Robbie loses his driving privileges when a girl on campus gets a ticket driving his car.

London Memories (4/28/66) *D:* James V. Kern. Steve falls for a widow after returning from a trip to Britain.

Season Seven

Stag at Bay (9/15/66) *D:* James V. Kern. A lovely female dancer stays with the Douglases after she is evicted from her apartment.

Fly Away Home (9/22/66) *D:* James V. Kern. Steve returns to his hometown and meets up with a former girlfriend, who he barely recognizes anymore.

Forget Me Not (9/29/66) *D:* James V. Kern. An ex-girlfriend of Steve's acts like Steve is on the verge of proposing to her. Joan Caulfield, who worked with Fred in *The Rains of Ranchipur,* guest stars.

Good Guys Finish Last (10/6/66) *D:* James V. Kern. Steve and Chip take part in a father vs. son quiz show, and Steve's team loses. Jay North guest stars.

Arrivederci, Robbie (10/13/66) *D:* James V. Kern. When Robbie takes an old-fashioned Italian girl for a walk in the park, tradition dictates he is supposed to marry her.

If at First (10/20/66) *D:* James V. Kern. Steve meets Robbie's new girlfriend, a meter maid who gives him a parking ticket. Yvonne (Batgirl) Craig guest stars.

Robbie's Underground Movie (11/3/66) *D:* James V. Kern. Robbie has to make a homemade movie for his cinema class.

Fiddler Under the Roof (11/10/66) *D:* James V. Kern. Uncle Charley attempts to teach Ernie how to play the violin.

Happy Birthday World (11/17/66) *D:* James V. Kern. Robbie's latest get-rich-quick scheme: starting a birthday cake company from home.

The Awkward Age (12/1/66) *D:* James V. Kern. Steve and Robbie both are interested in the same girl (played by Susan Oliver).

A Real Nice Time (12/8/66) *D:* James V. Kern. Chip gets his fifteen minutes when he dances with a movie star.

Falling Star (12/15/66) *D:* James V. Kern. Steve tries to help a fading singer resurrect her career by having her sing with Robbie's band. Jaye P. Morgan makes a second guest appearance.

Tramp or Ernie (12/22/66) *D:* James V. Kern. A decision has to be made when Ernie develops an allergy to Tramp. *The Brady Bunch* did a similarly-themed episode three years later involving Jan.

Grandma's Girl (12/29/66) *D:* James V. Kern. Chip rents a horse and buggy to impress a girl on a date. Jeanette Nolan plays the girl's old-fashioned grandmother.

You Saw a What? (1/5/67) *D:* James V. Kern. Ernie thinks he sees a flying saucer.

Both Your Houses (1/12/67) *D:* James V. Kern. Robbie falls for a neighbor girl in this Romeo and Juliet parody. Kevin Corcoran, who played Fred's youngest son in *The Shaggy Dog* and *Bon Voyage!*, appears.

My Pal Dad (1/19/67) *D:* James V. Kern. Robbie and Chip want to get out of the annual family fishing trip.

TV or Not TV (1/26/67) *D:* James V. Kern. The constant fights over what the family watches on television causes Uncle Charley to ban television for a week.

My Dad, the Athlete (2/2/67) *D:* James V. Kern. Steve competes against other fathers in a race.

The Good Earth (2/9/67) *D:* James V. Kern. Uncle Charley is cheated when he buys a vacation lot.

My Son, the Bullfighter (2/16/67) *D:* James V. Kern. To impress a girl (naturally) Robbie agrees to compete in a bullfight. Alejandro Ray guest stars.

The Best Man (2/23/67) *D:* James V. Kern. Robbie is asked to be best man at the wedding of a girl he once wanted to marry.

Now, In My Day (3/2/67) *D:* James V. Kern. Chip tries going steady with two girls at once.

Melinda (3/9/67) *D:* James V. Kern
Steve fixes Chip up with the daughter of a woman he is dating.

Charley O' The Seven Seas (3/16/67) *D:* James V. Kern. Uncle Charley's tales of adventure on the high seas prompt Ernie's teacher to quit her job and seek adventure. Jan Clayton guest stars.

Help, The Gypsies are Coming (3/23/67) *D:* James V. Kern. A band of gypsies takes over the Douglas' front yard.

Ernie's Folly (3/30/67) *D:* James V. Kern. Steve can't find the time to help Ernie with a science project, which leads to disaster.

Ernie's Crowd (4/6/67) *D:* James V. Kern. Ernie becomes a third wheel when he starts accompanying Chip, Robbie and Steve on their dates.

Ernie and the O'Grady (4/13/67) *D:* James V. Kern. Kind-hearted Ernie brings home a hobo (Eddie Foy, Jr.) who decides to stay.

The Sky is Falling (4/20/67) *D:* James V. Kern. Robbie works part time selling real-estate and the windfall is so good he contemplates quitting college.

So Long, Charley, Hello (4/27/67) *D:* James V. Kern. An old friend of Charley's wants him to join him for a job on a fishing boat.

Weekend in Paradise (5/11/67) *D:* James V. Kern. The family spends the weekend in Hawaii and each finds adventure and even a bit of romance.

Season Eight

Moving Day (9/9/67) *D:* Fred de Cordova. The Douglases have relocated to California (where Steve's job has transferred him) and they all feel initial homesickness.

Robbie Loves Katie (9/16/67) *D:* Fred de Cordova
Robbie thinks he should end his relationship with Katie but ends up proposing instead.

Inspection of the Groom (9/23/67) *D:* Fred de Cordova. Katie's family inspects the groom to be, Robbie.

Countdown to Marriage (9/30/67) *D:* Fred de Cordova. On the eve of their wedding both Katie and Robbie get cold feet.

Wedding Bells (10/7/67) *D:* Fred de Cordova. Katie and Robbie get married.

The Homecoming (10/14/67) *D:* Fred de Cordova. The honeymoon is over when Katie moves into the formerly all-male Douglas household.

My Wife, the Waitress (10/21/67) *D:* Fred de Cordova. Katie gets a job as a cigarette girl to help with expenses.

The Computer Picnic (10/28/67) *D:* Fred de Cordova. A computer is used to select mates to a school picnic.

The Chameleon (11/4/67) *D:* Fred de Cordova. Ernie is girl-shy even when it comes to having them as a friend.–

Designing Woman (11/11/67) *D:* Fred de Cordova. Steve falls for an attractive woman but only Katie sees her for what she really is. Yet another MacMurray film co-star Anne Baxter (*Smoky*) guest-stars.

Ernie, The Bluebeard (11/18/67) *D:* Fred de Cordova. Girl-shy Ernie ends up with two dates to a school dance. Maureen (Marcia Brady) McCormick guest stars.

Heartbeat (11/25/67) *D:* Fred de Cordova. Shades of Poe's *The Tell-Tale Heart* when Katie, alone at home, thinks she hears a loud heartbeat.

The Aunt Who Came to Dinner (12/2/67) *D:* Fred de Cordova. Marsha Hunt plays Katie's Aunt who takes over the Douglas household when she pays a visit.

Leaving the Nest (12/9/67) *D:* Fred de Cordova. Robbie and Katie decide it's time to move to an apartment of their own.

You're Driving Me Crazy (12/16/67) *D:* Fred de Cordova. Katie and Chip both have recently gotten their drivers license, so who caused the big scratch on the family car?

Liverpool Saga (12/23/67) *D:* Fred de Cordova. Chip asks a long-haired boy from Liverpool to join his rock 'n' roll band. Jeremy Clyde of "Chad and Jeremy" fame guest stars.

The Chaperones (12/30/67) *D:* Fred de Cordova. Chip and his friends want to spend a weekend at a cabin, so Robbie and Katie chaperone.

Green-eyed Robbie (1/6/68) *D:* Fred de Cordova. Katie agrees to tutor a former boyfriend.

Charley's Tea (1/13/68) *D:* Fred de Cordova.

Ernie, the Jinx (1/20/68) *D:* Fred de Cordova. Ernie feels he has become a jinx when bad things begin to happen to people he encounters.

Ernie and Zsa Zsa (1/27/68) *D:* Fred de Cordova. Ernie and Tramp end up spending the day with Zsa Zsa Gabor when they go out exploring Hollywood.

A Horse for Uncle Charley (2/3/68) *D:* Fred de Cordova. Uncle Charley buys a race horse.

Dear Enemy (2/10/68) *D:* Fred de Cordova. Robbie is on military maneuvers, and somehow each Douglas family member ends up becoming a military prisoner during the war games.

Uncle Charley's Aunt (2/17/68) *D:* Fred de Cordova. Here's your chance to see William Demarest in drag when he is forced to walk home from a lodge club variety show dressed as a chorus girl!

The Standing Still Tour (2/24/68) *D:* Fred de Cordova. Ernie and Uncle Charley are left at home while everybody else is out on a romantic date.

Honorable Guest (3/2/68) *D:* Fred de Cordova. The Douglas' planned camping trip is cancelled when their old Chinese friends from Bryant Park pay a visit.

The Perfect Separation (3/9/68) *D:* Fred de Cordova. A relationship goes astray during Robbie and Katie's first dinner party.

Gossip, Inc. (3/16/68) *D:* Fred de Cordova. Steve's co-workers get the idea he's a bigamist.

The Masculine Mystique (3/23/68) *D:* Fred de Cordova. Ernie and his best friend have a falling-out.

The Tire Thief (3/30/68) *D:* Fred de Cordova. The police think that Ernie and his friend are stealing car hubcaps.

Season Nine

The Great Pregnancy (9/28/68) *D:* Fred de Cordova. Katie learns she is pregnant and poor Robbie seems left behind.

Dr. Osborne, M.D. (10/5/68) *D:* Fred de Cordova. Katie wants one pediatrician (a woman), while Robbie wants another (a man).

Life Begins in Katie (10/12/68) *D:* Fred de Cordova. With a baby on the way, Robbie decides he must act very mature from now on. Butch Patrick guest stars.

The Grandfathers (10/19/68) *D:* Fred de Cordova. When a General finds out that Steve is an expected grandfather, he suddenly becomes easier to work with. Arthur O'Connell guest stars.

The Baby Nurse (10/26/68) *D:* Fred de Cordova. Uncle Charley decides to take up babysitting so he can gain experience in dealing with babies.

Big ol' Katie (11/9/68) *D:* Fred de Cordova. Katie can't believe how huge she has become, until she learns she is expecting triplets.

My Three Grandsons (11/16/68) *D:* Fred de Cordova. When Katie gives birth to triplets, Steve can't believe that he is a grandfather x three.

Tea for Three (11/23/68) *D:* Fred de Cordova. The triplets come home and Robbie is again feeling a bit left-out.

Back to Earth (11/30/68) *D:* Fred de Cordova. To help support his family, Robbie decides to quit school and get a full time job.

First Night Out (12/7/68) *D:* Fred de Cordova. Rose Marie plays a babysitter to the triplets.

Casanova O'Casey (12/14/68) *D:* Fred de Cordova. Uncle Charley suddenly finds himself with many dates after his last girlfriend marries another man.

Expendable Katie (12/21/68) *D:* Fred de Cordova. Katie is gone for the day and it takes three cleaning ladies to clean up the house!

The New Room (12/28/68) *D:* Fred de Cordova. The family decides to add on a room, but the contractor only seems to take to Katie.

The Fountain of Youth (1/4/69) *D:* Fred de Cordova. A widow seems to find Steve attractive at first, but then for some reason seems to cool on him.

Three's a Crowd (1/11/69) *D:* Fred de Cordova. The triplets go back to the hospital for proper identification when the family can't tell who is who.

Chip and Debbie (1/18/69) *D:* Fred de Cordova. Chip becomes engaged to a pretty classmate (Angela Cartwright).

What Did You Do Today, Grandpa? (1/25/69) *D:* Fred de Cordova. Steve goes undercover to help capture some enemy spies.

Chip on Wheels (2/1/69) *D:* Fred de Cordova. Steve gives Chip a used car for his birthday and expects his son to be more excited than he is.

Honorable Expectant Grandfather (2/8/69) *D:* Fred de Cordova. Steve's Chinese friend from Bryant Park days is concerned about the man his daughter has married, a hippy.

Other Woman (2/15/69) *D:* Fred de Cordova. Chip and Ernie think that Robbie may be cheating on Katie.

Goodbye Forever (2/22/69) *D:* Fred de Cordova. Ernie's best friend is moving away.

The O'Casey Scandal (3/1/69) *D:* Fred de Cordova. Uncle Charley starts paying attention to Ernie's girlfriend's grandmother.

Ernie's Pen Pal (3/8/69) *D:* Fred de Cordova. A pen pal of Ernie's from Latin America shows up at the Douglas home unexpectedly.

Ernie the Transmitter (3/15/69) *D:* Fred de Cordova. Ernie thinks he has ESP and tries to avert disaster for Robbie and Katie.

The Matchmakers (3/22/69) *D:* Fred de Cordova. Steve and a business buddy try to bring their kids together only to discover that they can't stand each other. Don DeFore guest stars.

Ernie is Smitten (3/29/69) *D:* Fred de Cordova. Ernie tries to change his image to attract a girl. The little girl is played by Jennifer Edwards, the daughter of director Blake Edwards and stepdaughter of Julie Andrews.

Two O'Clock Feeding (4/12/69) *D:* Fred de Cordova. A young couple turns to Steve to help save their marriage.

Teacher's Pet (4/19/69) *D:* Fred de Cordova. Sylvia Sidney, who worked with Fred in the 1936 film *The Trail of the Lonesome Pine,* guest stars as Ernie's strict English teacher.

Season Ten

The First Meeting (10/4/69) *D:* Fred de Cordova. Ernie complains about his new "mean" teacher and so Steve goes to investigate and discovers he is attracted to the widowed Mrs. Harper. Beverly Garland joins the cast.

Instant Co-Worker (10/11/69) *D:* Fred de Cordova. Robbie gets a job at Steve's firm.

Is it Love? (10/18/69) *D:* Fred de Cordova. The family tries to convince Steve that Barbara is the one.

A Ring for Barbara (10/25/69) *D:* Fred de Cordova. While detained at a police station, Steve proposes to Barbara.

The Littlest Rebel (11/1/69) *D:* Fred de Cordova. Barbara tries to gain acceptance from the Douglas clan.

Two Weeks to Go (11/8/69) *D:* Fred de Cordova. Steve and Barbara try to decide what form their wedding ceremony will take.

One Week to Go (11/15/69) *D:* Fred de Cordova. An argument causes Steve and Barbara to consider calling off their wedding.

Came the Day (11/22/69) *D:* Fred de Cordova. It's the wedding day for Steve and Barbara.

Mexican Honeymoon (11/29/69) *D:* Fred de Cordova. Steve and Barbara share their honeymoon at a resort with many younger just married couples.

After You, Alfonse (12/13/69) *D:* Fred de Cordova. Katie decides that Uncle Charley needs help with his manners, and puts Robbie up to the task of talking to him about it.

Rough on Dodie (12/20/69) *D:* Fred de Cordova. Dodie finds that having all-male stepbrothers can be physically rough.

Silver Threads (12/27/69) *D:* Fred de Cordova. Katie discovers she has some gray hairs.

It's a Woman's World (1/3/70) *D:* Fred de Cordova. Dodie has a school play and Steve is cast as a tree.

Table for Eight (1/10/70) *D:* Fred de Cordova. It's Barbara's first dinner party as Mrs. Steve Douglas.

Double Jealousy (1/17/70) *D:* Fred de Cordova. Rob's new secretary may be too good looking for Katie's liking.

Dodie's Tonsils (1/24/70) *D:* Fred de Cordova. Dodie needs her tonsils out and wants Steve to stay overnight with her at the hospital.

Who is Sylvia? (1/31/70) *D:* Fred de Cordova. An old girlfriend of Steve's comes to down and causes Barbara some jealous moments. Jane Wyman guest stars.

You Can't Go Home (2/7/70) *D:* Fred de Cordova. Robbie pays a visit to Bryant Park, where he grew up.

Guest in the House (2/14/70) *D:* Fred de Cordova. Steve is out of town so it is up to new step-mom Barbara to meet with one of Chip's teachers.

Charley's Cello (2/21/70) *D:* Fred de Cordova. Charley plays his cello alone, causing Barbara to think he is lonely.

The Honeymoon is Over (2/28/70) *D:* Fred de Cordova. Steve and Robbie are kept busy at work, causing Barbara and Katie to pay them a late-night visit.

Baubles, Bangles and Beatrice (3/7/70) *D:* Fred de Cordova. Dodie's six-year-old friend falls for Ernie.

Mister X (3/14/70) *D:* Fred de Cordova. Who is the bearded man hanging around the Douglas house?

Dodie's Dilemma (3/21/70) *D:* Fred de Cordova. Dodie needs her big, older brother's help with a school bully. Erin Moran (Joanie on *Happy Days)* guest stars.

Love Thy Neighbor (3/28/70) *D:* Fred de Cordova. Robbie and Katie clash with the new young couple next door. Jerry (Beaver) Mathers guest stars.

J.P. Douglas (4/4/70) *D:* Fred de Cordova. Chip tries to get rich quick while he is still young and can enjoy it.

Season Eleven

The First Anniversary (9/19/70) *D:* Fred de Cordova. Dodie tries to throw a surprise party for Steve and Barbara on their anniversary.

The Once-Over (9/26/70) *D:* Fred de Cordova. Chip's girlfriend Polly (Ronne Troup) suggests that they elope.

The Return of Albert (10/3/70) *D:* Fred de Cordova. One of Barbara's ex-flames (played by Craig Stevens) arrives in town.

The Non-Proposal (10/10/70) *D:* Fred de Cordova. Polly thinks that she is engaged to Chip.

Polly Wants a Douglas (10/17/70) *D:* Fred de Cordova. Polly again suggests to Chip that they elope, only to have Chip turn her down.

The Cat Burglars (10/31/70) *D:* Fred de Cordova. Steve is dressed up for a costume party, but police think he's a cat burglar.

The Elopement (11/7/70) *D:* Fred de Cordova. Chip and Polly decide to ask their parents permission to elope!

The Honeymoon (11/14/70) *D:* Fred de Cordova. After their elopement Polly and Chip go to Las Vegas for their honeymoon.

One by One They Go (11/21/70) Chip has to face his father-in-law now that Chip has eloped with his daughter.

My Four Women (11/28/70) Steve is recruited to be a model in a fashion show, but gets last-minute jitters.

The Bride Went Home (12/5/70) After Chip gets ill eating Polly's cooking, she decides to leave him.

The Power of Suggestions (12/12/70) Ernie uses the Douglases as guinea pigs in a psychology experiment, without their knowledge.

St. Louis Blues (12/19/70) Katie's mother takes the triplets to St. Louis for a month, and Katie and Rob find they miss their offspring.

The Liberty Bell (1/2/71) Rob is into motorcycles and his friend (played by Sal Mineo) suggests they take a motorcycle trip together.

The Love God (1/9/71) Dodie gets a crush on her teacher, who was once one of Barbara's students! Jodie Foster guest stars.

The New Vice President (1/16/71) Steve is up for a promotion, but there may be a roadblock in the way.

Robbie's Honey (1/23/71) Robbie is observed kissing his secretary, and without his wedding ring on.

Ernie's Drives (1/30/71) Ernie and his friend try to come up with a way to take their dates to the school dance.

Dodie Goes Downtown (2/6/71)Ernie has to take care of Dodie, but she disappears on a bus headed downtown while he wasn't looking.

The Recital (2/20/71)Dodie and two other little girls rehearse for a recital at the Douglas house.

Debbie (2/27/71)A young woman has the Douglas men wrapped around her finger while the Douglas women fume.

Fit the Crime (3/6/71) Ernie is again Dodie's babysitter and once again things don't go right, so he gets grounded along with Dodie.

The Return of Terrible Tom (3/13/71) Charley can't believe that his old shipmate has found manners.

After the Honeymoon (3/20/71) It's hard finding a place to live with three babies. This was a proposed pilot for a series for Don Grady and Tina Cole.

Season Twelve

The Advent of Fergus (9/13/71) Steve's Scottish cousin Fergus arrives. Fred MacMurray plays Fergus, but his voice is dubbed by Alan Cailou.

Fergus for Sale (9/20/71) Charley and Fergus feud, meanwhile Fergus is looking for a wife.

Lady Douglas (9/27/71) Anne Francis plays the waitress that Fergus falls in love with.

Goodbye Fergus (10/4/71) Fergus and his new bride leave for Scotland. Anne Francis guest-stars.

Four for the Road (10/18/71) The triplets run away when their sitter isn't looking.

Polly the Pigeon (10/25/71) Polly can't resist buying when a door-to-door salesman arrives.

Happy Birthday Anyway (11/1/71) The Douglas women are sick and tired of the Douglas men forgetting their birthdays.

Proxy Parents (11/8/71) Chip and Polly look after Dodie and the triplets over a long weekend.

The Enthusiasts (11/15/71) Steve is embarrassed by Barbara when she gets over enthusiastic at a dinner party.

Katie's Career (11/22/71) Katie gets a job singing at a coffee house.

Polly's Secret Life (11/29/71) Polly thinks that Chip is losing interest in her.

The Sound of Music (12/6/71) Uncle Charley fills in as a cello teacher.

The Triplets (1/13/72) The triplets are selected for a television commercial.

Three for School (1/20/72) Katie gets a temporary job as a secretary and enrolls the triplets into nursery school.

Alfred (1/27/72) A little boy in Dodie's class develops a crush on her.

Buttons and Beaux (2/3/72) The guys try to cheer Katie up, who is down in the dumps with Robbie away.

Peanuts (2/17/72) The Douglases have to roast lots of peanuts to help Dodie at a school sale.

Bad Day for Steve (2/24/72) Steve is having an accident-prone day. Is it in the stars?

Second Banana (3/2/72) Barbara wins a trip to Hawaii, thanks to her cooking skills.

Bad Day for Barbara (3/16/72) Now it's Barbara's turn for a bad day.

The Birth of Arfie (3/23/72) When Dodie is traumatized by Tramp's disappearance, Barbara takes her to a child psychologist. (Don't worry, Tramp will be okay.)

Lonesome Katie (3/30/72) The wife of one of Robbie's colleagues files for divorce due to her husband's frequent absences, which causes Katie distress.

Barbara Lost (4/6/72) Chip has to choose between college and being in a rock band.

Whatever Happened to Ernie? (4/13/72) Steve's boss thinks that Steve and Barbara are model parents, until Ernie suddenly takes a change for the worse.

Reviews

"*My Three Sons,* the new Fred MacMurray-Bill Frawley comedy out of Don Fedderson's packaging outfit, shapes up as an amiable, leisurely family comedy." *Variety,* 10/5/60.

"Assets of the show remain its characters and players. Led by Fred MacMurray, the people are likable and attractive. That praise goes for the big mutt, too, a member of the all-male family. No one expects anything big to happen in this situation comedy series, but the wrinkles in the proceedings should produce laughter ripples." *Variety,* 10/4/61.

"As situation comedies go, *My Three Sons* is pleasant and at times even humorous ... The series has, of course, a great deal going for it in a couple of old hands, Fred MacMurray and Bill Frawley, who have real comedy style and, amazingly, can still go through the hackneyed paces as though genuinely inspired. Some of their professionalism seems to have rubbed off on MacMurray's three video sons, Tim Considine, Don Grady and Stanley Livingston, and that makes for a happy outlook for several seasons to come." *Variety,* 9/25/63.

"In the ABC-TV trend to veteran, established Hollywood stars - Bing Crosby, Mickey Rooney, George Burns - fronting situation comedy, Fred MacMurray stands out as a genuine pioneer. He's been the main attraction of *My Three Sons,* and the comedy last week started its fifth season." *Variety,* 9/23/64.

"... Fred MacMurray ... continues to deliver in topnotch fashion, underplaying it nicely, to let the other participants deliver some of the zanies and reap the yocks. William Demarest is first rate as the irascible uncle whose bark covers the heart of gold ... Don Grady as the oldest son who is on the verge of maturity, and Stanley and Barry Livingston as the two younger offspring, all bring to the show a naturalness that wears well and lends credibility to a format that could easily become cute." *Variety,* 9/21/66.

"...With the aid of Mr. MacMurray's attractively relaxed performance, the weekly situations catch the humor of growing up. Without becoming stuffy about it, the program also often delicately points up a wholesome moral." Jack Gould, *The New York Times,* 12/17/67.

"*My Three Sons* remains good entertainment for three year olds; however, it's embarrassing for an adult. The laugh track's sense of humor is very strange indeed. This show is bland and innocuous to the point of nothingness. Which is not gainsaying the fact that 'Sons' is a big hit in silent majorityland, and undoubtedly will remain so." *Variety,* 9/23/70.

"If demographics continue to be the name of the video game this season, then, for better or worse, CBS has staked out its claim on the Golden Agers on Monday nights. For those who remember when Fred MacMurray starred in 40 years of sex comedies with the likes of Carole Lombard and Madeleine Carroll, it's a shoo-in … MacMurray and Demarest manage to lug the cumbersome vehicle along, sloughing off pieces of the scripters' maudlin sentimentality along the way … *My Three Sons* has been altered more times than it has been changed over the years, and each time the cast gets bigger and its plots get smaller … Growing in numbers though it is, the supporting cast is easily obscured by the stars." *Variety,* 9/22/71.

Seasonal Rankings

1960-61 Season: # 13	*1960-61 Season:* # 31
1961-62 Season: # 11	*1967-68 Season:* # 24
1962-63 Season: # 28	*1968-69 Season:* # 14
1963-64 Season: # 27	*1969-70 Season:* # 15
1964-65 Season: # 13	*1970-71 Season:* # 19
1965-66 Season: # 15	

Selected Fred MacMurray Television Appearances

1952 *All Star Revue* (NBC)
The Colgate Comedy Hour (NBC)
1953 *The Bob Hope Buick Show* (NBC)
All Star Revue (1953)
1954 *The George Gobel Show* (NBC)
The Jack Benny Program (CBS)
1955 *GE Theater: The Bachelor's Bride* (CBS)

The George Gobel Show (NBC)
The Colgate Comedy Hour (NBC)
1956   *Climax! The Louella Parsons Story* (CBS)
       Screen Directors Playhouse: It's a Most Unusual Day (NBC)
       The George Gobel Show (NBC)
1957   *The 20th Century-Fox Hour: False Witness* (CBS)
       The Dinah Shore Chevy Show (NBC)
       The George Gobel Show (NBC)
       The $64,000 Question (CBS)
       Shower of Stars (CBS)
       What's My Line, Mystery Guest (CBS)
1958   *The Lucille Ball-Desi Arnaz Show:* "Lucy Hunts Uranium"
       (CBS)
       December Bride (CBS)
       The George Gobel Show (NBC)
       GE Theater: One is a Wanderer (CBS)
       Cimarron City: I, The People (NBC)
1959   *The Ed Sullivan Show* (CBS)
       I've Got a Secret (CBS)
       What's My Line, Mystery Guest (CBS)
       Disneyland '59 (ABC)
1960   *U.S. Steel Hour: The American Cowboy* (CBS)
       The Steve Allen Plymouth Show (NBC)
1961   *This is Your Life: William Frawley* (ABC)
1963   *The Andy Williams Show* (NBC)
       Art Linkletter's House Party (CBS)
       The Bob Hope Show (NBC)
       Andy Williams' New Year's Eve Special (NBC)
1964   *Opening Night at the World's Fair* (NBC)
       Hollywood Palace (ABC)
       The Andy Williams Show (NBC)
       The 36th Annual Academy Awards, Presenter, Best Art
       Direction/Set Decoration (ABC)
1967   *The 39th Annual Academy Awards*, Presenter, Best Special/
       Visual Effects (ABC)
1970   *The Carol Channing Special*
1973   *Walt Disney: A Golden Anniversary Salute* (NBC)
1974   *Herbie Day at Disneyland* (NBC)
       The Chadwick Family, TV Movie (ABC)
1975   *Beyond the Bermuda Triangle*, TV Movie (ABC)
1976   *The Bob Hope Special: Joys*
       The Ted Knight Musical Variety Special (CBS)
       The Tony Orlando and Dawn Rainbow Hour (NBC)

1977 *Reunion with The Partridge Family and My Three Sons* (ABC)

1978 *Bing Crosby: His Life and Legend* (ABC)
The Mike Douglas Show (Syndicated)
The Wonderful World of Disney 25th Anniversary Spectacular (NBC)
Dinah! (Syndicated)
All Star Tribute to James Stewart (CBS)
Happy Birthday, Bob [Bob Hope Special] (NBC)
The American Film Institute Salute to Henry Fonda (CBS)

1979 *The Mike Douglas Show* (Syndicated)

1980 *The American Film Institute Salute to James Stewart* (CBS)

1982 *The American Film Institute Salute to Frank Capra* (CBS)

1984 *Bob Hope's Unrehearsed Antics of the Stars* (NBC)

1986 *The American Film Institute Salute to Billy Wilder* (NBC)

1987 *The American Film Institute Salute to Barbara Stanwyck* (ABC)

Notes and Sources

Prolog: Hollywood, 1938

The story of Ray Bayley meeting Fred in Hollywood in 1938 is told in *Good Old Days*, a nostalgia magazine in the January, 2006 issue on pages 48-49. Mr. Bayley also kindly shared additional thoughts with me in an e-mail correspondence.

Chapter 1
Small Town Boy Makes Good (1908-1934)

"Man, how I hated 'Frederick' as a kid," *Saturday Evening Post*, 3/3/45
"Mr. Martin received his education in the public schools...," Obit, *Beaver Dam Angus*, 12/15/11
"...through his energetic efforts...," ibid.
"Will you kindly give the enclosed clippings to Fred MacMurray...," Letter from Ida Bird Holmes to Hedda Hopper, Hedda Hopper Collection, Academy of Motion Pictures Arts and Sciences Library, Los Angeles, CA.
"I wept because a clown knocked another clown's head off," *Saturday Evening Post, 2/24/62*
"I played a duet with my father...," ibid
"He was always himself; he never was a big shot...," *Beaver Dam Daily Citizen*, 11/6/91
"...McKinstry would pull on the string hanging outside of Fred's window...," ibid.
"We lived on Washington Street in Beaver Dam...," *Milwaukee Sentinel*, 11/6/91.
"...was not in awe of Fred...," Randall McKinstry to author, 6/26/06.
"Life was fun...," *TV Guide*, 11/12/60.

"A nice guy, and he always treated everybody the same...," *Beaver Dam Daily Citizen*, 11/6/91.

"Heck, nobody kicked 45-yard dropkicks...," ibid.

"All the kids in the big classroom on the second floor...," *Beaver Dam Daily Citizen*, 6/28/77.

"...the wages were twenty-five cents an hour...," *Colliers*, 6/20/36.

"No, I have no complaints against the saxophone...," *New York Herald*, 7/16/44.

"My first two lines were...," *Saturday Evening Post*, 2/24/62.

"Isn't it funny?...," *Milwaukee Sentinel*, 11/6/91.

"He was considered very handsome by us girls...," Lyda Fischer to author, 7/28/05.

Bartell would recall that they played in a 'gin joint'..., *Beaver Dam Daily Citizen*, 11/6/91.

"...he became tangled up with one Mynie Bartell...," *Colliers*, 6/20/36.

"The largest of Beaver Dam High School...," *Beaver Dam Argus*, 6/4/25.

"I'd be working my head off around there...," *Colliers*, 6/20/36.

"I didn't have to tell them I couldn't...," ibid.

With Higgins and the Royal Purples Fred played several months..., ibid.

"I was looking ahead to the time when I'd have to support my mother...," *Los Angeles Times*, 6/27/48.

Back ground on why Fred's grandmother moved to California, Lester Martin to author, 11/2/06.

"I just crawled in...," *Los Angeles Times*, 4/30/72.

"Well, there was one thing, Woods said...," *Saturday Evening Post*, 3/3/45.

"You! Do you think you can come up here...," ibid.

"That was a film everybody's forgotten but for me...," *New York Herald Tribune*, 7/16/44.

He is first seen with a group of school boys..., *Colliers*, 6/20/36.

By 1930 he was playing sax with a pit band in a Los Angeles theater...," *TV Guide*, 11/12/60.

"The vaudeville part of the Collegians' act was real wild...," *Saturday Evening Post*, 2/24/62.

The boys made their way to New York where they found work in a revue...," *Pictoral TView*, 4/16/61.

"There was an actor who was to stand on stage with Libby Holman...," Lester Martin to author, 11/2/06.

"...the hottest torch singer of the day," ibid.

"...the first three nights my hands shook...," *Saturday Evening Post*, 2/24/62.

"...was such a nice guy we all loved him," *Say...Didn't you used to be George*

Murphy by George Murphy with Victor Lasky, Barthomew House, 1970.
"I knew we were in real trouble...," ibid, pg. 150.
"The Collegians wore gloves which looked like organ keys...," *Have Tux Will Travel*, by Bob Hope as told to Pete Martin, Simon & Schuster, 1954, pg. 125.
"Hope started stepping on toes right from the first...," *Bob Hope: The Road Well-Traveled*, by Lawrence Quirk, Applause books, 11/1/00
"He was tough—very tough...," ibid.
"I saw a girl named Lillian Lamonte," *Los Angeles Times*, 6/27/48.
"Courtship of quiet dinners in cheap tearooms...," *Photoplay*, November, 1936.
"There must be at least four rooms...," ibid.
"You'll get money Frederick...," *Los Angeles Times*, 6/27/48.
"If Fred had ever gotten drunk by his band mates...," *Claudette Colbert*, Laurence Quirk, Crown Publishers, 1985.
...Fred went to pick up his mail, *Christian Science Monitor*, 1/24/56
"...a young fella, Dave Jonas...," *Saturday Evening Post*, 2/24/62.
"So...I went into Bob's dressing room...," *Bob Hope: Portrait of a Superstar*, by Charles Thompson, Harpers-Collins, 1982, pg. 36.
"When MacMurray told Hope about the offer...," *The Secret Life of Bob Hope*, by Arthur Marx, Barricade Books, 1993, pg. 76.
"Of course it will be terrible...," *Photoplay*, November, 1936.
"Word came back...send him out," *Saturday Evening Post*, 2/24/62.
"I...played a truck driver...," ibid.

Chapter 2
Paramount Leading Man (1935-1940)

"Later, in Hollywood I helped Fred get started in pictures...," *Say...Didn't You Used to be George Murphy?*
"We've got a new fellow here and all the girls on the lot are just crazy about him...," *Newsday*, Claudette Colbert to Liz Smith, 11/7/91.
"Me? You're kidding," *National Enquirer* ("My Most Frightening Moment"), 3/1/88.
"Now, what are you so frightened about," ibid.
"Relax, the camera is a mile away," *Newsday*, 11/7/91.
"We had a big emotional scene...," *Saturday Evening Post*, 2/24/62.
"Sometimes a writer writes in scenes for people who just say 'hi', ibid.
Ruggles, a 'morose' man..., *Wide Eyed in Babylon*, Ray Milland, Morrow, 1974, pg. 188.
"I hate to follow Clark Gable...," *Oakland Tribune*, 4/28/35.
"I'll never forget how kind Claudette was...," *Claudette Colbert*, Laurence Quirk, Crown Publishers, 1985, pg. 73.

"The secret of the successful MacMurray-Colbert chemistry...," ibid.

"Colbert may have felt a 'little disappointed...," ibid, pg. 75.

"A little rich for my blood," ibid.

"I remember a scene on a porch...," *Kate*, Charles Higham, Signet, 1976, pg. 71.

"Miss Hepburn helped me all through *Alice Adams*...," *Kingston (NY) Daily Freeman*, 4/10/36.

Fred "was perfect in *Alice Adams*," Claudette Colbert, pg. 75.

Stevens and Hepburn considering Fred for *Quality Street, Giant: George Stevens A Life in Film*, Marilyn Ann Moss, University of Wisconsin Press, 2004.

Lombard known as the "profane angel...," *Hollywood Director*, Curtis Books, 1973, pg. 108.

"Leisen was competent and stylish at his best...," *Marlene Dietrich: Life and Legend*, Steven Bach, Harper Collins, 1992.

Leisen gets a "bad rap...," Leonard Maltin in e-mail interview with author, 9/26/05.

"I know Leisen's passes troubled Fred MacMurray a great deal," *Behind the Screen: How Gays and Lesbians Shaped Hollywood*, William Mann, Penguin, 2002, pg. 174.

"You look at Leisen's movies...," ibid, pg. 175.

"Carole certainly knew who Fred MacMurray was...," *Screwball: The Life of Carole Lombard*, Larry Swindell, Morrow, 1975.

"I took a flying leap and put Fred MacMurray in...," *Hollywood Director*, pg. 93.

Fred "the typical American guy...," *The Post Standard*, 7/2/47.

Fred "had a natural flair for comedy...," ibid

"Now Uncle Fred, you be funny now...," ibid, pg. 94.

"loosen up you big ape! It isn't going to hurt," *TV Guide*, 8/17/63.

"When they finished that take, Carole and Fred collapsed...," *Hollywood Director*, pg. 96.

"Well, how did it go with Carole Lombard...?," ibid, pg. 97.

"If Fred couldn't get a laugh out of the beloved Lombard...," *TV Star Parade*, May, 1965.

"Really the most decent person I've met in Hollywood," *Long Live the King*, Lyn Tornabene, G.P. Putnam's Sons, 1976.

Trail of the Lonesome Pine financial/salary information, *Walter Wanger Papers*, Wisconsin State Historical Society Archives, Madison, Wisconsin.

"the first color film to be shot outdoors...," *Close Ups*, Sylvia Sidney interviewed by Karyn Kay, Workman Publishing, 1978.

"Actually it took at least fifteen hours...," *Hollywood Director*, pg. 99.

"How do I feel...," *Colliers*, 6/20/36.

"...Fred had the first buck he ever made," *Hollywood Director*, pg. 94.

"I think he always gives a good performance…," *TV Guide*, 8/17/63.

"Could I bring my date, my fiancé…," *Saturday Evening Post*, 3/3/45.

Raft was looking for excuses to get out of the picture…, *Screwball*, pg. 204.

"I was living with my mother…," *Hollywood Director*, pg. 97.

Lombard and Fred would "establish the pace…," *Screwball*, pg. 205.

Fred got "busy and practiced riding for a month…," *King Vidor*, By Nancy Dowd, Scarecrow, 1988 pg. 160.

"We had to set up three separate camps…," ibid.

"…Paramount shipped 50,000 rounds of blank cartridges…," *The Marion (OH) Star*, 9/5/36.

"I stood there and waited for Oakie to say goodbye and leave…," *Double Takes*, Jack Oakie, Strawberry Hill Press, 1980.

"Neither Oakie nor MacMurray recall that story," *My Side of the Road*, Dorothy Lamour, Prentice-Hall, 1980.

"…they got a judge up a little early and had a sort of sunrise ceremony…," *Winnipeg Free Press*, 1/4/45.

Fred acted as a "nurse for the sick Lillian Lamont…," *Kansas City Star*, 1/23/38.

Information regarding Lillian suffering from Bulimia, Lester Martin to author, 11/2/06.

"Competition" in roles between Fred and Gary Cooper, *Los Angeles Times*, 4/15/36.

"Do as little talking as possible…," *Olean Times-Herald*, 5/23/41.

Fred emerging as Robert Taylor's chief rival among new film stars, *Los Angeles Times*, 8/23/36.

Background on *Maid of Salem*, *Oakland Tribune*, 11/22/36 and AFI production notes.

Skid "just a shadow of…his former glory…," *Hollywood Director*, pg. 108.

Lombard later placed her performance as Maggie King…," *Screwball*.

Fred "walked up and down the set…," *Hollywood Director*, pg. 110

As usual Fred had a hard time with love scenes…, ibid, pg. 111.

"We went to the projection booth the next morning," ibid.

"Not only a great star, Carole was a beautiful woman…," *My Side of the Road*.

Breen letter to Hummel, AFI notes.

Paramount inter-office communication dated 9/3/37, *Claude Binyon Papers*, Wisconsin State Historical Society Archives, Madison, Wisconsin.

Fred "kept blowing his lines…," *Three Phases of Eve*, Eve Arden, St. Martin's Press, 1985, pg. 44.

Initially Fred's role was to be played by Don Ameche…," *Bing Crosby: A Pocketful of Dreams*, Gary Giddens, Back Bay, 2002, pg. 495.

"*Sing You Sinners* was Claude Binyon's baby…," ibid.

"The only break I get in the picture…," ibid, pg. 498.

A visiting reporter recorded the following exchange…, *Lowell Sun*, 8/4/38.

"We wanted to get that feeling that every man has…," *William A. Wellman*, Frank Thompson, Scarecrow Press, 1983.

Talk of Fred being cast in *Beau Geste*, ibid.

Fred "didn't particularly care" for Carroll…, author interview with Sid Bloomberg, 5/21/05.

"We had to do a session once with Fred MacMurray…," *People Will Talk*, John Kobal, Knopf, 1986, pg. 525.

Fred on slapping his leading ladies, *NY Post*, 5/27/39.

Chapter 3
"The Highest Paid Actor in Hollywood" (1940-1944)

Kissing techniques of Fred's co-stars, "Movie Girls' Kissing Techniques Difffer," *New York World Telegram*, 3/8/40

"They had to squeeze the work out of him…," *Madcap: The Life of Preston Sturges* By Donald Spoto, Little Brown & Co., 1990.

"…it might be assumed that Sturges and not Leisen was…," *Hollywood Director*, pg. 136-137.

"We all dreaded having to shoot the love scene…," *Hollywood Director*, pg. 142.

Sturges writing a "great comic role" for Stanwyck, *Xmas in July: The Life & Art of Preston Sturges*, By Diane Jacobs, University of California Press, 1992.

"…showed neither the nimble wit nor commanding presence…," ibid.

"I wish I could say the same about you," *Forties Film Talk* By Doug McClelland, McFarland, 1992 (also quoted in *Movie Talk*, David Shipman, St. Martin's Press, 1988, pg. 198.)

"Ironically Fred did work again briefly with Sturges…," *Between Flops: A Biography of Preston Sturges* By James Curtis, Harcount, Brace& Co, 1982, pg. 151.

"Her insecurities continued to spill over onto the shooting set…," *Jean Arthur: The Actress Nobody Knew* By John Oller, First Limelight, Feb, 1997, pg. 120.

"Captain Marvel was himself based on the actor, Fred MacMurray…," "The Human Qualities of Captain Marvel Characters", P.C. Hammerlinck, Fawcett Companion, Two Morrows Publishing, 2001.

"At the time Fred MacMurray was a very popular actor…," "The Worlds Mightiest Opinions: C.C. Beck Remembered", P.C. Hammerlinck, Fawcett Collectors of America, Winter '97.

"John Wayne told of Roos...," *Shooting Star,* pg. 174.

"MacMurray never had any idea of going Hollywood," "Hollywood's Ho-Hum Boy," *Saturday Evening Post,* 3/3/45.

"It's stocked with a bread of Hereford cows...," *LA Times,* 7/22/45.

"Fred never has to sign a check or look at a bank statement...," *Saturday Evening Post,* 3/3/45.

"In August, 1941 Roos...took Fred, John Wayne, Ray Milland and Ward Bond...," *Shooting Star,* pg. 176.

"The MacMurray's weren't much for going out on the town either...," "Hollywood's Ho-Hum Boy," *Saturday Evening Post,* 3/3/45.

"If I want my dance right away or if I'd rather wait...," *NY Post,* 10/3/65.

"...one of the few happy and well-adjusted marriages in Hollywood," *Joan Crawford* by Charles Higham

"The Gable's threw parties for only close friends..." *Long Live the King* By Lyn Tornabene, G.P. Putnam's Sons, NY, 1976, pg. 263.

"It's just that we want her to grow up like any other normal child...," *LA Times,* 4/23/42.

"Fred traveled overnight with his mother...," "Fred MacMurray to Attend Centennial Event," *Beaver Dam Daily Citizen,* 7/3/41.

"He choose *On Wisconsin*...," "Hollywood's Ho-Hum Boy," *Saturday Evening Post,* 3/3/45.

"He showed his support and loyalty for Beaver Dam," Interview with author by Randall McKinstry.

"Shortly after the centennial...," "Screen Star Stops Traffic," *Winnipeg Free Press,* 7/12/41.

"Much of the film was made on location at the San Diego Naval Station...," *Errol Flynn: The Spy Who Never Was* By Tony Thomas, A Citadel Press Book, 1990.

"Curtiz had to be on his best behavior...," ibid.

"...she accepted without knowing the director, full script or leading man," *Marlene Dietrich,* by Maria Riva,

"Poor Fred MacMurray...", ibid.

"One thing she couldn't understand...," *Hollywood Director,* pg.177.

"Marlene hit on everybody..." Interview with Sid Bloomberg, 5/21/05.

"Marlene was amazing...," *Marlene* by Charles Higham, Pocket Books, NY, 1977, pg. 149.

"Fred became a good friend, a sort of mentor...," *40's Film Talk* By Doug McClelland, McFarland, 1992.

"Fred never fell in love with acting as acting himself...," *The Days of My Life* By McDonald Carey, St. Martin's, 1991, pg. 102.

"...worth adoration...," ibid, pg. 101.

"...she likes him in person as much as she thought...," ibid, pg. 102.

"Nobody's looking. You can let go," *Hollywood Director,* pg??

"A wonderful girl. Swore like a man...," *Movie Talk*, David Shipman, St. Martin's Press, 1988, pg. 129.

"Fred also joined the Hollywood Anti-Nazi League...," *Radical Hollywood*, Paul Bohle & Dave Wagner, New Press, 2002.

"Joan enjoyed working with Fred MacMurray...," *Joan Crawford* by Lawrence Quirk & William Schoell, University of Kentucky Press, 2002, pg. 120.

"Claudette, the trouble with this picture is that we're both too goddam old for it!," *Hollywood Director*, pg. 216.

"Quite a few Hollywood folk make more than I do...," *LA Times*, 7/22/45.

Chapter 4
"Double Indemnity"

Backstory on the making of *Double Indemnity* come from several sources including:

"Making and Remaking Double Indemnity" by James Naremore, *Film Comment*, Jan/Feb, 1996

"The Making of Double Indemnity" by Jay Rozgonyi, *Films in Review*, June/July, 1990

"Double Indemnity: A Policy That Paid Off" by John Allyn, *Film Quarterly*, Spring, 1978

On Sunset Boulevard: The Life and Times of Billy Wilder by Ed Sikov, Hyperion, 1998

Nobody's Perfect by Charlotte Chandler, Simon & Schuster, 2002

"Chandler liked to smoke his pipe constantly...," *Films in Review*, pg. 342.

"...idea was to write a love story between the two men...," *Film Quarterly*, pg. 120.

"Stanwyck wasn't so certain at first if she wanted to play an 'out and out bitch,'" *Barbara Stanwyck: A Biography* by Al DiOrio, Coward-McCann, 1983, pg. 136.

George Raft refusal to play Neff, *On Sunset Boulevard*, pg. 202.

"What Wilder saw was MacMurray's grinning, guy-next door affability...," Ibid, pg. 202.

"I just wanted the audience to go with Walter...," *Film Quarterly*, pg. 120.

"You're making a mistake--that part requires acting...," *On Sunset Boulevard*, pg. 202.

"I held off saying I would do it...," *American Classic Screen*, March/April, 1974

"I was used to being the bad girl...," *Nobody's Perfect*, pg. 118.

"There being nobody, then or now whom I respect more...," *Barbara*

Stanwyck: A Biography, pg. 136.

"It was designed to be MacMurray's film," *Little Caesar: A Biography of Edward G. Robinson*, Alan L. Gansberg, Scarecrow Press, 2004, pg. 112.

"We hire Barbara Stanwyck and here we get George Washington!," *On Sunset Boulevard*, pg. 203.

"Fred was very very unsure about whether he should be doing Double Indemnity," *Nobody's Perfect*, pg. 118.

"Fred was a 'notorious line-muffler...,'" *On Sunset Boulevard*, pg. 208.

"I don't know about you, but I was wonderful!," *Stanwyck*, by Axel Madsen, pg. 219.

"Billy left the set to meet a starlet...," *Film Quarterly*, pg. 121.

"I remember we did it on a process stage...," *Billy Wilder in Hollywood*, by Maurice Zolotow, G.P. Putnam's, NY, 1977, pg. 116.

"I shot an ending which I chopped off...," *Conversations With the Great Moviemakers of Hollywood's Golden Age*, by George Stevens, Jr., Alfred A. Knopf, 2006, pg. 331.

"Wilder photographed the step by step procedure of execution...," *Film Comment*, pg. 30.

Reviews cited:

Variety, 4/26/44

PM, 9/7/44

New York World Telegram, 9/5/44

Brooklyn Eagle, 9/7/44

"A definitive film noir...," *Film Comment*, pg. 23.

Recollection of the Glendale preview, *People*, 12/9/91, letters to the editor.

"The way you found tragedy...," *Cain* by Roy Happe, Holt, Reinhardt, & Winston, 1982, pg. 347.

"I'd make any picture Billy wanted me to...," *New York Post*, 7/29/62.

"I enjoy comedy more than anything, I guess...," *American Classic Screen*, March/April, 1974.

Chapter 5
Leaving Paramount, Fox Trilogy and Career Doldrums (1945-1949)

Turning down *The Best Years of Our Lives*, *Goldwyn: A Biography*, A. Scott Berg, Knopf, 1989.

Leisen "ashamed" of *Practically Yours*, *Hollywood Director*, pg. 216.

"Claudette, the trouble with this picture...," ibid.

"A neglected masterpiece and perhaps the forties' funniest farce," *Hollywood in the Forties*, Charles Higham & Joel Greenberg, A.S. Barnes & Co., 1968.

Fox Attempts to lure Fred from Paramount, *Saturday Evening Post*, 3/3/45.

Background on the making of *Murder, He Says*, "Making Murder" by George Marshall, *Film Fan Monthly*, March 1971, pg. 20-23.

"But nobody paid much attention to a funnier...," *Kiss Kiss Bang Bang*, Pauline Kael, Bantam, 1968.

"Fox hung out the STAR WANTED sign...," *Saturday Evening Post*, 3/3/45.

June Haver wishing she too could marry a man like Fred MacMurray, *The Guy Next Door*, A&E Home Video.

Recollections of Joan Leslie, interview with author, 3/30/06.

"Fred read some 765 pages of biographical notes...," *Harrisburg (IL) Daily Register*, 1/19/45.

"He said his love-making was persistent...," ibid.

"Nope. I played that my regular way...," *LA Times*, 7/22/45.

Recollections of Darryl Hickman, interview with author, 9/29/06.

"Syrupy melodrama...," *Eddie Rickenbacker: An American Hero in the 20th Century*, W. David Lewis, Johns Hopkins University Press, 2005, pg. 497.

"...bringing out nothing of the intensity of Rickenbacker's life and experiences," ibid.

Rickenbacker was "proud of it...," ibid.

"Miss Hazel Martin, takes care of this avalanche of words...," *Saturday Evening Post*, 3/3/45.

Fred being sued by tenants of an apartment he owned, *LA Herald & Express*, 12/3/48.

"Which is your favorite side...," *Forties Film Talk*, pg. 31.

"Fox readying another picture for Fred...," *LA Times*, 1/20/46.

"Claude Binyon was Fred MacMurray's favorite writer...," *Hollywood Director*, pg. 256.

"Binyon was very shy...," ibid, pg. 257.

"Fred MacMurray was expert at comedy timing, but Paulette wasn't...," *Paulette: The Adventurous Life of Paulette Goddard*, Joe Morella & Edward Z. Epstein, St. Martin's Press, 1985, pg. 148.

"Fred MacMurray turns in the best comedy performance of his career...," *Burlington Daily Times*, 12/20/46.

"Claudette and I worked darn hard...," *Claudette Colbert*, pg. 74.

"Ma was good for a lot of laughs...," *Saturday Evening Post*, 11/12/49.

Marjorie Main believing Fred "lacked warmth," *Marjorie Main*, Michelle Vogel, McFarland, 2006, pg. 43.

"The lady is absolutely right...," "So He Won't Talk," *This Week*, 6/8/47.

"She was rushed to Universal..." *Ava*, Roland Flamini, Berkley Publishing Group, 1984, pg. 97.

"...Fred's white tropical suit on fire...," *Ava Gardner*, John Daniell, St. Martin's Press, 1983, pg. 70.

Gardner believing Fred was "great" to work with, *Ava Gardner: Love is*

Nothing, Lee Server, St. Martin's Press, 2006.

"...Fred had the rather innocuous coded name...," *Ava: My Story*, Ava Gardner, Bantam, 1990, pg. 320.

"Aware of the sensitive feelings surrounding their production...," *The Films of Frank Sinatra*, Daniel O' Brien, Butler & Tanner, LTD, 1998 pg. 34-38

"If *Double Indemnity* depicted the dark side of MacMurray's regular guy persona..." ibid.

"We had been getting together for 14 years...," *Claudette Colbert*

"Mr. Stahl, is there something we should change...," *Natasha: The Biography of Natalie Wood*, Suzanne Finstad, Three Rivers Press, 2002, pg. 69.

"never saw a child of such energy and delightful innocence...," ibid.

"Wood as overly ambitious...," ibid, pg. 74.

Fred being considered for the lead in a stage version of *The Maltese Falcon*, *The Lost One: The Life of Peter Lorre*, Stephen D. Younglain, University of Kentucky Press, 2005, pg. 184.

Fred turning down *Sunset Boulevard*, *Hollywood's First Choices*, Jeff Burkhart & Bruce Stuart, Three Rivers Press, 1994, pg. 17.

Chapter 6
From Despair to Happiness (1950-1954)

"William Boyd's manager demanded to see a print of the film...," *Variety*, 11/15/51.

"Kid, it won't work today...," *Only Make Believe: My Life in Show Business*, Howard Keel & Joyce Spizer, Barricade Books, 2005, pg. 140.

"Fred MacMurray used to park there...," ibid, pg. 35.

"I already know you, Fred...," ibid, pg. 140.

Cary Grant and Fred having dinner together, *Johnny Came Lately*, Fred De Cordova, Simon & Schuster, 1988, pg. 248.

"Another movie star who was frugal...," *Hollywood Trail Boss: Behind the Scenes of the Wild Wild West*, Burt Kennedy, Boulevard Books, 1997.

Ed Hartmann recollections, *Film Fax*, Interview by Robert Nott, Feb/March, 1994, issue # 43.

"I was amused by Fred's frugality...," interview with Gene Reynolds, 1/23/06.

"He was supposedly very tight with the dollar...," e-mail from Mel Shavelson to author, 3/2/06.

John Stephens' recollections, *From My Three Sons To Major Dad*, John Stephens, The Scarecrow Press, 2005. pg. 44-46.

"His frugality was certainly a part of his reputation...," Don Grady to author.

"I remember once the wardrobe man…," *People,* 11/18/91.

"Sheila, you keep building this myth…," *NY Mirror,* 12/27/59.

"Fred was not frugal…," Lester Martin to author, 11/2/06.

"Mrs. Fred MacMurray, who has been sick since Christmas…," *LA Examiner,* 4/4/48.

"I was ready to walk out…," *Close Up: The Contract Director,* Jon Tuska, Scarecrow Press, 1976, pg. 167.

"My idea was to shoot aboard ship on the way to Hawaii…," ibid, pg. 168.

Recollections of Claude Jarman, Jr. to author, 4/7/06.

"I saw Fred blow up only once…," Sid Bloomberg to author, 5/21/05.

"I might as well…No reason why those guys should keep adventure pictures to themselves…," *Panama News Herald,* 8/5/52.

"…Lily was in grave condition…,"
Information regarding Lily suffering from bulimia, interview with Lester Martin, 11/2/06.

"Everybody had the wrong idea about Lily's illness…,""A Real Hollywood Love Story," Louella Parsons, *LA Examiner,* 12/53.

"Stricken with grief, Fred occupied his mind…," *The All-Americans,* John Robert Parish & Don Stanke, Arlington House, 1977, pg. 278.

"I knew he was sad, but he didn't want to discuss it," Lester Martin to author.

"What I liked best about *The Caine Mutiny*…," *A Mad, Mad, Mad, Mad World,* Stanley Kramer with Thomas Coffey, Harcourt Brace & Co., 1997.

"Fred MacMurray was a spectator in the scene of life…," ibid.

"…the cast was not a chummy one…," *Bogart,* A.M. Sperber & Eric Lax, Morrow, 1997, pg. 481.

"We got down to the business of shooting our dialogue scenes outside the bridge…," *It's a Hell of a Life But Not a Bad Living,* Edward Dmytryk, NY Times Books, 1978, pg. 178.

"Initially, Fred felt that piece of business seemed…," *National Enquirer,* 5/8/73.

Bogart was "rather well satisfied with his performance…," *Bogart: A Life in Hollywood,* Jeffrey Meyers, Houghton Mifflin Company, 1997, pg. 280.

"The producer knew he needed somebody who could hold her own against…Fred MacMurray," *Kim Novak: Reluctant Goddess,* Peter Harry Brown, St. Martin's Press, 1986.

"…it offered Kim a showy role…," *King Cohn,* Bob Thomas, G.P. Putnam's Sons, 1967.

"As sweet a human being…," Darryl Hickman to author, 9/29/06.

"Cute as a button…," Sybil Jason to author, 10/30/06.

"I think I made the right decision to go into the convent…," June Haver Obit, *Newark (NJ) Star Ledger,* 7/2/05.

Haver recollections of the Gay Nineties party where she met Fred, "I tricked my Husband Into Becoming a Father—Twice!" *Photoplay*, June Haver MacMurray as told to Jane Ardmore, September, 1967.

"Ann is an old friend of Lillian's…" *NY Daily Mirror*, 1/24/54.

"We explained that June and Fred had gotten off in Panama…," *Modern Screen*, June, 1954.

"I don't know what could have made Joan say such a thing…," *NY Daily News*, 3/23/54.

"It could happen," *Modern Screen*, June, 1954.

"I wouldn't run off and get married without taking you into my confidence…," *NY Daily News*, 3/23/54.

Memo from Darryl Zanuck to Claude Binyon regarding *Women's World*, Claude Binyon Papers, Wisconsin State Historical Society Archives, Madison, Wisconsin.

Recollections of Arlene Dahl, Interview with author, 10/21/06.

Fred taking a thermometer on the set, *The Glamour Factory*, Ronald L. Davis, Southern Methodist University Press, 1993, pg. 239.

"All I'm going to say is that June is a fine girl," *Modern Screen*, June, 1954.

"When are we going to get married?" *Photoplay*, September, 1967.

"Say, there's something for you in the pocket…," ibid.

"…a great decision—one of the greatest of my life…," *NY Journal American*, 6/24/54.

Account of MacMurray-Haver wedding, *NY World Telegram*, 6/29/54.

"Honeymooning on company time…," *NY World & Sun*, 8/16/54.

"shiny bright light, so tiny and beautiful…," Joan Leslie to author, 3/30/06.

"Where Lillian was reserved…," Lester Martin to author, 11/2/06.

Chapter 7
Career Resurrection (1955-1959)

Details on Lily's will, *LA Times*, 11/2/54.

"The Merle Miller script is wordy and heavy…," *The All Americans* (Parish)

"I've been carrying Lana Turner all day…," *NY Herald Tribune*, 9/30/55.

"For the greater part of his career, Werker's work was routine…," *The Western*, Phil Hardy, Morrow & Company, 1983.

"In every city where I appeared…," *Los Angeles Times*, 1/31/56.

Tony Curtis's comments on Abner Biberman, *Tony Curtis: The Autobiography*, Tony Curtis & Barry Paris, Morrow & Company, 1993, pg. 82.

Contrasting acting styles between leads, particularly Fred and Stockwell, *The Western*.

Comments by Joan Weldon come from an interview that Robert Nott conducted with Miss Weldon which ran in "Western Clippings, Western Ladies #4", March 1999.

"Why don't you get back into the movies?" *NY Post*, 10/3/65.

"One of the least discussed of Sirk's great melodramas of the 50's," *Senses of Cinema*, "The Far Side of Paradise: Douglas Sirk's *There's Always Tomorrow*," by Adrian Dank.

"...A very good actor...," *Sirk on Sirk*, Jon Halliday, Seeker & Warbury, London, 1971, pg. 120.

Recollections of William Reynolds, *Classic Images*, "The Perfect Son", Michael Barnum.

"It should have frightened me but it didn't...," *NY Daily News*, 10/6/57.

"And I learned to love them because...," ibid.

"No, I do not feel I submerged a career," ibid.

"Here I am in the twilight of my life!," *Photoplay*, September, 1967.

"No, I want you to be free...," *Pictorial TView*, 5/8/60.

"I wish you'd thought of us...," *Photoplay*, September, 1967.

"What are we going to do with twins that were born yesterday?" ibid.

"Fred MacMurray was a nice enough guy...," *The Lucy Book*, Geoffrey Mark Fidelman, Renaissance Books, 1999, pg. 122.

"And now I won't use a cook...," *NY Mirror*, 12/27/59.

Walt Disney outlining plot of *The Shaggy Dog* to Roy and Edna Disney, *Building a Company*, Bob Thomas, Hyperion, 1998, pg. 227-228.

Recollections of Tom Kirk in this chapter are from an interview with the author, 3/28/06.

"One of the most underestimated actors of all-time...," *Fred MacMurray with Fondness*, comment from Kevin Corchoran, *Shaggy Dog* DVD, 2006.

"A curious film...," *The Disney Films*, Leonard Maltin, Disney Editions, 2000, pg. 157.

Impressed by Fred's ability to do take after take...," Tim Considine in Disney documentary *Fred MacMurray with Fondness*, *Shaggy Dog* DVD, 2006.

"It's an interesting role...," *NY Journal American*, 3/12/59.

"I worked with Kim Novak in her first movie...," *A Dream is a Wish Your Heart Makes*, Annette Funicello & Patricia Romanowski, Hyperion, 1994, pg. 70.

"Fred, I'm in trouble...," *Nobody's Perfect*, pg. 227.

"Fred MacMurray, on the other hand...," *On Sunset Boulevard: The Life & Times of Billy Wilder*, pg. 438.

"I played a real stinker in it...," *American Classic Screen*, March/April, 1974.

"There was a great deal of Fred and his persona...," Jack Lemmon in "The Guy Next Door", *Biography*, A&E.

"I was playing around in my dressing room...," *Lemmon,* Don Widener, MacMillan, 1975, pg. 182.

"I'll tell you a very funny story about him...," *Conversation with Wilder,* Cameron Crowe, Knopf, NY, 1999, pg. 50.

MacMurray gives Shirley MacLaine a hundred-dollar bill..., *Billy Wilder in Hollywood,* pg. 246.

"I saw you in *The Apartment* last night...," *On Sunset Boulevard,* pg. 438.

Chapter 8
"The MacMurray System" (1960-1965)

"I was shooting the breeze with Randy Scott...," *TV Guide,* Feb, 1960.

"Those husband-wife TV series are for the birds...," *NY Post,* 3/14/59.

Plot and sketch descriptions of *The American Cowboy, Modesto Bee,* 2/7/60.

"I've played a lot of cowboys...," *Newark (NJ) Evening News,* 2/7/60.

"Now 50% of the profits meant not only profits from the show...," *Television Chronicles* #3, "My Three Sons: The Mike Years", October, 1995.

"A couple of days later Fedderson sent me a story outline...," *Saturday Evening Post,* 2/24/62.

"Why not think of a television series...," *TV Guide,*

"Walt advised against TV," *TV Guide,* 8/17/63.

"If the series was called The Fred MacMurray Show...," *NY World Telegram & Sun,* 8/11/60.

"It impacted everyone...," *Television Chronicles* #3

Frawley, "A great guy—they don't make people like him...," *From My Three Sons to Major Dad,*

"He would have a couple of nips with his lunch...," Cynthia Pepper to author, 11/27/05.

"Boy, would I like to fuck her...," *From My Three Sons to Major Dad,* pg. 49.

"The real treat for me...," Hank Jones to author, 12/21/05.

"Who wrote this shit," Gene Reynolds to author, 1/23/06.

"My name is Stanley Livingston and no cracks," *From My Three Sons to Major Dad,* pg. 46.

Ryan O' Neal was originally signed to play eldest son Mike..., ibid.

"Billy Chapin "was a little too rebellious...," Don Grady to author.

"I know we had a kind of confrontation early on...," *Television Chronicles* #3 pg. 30-31.

Grady believing he got role because of 'dimple' "just like MacMurray's," Don Grady to author, 11/6/05.

"Don was an extremely likable young man...," Hank Jones to author, 12/21/05.

"I was really concentrating on who this 'Robbie' character...," Don Grady to author.

"I was feeling that the show was something special...," ibid.

"Fred did not hang...," ibid.

"The strangest show...," Beverly Garland to author.

"I do all my work in about three months...," *Saturday Evening Post*, 2/24/62.

"No-nonsense guy, kind of like your parent...," Don Grady to author.

"Fred was not a proponent of 'method' acting...," ibid.

"I have no theories...," *Western Kansas Press*, 12/16/62.

"After a scene, they talk it over with him...," *Panama City News Herald*, 6/16/63.

"He was a very private person...," Cynthia Pepper to author.

"I remember Mr. M being very quiet and reserved...," hank Jones to author.

"Quick Daddy, come look at yourself when you had hair," *TV-Star Parade*, May, 1965.

Fred embracing "carnegaine sweater" roles, Don Grady to author.

"Armed with a detailed description of our TV family...," *Saturday Evening Post*, 2/24/62.

"My wife June was upset about it...," *Oakland Tribune*, 5/21/69.

"It bothered Fred, it bothered the producers...," Don Grady to author.

Clause in contract where Fred was paid $5000 for every day he worked over his contracted days, *From My Three Sons to Major Dad*, pg. 43.

"He sent me a telegram asking for the job," *Hollywood Director*, (1994 edition)

"Fred was right about things a lot of times...," *From My Three Sons to Major Dad*, pg. 51.

"The best actor and star I ever had the pleasure of working with," ibid, pg. 44.

"John Stephens used to scare the bejesus out of me," Don Grady to author.

Most child actors could be "monsters, but not these boys," *TV Guide*, 8/17/64.

"I want to start spending more time with them while they're young...," *NY Herald Tribune*, 10/21/62.

"Richly deserved designation...Television Father of the Year," *Panama City News*, 6/16/63.

"The father in our show isn't a dope...," *TV Guide*, 7/31/65.

"One year would have been enough...," Gene Reynolds to author.

"My hair had to be the same six months from now in a close-up...," *Television Chronicles* #3, pg. 28.

Vera Miles anecdote, *From My Three Sons to Major Dad*, pg. 38-39.

"Fred was never involved with scripts or story conferences...," Gene

Reynolds to author.

"The kids just adored him…," *From My Three Sons to Major Dad,* pg. 53.

"great empathy for the pressures we were under to deliver…," Hank Jones to author.

"I really consider myself very blessed and lucky…," *Meet the Mertzes,* Rob Edelman & Audrey Kupferberg, Renaissance Books, 1999, pg. 197.

Jimmy Stewart anecdote, *From My Three Sons to Major Dad,* pg. 55-57.

"Fred occasionally liked to send a laugh up to the execs…," Don Grady to author.

"We had a scene in a schoolroom…," Hank Jones to author.

"I remember dancing at this party that was given by the advertising company…," *Television Chronicles #4,* pg. 27.

"Fred would come up to me and say he was worried that Bill…," Gene Reynolds to author.

Frawley "didn't take it well," *From My Three Sons to Major Dad,* pg. 50.

"It was a rather ugly scene on the set," ibid.

"Frawley would occasionally come back…," *Meet the Mertzes,* pg. 226.

"Fred MacMurray and I were paired as pallbearers…," *A Book,* Desi Arnaz, Buccaneer Books, 1994.

"I was pretty upset…the fact that he wasn't coming back…," Stanley Livingston to Dan Falatico, *Television Chronicles* #4.

"He did one of his patented pratfalls…," *Television Chronicles* #3, pg. 33.

"Frawley may have been a cantankerous old guy…," *From My Three Sons to Major Dad,* pg. 51.

Chapter 9
The 60's Disney Films

"Fred could express the things which Disney felt but couldn't articulate…," Tom Kirk to author.

"The Disney Studios were one of the best studios to work at…," *I Love the Illusion: The Life and Career of Agnes Moorehead,* Charles Tranberg, Bear Manor Media, 2005.

Everyone smiled, really because everyone was just plain glad…," Hank Jones to author.

"He (Disney) was a charming man…," Eliott Reid to author, 2/19/05.

"When Disney was still alive it was very clean, very wholesome…," Tom Kirk to author.

"Victorian, prudish—that whole generation of our family was…," *Remembering Walt,* Amy Booth Green & Howard Green, Diane Publishing, 1999, pg. 88.

"There's a lack of tremendous pressure in the Disney studios…," *Christian Science Monitor,* 2/2/66.

"Disney liked Fred enormously…," Tom Kirk to author.

"He's a down-to-earth, practical actor...," *Charleston (WVA) Sunday-Gazette,* 7/2/61.

"Three years ago kids never knew who I was...," *Western Kansas Press,* 12/6/62.

"I didn't know Walt very well then...," *St. Joseph (MI) Herald-Press,* 6/8/60.

"We had a technical advisor on *The Absent Minded Professor...,*" *Man Behind the Magic: The Story of Walt Disney,* Richard Greene & Katharine Barret, Viking Juvenile, 1991, pg. 130.

"If there was pain in his life—tragedy—he didn't reveal that...," Nancy Olson quoted from "The Guy Next Door" *Biography,* A&E.

"The most important casting of all...was that of Fred MacMurray...," *The Disney Films,* pg. 187.

"Reticent person of Scottish background...," Elliott Reid to author.

"We both sensed that we were comfortable with each other," ibid.

"Somewhat reserved, but with a noticeable twinkle in his eye...," Hank Jones to author.

"As much as I wanted Fred's friendship and approval...," Tom Kirk to author.

"Wynn's memory was failing...," *Film Crazy: Interviews with Hollywood Legends,* Patrick McGilligan, St. Martin's Griffin, 2001, pg. 217.

"We left home before 7 and didn't' get home until after 9...," *Charleston (WVA) Sunday-Gazette,* 7/2/61.

"I'm glad to be in a picture...," ibid.

"The children should have a fine time...," *New York Times,* 3/17/61.

"Enjoyable as an absurd, uncomplicated...," *Variety,* 2/22/61.

"A critic had written a snide article in some high-profile...," *Remembering Walt,* pg. 129.

"Somehow Disney let the sequence pass...," *The Disney Version,* Richard Schickel, Avon, 1969, pg. 303.

Fred running out of gas as he attempts to "rescue" Wyman, *The Odessa American,* 9/2/58.

"She admired MacMurray's talents...," *Jane Wyman: The Actress & Woman,* Lawrence Quirk, W.W. Norton, 1987.

"Many people assume that the prima-donnas are actresses...," Jane Wyman to author, 2002.

Recollections of the making of *Bon Voyage!* Tom Kirk to author.

"Bon Voyage is a hackneyed and tremendously overlong film..." *The Disney Films,* pg. 198.

"Competent, super clean and efficient," *NY Post,* 5/18/62.

"We can't lose the ball with an incomplete forward pass...," *NY World Telegram,* 7/14/62.

"I could find no law against it...," ibid.

"Some people think it was the most enjoyable of the pictures...," Elliott

Reid to author.

"That's the kind of question I hate," Tom Kirk to author.

"...as a light comedian he was as good as it gets...," ibid.

"crazy...in the spirit of an old-fashioned sight gag...," *NY Times*, 2/9/63.

"I knew his agent Arthur Parks...," *Curtis Bernhardt: Oral History Directors Guild of America* #3, Mary Kiersch, Scarecrow Press, 1986.

"I felt the worst problem with the film was the casting of Polly Bergen...," ibid.

"You never gave me a nose bleed," *TV Star Parade*, May, 1965.

Arlene Dahl's recollections of *Kisses For My President*, interview with author, 10/21/06.

"There were a lot of reasons I made concessions and compromises...," *Curtis Bernhardt: Oral History Directors Guild of America* #3.

"You know the bad luck...," ibid.

"To give the picture an authentic feeling of the thirties...," Disney press kit for *Follow Me, Boys!*

"Very much in tune with this film and this character...," Elliott Reid to author.

"I play a scoutmaster in the movie...," *Newark (NJ) Evening News*, 8/8/65.

"Disney's tribute to the boy scouts..." Elliott Reid to author.

"When I got the picture and found out Lillian Gish was in it...," ibid.

"Sometimes he'd come down to the set and ask...," *Remembering Walt*, pg. 45.

"Two hour commercial for the Boy Scouts of America...," *NY World Journal Tribune*, 12/21/66.

An "orgy of sentiment unparalleled in our day and age," The *Disney Version*, pg. 303.

"Fred MacMurray's simple, honest approach...," *The Disney Films*, pg. 246.

"Walt Disney chose his favorite, Fred MacMurray...," *Disney A-Z*, Dave Smith, Hyperion, 1996, pg. 255.

Fred sprained his ankle rehearsing..., *A Rose for Mrs. Miniver*, Michael Troyan, University Press of Kentucky, 1999.

Fred being a father figure, recollection of Lesley Ann Warren, "Fred MacMurray with Fondness, *Shaggy Dog* DVD, 2006.

"We did a scene I didn't think was particularly good...," *Great Bend (KS) Daily Tribune*, 7/6/66.

"The most laid back guy...," John Davidson, "Fred MacMurray with Fondness," *Shaggy Dog* DVD, 2006.

"I always hoped Mr. Disney would invite me to come to his studio...," *NY Morning Telegram*, 7/4/66.

"Fred and I have something in common...," *NY Daily News*, 8/3/66.

"We were filming the big dinner scene...," *Burlington (NC) Times-News*,

7/20/71.
"You didn't get anything for nothing from Old Walt," *Man Behind the Magic*, pg. 129.
"My personal theory about *The Happiest Millionaire…*," Leonard Maltin to author, 9/26/05.
"Fred MacMurray, a modestly gifted farceur…," *The Disney Version*, pg. 304."
"I haven't heard any reason why there was the four year gap in the films…," Dave Smith to author, 8/14/06.

Chapter 10
My Three Sons Part Two (1966-1972)

"One year later, there was never any talk of an adoption…," Television Chronicles #4 pg. 19.
"Color won't change the show very much…," *Newark (NJ) Evening News*, 8/8/65.
"We'll be in color next season…," *New York Times*, 8/22/65.
"He just revitalized the whole show…," ibid, pg. 21.
"de Cordova was a unique man…," *From My Three Sons to Major Dad*, pg. 53-54.
"I absolutely idolized him…," *Television Chronicles* #4, pg. 21.
"Fred de Cordova loved to kid people including Fred MacMurray…," Beverly Garland to author, 7/15/05.
"The devil himself must have negotiated Fred's contract," *Johnny Came Lately*, pg. 112.
"Hey, who was that girl who went out with Robbie…," *TV Guide*.
"I think they wanted to get Robbie married quickly…," *Television Chronicles* #4, pg. 21.
"I opposed Tina Cole for the role," ibid.
"I had a crush on Ronne Troup!" Don Grady to author.
"It was difficult for the others to realize that a woman takes much longer to get ready…," *TV Guide*, 2/17/68.
"The idea that Robbie and Katie would sleep in separate beds…," Don Grady to author.
"I thought this might have been our last year…," *Oakland Tribune*, 5/21/69.
"That was probably, in the entire 12 years…," *Television Chronicles* #4, pg. 22.
"The writers were running out of ideas for the male household…," Don Grady to author.
"If there is an explanation…," *TV Guide*, 7/31/65.
"No! No! Beverly…," Beverly Garland to author.
"There was a meeting between me and three others…," ibid.

"Good enough for good 'ol Bing…," *TV Guide,* 1/10/70.

Dawn Lyn testing for *Nanny and the Professor, Television Chronicles* #4, pg. 23.

"You act like you belong here," Beverly Garland to author.

"I saw Barbara as not afraid to speak up…," ibid.

"Very quiet and formal…," Dawn Lyn to author, 2/3/05.

MacMurray didn't like her "precociousness…," *Television Chronicles* #4, pg. 24.

"I was so young at the time…," Dawn Lyn to author.

"A real sweetie…just a little pumpkin," Beverly Garland to author.

"Demarest was great fun…," Dawn Lyn to author.

"Had been in nearly every movie ever made…," Beverly Garland to author.

"Bing was often in his own little world—Fred was not…" ibid.

"He just adored all the boys and they adored him…," ibid.

"…you could tell he didn't approve," *People,* 7/17/97.

"You might say that Fred sort of became a replacement dad for me…," Don Grady to author.

"He's at an age where it's hard to communicate…," *TV Guide,* 10/5/68.

"Attempting to distance himself from his father…," Don Grady to author.

"I was invited to his home once…," ibid.

"My politics started to differ from his…," ibid.

"Every year I think we ought to quit…," *Long Beach Press-Telegram,* 7/24/70.

"It was a very emotional experience…," *Television Chronicles* #4, pg. 25.

"Well, the network didn't like that," *Burlington (NC) Times-News,* 7/20/71.

"He wished me well," Don Grady to author.

"I can understand why he wanted to leave…," *Burlington (NC) Times-News* 7/20/71.

Jimmy Stewart being wooed for a new series, *Jimmy Stewart: A Biography,* Marc Eliot, Rebel Road Inc., 2006, pg. 378-379.

Recollections of Anne Francis regarding 12th season trilogy from letter from Anne Francis to author.

"Fred Silverman took over at CBS…," Beverly Garland to author.

Fred was "absolutely livid…," ibid.

"If you're an actor…," Don Grady to author.

Chapter 11
The Twilight of a Saxophone Player (1973-1991)

George Lindsey recollections, George Lindsey to author, 2/6/06.

"It's a miracle to me that I ever got into pictures…," *National Enquirer,* September, 1972, Jimmy Starr Papers.

"He's not dull at all…," ibid.

"You know, Daddy is always calling himself dull…," *The MacMurrays: Old Fashioned and Loving It,* Margaret Rau, pg. 10-11.

Surprised to see the girls in starched dresses and wearing white gloves, Dawn Lyn to author.

"All the kids at school like the old clothes and music…," *The MacMurray's: Old Fashioned and Loving It,* By Margaret Rau, pg. 10.

"We can talk to our parents where a lot of kids can't," ibid.

Fred's camper, *Austin (MN) Herald,* 11/19/65.

Fred and the family taking the camper to the wedding, Lester Martin to author.

"Dad put me on a saddle in front of him…," *California Country,* "From Hollywood to Healdsburg, With Love, Jim Morris, September/October, 2005.

One of Fred's favorites was tomatoes…, *Savor Wine Country Magazine,* Q&A Kate MacMurray, 12/5/04.

"Mom and Dad worked hard for us to have dinner…," *San Francisco Chronicle,* 3/6/03.

"Being in Los Angeles…," *Savor Wine Country Magazine,* 12/5/04.

Famous guests at the ranch, *San Francisco Chronicle,* 3/6/03.

"The fog rolling in and out of the redwoods…," ibid.

"I remember the first time I played Bel-Air…," *Who's Your Caddy,* Rick Reilly, Doubleday, 2003, pg. 206.

"It was a close thing…," *Bob Hope: Portrait of a Superstar,*

"Fred played golf with presidents…," Lester Martin to author, 11/2/06.

"So I was all set to fix it when June…," *Detroit News,* 5/25/65.

Fred considered for lead in *Yours, Mine & Ours,* Mel Shavelson to author.

Information regarding *The Chadwick Family, Detroit News,* "Judging It", Frank Judge, December, 1974.

Information regarding *Fire! The Hollywood Reporter,* 12/8/76, 12/9/76.

"staring at me were Fred MacMurray…," *Candidly Caine,* Elaine Gallagher, Robson Books, 1990, pg. 171.

"We don't talk about that one," *Frederick (MD) Post,* 5/28/87.

Fred turning down *Cocoon,* ibid.

"I'm going through all the standard treatment," *Annapolis (MD) Capital,* 10/24/77.

"Homosexuality, drugs, violence…," *NY Daily News,* 11/15/77.

"I'm no prude…," ibid.

"Fred was eager to show June how to catch bullhead…," *Beaver Dam Daily Citizen,* 11/6/91.

"Bud didn't forget how to take bullheads off the hook…," *Beaver Dam Daily Citizen,* 6/28/77.

Fred's visit to Wilson Elementary School, *Beaver Dam Daily Citizen,*

7/14/79.

Background of attempted land theft, *New York Times,* 8/17/81.

"I feel very often I'm a bad citizen…," *TV Guide,* 10/5/68.

June not allowing Fred to become a "hermit…," Beverly Garland to author.

"I was lucky enough to make four pictures with Barbara…," *Movie Talk,* pg. 192.

Fred winning the "Popscar, *American Classic Screen,* March/April, 1974.

Fred chatting with Marilyn Chambers at a Sammy Davis, Jr. party, *In Black and White: The Life of Sammy Davis, Jr.,* Wil Haygood, Knopf, 2003.

"Fred was the first person presented with the Disney Legends Award," Dave Smith to author.

Fred inducted into the Wisconsin Hall of Fame, *Beaver Dam Daily Citizen,* 6/19/87.

Details re: his 1987 stroke, *National Enquirer,* 1/19/88, Jimmy Starr Papers.

"We are just going to have the family…," *Newsday,* 8/30/88.

"I could see that it was painful for her to talk about him…," *Forties Film Talk,* MacDonald Carey interview.

"He couldn't make it down the stairs to the phone…," Don Grady to author.

"The light of Fred's life…," ibid.

"She took wonderful care of him," *People,* 11/18/91.

"I knew Fred was ill…," Lester Martin to author, 11/2/06.

"All I could think of was 'how sad,'" Beverly Garland to author.

"To know this, meant a great deal to me," Elliott Reid to author.

"The movie camera, with its undeniable capacity…," *LA Times,* 11/7/91.

"You suddenly heard the whole bowl go 'Ahhhh!'," *People,* 11/18/91.

"Fondly", *Chicago Tribune,* 11/6/91.

Index

Crosby, Bing, 22, 53, 55, 63-64, 75, 91, 93, 106, 120, 244, 246
Curtiz, Michael, 81, 82
Dahl, Arlene, 152, 154-155, 225-226
Davidson, John, 230, 232
Davis, Sammy, Jr., 264
Day of the Bad Man (film), 164-165
De Cordova, Fred, 136, 239-240, 244
De Havilland, Olivia, 81, 109, 260
Demarest, William, 117, 125, 137, 203-204, 205, 238, 246
Dietrich, Marlene, 32, 75, 82-84, 90
Disney, Walt, 172, 174-175, 178, 181, 182, 183, 186, 207, 208, 209, 211, 216, 221, 222, 227, 228, 229, 230, 231, 234-235
Dive Bomber (film), 46, 64, 80-82
Dmytryk, Edward, 144, 145, 146, 147
Double Indemnity (film), 56, 95-105, 106, 107, 109, 111, 261, 265, 269
Douglas, Melvyn, 73, 74
Douglas, Paul, 178
Dunne, Irene, 65, 68, 120, 124, 133, 139, 233
Eddy, Nelson, 159
Egg and I, The (film), 122-124, 133
Engstead, John, 66-67
Exclusive! (film), 33, 62
Face of a Fugitive (film), *165*
Fair Wind to Java (film), *139-143*
Far Horizons, The (film), *156-157, 159, 160*
Father Was a Fullback (film), *129*
Family Honeymoon (film), 128
Farmer, Frances, 62, 70
Fedderson, Don, 184, 185, 186, 189, 193, 197, 203, 239, 241, 243, 244, 249
Fenton, Leslie, 118, 125
Ferrer, Jose, 144, 146, 147
Fischer, Lyda, 20
Flynn, Errol, 81, 142, 151, 152
Follow Me, Boys! (film), 33, 207, 227-230, 234, 268
Fonda, Henry, 44, 88, 111, 119, 125, 126, 245, 256, 258, 260, 261
Fontaine, Joan, 151-152
Francis, Anne, 250
Friends of Mr. Sweeney (film), 27-28, 33
Frawley, William, 64, 137, 171, 184-185, 188-189, 192, 194, 203-204, 205
Funicello, Annette, 175, 177, 233, 258
Gable, Clark, 31, 35, 43, 79, 87, 116, 124, 135, 136-137, 261

Gardner, Ava, 120, 124-125
Garland, Beverly, 138, 193, 240, 244-246, 247, 250, 151, 264, 268
Garson, Greer, 230, 231, 232
Geiger, Charles, 16
Gilded Lily, The (film), 32-37, 38, 39, 41
Girls Gone Wild (film), 22
Gish, Lillian, 228-229
Gobel, George, 183
Goddard, Paulette, 40, 91, 120, 121-122, 125
Good Day for a Hanging (film), 165
Gordon, Max, 24, 25
Grady, Don, 138, 189, 190, 191-192, 193, 194, 196, 197, 198-199, 201, 202, 241-242, 243, 247, 248-249, 250, 251, 267, 269
Grand Old Girl (film), 28-29, 33, 34
Grant, Cary, 32, 46, 50, 64, 80, 88, 106, 136, 224
Greenstreet, Sydney, 25
Gun for a Coward (film), 163-164
Hagen, Jean, 173, 175
Hands across the Table (film), *38-39, 41-43*
Happiest Millionaire, The (film), 230-235
Hartmann, Edward, 137, 188, 196, 200
Hathaway, Henry, 44
Haver, June, 17, 39, 114, 136, 149-152, 154, 155, 156, 157, 159, 160, 163, 168-172, 183, 186, 195, 196, 225-226, 233, 241, 243, 253, 255, 256, 257, 262, 264, 265, 266, 267, 268, 269
Heflin, Van, 152
Hepburn, Katharine, 37-38, 43, 54, 68, 69
Heston, Charlton, 156, 159, 263
Hickman, Darryl, 116, 149-150, 156
Hilliard, Harriet, 62-63
Holman, Libby, 23-24
Honeymoon in Bali (film), 66
Hooper, Hedda, 16, 128, 217
Hope, Bob, 24, 25-26, 27, 35, 53, 139, 257, 261, 262, 264, 267
Howard, William K, 50
Hunter, Jeffery, 163, 164, 165
Hutton, Betty, 91
Invitation to Happiness (film), 68
Jarman, Claude, Jr., 142
Johnson, Van, 144, 145-146, 147
Jones, Allan, 66
Jones, Dean, 235, 258
Jones, Hank, 187, 189, 191, 193, 194, 200, 202, 205, 207-208, 214

About The Author

Charles Tranberg lives in Madison, Wisconsin and is the author of *I Love the Illusion: The Life and Career of Agnes Moorehead* which was selected as one of the Ten Best books of 2006 by *Classic Images*. He is also the author of *Not so Dumb: The Life and Career of Marie Wilson.*

BearManorMedia

PO BOX 71426 · ALBANY, GEORGIA 31708

THE PHILIP RAPP JOKE FILE

For the first time ever, be privy to the open caverns of mirth that is the profilic Philip Rapp joke file! Rapp, writer for Baby Snooks, Eddie Cantor and creator of the *Bickersons*, wrote and collected jokes for years, drawing from it during his classic radio and TV years. Now we've taken the best quips and put them together for one great and funny book! Illustrated.
ISBN: 1-59393-102-6. $14.95

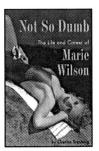

NOT SO DUMB
THE LIFE AND CAREER OF MARIE WILSON
by Charles Tranberg

Ready for the first biography on blonde, bubbly Marie Wilson? Was she really that vapid? Well — read the book on this *My Friend Irma* star!
ISBN: 1-59393-049-6. $19.95

TWENTY QUESTIONS
by Robert VanDeventer

A novelized memoir of *Twenty Questions*, one of the first weekly panel quiz shows on the radio.
ISBN: 1-59393-077-1. $19.95

INCORRECT ENTERTAINMENT
by Anthony Slide

Cultural Historian Anthony Slide, who has been described by the *Los Angeles Times* as a one-man publishing phenomenon, strikes again with a book guaranteed to contain something OFFENSIVE for everyone. From FASCISM in Hollywood to the latest topical jokes on the *Challenger* disaster & more.
ISBN: 1-59393-093-3. $19.95

FRED MACMURRAY: A BIOGRAPHY
by Charles Tranberg

A biography of Hollywood's most famous dad! Features an introduction by Don Grady of *My Three Sons*.
ISBN: 1-59393-099-2. $24.95.

ANGELIC HEAVEN
A Fan's Guide To Charlie's Angels
by Mike Pingel

The ultimate fan's guide to the hit 70s/80s television series by legendary producer Aaron Spelling. Filled with facts about the show, behind-the-scenes tidbits, rare photos and forewords by Farrah Fawcett and Cheryl Ladd, *Angelic Heaven* will have you rushing out to buy the DVDs!
$19.95

WHO'S WHO OF STAGE & SCREEN
by C. Elizabeth Lalla

Who's Who of Stage and Screen will make a beautiful addition to any Hollywood lover's collection! Filled with photos, profiles, resumes and contact information for the artists included. Nearly 600 pages, 8x10 size!
$35.00

THE FILMS OF THE DIONNE QUINTUPLETS
by Paul Talbot

An emphasis on their interesting film career of the famous five. Packed with photos and priceless information, every film fan will marvel at their story.
ISBN: 1-59393-097-6. $19.95.

ADD $3.00 POSTAGE FOR EACH BOOK

RDER THESE BOOKS AND MORE! VISIT WWW.BEARMANORMEDIA.COM

Printed in the United States
113919LV00004B/210/A